TRAVELS IN THE OLD SOUTH

A Bibliography

VOLUME THREE

The Ante Bellum South, 1825–1860

TRAVELS IN
THE OLD SOUTH

A Bibliography

VOLUME THREE

The Ante Bellum South, 1825-1860

Cotton, Slavery, and Conflict

EDITED BY THOMAS D. CLARK

UNIVERSITY OF OKLAHOMA PRESS : NORMAN

Library of Congress Catalog Card Number: 56–8016

Copyright 1959 by the University of Oklahoma Press, Publishing Division of the University. Manufactured in the U.S.A. First edition, April, 1959. Second printing, September, 1969.

IN MEMORY OF

Charles Sackett Sydnor

ACKNOWLEDGMENTS

THE PERIOD 1826–60 covers one of the most fascinating eras in Southern history. More people visited the region during these three decades than ever again in so short a time. This intensive visitation resulted in the writing of a large number of travel accounts, and many of these exist only in single or few copies. Many libraries and individuals have been exceedingly generous to both the compilers and the editor in allowing us to use their materials. Individual scholars have called our attention to books which might otherwise have gone undiscovered.

Again we wish to express appreciation to the Rockefeller Foundation for the necessary funds to finance the research for these volumes. It would be difficult to say how much funds provided by the Research Fund Committee of the University of Kentucky have served to finance checking and refining of the entries in this volume.

Publication of *Travels in the Old South* would have been impossible had it not been for the generosity of the late J. W. Carnahan of Chicago, a distinguished publisher himself.

Among the people who have given of their time and rich knowledge of Americana and the mysteries of bibliography are Miss Jacqueline Bull, Miss Katherine Katterjohn, Mr. Lawrence S. Thompson of the University of Kentucky Library, Mr. John Cook Wyllie of the McGregor Library, University of Virginia, Mr. Stanley Pargellis of the Newberry Library, and that sage bibliographer, Mr. Wright Howes of Chicago. Miss Ada Nisbet of the University of California is our generous creditor. She read the manuscript and made useful suggestions.

As general editor of this series, I find myself exceedingly grateful to the four contributors who labored diligently to present these three decades in their full measure as the travelers formed this intricate profile of the ante bellum South. Behind volumes of this sort are those patient laborers who give so much and receive so little for their efforts. The University of Oklahoma Press deserves the scholars' acclaim for its willingness to publish bibliography, and its staff a word of appreciation for helping to see that some consistency is served and that the rules of bibliographical craftsmanship are observed.

Thomas D. Clark

Lexington, Kentucky

CONTENTS

ILLUSTRATIONS

EDITOR'S PREFACE

IN THE second quarter of the nineteenth century the South was a land of constant change. Pioneers of several nationalities from the beginning of the sixteenth century on broke trail into the region. With the Gulf of Mexico, the Atlantic Coast, and the great interland river system surrounding and penetrating the region it often received visitors who otherwise would have passed it. After 1825 the pioneering efforts of the first settlers produced a more or less settled society. Steamboat transportation had become a dependable means of travel. Highways across the region were opened. Rickety stage coaches jostled passengers overland from Baltimore to the Río Grande and from Cincinnati to Mobile. The cotton and sugar industries were rising staple crops in the nation's agricultural system. At the same time the region below the Potomac was beginning to consider itself a distinct entity bound by ties of a homogeneous population, a kindred geographical and economic interest, and a local political system of common form and origin.

Aside from its frontier nature, homogeneous ties, and political and sectional awareness, the South had become a land of expanding slavery. By 1825 slavery was taking a new lease on life. The "peculiar institution" itself was undergoing a change in both geographical location and nature. As settlers pushed down the great valleys to claim fresh lands in the frontier delta and hill sections of the backwoods, they not only brought family slaves with them, but they sent back for the surplus laborers in the faltering agricultural system of the old South. Expansion of the cotton belt and of slavery were, of course, simultaneous. At the same time criticism of the institution reached national proportions. The summer campaign following discussion of the Missouri Compromise in 1820 made slavery a sectional, political, and moral issue. To a significant extent the local and national press found in the rising slavery issue a new source of sensational news, and a boon to sluggish editorial imaginations.

Publicity relating to slavery not only piqued the national curiosity, but likewise that of foreigners. Visitors of all sorts streamed across the

South to see the Southerners and their slaves at home. English, French, German, Italian, and many others came visiting to see slavery, the frontier, staple crops of the South, to gain a sense of American sectional differences at firsthand, and to prepare materials for almost countless books. So common did this visitation become that patterns of a "grand tour" were outlined, and visitors virtually stumbled on each other's heels on their round of the circuit.

At no period in Southern history is it possible to lay hand on a larger volume of comparative material. Possibly there is no important locality or subject relating to the South which cannot be examined with an adequacy of firsthand accounts. At no time in Southern history, except that following World War II, did more critical visitors come south. At the same time there was a generous stream of defenders and apologists. The existence of a staple economy, a slave society, and a planter hierarchy made a strange romantic appeal to visitors. Showing through the introductions of many of the works are the ribs of romantic concepts of the Southern way of life.

Realities of Southern existence often hit travelers a stunning blow. Even so well conditioned a traveler as Frederick Law Olmstead found the region's economic and social systems more realistic than he had conceived them to be back in New York. His standards of labor were high, even for his native New York, and his visit below the Potomac revealed much for him to question and criticize. Many New England travelers possibly saw the South in no better perspective than did Englishmen who arrived on the American shore with wonderfully developed prejudices and standards of misjudgment. The rawness of the Southern frontier, conditions of Southern yeomen, the carelessness and laziness of Negro slaves, and the airs and manners of planters all make excellent grist to the travelers' literary mill. Fannie Kemble, Harriet Martineau, Charles Dickens, Fredericka Bremer, Mrs. Frances Trollope, and scores of others viewed the Southerners with something approaching disdain. Sympathetic and detached views were often waifs indeed in this literary forest of travel accounts.

Frenchmen came looking for excitement in the woods, in search of traces of Gallic civilization, and generous amounts of undigested historical data. They wrote strictly for their fellow countrymen, and most of them felt under great compulsion to set the historical stage. As a result American history has seldom been so successfully mangled as in their vague Latin travel accounts. It was a rare thing indeed that a French visitor could stand off and look at America and see it for what it was. Although French travelers generally lacked the biting critical nature of English observers, they also lacked the spiciness and appeal even in error.

German travelers were motivated almost always by a single purpose —a search for an immigrant haven. In their methodical plodding way they garnered data in bales, made close economic observations, and presented their countrymen with evaluations which approached objective scholarship. This was not true, of course, in all cases. Karl Theodor Grieseinger gave a picture of aspects of American social life which has possibly not been equaled. That is, he saw a side of life which most travelers either never saw or were too discrete where their personal reputations were concerned to mention.

In resorting to the travel accounts, 1825–60, as sources of Southern history, the scholar must be warned that he is examining a huge volume of highly personal and prejudiced literary materials. These accounts run almost the full gamut of national and sectional points of view, of defense and attack of a way of life, of political and religious bigotry, of national and international prejudices, of smugness and self-righteousness, of objectivity and honesty, and finally of gross misinformation. The user of this material must beware. His judgment of the validity of individual accounts must be based squarely upon a capacity to learn about each observer and the conditions under which he prepared his account. Likewise, he must determine, if he can, whence the traveler came, why he came, and where he went. This last fact is not an easy one to elicit from many of the accounts.

The contributors to the several sections of this volume have made diligent efforts to determine some of the more meaningful facts about the travel accounts and their authors in their periods. Judgments expressed in these accounts are what the contributors consider to be objective and trustworthy appraisals. They were unable to anticipate the various purposes to which this material might be used by various scholars, and possibly their appraisals do not always portray a comprehensiveness of the full contents of many of the accounts. They do, however, give adequate suggestion of the meager contents, itinerary, and reliability of the materials.

This volume contains an appraisal of what might well be considered the most valid part of the huge collection of American travel literature. Although it bears a regional title, its scope becomes almost national in meaning. Except for limiting the descriptions of the travelers' itineraries these appraisals consider a vast portion of national travel materials.

Again the editor wishes to emphasize the fact that this is a tool for scholars in search of contemporary views of America. Every effort has been made to follow the established rules of bibliography which make for clarity and usability. No pretense is made that this is a precise exercise in bibliographical organization and collation. By the same token it would be rash indeed to pretend anything approaching completeness. Sincere efforts have been made to include every work of a travel nature which in any way applies to the South. This, however, is one of the most fertile areas for fugitivism. Like stray steers hiding in deep Southern pine forests, travel strays come wandering in from the most unexpected places. A member of a family discovers an old manuscript travel account of a forebear and has it printed in a severely limited edition, or almost entire editions of books are packed away and forgotten before they had appreciable distribution. But the most fertile area for the creation of incompleteness in a bibliography of this sort is the appearance of newly printed accounts and editions after this manuscript was prepared for the printer.

A great deal of peripheral material is included because of its pertinency in regional descriptive literature. There is a generous amount of negativism sprinkled through the various sections. This has seemed, to both compilers and editor, a necessary approach in order to set the user's mind at ease about whether or not certain works should have been considered. This bibliography does present the great body of descriptive materials relating to the South. In this volume is contained a bold outline of the regional growth and change, and an appreciable portion of the material appraised can be accepted within reasonable bounds as a dependable historical source.

Thomas D. Clark

[xviii]

PART I

The Cotton South, 1826–1835

INTRODUCTION

D URING the years 1826–35 approximately ninety-five travelers passed through some one or another portion of the Southern states and wrote accounts of their observations and experiences which were published in book form. Of those here considered, twenty-four were from the North, fifteen were white Southerners traveling in their own or other Southern states, four were absconding slaves, and the remainder were foreigners—twenty-six British subjects, ten Germans, nine Frenchmen, four Mexicans, and one each from Austria, Sweden, and Greece.

The accounts vary greatly in length and in the relative amount of attention they give to the South, since a large number include travels in other parts of the United States and even in foreign countries. Some fifteen or twenty touched the South only while passing up or down the Ohio River or merely dipped down from the North to visit the nation's capital as a part of an American tour not otherwise concerned with the region below the Mason and Dixon Line. Others traveled for hundreds or even thousands of miles in the South, observing the region in the greatest detail and recording impressions both serious and cynical, favorable and critical. It should be noted, however, that the length of an account often bears little relation to its importance as source material. Jared Sparks, for example, was able to compress into the 96 pages of his "Journal of a Southern Tour in 1826" careful notes on Southern archives and manuscript collections and significant comments upon Southern life and manners more valuable to the historian than the 1,060 pages of repetitious vituperation and violent personal prejudices to be found in the five volumes of Southern travel written by Mrs. Anne Royall.

The motives which impelled the travelers of this period to undertake their respective journeys are numerous, sometimes fanciful and trivial, but they are important in shedding light upon the frame of reference in which the traveler would be likely to couch his account. Interest in or preoccupation with the Texan war for independence and the possibility of settling in the resulting Republic were significant factors in stimulating travel into that region. All five of the above-mentioned Mexican accounts were concerned with this area, as were German works by Hermann Ehrenberg and Charles Sealsfield. Ehrenberg came originally to New Orleans, but there he immediately joined a band of volunteers and with this outfit participated in the storming of the Alamo under Milam and was among those captured with Fannin at Goliad. One of the few to escape this massacre, he prepared an account of his experiences, entitled *Texas und Seine Revolution,* which he sent to Leipzig and had published in 1843. Written graphically and perhaps with greater detachment than a citizen of the United States could have shown, his work deals largely with military events, but it also contains descriptive material relating to the prairies and other features of Texas geography. It is possible that this book, which was reissued in 1844 and again in 1845, may have played some part in attracting German immigration to Texas in the forties and fifties. Sealsfield's most thoughtful work, *The Americans as They Are* (London, 1828), relates primarily to a trip down the Ohio and Mississippi; but he also traveled in Texas, observing the region with the eye of an artist, historian, and ethnographer, and from these experiences drew the materials for his masterpiece of fiction, *The Cabin Book* (New York, 1844), a vivid picture of Texas and its society in the early days and during the war for independence.

To Texas also went S. W. Cushing, a Boston sailor who in 1836 took service in the Texas Navy, and later in his autobiographical *Wild Oats Sowings* (New York, 1857) left an account of gambling, fighting, and other escapades characteristic of an adventurous seaman. More serious reasons motivated Benjamin Lundy, who made three trips to Texas in the early thirties searching for suitable places for the settling of emancipated slaves and working at the trade of saddler while pursuing his unsuccessful colonization schemes. Mrs. Mary Austin Holley, widow of the president of Transylvania College and a cousin of Stephen F. Austin, visited the latter's colony in 1831 and on the basis of this experience published her *Texas: Observations, Historical, Geographical, and Descriptive* (Baltimore, 1833), the first work on Texas in the English language. Mrs. Holley's book was a factor of importance in stimulating homeseekers to locate in Texas and in providing the basic geographical and agricultural information for many other works on that state in the thirties and forties. Similar in content as well as the use to which it was later put was a *History of Texas* (Cincinnati, 1836), by David B. Edward, a Scottish schoolmaster, who explored the region in 1830 and again in 1835. Whole passages from these two books were incorporated into the redoubtable Davy Crockett's *Exploits and Adventures in Texas* (Philadelphia, 1836), which was alleged to have been, but in all probability was not, the work of this defender of the Alamo.

Interest in prisons and penitentiaries was a factor leading many Europeans to visit the United States during this period, and several of these extended their itineraries into the South. From England, by order of the Home Secretary, came William Crawford, whose *Report* (London, 1834) included descriptions of penitentiaries in Virginia, Kentucky, and Tennessee. The Frenchman Frédéric Demetz and Guillaume Blouet came South to visit the penitentiary at Richmond, as did the German Dr. Nicolaus Heinrich Julius, who tarried at this old prison, not because it was worth investigating but because it had been omitted by Beaumont and Tocqueville. More significant, so far as the South is concerned, were certain by-products of these prison investigations. Edward Strutt Abdy accompanied William Crawford but remained for an independent tour, on which he passed through Virginia and Kentucky, leaving an account critical of nearly everything he saw in these two states, especially slavery and excessive drinking. Beaumont and Tocqueville were sent by the French government to study prison systems and recorded their findings in *Du Système Penitentiaire aux États-Unis* (Paris, 1833); but they are better known for the respective accounts they wrote of travels undertaken after their official task had been completed—Beaumont's *Marie* (Paris, 1835) and Tocqueville's widely read *Democracy in America* (French ed., Paris, 1835–1840, and various English translations).

Religious duties of one type or another were likewise important causes of travel. Thomas Shillitoe, a London Quaker, came on a fraternal visit to the churches of his faith, including those of the South, in 1826, leaving a good account of religious conditions among the Friends of North Carolina and of the Moravian community at Salem, where he had some difficulty in securing permission to hold services; Andrew

[5]

Reed and James Matheson made a similar visit to the Presbyterian and Congregational bodies of the United States in 1834, being among other things unfavorably impressed with the camp meetings they observed in Virginia; and Stephen Davis, an English Baptist, included Virginia in a tour made in 1833 for the purpose of raising funds for a society to promote a knowledge of the Bible in Ireland. Among native Americans, James Weddel Alexander came from Princeton for a brief Presbyterian pastorate in Virginia during the late twenties, finding himself an Adams man in the midst of Jacksonians but otherwise enjoying his experiences—riding, visiting, and drinking with the planters; and Isaac McCoy, a native of Pennsylvania, made several trips to Baptist Indian missions in what is now the state of Oklahoma. Timothy Flint and John Mason Peck were others whose religious activities were associated with travel and whose accounts, more or less significant, have been published.

The multiplicity of interests manifested by travelers can, indeed, only be suggested: Michel Chevalier was sent by the French government to study railroads and other public works, while his more romantic compatriot, Theodore Pavie, came in the hope of imitating the writings of Chateaubriand and to gratify a long-cherished desire to stand where the Ohio joined the mighty Mississippi. Tyrone Power, an Irish comedian, came in the pursuit of his profession, twice touring the South, with which he was favorably impressed; and, quite unlike most foreigners, was not disturbed by slavery. Rich Short, an English laborer, came in search of employment; in Virginia and North Carolina he found much trouble in securing work and more difficulty in getting his pay. Henry Tudor came for reasons of health, to visit the only quarter of the globe he had not yet seen, and "to behold . . . the magnificent Cataract of Niagara." Godfrey T. Vigne, another Englishman, came with "note book, sketch book, gun, and fishing rod—alone, unbewifed, unbevehicled . . . with the determination of being, so far as an Englishman can be, unprejudiced; and of seeing all I could of the United States in the space of about six months."

Ethan Allen Andrews was sent down from the North to investigate slavery and the slave trade in Maryland and Virginia, of which he wrote an account that was naturally prejudiced but nevertheless acute and penetrating. Constantine Samuel Rafinesque botanized and visited mineral springs in Kentucky and Tennessee, and Elisha Mitchell explored the geological formations of western North Carolina. William F. Pope described a trip from Louisville to Little Rock, where he went in 1832 as secretary to the territorial governor of Arkansas. Philip St. George Cooke and George Archibald McCall wrote of their experiences at various army posts; Thomas L. McKenney went to Mississippi to negotiate removal treaties with the Indians; and Barton Griffith supervised the shipment of a steamboat-load of pork from Indiana to New Orleans, where he contracted dysentery from which he died shortly after returning home. For the most part Mrs. Anne Royall traveled for the eminently practical purpose of selling her books. As soon as one of her volumes was printed, she would load several trunks full of copies on the stage and set out on a tour, disposing of the book just printed and collecting material for a succeeding one.

Certain accounts of this period have importance as a result of the reputations of their authors or of literary distinction, although they may be of less value to the social historian because of excessive preoccupation with descriptive material. Among these are Charles Fenno Hoffman's *A Winter in the West* (2 vols., New York, 1835), the second volume of which includes a tour through Kentucky and Virginia; and to a lesser extent Joseph Holt Ingraham's *South-West, by a Yankee* (2 vols., New York, 1835), concerned largely with descriptions of New Orleans and of the state of Mississippi. James Fenimore Cooper's *Notions of the Americans: Picked up by a Travelling Bachelor* (2 vols., London, 1828) is a series of letters, three of which relate to the South, purporting to have been written by an Englishman traveling in the United States, but in reality it is the work of the homesick Cooper defending his country against the misunderstandings he had encountered in Europe, where he had been living for two years. Washington Irving's *A Tour on the Prairies* (Philadelphia, 1835) is too well known to require appraisal here. In addition to its literary value, it is also unique in being an account of a tour of which two other accounts were written. Charles Joseph Latrobe, an Englishman who accompanied Irving, recorded his account in *The Rambler in North America* (2 vols., London, 1835), while Henry Leavitt Ellsworth, an Indian commissioner from New England who acted as host to the party, preserved his narrative in the form of a long letter to his wife, eventually published as *Washington Irving on the Prairie*, edited by Stanley T. Williams and Barbara D. Simison (New York, 1937). In contrast to Latrobe's expansive recital of the same events and to Irving's elegant narrative, Ellsworth's account is without literary embellishment; but it is significant in that its pages depict the author of *The Alhambra* and *The Sketch Book*, not as he was seen in Paris and on Broadway, but as he appeared in the company of Indian guides and other companions on the actual frontier of a hundred years ago.

So much similarity is observable in the accounts of the better-known British travelers of the period that they may be conveniently treated as a group. These include James Edward Alexander, George William Featherstonhaugh, Thomas Hamilton, Simon Ansley O'Ferrall, Charles Augustus Murray, James Stuart, and Captain Basil Hall and his wife Margaret Hunter Hall, whose account, published one hundred years later, supplements that of her husband by naming many persons and places which in his narrative are described without identification. In the same category might also be placed the German duke, Bernhard of Saxe-Weimar-Eisenach, and the Swede Carl David Arfwedson. For one thing, these visitors had no particular purpose in mind other than the experience of travel itself. On the whole they were either wealthy or members of the upper classes of society, accustomed to the refinements of European life and therefore critical of the primitive agriculture, crude conveyances, and inadequate inn and tavern accommodations they encountered. To a man, they were opposed to slavery, typical of their comments being that of Murray, who regarded the institution as "a foul stain upon the honour, humanity, and justice of the United States." At the same time, they were critical of American democratic customs, as instanced by Alexander's displeasure with the hasty eating at a Nashville inn and with the equalitarianism which placed him at the same table with a tailor who had just previously pressed his coat; and by Featherstonhaugh's reaction when, upon calling at the executive mansion at Little Rock, he was informed by the wife of the Governor that the latter had gone into the woods to search for a stray sow and pigs.

A single route was followed by these and other travelers to an extent sufficient to characterize it as a sort of American "Grand Tour." This route led from Washington to New Orleans, usually by way of Richmond and Norfolk, Fayetteville, Camden, Columbia, Augusta, Mill-edgeville, Columbus, and through the Creek Indian country to Montgomery, whence the journey was continued by steamer to Mobile and on to New Orleans. A variation led from Columbia to Charleston and Savannah and thence either by river to Augusta or directly overland to Macon and Columbus, the latter being the route of Captain Hall, whose party traveled across the state of Georgia in privately hired equipages, through pine barrens and over swollen streams, with nightly accommodations to be secured only at rude farmhouses along the way. The passage through the Creek country afforded an opportunity to visit these Indians, whose ceremonies are described at some length in the works of Captain Hall and Arfwedson. The return trip from New Orleans was generally taken by river, up the Mississippi and Ohio to Louisville or Cincinnati and thence eastward overland. Not infrequently these routes were transposed, the traveler going by way of Cincinnati and the rivers to New Orleans and returning to Washington by land.

If, as indicated, the length of an account often has little relation to its importance, the same may be said of the relation between the general importance of an account and its significance as Southern travel, even though it may include the South. Mrs. Frances Trollope, for example, was perhaps the best known, as well as the most bitterly resented, of all the foreign travelers of her period, yet her experiences in the South were not an important phase of her American sojourn. Landing at New Orleans in late December, 1827, she went almost immediately up the river to Memphis, tarried there for a short time in order to visit Fanny Wright's near-by Nashoba community, and then proceeded to Louisville and Cincinnati. Although she was opposed to slavery, it is not apparent that she held any other grudge against the South except so far as this region was a part of a nation which she disliked; and therefore her comments upon the Southern phases of her experiences are incidental as compared with her reactions to Cincinnati and other portions of the United States.

In contrast to this widely read book, that of Gustave de Beaumont has never been translated into English and is therefore relatively unknown in the United States, although it contains many acute and penetrating observations on the race problem as it existed, both North and

South, in the 1830's. As will be recalled, Beaumont and Alexis de Tocqueville, after completing their prison studies, set out upon a tour of the West and South. In the South they traveled down the Ohio to West Point, Kentucky, where the December ice in the river compelled a continuation of their journey by land back to Louisville and thence by way of Nashville to Memphis. Here they remained for a week and on Christmas Day, 1831, took passage for New Orleans. On the same boat was a party of emigrating Choctaw Indians, and also Sam Houston, with whom the two Frenchmen held a long conversation. At New Orleans, slavery, which had been observed at Memphis, was again encountered, along with its various effects, and unfavorably appraised. Turning eastward again, they went to Mobile and Montgomery and thence to Norfolk and Washington, apparently passing through Macon, Milledgeville, Augusta, Columbia, and Fayetteville. Slavery and the Indian problem continued to confront them along this route; and somewhere in South Carolina, presumably at a tavern where they were detained by a travel mishap, they spent some time in company with Joel R. Poinsett, whom they had previously met in Philadelphia and who was now acting as one of the organizers of anti-nullification sentiment in his native state.

Beaumont's reflections upon these experiences appeared in the form of a novel, the full title of which was *Marie, ou l'esclavage aux États-Unis, Tableau de Moeurs Américaines* (2 vols., Paris, 1835). The plot, relatively simple, involves a young Frenchman who falls in love with a beautiful girl in Baltimore, only to learn from her father that she is of mixed blood, although she does not appear to be. The father refuses to give his consent to the marriage until the Frenchman has made a tour of the country to observe with his own eyes the true position of Negroes in America. Despite his experiences on the tour, with race riots and other forms of discrimination, the young man returns, and the two are married. They are almost mobbed at the wedding ceremony and flee to the wilderness of Michigan, where the wife soon dies, just prior to the news that her brother has been killed in Georgia while leading a conspiracy of Cherokee Indians and enslaved blacks against their white oppressors. Beaumont's primary aim was not to create a romance, but to reproduce the impressions that he had received in America. To this end he also included in the book many notes, references, and citations, relegated to appendices in order to avoid doing violence to the literary form he had chosen; and three long essays on "The Social and Political Conditions of Negro Slaves and Freedmen," "Religious Movements in the United States," and "The Early State and Present Condition of the Indian Tribes of North America." Except for Baltimore and a few references to New Orleans, the scene of *Marie* is laid in the North; but it is unquestionable that slavery as Beaumont observed it in the South and the party of emigrating Choctaw Indians which he encountered at Memphis are a part of the materials out of which he constructed his imaginary story.

JAMES W. PATTON
The University of North Carolina

The Cotton South, 1826–1835

1. ## Abdy, Edward Strutt (1791–1846)

Journal of a residence and tour in the United States of North America, from April, 1833, to October, 1834, by E. S. Abdy . . . 3 vols. London, J. Murray, 1835.

> Vol. I, xii, 395 p.; Vol. II, viii, 415 p.; Vol. III, viii, 408 p.   19½ cm.
> *Inclusive dates:* April and May, 1834.
> *Location of copy:* Library of Congress.

Abdy was an English traveler who accompanied William Crawford on the latter's tour of prison inspection in the United States and remained for a time after Crawford had returned to England. He kept a journal which "he thought might essentially serve the cause of humanity . . . and give a true and faithful picture of the cruelties he had witnessed" (I, v). In the South he went from Washington by way of Alexandria, Warrenton, Charlottesville, Richmond, Scottsville, Staunton, Lexington, and Charleston, Virginia, to Maysville, Kentucky, and thence to Frankfort and Louisville and on into Indiana, all of this being described in II, 173–362. He was strongly anti-slavery and therefore anti-Southern, in addition to being considerably anti-American. His account is critical of nearly everything he observed in the two Southern states through which he passed, especially slavery and excessive drinking. Descriptions of Armfield's slave-trading establishment at Alexandria (II, 179–80) and the behavior of University of Virginia students at Charlottesville (II, 238–39) are colorful. There are relatively few direct accounts of the author's experiences in the South, but a large amount of secondary information on slavery, government, and history, based on newspapers, statutes, and other works.

2. ## Adams, Herbert Baxter (1850–1901)

The life and writings of Jared Sparks, comprising selections from his journals and correspondence, by Herbert B. Adams. 2 vols. Boston and New York, Houghton, Mifflin and company, 1893.

> Vol. I, li, 572 p.; Vol. II, xviii, 639 p.   6 ports. (incl. fronts.).   23 cm.
> *Illustrations:* Vol. I, 2 ports.; Vol. II, 4 ports.
> *Inclusive dates:* March–May, 1826.
> *Location of copy:* University of North Carolina Library.

Includes Sparks's "Journal of a Southern Tour in 1826" (I, 414–510). Among the objectives sought by Sparks were "health, interests of the 'Review,' historical researches, and knowledge of men and things." His itinerary south of Washington was Fredericksburg, Richmond, Norfolk, Charleston, Augusta, and Milledgeville, and thence back to Richmond by way of Augusta, Columbia, Camden, Fayetteville, and Raleigh. The journal contains valuable notes on Southern archives and manuscript collections and interesting comments upon Southern life and manners. At Richmond he called on John Marshall, at Columbia he saw Thomas Cooper, and upon his departure from Richmond on the return trip he took a stage in which John Randolph was also a passenger. He was saddened by the sight of a slave-whipping at Milledgeville, and found the country between Charleston and Augusta "disheartening and revolting"; but he was favorably impressed with Raleigh.

"Although hastily written at odd moments, and never intended for publication, Mr. Sparks' notes of travel and observations contain little that is purely personal or ephemeral. He had a useful purpose in mind when he recorded the results of each day's experience" (Adams, I, 510).

3. Alexander, James Edward (1803–1885)

Transatlantic sketches, comprising visits to the most interesting scenes in North and South America, and the West Indies. With notes on Negro slavery and Canadian emigration. By Capt. J. E. Alexander . . . 2 vols. London, R. Bentley, 1833.

Vol. I, xxiii, 384 p.; Vol. II, xiii, 320 p. fronts., plates, map. 21½ cm.
Maps: Sketch map of parts of North and South America and the West Indies.
Illustrations: Six in Vol. I; four in Vol. II, only one of which, "Squatter, Mississippi," is concerned with the South.
Inclusive dates: 1831.
Other editions:
Philadelphia, Key and Biddle, 1833. vii, [9]–378 p. 25 cm.
Location of copy: Duke University Library.

The author, a captain in the Forty-second Royal Highlanders, passed through the South en route to the East and Canada after touring British South America and the West Indies. He landed at New Orleans and traveled up the Mississippi to Memphis, thence overland in a four-horse wagon to Nashville, and by stage to Louisville and Cincinnati. Alexander was too much a soldier and too well-seasoned a traveler to be greatly disturbed by the primitive conditions he found in the South, particularly in Tennessee and Kentucky; and on the whole he was not unfriendly, although he disliked slavery and the republican form of government. He was amused by the hasty eating at a Nashville inn and by the equalitarianism which placed him at the same table with a tailor who had just previously pressed his coat (II, 100–103).

4. Alexander, James Weddel (1804–1859)

Forty years' familiar letters of James W. Alexander, D.D., constituting, with the notes, a memoir of his life. Edited by the surviving correspondent, John Hall. 2 vols. New York, C. Scribner; London, Sampson Low, son & company, 1860.

> Vol. I, viii, 412 p.; Vol. II, 379 p. fronts. (ports.). 22½ cm.
> *Inclusive dates:* 1825–1828.
> *Location of copy:* Library of Congress.

The author was born in Virginia but was carried to Philadelphia by his parents at the age of three. After graduating from Princeton, he served as a Presbyterian pastor in Virginia from 1825 to 1828. The above work contains about twelve letters written during this period (I, 89–118), mainly from Petersburg and Charlotte Court House. Some travel is described, in Halifax, Prince Edward, and other Virginia counties.

Alexander apparently enjoyed his sojourn in Virginia, where, in addition to his preaching, he passed considerable time in riding, visiting, and drinking with the planters. He was an Adams man in the midst of Jacksonians. Apparently he saw something of John Randolph. He was friendly to slavery and saw no remedy for it, although he regretted the ignorance that attended it.

There are some good descriptions of Virginia eating, wild life, and an interesting account of a Virginia election held on a court day at Charlotte Court House (I, 100–102).

5. Almonte, Juan Nepomuceno (1803–1869)

Noticia estadistica sobre Tejas, por Juan N. Almonte. Mexico, Impreso por Ignacio Cumplido, 1835.

> 96, [4] p. 3 fold. tables. 14½ cm.
> *Maps:* Folded table of Texas imports and exports.
> *Inclusive dates:* 1834.
> *Location of copy:* Library of Congress.

This was Almonte's official report as an aide to Santa Anna after extensive travels in Texas in 1834. It is mainly a description of Texas, its location, climate, products, history, political divisions, geology, rivers, and Indians. The account is complete, but there is no reference to an itinerary.

6. Andrews, Ethan Allen (1787–1858)

Slavery and the domestic slave-trade in the United States. In a series of letters addressed to the Executive committee of the American union for the relief and improvement of the colored race . . . By Prof. E. A. Andrews. Boston, Light & Stearns, 1836.

xii, [9]–201 p. 16½ cm.
Inclusive dates: July, 1835.
Location of copy: Library of Congress.

Andrews, a Yale graduate of 1810, a teacher of ancient languages at the University of North Carolina, 1822–28, and later head of a school at New Haven, Connecticut, was sent in 1835 as an agent of the American Union to investigate slavery and the slave trade in Maryland, Virginia, and the District of Columbia. His itinerary included Baltimore, Washington, Alexandria, Fredericksburg, Richmond, and thence back to Baltimore by boat. He found no strong attachment to slavery in Maryland. At Alexandria he visited the establishment of Franklin and Armfield, of which he gives a good description (pp. 135–43). En route from Alexandria to Fredericksburg he held an interesting conversation with a slave trader carrying slaves to South Carolina (pp. 145–53).

The author's interest was in slavery and the slave trade, both of which he observed wherever possible and discussed with numerous people, none of whom he seems to have antagonized. He was naturally prejudiced, but his account is judicious, acute, and penetrating.

7. Arfwedson, Carl David (1806–1881)

The United States and Canada, in 1832, 1833, and 1834 . . . By C. D. Arfwedson. 2 vols. London, R. Bentley, 1834.

Vol. I, vii, 433 p.; Vol. II, vii, 418 p. fronts. 21 cm.
Illustrations: Two: fronts.
Inclusive dates: 1832–1833.
Other editions:
Förenta Staterna och Canada, åren 1832, 1833 och 1834 . . . Stockholm, L. J. Hjerta, 1835. 2 vols., paged continuously. 674 p. 14½ cm.
Location of copy: Library of Congress.

Arfwedson was a Swedish scholar and a prolific writer on a variety of subjects. On his American tour he was in the South from November, 1832, until February, 1833, traveling by way of Washington, Richmond, Norfolk, Fayetteville, N. C., Charleston, Savannah, Augusta, Macon, Montgomery, and Mobile to New Orleans and thence up the Mississippi and Ohio to Cincinnati. He discusses slavery at some length (I, 323–52), being opposed to the institution on principle but observing that on the whole the slaves were well treated. The North Carolina landscape depressed him, with its primitive dwellings, bad roads, swamps, dangerous ferries, and poor soil. His account of Charleston deals largely with the Nullification Controversy, but is taken from documents rather than from observations. From Charleston to Savannah and thence to Augusta he traveled by boat, without much convenience, and he was further annoyed by the rawness of the country between Augusta and Montgomery—bad roads, bad stages and worse drivers, and unpleasant food. There is a good description of the Indian country around Fort Mitchell, Alabama, through which he made a side tour on horseback with an Indian guide and took part in an Indian hunting expedition (II, 16–23). His observations on New Orleans (II, 52–71) are not particularly unique, and his account of the voyage up the Mississippi is similar to that of other travelers of the period.

As above indicated, Arfwedson was critical of slavery; and like most Europeans he was not well pleased with the South. He was especially plagued with bad roads and inadequate accommodations for travelers.

8.   Atwater, Caleb (1778–1867)

Remarks made on a tour to Prairie du Chien; thence to Washington city, in 1829. By Caleb Atwater. Columbus, O., Isaac N. Whiting, 1831.

vii, 296 p.   17 cm.
Inclusive dates: 1829.
Other editions:
   (1) Columbus, [O.], printed by Jenkins and Grover, 1831.   vii, 296 p.   17 cm.
   (2) The Writings of Caleb Atwater. Published by the Author. Columbus, Scott & Wright, 1833.   7, [1] p., 1 l., [9]–408 p., incl. illus., 10 plates.   20 cm.
   (3) The Indians of the Northwest, their manners [!] customs, &c., &c., or Remarks made on a tour to Prairie du Chien and thence to Washington city in 1829 . . . Columbus, [O.], 1850.   vii, 296 p.   18 cm.
Location of copy: Library of Congress.

The author, a resident of Ohio, was one of three commissioners appointed in 1829 to treat with the Winnebago and other Indian tribes in the vicinity of Prairie du Chien, Wisconsin. En route to this assignment he traveled down the Ohio River, stopping briefly at Maysville and Louisville (pp. 9–24) but going no farther south.

9.

Auszüge aus Briefen aus Nord-Amerika, geschrieben von zweien aus Ulm an der Donau gebürtigen, nun im Staate Louisiana ansässigen Geschwistern. Nebst Beschreibung einer Reise durch mehrere der Nördlichen und westlichen Staaten von Nord-Amerika. Zur Unterhaltung und Belehrung hrsg. von dem Vater der beiden Geschwister. Ulm, E. Nübling, 1833.

> [4]–214 p. front. 17 cm.
> *Inclusive dates:* 1824–1832.
> *Location of copy:* Library of Congress.

These are abstracts from letters written by two natives of Ulm, Germany, one Max and his sister Thekla (a Mrs. Dobbs), who settled in Louisiana. The travels and adventures of the brother and sister are related, as well as the experiences of an uncle who undertook a journey through the majority of the Northern and Western states in 1824. A large number of the letters were written from St. Francisville, Louisiana. Although travel is described, it is difficult to determine the extent to which the writers were travelers as distinguished from sojourners, and also the extent to which the editor intended his work for *Belehrung* as compared with *Unterhaltung*.

10. [Baird, Robert, (1798–1863)]
View of the valley of the Mississippi; or, the emigrant's and traveller's guide to the West . . . Philadelphia, H. S. Tanner, 1832.

> xii, 341 p. fold. front., fold. maps, plans. 18½ cm.
> *Maps:* Several folding maps.
> *Other editions:*
> 2d ed. Philadelphia, H. S. Tanner, 1834. xi (i.e., xii), [13]–372 p. fold. maps (incl. front.), plans. 18 cm.
> *Location of copy:* Library of Congress.

A guidebook prepared for (1) those who desire to migrate to the Mississippi Valley; (2) those who wish to travel there for amusement, health, or business; and (3) those who wish to know more about the Valley, although they never expect to travel there. The first ten chapters present a general view of the geography, history, manners and customs, climate, soil, and other aspects of the entire Valley, followed by chapters on individual states and territories, including lists of their colleges, schools, and other institutions.

11.   Ball, Charles

Slavery in the United States; a narrative of the life and adventures of Charles Ball, a black man, who lived forty years in Maryland, South Carolina and Georgia as a slave, under various masters, and was one year in the Navy with Commodore Barney, during the late war. Containing an account of the manners and usages of the planters and slaveholders of the South. A description of the condition and treatment of the slaves, with observations upon the state of morals amongst the cotton planters, and the perils and sufferings of a fugitive slave, who twice escaped from the cotton country. Lewistown, Pa., J. W. Shugert, 1836.

> 400 p.   18 cm.
> *Inclusive dates:* 1805–1835.
> *Other editions:*
>   (1) New York, J. S. Taylor, 1837.   2 p.l., xii, ₁13₁–517 p.   18 cm.   (Added t.p.: The cabinet of freedom . . . 1836).
>   (2) Pittsburgh, J. T. Shryock, 1853.   1 p.l., ₁v₁–vi, ₁9₁–446 p.   19 cm.
>   (3) 3d ed. Pittsburgh, J. T. Shryock, 1854.   vi, 9–446 p.   12mo.
>   (4) Fifty years in chains; or, the life of an American slave . . . New York, H. Dayton; Indianapolis, Ind., Dayton & Asher, 1859.   2 p.l., ₁9₁–430 p.   19 cm.
> *Location of copy:* Duke University Library.

According to this account, the author was born in Maryland, sent south after his marriage, and purchased by a planter somewhere near Columbia, South Carolina. About 1806 he was sold again and carried to Morgan County, Georgia, from which he escaped and fled back to Maryland about 1813. After living there as a free man until 1830, he was kidnapped by a brother of his former owner and returned to Georgia, near Milledgeville. Escaping a second time, he was caught and sold; but in a third attempt he was successful, fleeing to Savannah where he stowed away on a ship and finally reached Philadelphia.

There are extended descriptions of Ball's first trip South—across Virginia and North Carolina and into South Carolina—and of his return trip to Maryland from Georgia in 1813; also numerous accounts of whippings and other unfavorable aspects of slavery. The preface states that "the narrative is taken from the mouth of the adventurer himself; and if the copy does not retain the identical words of the original, the sense and import, at least, are faithfully preserved." It was obviously published as abolition literature, but may have some basis in fact.

12.   [Banks, John (1797–1870)]

Autobiography of John Banks, 1797–1870, Columbus, ₁Georgia?₁, privately printed, ₁1936?₁.

38 p. 21½ cm. (On fly leaf: A short biographical sketch of the undersigned by himself, John Banks).
Inclusive dates: 1830–1865 (1818).
Location of copy: University of Virginia Library.

This is an autobiography in the form of a diary kept between 1830 and 1865 with many years omitted. It includes, apparently written from memory, an account of the author's services in the war against the Seminole Indians in Florida, January–May, 1818 (pp. 9–16). Banks enlisted at Elberton, Georgia, in January, 1818, was elected first lieutenant, and marched with the troops to Florida and back. The itinerary was through Lexington, Milledgeville, Hartford, Fort Scott, Tallahassee, and St. Marks, which was captured. After this the Georgia soldiers returned home, while General Jackson and the regulars proceeded against Pensacola. The account of the expedition is brief and relates chiefly to daily marches, lack of food, Indian fights, and similar episodes.

13.   Beaumont de la Bonninière, Gustave Auguste de
      (1802–1866)

Marie; ou, L'esclavage aux États-Unis, tableau de moeurs américaines, par Gustave de Beaumont . . . 2 vols. Paris, Charles Gosselin, 1835.

Vol. I, viii, 396 p.; Vol. II, 334 p.   21 cm.
Other editions:
  (1) Bruxelles, L. Hauman, 1835.
  (2) Second edition, revue et corrigée. Paris, 1835.
  (3) Troisième édition, corrigée. Paris, 1836.
  (4) Quatrième édition. Paris, Charles Gosselin, 1840.
  (5) Cinquième édition. Paris, Charles Gosselin, 1842. 2 p.l., 388 p. 17½ cm.
  (6) Bruxelles, 1844.
  (7) Marie oder die Sklaven (Vol. II of Nordamerikanische Bilder und Zustände nach Gustav v. Beaumont und Alexis v. Tocqueville. Deutsch von Otto Spazier. 2 vols. Weimar, B. F. Voigt, 1836.). iv, 268 p. 17 cm.
Location of copy: Library of Congress.

Beaumont and Alexis de Tocqueville were sent by the French government to study the prison system of the United States. They remained in America from May, 1831, to February, 1832, and published the results of their investigation in *Du système penitentiaire aux États-Unis, et de son application en France,* a widely read work but not concerned with the South (Paris, H. Fournier jeune, 1833. 21½ cm. viii, 439 p. American edition, *On the Penitentiary System in the United States, and its Application in France.* Translated with introduction, notes, and additions, by Francis Lieber. Philadelphia, Carey, Lea & Blanchard, 1833. 22½ cm. xlvii, 301 p.).

After completing their prison studies, the two investigators set out upon a tour of the West and South, and although their itinerary was detailed in the introduction, it is worth repeating here. In the South they traveled down the Ohio to West Point, Kentucky, where the December ice in the river compelled a continuation of their journey by land back to Louisville and thence by way of Nashville to Memphis. At Sandy Bridge, a remote tavern in western Tennessee, Tocqueville was taken desperately ill, almost losing his life. Arriving at Memphis, they remained for a week and took passage for New Orleans on Christmas Day, 1831. On the same boat were a party of emigrating Choctaw Indians and also Sam Houston, with whom the two Frenchmen held a long conversation. New Orleans detained them only three days; here slavery, which had been observed at Memphis, was again encountered, along with its various effects, and unfavorably appraised. Turning eastward again, they went to Mobile and Montgomery and thence to Norfolk and Washington, apparently passing through Macon, Milledgeville, Augusta, Columbia, and Fayetteville. Slavery and the Indian problem continued to confront them along this route; and somewhere in South Carolina, presumably at a tavern where they were detained by a travel mishap, they spent five days in company with Joel R. Poinsett, whom they had previously met in Philadelphia and who was now acting as one of the organizers of anti-nullification sentiment in his native state.

In addition to their joint work on prisons, Beaumont and Tocqueville wrote individually of their experiences in America. Beaumont's reflections appeared in the form of a novel, entitled *Marie, ou L'esclavage aux États-Unis*. Although never translated into English and therefore relatively unknown in the United States, this work contains many acute and penetrating observations on the race problem as it existed, in both the North and the South, in the 1830's. The plot has been related in the introduction to this section of *Travels in the Old South*.

Beaumont apparently kept a diary which included his Southern travels, but it has been lost. Thirty years later while editing the correspondence of Tocqueville, he undertook to reconstruct from some pencil notes, which he claimed to have made in America, a journal of the tour from Wheeling to New Orleans. This he published in pages 28–34 of Tocqueville's *Correspondence et Oeuvres Posthumes* (Paris, 1860). (This is Vol. V of *Oeuvres Complètes d'Alexis de Tocqueville*. 9 vols. Paris, Michel Lévy Frères, 1864–1867. 21 cm. Copy in the Library of Congress.) English translation of this volume, together with Vol. VI, published as *Memoir, Letters, and Remains of*

Alexis de Tocqueville (2 vols. London, Macmillan & Co., 1861. Vol. I, xii, 455 p.; Vol. II, ix, 470 p. 18 cm. Copy in the Library of Congress). American edition (2 vols. Boston, Ticknor and Fields, 1862. Vol. I, x, 430 p.; Vol. II, xi, 442 p. 17 cm. Copy in The New York Public Library). Internal evidence, however, casts considerable doubt on the contemporaneous character of this sketch. (See George W. Pierson, *Tocqueville and Beaumont in America* [New York, 1938], 546–47.)

14. Bernhard, Karl, Duke of Saxe-Weimar-Eisenach (1792–1862)

Reise sr. Hoheit des Herzogs Bernhard zu Sachsen-Weimar-Eisenach durch Nord-Amerika in den Jahren 1825 und 1826. Hrsg. von Heinrich Luden . . . Weimar, Wilhelm Hoffmann, 1828.

> 2 vols. in 1: Vol. I, xxxi, 317 p.; Vol. II, 323 p. fold. front., illus., plates, maps (part fold.), fold. plans. 23½ cm.
> *Inclusive dates:* 1825–1826.
> *Other editions:*
> (1) Travels through North America, during the years 1825 and 1826. By His Highness, Bernhard, duke of Saxe-Weimar-Eisenach . . . 2 vols. Philadelphia, Carey, Lea & Carey, sold in New York by G. & C. Carvill, 1828. Vol. I, iv, [9]–212 p.; Vol. II, [3]–238 p. 21½ cm. Trans. from the German.
> (2) Reize naar en door Noord-Amerika 1825–1826, in twee deelen. Te Dordrecht, Bij Blusse en van Braam, 1829.
> *Location of copy:* North Carolina State College Library.

These travels included an extensive tour of the South. After a visit to Mount Vernon, made while visiting Washington City, Bernhard entered Virginia in November, 1825, passing through Harpers Ferry, Winchester, Staunton, Natural Bridge, Lexington, Charlottesville, and Richmond, and thence proceeding by steamer to Norfolk. In the Carolinas his itinerary included Murfreesboro, Tarboro, Fayetteville, Cheraw, Camden, Columbia, and Charleston. Turning then westward, his route continued by way of Augusta, Milledgeville, Macon, and Fort Mitchell, to Montgomery, from which he went by steamboat to Mobile. A side trip to Pensacola was taken in company with Colonel John E. Wool, who was going to inspect the garrison there. Returning to Mobile, Bernhard resumed his tour, going on to New Orleans and later ascending the Mississippi to St. Louis, where he ended the Southern phase of his tour in April, 1826.

Bernhard was a shrewd observer and described his experiences in considerable detail. He disliked slavery and, like most travelers of this period, was critical of the bad roads and poor accommodations

Reise

Sr. Hoheit

des

Herzogs Bernhard

zu Sachsen-Weimar-Eisenach

durch

Nord - Amerika

in den Jahren 1825 und 1826.

Karl Bernhard

Herausgegeben

von

Heinrich Luden.

Erster Theil.

Mit 16 Vignetten, 4 Kupfern, 3 Planen und 2 Charten.

Weimar, 1828.

bei Wilhelm Hoffmann.

[22]

in Georgia and Alabama. He was not impressed with the farming he saw in North Carolina and was somewhat amazed at the primitive types of dwellings he encountered there. As became his station, he was more at home in cities and with the upper classes of society. He particularly enjoyed a night spent with Jefferson at Monticello, his contacts with the faculty of the South Carolina College at Columbia, his entertainment by the German community in Charleston, and his experiences in New Orleans, where he spent nine weeks in a round of balls, dances, the theater, and other diversions. As a military man he was especially interested in forts, arsenals, garrisons, and weapons, observing these wherever possible, as at Harpers Ferry and Fortress Monroe, noting their features in detailed and often technical military phraseology.

15.

Bilder aus dem gesellschaftlichen Leben der Nord-Amerikaner ... Von einer Deutschen. Reutlingen, M. Mäcken, 1835.

> 254 p. 21½ cm.
> *Illustrations:* One: Capitol at Washington.
> *Inclusive dates:* c.1833–1834.
> *Other editions:*
> Erzählungen aus dem gesellschaftlichen Leben der Nord-Amerikaner. Reutlingen, Beck'sche Antiquariats-Buchhandlung, 1842.
> *Location of copy:* Harvard University Library.

This book relates mainly to New York and Philadelphia. The last chapter has a brief account of Charleston, South Carolina, to which the author traveled from Philadelphia by sea sometime in 1833 or 1834 (pp. 245–54).

16.   Bromme, Traugott (1802–1866)

Reisen durch die Vereinigten Staaten und Ober-Canada. Von Tr. Bromme. 3 vols. Baltimore, C. Scheld & co., 1834–35. [Actually printed in Dresden by Waltheresche Hofbuchhandlung for Scheld, a German bookseller in Baltimore.]

> Vol. I, xii, 334 p.; Vol. II, x, 381 p.; Vol. III, xvi, 466 p.   fold. map., tables (part fold.).
> *Inclusive dates:* c.1831–1833.
> *Location of copy:* Library of Congress.

The second and a portion of the third volume relate to the Southern states. After a tour of New York, New England, and Pennsylvania, Bromme entered the South at Baltimore and there set out upon an extensive itinerary which included Lexington and other Kentucky towns; Gallatin, Nashville, Lebanon, Carthage, Knoxville, and Rogersville, Tennessee; Abingdon, Staunton, Harrisonburg, Winchester, and Norfolk, Virginia; Elizabeth City, Edenton, New Bern, and Wilmington, North Carolina; Georgetown, Charleston, and Beaufort, South Carolina; Savannah and Darien, Georgia; and St. Augustine, Pensacola, Mobile, New Orleans, Natchez, and Memphis, from which point he went to St. Louis and thence to the Northwest and Canada. His motives were to observe a young nation which was not at "the end of centuries but beginning" in political development, whose economy was nascent and not mature, and where he hoped to help poor German peasants find a new and better land of opportunity. His observations and comments are presented in great detail, especially those regarding economic conditions, distances, counties, towns, and other factors that would be of interest to German travelers or emigrants.

Bromme's *Reisen* was the foundation upon which he based other extensive works on the United States, including the South. Among these were:

(1) Louisiana. Ein Taschenbuch für Auswanderer und Freunde der Länder- und Völkerkunde. A reprint of the section on Louisiana in Bromme's Reisen durch die Vereinigten Staaten. Baltimore, C. Scheld und co., 1837.
54 p. 20 cm.
Inclusive dates: c.1832.
Location of copy: The New York Public Library.

(2) Reise durch die Floridas von St. Augustine durch die Halbinsel nach Pensacola. A reprint of the Florida portion of Bromme's Reisen durch die Vereinigten Staaten. Baltimore, C. Scheld und co., 1837.
[3]–80 p. 19½ cm.
Inclusive dates: c.1832.
Location of copy: The New York Public Library.

(3) Mississippi und Alabama. Taschenbuch für Einwanderer und Freunde der Länder- und Völkerkunde. Two parts, each with separate titles, *viz.*: Mississippi, eine geographisch-statistisch-topographische Skizze für Einwanderer und Freunde der Länder- und Völkerkunde; Alabama, eine geographisch- . . . und Völkerkunde. These are reprints of the portions dealing with Mississippi and Alabama in Bromme's Reisen durch die Vereinigten Staaten. Baltimore, C. Scheld und co., 1837.

[24]

Part I, 24 p.; Part II, 22 p. 19 cm.
Inclusive dates: c.1832.
Location of copy: The New York Public Library.

(4) Neustes vollständigstes Hand- und Reisebuch für Auswanderer aus allen Klassen und jeden Stande nach den Vereinigten Staaten von Nord-Amerika. Contains advice to immigrants—where to go and not to go, what to take, and what to do. Includes information on the South, especially Florida and Texas. Bayreuth, Buchner'schen Buchhandlung, 1846.

viii, 387 p. 20 cm.
Other editions:
    1847, 1848, 1849, 1853, 1866, 1875, and at least two others. Among these were:
    1) Hand- und Reisebuch für Auswanderer nach den Vereinigten Staaten von Nord-Amerika, Texas, ober- und unter Canada . . . Bayreuth, Buchner'schen Buchhandlung, 1848. xii, 555 p. 19 cm.
    2) Hand- und Reisebuch für Auswanderer und Reisende nach den Vereinigten Staaten von Nord-Amerika. Bamberg, Buchner'schen Buchhandlung, 1875. xi, 727 p. 18½ cm.
Location of copy: The New York Public Library.

(5) Gemälde von Nord-Amerika in allen Beziehungen von der Entdeckung an bis in die neueste Zeit. Eine pittoreske Geographie für alle, welche unterhaltende Belehrung suchen und ein umfassendes Reisehandbuch für jene, welche in diesem Lande wandern wollen. A geographical work, containing a physical, ethnographic, and political account of North America and including some material on the South. 2 vols. Stuttgart, J. Scheible's Buchhandlung, 1842.

Vol. I, [5]–796, and xxxxviii p. of illus.; Vol. II, ix, 800, and 39 p. of illus. 22 cm.
Other editions:
    Vol. I of this work was also issued as:
    1) Des Universums Neue Welt; Nord-Amerika, in allen Beziehungen geschildert. Stuttgart, J. Scheible's Buchhandlung, 1838–42. [5]–796, and xxxxviii p. of illus. 22 cm.
    2) Nordamerikas Bewohner, Schönheiten und Naturschätz im allgemeinen und die britischen Besitzungen insbesondere. Stuttgart, J. Scheible's Buchhandlung, 1839. [5]–796, and xxxxviii p. of illus. 22 cm.
Location of copy: The New York Public Library.

17. Brown, William Wells (b. 1815)

Narrative of William W. Brown, a fugitive slave. Written by himself. Boston, The Anti-slavery office, 1847.

        xi, [13]–110 p. front. (port.). 17½ cm.
        Inclusive dates: c.1830–1835.

Other editions:

    (1) London, Charles Gilpin, 1849. ix, ₁13₁–168 p. 17 cm.

    (2) Twelfth thousand. ₁With a portrait₁. London, Charles Gilpin, 1850.

    (3) ₁With an appendix₁. London, ₁Dublin printed₁, 1850.

    (4) With additions by the Rev. Samuel Green. London, W. Tegg & co., 1853. 176 p. 12mo.

    (5) Levensgeschiedenis van den Amerikaanschen slaaf, W. Wells Brown, Amerikaansch afgevaardigde bij het vredescongres te Parijs, 1849, door hem zelven beschreven. Naar den 5. Engelschen druk vertaald door M. Keijzer. Zwolle, W.E.J. Tjeenk Willink, 1850. x, 119, ₁1₁ p. front. (port.). 23½ cm. *Location of copy:* Library of Congress.

The author of this work was born a slave in Kentucky about 1815 and was carried to Missouri as a child. During his youth he made several trips from St. Louis to New Orleans as a member of the crew of a steamboat carrying cargoes of slaves. These episodes, together with his escape from the South into Ohio in 1834, are described in typical abolitionist fashion, but the main emphasis is upon his life in Missouri and his experiences after reaching the North. In Ohio, he took the name of William Wells Brown and later achieved some distinction as a reformer and historian of the Negro race.

18.   Bullock, William (fl. 1808–1828)

Sketch of a journey through the western states of North America, from New Orleans, by the Mississippi, Ohio, city of Cincinnati and Falls of Niagara, to New York, in 1827. With a description of the new and flourishing city of Cincinnati by Messrs. B. Drake and E. D. Mansfield. And a selection from various authors . . . useful to persons desirous of settling in America. London, John Miller, 1827.

    3 p.l., ₁v₁–xxxi, viii, 135 p. front. (fold. plan), fold. map. 18½ cm.
Maps: Fold. map of the U. S.
Illustrations: Frontispiece: folded chart of proposed town of Hygeia.
Inclusive dates: 1827.
Other editions:

    (1) London, John Miller, 1827. 2 pts. 12mo.

    (2) Bullock's journey from New Orleans to New York, in 1827 . . . Cleveland, O., 1905. fold. plan. (In Reuben G. Thwaites [ed.], Early western travels, 1748–1846. Cleveland, 1904–1907. Vol. XIX, pp. ₁113₁–154. 24½ cm.).
Location of copy: Library of Congress.

Bullock was a proprietor of a London museum, to secure material for which he had visited Mexico in 1822, later publishing a widely read book on that country. On a second trip to Mexico in 1827, he returned by way of the United States, landing at New Orleans and going up the Mississippi and Ohio to Cincinnati. From Cincinnati he went over into Kentucky and spent about two weeks at Elmwood, an estate which he purchased and to which he returned from England with his family to make his home in 1828. The Southern phase of his 1827 visit to the United States is described on pages v–xxi. The remainder of the book deals with the North and East. There is a brief description of New Orleans, reprinted from Timothy Flint's *Recollections* (*q.v.*) and a good account of the steamboat upon which Bullock ascended the Mississippi.

19.   [Burlend, Mrs. Rebecca (1793–1872)]

A true picture of emigration: or fourteen years in the interior of North America; being a full and impartial account of the various difficulties and ultimate success of an English family who emigrated from Barwick-in-Elmet, near Leeds, in the year 1831. London, G. Berger; ɩetc., etc., 1848ɩ.

> 1 p.l., ɩ5ɩ–62 p.   17½ cm.
> *Inclusive dates:* 1831–1845.
> *Other editions:*
>   Edited by Milo Milton Quaife . . . Chicago, The Lakeside Press, R. R. Donnelley & sons co., 1936. xxxi, 167 p.   front. (port.), fold. map.   17½ cm. (Lakeside classics ɩ34ɩ).
> *Location of copy:* The New York Public Library.

This is an account of the experiences of a family of English emigrants who settled in Pike County, Illinois, as narrated by the mother. They landed at New Orleans, spent one day there, and then traveled by steamboat up the Mississippi River. There is a brief description of New Orleans, and a few references to the trip up the river. The author was unfriendly to slavery. The narrative relates almost entirely to Illinois, less than three pages being devoted to the South.

20.   Chevalier, Michel (1806–1879)

Lettres sur l'Amérique du Nord, par Michel Chevalier, avec une carte des États-Unis d'Amérique . . . 2 vols. Paris, C. Gosselin et cie., 1836.

> Vol. I, 2 l., xv, 470, ɩ2ɩ p.; Vol. II, 2 l., 527, ɩ1ɩ p.   fold. map.   22 cm.
> *Inclusive dates:* 1833–1835.
> *Other editions:*
>   (1) Edition spéciale revue, corrigée et augmen. de plusieurs chapitres. 2 vols. Paris, Charles Gosselin et Cᵉ., M DCCC XXXVII.   Vol. I, 2 l., xvi, 438 p.; Vol. II, 2 l., 531 p.
>   (2) Troisième edition. Paris, 1836.
>   (3) 3. éd., rev., cor., augm. de plusieurs chapitres et d'une table raisonnée des matières. Paris, C. Gosselin et Cⁱᵉ., 1838.
>   (4) Quatrième edition. Paris, 1837.
>   (5) 2 vols. Bruxelles, Société belge de librairie, etc., Hauman, Cattoir et cᵉ., 1837.   Vol. I, 2 l., 484 p.; Vol. II, 2 l., 531 p.   fold. map.   16 cm.

(6) 3 vols. Bruxelles, 1837. 12mo.

(7) 3d., rev., cor., augm. de plusieurs chapitres et d'une table raisonnée des matières . . . 3 vols. Bruxelles, Société belge de librairie, 1838. fold. map. 16 cm.

(8) Troisième ed. 3 vols. Bruxelles, 1839. 12mo.

(9) Society, manners and politics in the United States: being a series of letters on North America . . . Tr. from the 3d Paris ed. Boston, Weeks, Jordan and company, 1839. iv, 467 p. 22 cm. (Tr. by Thomas Gamaliel Bradford).

(10) Lettres sur l'Amérique du Nord; extraits avec une introduction par Robert G. Mahieu. Princeton, Princeton university press for Institut français de Washington, 1944. xx, 51 p. 21½ cm. (Petite bibliothèque américaine. Institut français de Washington).

(11) Briefe über Nord-Amerika . . . Aus dem Französichen. Leipzig: P. Reclam, junr., 1837.

These letters originally appeared in the Journal des debats; cf. Sabin. *Location of copy:* Duke University Library.

Chevalier, later to become a celebrated French economist, was sent to the United States, under the patronage of the French ministry of the interior, to study railroads and other public works. He arrived in December, 1833, and was so attracted by the country that he remained until October, 1835. During this time he traveled extensively in all parts of the Union, studying the social and political system and recording his observations in a series of letters which gave him a reputation among his contemporaries equal to that of Tocqueville and Beaumont, and which still remains as one of the most important French commentaries on the United States.

Chevalier's itinerary in the South is difficult to trace, and if the letters were written in the order of their dates, he must have visited the section more than once. It appears certain that he stopped at Richmond, Charleston, Augusta, New Orleans, Memphis, and Louisville. The letters, presumably written from various towns along his route, are general and philosophical in nature; and, except in a few instances, are not descriptive of any particular locale. There is a brief description of a tobacco works at Petersburg, Virginia (p. 83); a penetrating analysis of the contrast between Yankees and Virginians (pp. 109–24); further comments upon the differences between the North and South (pp. 150–57); a description of Richmond (pp. 325–29); and incidental comment upon social and economic conditions in the South (pp. 399–400).

21. Church, Jeremiah

Journal of travels, adventures, and remarks, of Jerry Church. Harrisburg, 1845.

72 p.   15 cm.
Inclusive dates: c.1831.
Other editions:
   Reprint of 1845 edition. Edited with notes, &c., by A. Monroe Aurand, jr. Harrisburg, Pa., priv. print. by the Aurand press, 1933. 2 p.l., [7]–89 p. 23½ cm.
Location of copy: Library of Congress.

The author made three trips to the South about 1831. On the first of these he traveled from Pennsylvania by way of Washington and Richmond to North Carolina, where he engaged for a short time in gold mining, and then continued on through East Tennessee, Nashville, and Smithland, Kentucky, to St. Louis (pp. 18–22). Later he passed down the Mississippi River en route from Chicago to New Orleans (pp. 31–33). On the third trip he spent a short time in Tennessee as a land speculator. Except for a description of gold mining in North Carolina (pp. 19–20), his references to the South are casual. The account is bold and rollicking, leading the reader to question its reliability.

22.   Coke, Edward Thomas (1807–1888)

A subaltern's furlough; descriptive of scenes in various parts of the United States, upper and lower Canada, New Brunswick, and Nova Scotia, during the summer and autumn of 1832. By E. T. Coke . . . 2 vols. New York, J. & J. Harper, 1833.

   Vol. I, [13]–222 p.; Vol. II, iv, 188 p.   17½ cm.
Inclusive dates: June, 1832.
Other editions:
   (1) London, Saunders and Otley, 1833.   xi, 485 p.   plates, fold. map, fold. facsim.   22½ cm.
   (2) A subaltern's furlough . . . (In The select circulating library . . . Philadelphia, 1833.   29½ cm.   Vol. II., pp. 378–426).
Location of copy: University of North Carolina Library.

Coke's travel in the South (I, 68–122) was only a minor incident of his American tour and was centered around Washington and Baltimore, including Mount Vernon, Winchester, and Harpers Ferry, Virginia, and Point of Rocks, Maryland. He confined his remarks "to those things which require but a short residence, in a country . . . merely pointing out some of the most interesting objects and places of greatest historical note," and leaving "the full definition of Republican, National Republican, Federalist, Nullifier, Democrat, and all the other various shades and sects of the political world, to those who have made state affairs their study."

[29]

23. Conder, Josiah (1789–1855)

. . . [United States of America and Canada] by Josiah Conder . . . 2 vols. London, J. Duncan, 1830.

> Vol. I, v, 372 p.; Vol. II, iv, 335 p. fronts. (fold. maps), plates. 16 cm.
> (Half-title: The modern traveller, Vol. 23–24).
> *Maps:* Two: folding maps of North America (Vol. I) and United States (Vol. II).
> *Illustrations:* Fine landscapes.
> *Location of copy:* Library of Congress.

Conder's work is really a sort of history of the world drawn from accounts of British travelers. The second of these volumes includes several long descriptions of travel in the South in the form of long quotations or digests of the accounts of Hall and Hodgson.

24. Cooke, Philip St. George (1809–1895)

Scenes and adventures in the army; or, romance of military life. By P. St. G. Cooke . . . Philadelphia, Lindsay & Blakiston, 1857.

> xii, [13]–432 p. 18½ cm.
> *Inclusive dates:* 1833.
> *Other editions:*
> Philadelphia, Lindsay & Blakiston, 1859.
> *Location of copy:* Library of Congress.

This book covers the period 1827–45 and relates mainly to the West—Missouri, Kansas, Wisconsin, and the territories. One chapter (pp. 197–204) describes Cooke's experiences as a recruiting officer in Tennessee in 1833. He passed through Clarksville, Perryville, Lexington, and Jackson to Nashville, where he spent a week and then took his recruits by keelboat to Paducah and thence by steamboat to Jefferson Barracks.

25. Cooper, James Fenimore (1789–1851)

Notions of the Americans: picked up by a travelling bachelor . . . 2 vols. Philadelphia, Carey, Lea & Carey, 1828.

> Vol. I, xii, 340 p.; Vol. II, [3]–359 p. 18 cm.
> *Other editions:*
> (1) 2 vols. London, Henry Colburn, 1828. Vol. I, xxiv, 459 p.; Vol. II, xi, 477 p. 22 cm.
> (2) Philadelphia, 1833.
> (3) New edition. Phila., 1838.
> (4) New edition. Phila., 1840.
> (5) New York, Stringer & Townsend, 1840.
> (6) New York, Stringer & Townsend, 1850.

(7) The travelling bachelor; or, Notions of the Americans, by J. Fenimore Cooper. Complete in one volume. New edition. New York, Stringer and Townsend, 1856. xii, 696 p. 19 cm.

(8) Lettres sur les moeurs et les institutions des États Unis de l'Amérique septentrionale. Par M. James Fennimore [*sic*] Cooper; traduit de l'Anglais par Mlle. H. Preble. 4 vols. Paris, 1828. 12mo.

(9) Die Nordamerikaner, geschildert von einem reisenden Junggesellen. Aus dem Englischen. 4 vols. Stuttgart, Frankh, Buchhdg., 1828. 8vo.

(10) Frankfurt am Main, 1929.

Location of copy: Library of Congress.

This purports to be a series of letters written home by an Englishman traveling in the United States, but in reality it is the work of a homesick American defending his country against the misunderstandings he had met in Europe, where Cooper had been living for two years. Three of the letters are on the South, dealing with (1) slavery, (2) Indians, and (3) general social and economic conditions. These are dated from Washington and New York, the author stating that he has just returned from a Southern tour; but this is obviously fictitious.

26. Cortambert, Louis Richard (1808?–1881)

Voyage au pays des Osages. Un tour en Sicile. Par Louis Cortambert. Paris, A. Bertrand, 1837.

94 p. 21 cm.
Inclusive dates: 1835–1836.
Location of copy: Library of Congress.

Mostly Indian material relating to Missouri and Oklahoma. After leaving Missouri, the author descended the Mississippi to New Orleans, this trip being briefly described, with casual references to Vicksburg, Natchez, and Baton Rouge (pp. 53–56).

The *Voyage* covers pages 5–56; *Un tour en Sicile,* pages 57–84. Pages 85–94 describe an "Excursion aux Cataractes du Niagara," taken in June, 1833, at the end of a previous visit made to the United States by Cortambert. He was in the South during the earlier trip, but this is not described here.

27.

The cousins' journey; or, sketches of American scenery. Boston, L. C. Bowles, 1833.

102 p. 15 cm.
Illustrations: One: front. (farmyard scene).
Inclusive dates: c.1830.
Location of copy: Library of Congress.

A book for young people. The preface states that "its descriptions are all conformed to reality, being taken from the letters of an intelligent traveler, pursuing the route pointed out in the work. It thus forms an authentic little book of travels for the young, of which the accounts are adapted to their comprehension, and related in such a manner as to excite their interest."

It purports to be a series of letters written by two young people to a cousin in Massachusetts while returning to their home in Louisiana after a visit to this relative. Their itinerary south of Washington includes Leesburg, Winchester, New Market, Lexington, Abingdon, Knoxville, Huntsville, the Choctaw country, and Natchez, and thence by boat to New Orleans. The material is almost entirely descriptive and may be based upon the letters mentioned in the preface, although it could have been taken from guidebooks and gazetteers.

28.   Crawford, William (1788–1847)

Penitentiaries (United States). Report of William Crawford, esq., on the penitentiaries of the United States, addressed to His Majesty's principal secretary of state for the Home department. Ordered, by the House of commons, to be printed, 11 August 1834. [London, 1834].

> 56, 229 p. 18 plans (partly fold.). 33½ cm.
> *Inclusive dates:* c.1833.
> *Other editions:*
>> Report of William Crawford, esq., on the penitentiaries of the United States . . . Ordered to be printed 13th March 1835. [London, 1835].
> *Location of copy:* Library of Congress.

Includes descriptions of penitentiaries in Virginia, Kentucky, and Tennessee. An official report, detailed and statistical.

29.   Crockett, David (1786–1836)

Col. Crockett's exploits and adventures in Texas: wherein is contained a full account of his journey from Tennessee to the Red River and Natchitoches, and thence across Texas to San Antonio; including his many hair-breadth escapes: together with a topographical, historical, and political view of Texas . . . The narrative brought down from the death of Col. Crockett to the battle of San Jacinto, by an eye-witness. Philadelphia, T. K. and P. G. Collins, 1836.

> viii, 13–216 p. front. (port.). 17½ cm.
> *Inclusive dates:* 1835–1836.
> *Other editions:*
>> (1) London, R. Kennett, 1837. vii, 152 p. 19½ cm.

(2) 6th ed. Philadelphia, T. K. & P. G. Collins, 1837. viii, 13–216 port. 12mo.

(3) Cincinnati, U. P. James, 1839.

(4) New York, 1845.

(5) New York, W. H. Graham, 1848.

Also in:

Life of Col. David Crockett, written by himself. Comprising his early life, hunting adventures, services under General Jackson in the Creek War, electioneering speeches, career in Congress, triumphal tour in northern states and services in the Texas war. To which is added, an account of Colonel Crockett's glorious death at the Alamo, while fighting in defence of Texas independence. By the editor. Philadelphia, G. G. Evans, 1860. pp. 239–405. front., plates. 19 cm.

Life of David Crockett, the original humorist and irrepressible backwoodsman . . . Philadelphia, Porter & Coates, [c.1865]. pp. 239–405. front., 4 plates. 19½ cm.

Life of David Crockett, the original humorist . . . Philadelphia, J. E. Potter and company, [c.1882]. 2 p.l., 3–404 p., 1 l. front., plates. 19½ cm.

Life of David Crockett, the original humorist . . . New York, The Perkins book company, [c.1903]. xxiv, 415 p. front. (port.), plates. 19 cm.

The autobiography of David Crockett, with an introduction by Hamlin Garland. New York, Chicago [etc.], C. Scribner's sons, [c.1923]. pp. 213–328. 16½ cm.

Davy Crockett and his adventures in Texas, told mostly by himself: with an introduction and illustration by John W. Thomason, jr. New York, Chicago [etc.], C. Scribner's sons, [c.1934]. pp. [135]–[260]. col. front., illus. 21½cm.

Location of copy: Library of Congress.

According to this account, Crockett traveled by canoe and on foot from his home in Weakley County, Tennessee, to the Mississippi, where he boarded a steamboat for Little Rock, at which he arrived in November, 1835. Thence by horseback he went to Fulton, on the Red River, took another steamer, and descended to Natchitoches, and from there continued by horseback to Nacogdoches and across the Texas prairies to San Antonio. Beginning at Natchitoches, he was successively joined by four other adventurers—a gambler referred to as Thimblerig, a bee hunter, and a former pirate and his Indian companion—all of whom accompanied him to San Antonio and died bravely at the Alamo. The account of the party's experiences in crossing the prairies contains descriptions of the regions they traversed and of Crockett's encounters with a buffalo herd, a Mexican cougar, and a band of Comanche Indians. The section relating to the Battle of the Alamo includes a journal purporting to have been kept by Crockett, February 19 to March 5, 1836 (pp. 182–202).

Whole passages from Mrs. Holley's *Texas*, David B. Edward's *History of Texas*, and other current frontier materials are incorporated into the narrative, thus leading to serious questions regarding its authenticity. According to the preface, the manuscript, which had presumably been taken from Crockett's baggage at the Alamo, was found in General Castrillon's effects at San Jacinto by one Charles T. Beale, who "added a chapter, and brought down the history of the events to the present time." More probably it was the work of hack writers who quickly assembled it at Philadelphia soon after word of Crockett's death was received in the East. For further discussion of this problem, see Constance Rourke, *Davy Crockett* (New York, Harcourt, Brace and Company, 1934), 247–76; and James Atkins Shackford, *David Crockett, the Man and the Legend* (Chapel Hill, University of North Carolina Press, 1956), 273–81.

30. Cushing, S. W. (b. 1818)

Wild oats sowings; or, the autobiography of an adventurer . . . By S. W. Cushing. New York, D. Fanshaw, 1857.

> 483 p.   19 cm.
> *Illustrations:* Four: Naval engagements.
> *Inclusive dates:* c.1830–1840.
> *Location of copy:* Library of Congress.

As a sailor, Cushing, a native of Boston, was in Charleston, Mobile, and New Orleans on various occasions during the 1830's and 1840's. Accounts of these visits are interspersed through his book, but in general they include little except descriptions of gambling, fighting, and other escapades characteristic of adventurous seamen. In 1836 he took service on the Texas schooner *Liberty* and saw some action in Matagorda Bay; and also served as a Texas soldier at San Jacinto. He deals at some length with his experiences in Texas, both before and after San Jacinto, but mainly in the form of descriptive material and adventure, having little value as a traveler's account.

31. Davenport, Bishop

A new gazetteer, or geographical dictionary of North America and the West Indies . . . Comp. from the most recent and authentic sources. By Bishop Davenport. Baltimore, G. M'Dowell & son; Providence, Hutchens & Shepard, 1832.

> 471 p.   illus., 2 fold. maps.   22½ cm.
> *Maps:* Folded colored maps of North America and of the United States.
> *Other editions:*
> (1) Baltimore, G. M'Dowell & son, 1833.
> (2) Baltimore, G. M'Dowell, 1835.

(3) A new edition with alterations and additions to 1836 . . . Philadelphia, B. Davenport & co., 1836. 518 p. illus., fold. map. 23 cm.

(4) A new edition with alterations and additions by Bishop Davenport. Philadelphia, B. Davenport & co., 1838.

(5) A pocket gazetteer, or Traveller's guide through North America and the West Indies . . . Baltimore, Plaskitt & co., ₍etc.₎, 1833. 468 p. front. (fold. map), illus., fold. plates. 15 cm.

(6) Trenton, N. J., the author, 1833.

(7) A history and new gazetteer, or geographical dictionary, of North America and the West Indies . . . Compiled from the most recent and authentic sources. A new and much improved edition. By Bishop Davenport. New York, S. W. Benedict & co., 1842. 592 p. illus. (incl. maps, coats of arms). 23½ cm.
Location of copy: Library of Congress.

Includes complete information on extent, boundaries, and products of each state; the bearing and distance of various places from each other and from Washington; population figures for 1830; and tables of commerce, revenue, the public debt, and various institutions of the United States.

32. Davis, Stephen

Notes of a tour in America, in 1832 and 1833. By Stephen Davis . . . Edinburgh, Waugh & Innes; ₍etc., etc.₎, 1833.

4 p.l., ₍vii₎–xii, ₍13₎–150 p. 14½ cm.
Inclusive dates: 1833.
Location of copy: Library of Congress.

The author was a Baptist minister, the object of whose tour was to raise funds for a society to promote a knowledge of the Bible in Ireland. He was in Virginia during February, 1833, visiting and preaching at Alexandria, Fredericksburg, Richmond, and Norfolk, and going thence by boat to Baltimore. This was only an incidental phase of his tour and is described very briefly. He was critical of slavery, which he regarded as a stain upon the South and a cause for that section's inferiority to the North and West. There is a description of a slave auction which he witnessed at Richmond (p. 101).

33. [Delius, Edouard]

Wanderungen eines jungen Norddeutschen durch Portugal, Spanien, und Nord-Amerika in dem Jahren 1827–1831. Hrsg. von Georg Lotz. 4 vols. Hamburg, Herold-schen Buchhandlungen, 1834.

Vol. I, vi, 192 p.; Vol. II, 192 p.; Vol. III, 184 p.; Vol. IV, 195 p.
Inclusive dates: 1830–1831.
Location of Copy: The New York Public Library.

Delius arrived in New York in December, 1829. He visited Boston, Philadelphia, and Baltimore (for some time), and Virginia in the spring of 1830. In the fall and winter of 1830–31 he went to Charleston, Savannah, Augusta, Macon, Columbus, Montgomery, Mobile, and New Orleans, and thence to Rapp's colony in Indiana. He refers to himself as wishing "above all things not to be ranked amongst those writers on America, who are reproached, with more or less reason, to have returned hospitality with ridicule" and states that he has described America "not to a practical matter of fact, but to an easy and abstractedly polished people,"—in short, that he wrote "for Germans with German notions" (IV, 194–95).

34. Demetz, Frédéric Auguste (1796–1873)

Rapports à m. le comte de Montalivet . . . ministre secrétaire d'état au Département de l'intérieur, sur les pénitenciers des États-Unis, par m. Demetz . . . et par m. Abel Blouet. Paris, Imprimerie royale, 1837.

> 2 p.l., 144, 114 p., 1 l. 45 plates. (part fold., incl. plans). 33 cm.
> *Illustrations:* Folded plans.
> *Other editions:*
> Paris, Imprimerie royale, 1839.
> *Location of copy:* Library of Congress.

An account of United States prisons. The only one described in the South was at Richmond, and that only briefly. There is no itinerary. This is really an official document, heavily charged with statistics.

35. Edward, David B.

The history of Texas; or, the emigrant's, farmer's, and politician's guide to the character, climate, soil and productions of that country: geographically arranged from personal observation and experience. By David B. Edward . . . Cincinnati, J. A. James & co., 1836.

> xii, 13–336 p. front. (fold. map). 17½ cm.
> *Location of copy:* Duke University Library.

The author was a Scottish schoolmaster, at the Gonzales Seminary, in Texas. He had lived in Texas for three years at the time he wrote this book. Also he was "one of four who explored it, in the year 1830, from side to side, and from settlement to settlement, during the space of six months, without once sleeping within the walls of a house." In 1835 he "had the curiosity to spend six months more, in examining the improvements made throughout every locality of that extensive province; in order that none should be able to detect a falsehood, or prove a material error, which could either mislead, or seriously injure those who may put confidence in this work."

The book itself is not a travel account, although the author, as above indicated, had traveled widely over Texas. It is historical, geographical, and statistical, including descriptions of boundaries, resources, water, timber, climate, Indians, Mexicans, and people of Texas; also documents, advice to emigrants, and a copy of the Mexican constitution of 1824.

Like Mrs. Holley's *Texas,* this work was extensively used as a basis for many other books on that state written in the 1830's and 1840's.

36. Ehrenberg, Hermann

Texas und seine Revolution, von Hermann Ehrenberg . . . Leipzig, Otto Wigand, 1843.

iv, 258 p. 21½ cm.
Inclusive dates: 1835–1836.
Other editions:

(1) Der Freiheitskampf in Texas im Jahre 1836. Von H. Ehrenberg . . . Leipzig, O. Wigand, 1844. 1 p.l., iv, 293, ₁1₁ p. 13½ cm.

(2) Fahrten und Schicksale eines Deutschen in Texas. Leipzig, 1845.

(3) A translation of H. Ehrenberg's Fahrten und Schicksale eines Deutschen in Texas, with introduction and notes . . . by Edgar William Bartholomae . . . M.A. thesis, University of Texas, Austin, 1925. 8 p.l., 335 num. l. 2 l. 28 cm.

(4) With Milam and Fannin; adventures of a German boy in Texas' revolution, by Herman Ehrenberg; translator, Charlotte Churchill; editor, Henry Smith; typographer, Mariana Roach; illustrator, Jerry Bywaters. Dallas, Tex., Tardy publishing company, inc., ₁c.1935₁. 1 p.l., vii–xv, 224 p., incl. plates. front. 19½ cm. ("Abridged translation").
Location of copy: New York Public Library.

Ehrenberg was a young German who came to the United States in 1835, reaching New Orleans in October. There he joined a band of Volunteers, known as the New Orleans Greys, and went with this outfit to Texas. Their route was up the Mississippi and Red rivers by steamboat to Natchitoches, on foot to Nacogdoches, and thence on horseback through Washington and Bastrop to San Antonio. They participated in the storming of the Alamo under Milam, witnessed the surrender of General Cos, and were among those who occupied the Alamo after Cos had gone back to Mexico. In December they joined the proposed expedition against Matamoras, going down the San Antonio River to Goliad and thence to Refugio to await Fannin. Upon the arrival of the latter the expedition was given up, and the troops returned to Goliad. After receiving news of the fall of the Alamo, they retreated from Goliad but were overtaken and captured by the Mexicans on the Coleto. Taken back to Goliad by their captors, they were imprisoned for a time and then treacherously massacred, Ehrenberg being one of the few to escape.

Ehrenberg's experiences in the above campaigns are described graphically and perhaps with greater detachment than a citizen of the United States could have described them. His account deals largely with military events, such as marches and battles, but there is considerable material relating to camp and prison life, and some descriptive material regarding the prairies and other features of Texas geography. Possibly the book may have played some part in attracting German immigrants to Texas in the forties and fifties.

37. Ellsworth, Henry Leavitt (1791–1858)

Washington Irving on the prairie; or, A narrative of a tour of the Southwest in the year 1832, by Henry Leavitt Ellsworth; edited by Stanley T. Williams and Barbara D. Simison. New York, American book company, 1937.

> xviii, 152 p.   map, facsims.   23 cm.
> *Maps:* One: showing route of the Irving party.
> *Illustrations:* Two: facsimile pages of Ellsworth's journal.
> *Inclusive dates:* October 8–November 17, 1832.
> *Location of copy:* University of North Carolina Library.

Ellsworth, a New Englander, was appointed in 1832 as one of three commissioners to superintend the settlement of the Indian tribes transplanted to the south and west of the Arkansas River. En route to this assignment he accidentally met Washington Irving, Charles J. Latrobe, and the latter's protégé, the youthful Count de Pourtales, all of whom decided to accompany him to the West. Upon reaching Fort Gibson and finding that the other two commissioners had not arrived, Ellsworth arranged an expedition, including himself, his three traveling companions, guides, and a party of mounted Rangers, to visit the buffalo country lying about a hundred miles farther on. It was thus that Irving obtained his material for *A Tour on the Prairies* and Latrobe composed a portion of his *Rambler in North America.*

Preserved in the form of a long letter to his wife, Ellsworth's narrative of this expedition parallels closely the accounts written by his two fellow travelers. It begins on October 8, 1832, at Fort Gibson and ends on November 17, at the same place, recording an itinerary which followed the Arkansas River up to its juncture with the Cimarron, westward to the Cross Timbers region in the vicinity of the

Canadian River, and back to Fort Gibson by way of what would later become Norman, Tecumseh, and Okmulgee. In contrast to Latrobe's expansive recital of the same events and to Irving's elegant narrative, it describes without literary embellishment the country through which the party traveled and their day-to-day experiences along the route. These include camping, buffalo hunting, capturing wild horses, contacts with the Osage Indians, and other adventurous episodes.

In addition to its significance as a chronicle of early Oklahoma, Ellsworth's account has indispensable value as a piece of Irvingiana. Here the author of *The Alhambra* and *The Sketch Book* is depicted, not as he was seen in Paris and on Broadway, but as he appeared in the company of Indian guides and other companions on the actual frontier of a hundred years ago. It is also interesting to compare the puritanical Ellsworth's candid description of Pourtales with the more gentlemanly accounts of this wild youth appearing in Irving's *Tour* and Latrobe's *Rambler*.

38.   [Evarts, Jeremiah (1781–1831)]

Through the South and the West with Jeremiah Evarts in 1826. Edited by J. Orin Oliphant. Lewisburg, Pa., Bucknell University Press, 1956.

viii, 143 p.   front.   23 cm.
Inclusive dates: January to May, 1826.
Location of copy: University of North Carolina Library.

Jeremiah Evarts entered the South at Charleston, South Carolina, on January 28, 1826. After a stay of two weeks in that city, he set out for the Cherokee, Choctaw, and Chickasaw Indian country, where he visited and reported upon a number of mission stations that were being operated by the American Board of Commissioners for Foreign Missions, of which he was the active and zealous corresponding secretary. Reaching Memphis on May 8, he proceeded by steamboat up the Mississippi and Ohio rivers to Louisville and thence to Marietta, Ohio, where on May 20 his boat was halted by shallow water and the account of his journey abruptly ends.

For reasons of health Evarts had already made four trips South—in 1818, 1822, 1824, and 1825—and he was therefore not entirely a stranger to the region through which he was traveling in 1826. At the same time, he was not altogether friendly in his comments upon the South. He was not fanatical on the subject of slavery, but like Olmsted in a later period, he was depressed by the casual and at times slovenly way of Southern life. "I have no doubt," he wrote, "the county of Worcester, Mass. contains more good houses, than the whole cotton growing country of the United States (not including the cities), although last year's crop of cotton will probably sell for $24,000,000" (p. 93). He also remarked unfavorably upon the state of religion, morality, and education that he encountered in the Southern interior. Augusta, Georgia, he considered to be "more given to idolatry of money than any other [place] which I can recollect" (p. 96); and in regard to Memphis and its neighborhood, he "could not learn there is any moral culture of the inhabitants" (p. 124).

The account of Evarts' journey is contained in a series of letters written by him on varying dates and at various places to officials of the American Board in Boston and preserved in the records of that organization, now in the Houghton Library at Harvard University. The editor has selected only the significant passages relating to the 1826 trip. These comprise an illuminating, although a partial, view of the South and West in the fiftieth year of American independence.

39.   Featherstonhaugh, George William (1780–1866)

A canoe voyage up the Minnay Sotor; with an account of the lead and copper deposits in Wisconsin; of the gold region in the Cherokee country; and sketches of popular manners; &c., &c., &c. By G. W. Featherstonhaugh . . . 2 vols. London, R. Bentley, 1847.

Vol. I, xiv, 416 p.; Vol. II, vii, 351 p.   fronts., illus., 2 fold. maps.   22 cm.
Maps: Folding map of the United States showing route.
Inclusive dates: July–October, 1836.
Location of copy: University of North Carolina Library.

In the same year that his *Excursion through the Slave States* ended, Featherstonhaugh embarked upon a similar journey through the central states and to the country watered by the principal tributaries of the Mississippi River. On his return he descended the Mississippi and ascended the Ohio to Paducah; continued by steamboat up the Tennessee to Tuscumbia, Alabama, from whence he went to Decatur by rail, and then by steamboat and canoe to Ross's Landing, in the vicinity of which he spent a few days among the Indians and at the Moravian mission at Brainerd. Proceeding thence to Cleveland and into Georgia, he again visited among the Indians and was present at a council held by the Cherokees and United States commissioners at Red Clay. Other Georgia points which he visited included Gainesville, Clarksville, and Dahlonega, where he met John C. Calhoun, whom he also visited later at Fort Hill. From Fort Hill he turned northward, toured western North Carolina, including Asheville and Hot Springs, and then proceeded eastward through Rutherfordton,

Lincolnton, Charlotte, Concord, and Hillsboro to Raleigh, and thence by way of Petersburg and Richmond to Washington.

Featherstonhaugh's principal interests on this portion of his tour were the Indians and the gold-mining operations in Georgia and North Carolina; and these items are described in considerable detail. Of his experiences on steamboats and stagecoaches and at inns and taverns, he was even more critical than in his previous account. On the other hand, he was much charmed with Calhoun and the latter's associates and surroundings at Fort Hill, the vicinity of which reminded him of Tuscany. It thus seems evident that he appreciated and was willing to recognize gentility when he found it, but that he regarded the rudeness and lack of discipline which he encountered on stages and steamboats as more typical of Southern society.

40. Featherstonhaugh, George William (1780–1866)

Excursion through the slave states, from Washington on the Potomac to the frontier of Mexico; with sketches of popular manners and geological notices. By G. W. Featherstonhaugh . . . 2 vols. London, J. Murray, 1844.

> Vol. I, xxix, 357 p.; Vol. II, x, 394 p. fronts., illus., fold. map. 21 cm.
> *Maps:* Folding map of U. S. (in Vol. I), showing route.
> *Illustrations:* Seven in Vol. I; three in Vol. II.
> *Inclusive dates:* August, 1834–February, 1835.
> *Other editions:*
> New York, Harper & brothers, 1844. 168 p. 24 cm.
> *Location of copy:* Duke University Library.

Featherstonhaugh left Baltimore on August 1, 1834, accompanied by his wife and son, and traveled by rail to Frederick and thence by stage through Harpers Ferry, Winchester, and Staunton, to the Virginia Springs. Here he remained for about three weeks and felt himself none too well treated, especially at White Sulphur, of which his account was critical (I, 52–84). Leaving his wife at Sweet Springs, he proceeded westward with his son, through Fincastle, Wytheville, Abingdon, and Saltville, to Blountville, Tennessee. On this trip he overtook a slave trader, now known to have been John Armfield, with three hundred slaves bound for Natchez, a circumstance which led to his inclusion of a vigorously critical reaction to slavery and the slave trade (I, 119–30). Other pertinent comments on this trip include a description of the landlord of an inn at Wytheville (I, 134–35); of the salt works at Saltville (I, 138–41); and of a fight he had in a tavern at Blountville (I, 156–57).

Continuing on in Tennessee he passed through Kingsport, Rogers-

EXCURSION.

THROUGH

THE SLAVE STATES,

FROM

WASHINGTON ON THE POTOMAC TO THE FRONTIER OF MEXICO; WITH SKETCHES
OF POPULAR MANNERS AND GEOLOGICAL NOTICES.

BY

G. W. FEATHERSTONHAUGH, F.R.S., F.G.S

NEW-YORK

PUBLISHED BY HARPER & BROTHERS,
No. 82 CLIFF-STREET.

1844

[42]

ville, Knoxville, Kingston, Sparta, and Lebanon to Nashville, on the road again overtaking Armfield and his coffle and proceeding to further castigation of the slave trade (I, 151–71). He was well pleased with Nashville, where he remained for some days, calling on various people and making geological expeditions into the surrounding country. Leaving on October 5, he proceeded by way of Bowling Green, Mammoth Cave, and Elizabethtown to Louisville, where he had planned to take a steamboat for St. Louis; but growing impatient with the captain's delay in getting started (I, 235–45), he went overland through Indiana and Illinois.

At St. Louis, still accompanied by his son, he bought a wagon, which he used in going to Little Rock, Hot Springs, of which there is a good description (II, 106–17), Washington, across the Red River for a few miles into Texas, and back to Little Rock, where he embarked for New Orleans on December 24. His references to Arkansas are critical in the extreme, including descriptions of violence and uncouth life at Little Rock (II, 42–64); bad food and a habit of never closing doors (II, 68–69); and a call at the executive mansion, where he was informed by the Governor's wife that the chief executive had gone into the woods to look for a sow and pigs (II, 53). He was equally displeased with the habits of the passengers he found on the boat going down the Mississippi (II, 227–55).

From New Orleans he took the Pontchartrain Railroad and Lake-Gulf route to Mobile; thence by boat to Montgomery and on through Macon, Milledgeville, and Augusta to Columbia, South Carolina. Here he called on Dr. Thomas Cooper, and was a guest at a dinner where several South Carolinians expressed their antirepublican sentiments (II, 340–41). The concluding lap of the journey passed through Chester, near which he visited a gold mine (II, 356–57), York, Charlotte, Lexington, Salisbury, Danville, and Richmond, where the tour ended in February, 1835.

Featherstonhaugh was one of the few important travelers of this period whose accounts were confined almost entirely to the South. His purpose in making the tour was "to supply, to a certain extent, the want of information which exists respecting some portions of the Southern states" (I, xi), and he assures the reader that his book is "a faithful and almost literal transcription from his original journals, the incidents of the tour having always been noted from day to day, and the journals having been regularly written up at least once a week" (I, xiii). He was opposed to American democratic institutions, and critical of the society and manners he encountered; but he thought highly of the South's physical resources.

[43]

41. Finch, John (fl. 1835)

Travels in the United States of America and Canada, containing some account of their scientific institutions, and a few notices of the geology and mineralogy of those countries. To which is added, an essay on the natural boundaries of empires. By I. Finch ... London, Longman, Rees, Orme, Brown, Green, and Longman, 1833.

> 3 p.l., [ix]–xv, 455 p.   21 cm.
> *Inclusive dates:* 1824.
> *Location of copy:* Library of Congress.

Finch's itinerary south of Washington, which he left in March, 1824, included Mount Vernon, Fredericksburg, Charlottesville, Richmond, Williamsburg, and Norfolk, after which he presumably left Virginia by sea, as his next reference is to New Jersey. He makes some remarks on slavery, mainly descriptive (pp. 235–42). While at Charlottesville he visited both Jefferson and Madison (pp. 243–58), and at Richmond he called on John Marshall. There are some references to the geology of Virginia and a few descriptions of travel facilities and agriculture, but the main concern is with accounts of the author's visit to prominent citizens. He was not displeased with his experiences in Virginia, probably because he was so cordially entertained.

42. Flint, Timothy (1780–1840)

Journal of the Rev. Timothy Flint, from the Red river, to the Ouachitta or Washita, in Louisiana, in 1835. [Alexandria? La., 1835?].

> 31 p.   16 cm.
> *Inclusive dates:* March, 1835.
> *Location of copy:* Library of Congress.

An account of a survey of the Maison Rouge grant on the Ouachita River made by Flint and his son, in the form of a letter to the owner of the grant. The journey was made on horseback and apparently lasted only a few days, beginning at Alexandria, on March 24, 1835. The itinerary includes Big Creek, Little River, Bowley's Tavern, and Prairie du Lait, after which it becomes vague. The work is mainly descriptive of forests, lands, waters, and general conditions along the route and on the grant itself. There is a good description of a ferryboat and the ferryman, an old Hollander of the Robinson Crusoe type (pp. 12–14).

43. Galveston Bay and Texas Land Company

Address to the reader of the documents relating to the Galveston Bay and Texas land company, which are contained in the appendix. New York, printed by G. F. Hopkins & son, 1831.

37, ₍1₎, 69 p. 20½ cm.
Location of copy: Library of Congress.

This book is promotional literature issued to attract immigrants to Texas. Contains information relating to the most suitable routes of travel to Texas; the climate and soil, products, religion and manners, and tariffs. Also a long letter from David G. Burnet, who had lived and traveled in Texas for two years at this time, describing the region (pp. 21–30). The appendix includes a copy of the deed made to the company by the Mexican government, the company's articles of association, and the colonization laws of Mexico.

44.

A geographical view of the United States. Boston, A. K. White, 1827.

130, ₍2₎ p. 19½ cm.
Other editions:
  A geographical view of the United States. Embracing their extent and boundaries, government, courts and laws, religion, divisions, population . . . New-York, W. W. Reed, 1829. 119, ₍1₎ p. 18 cm.
Location of copy: Library of Congress.

A gazetteer containing a brief account of every state in the Union: extent, boundaries, divisions, religion, population, literature, and other subjects.

45.   Griffith, Barton (d. 1834)

The diary of Barton Griffith, Covington, Indiana, 1832–34, now edited and published for the first time by permission of his great great nephew, J. Barton Griffith, M.D. Crawfordsville, Ind., R. E. Banta, 1932.

2 p.l., 17 p. illus. (map). 19 cm.
Maps: One: showing Griffith's itinerary.
Inclusive dates: 1834.
Location of copy: Library of Congress.

Griffith traveled by steamboat from Louisville to New Orleans in 1834 to supervise the sale of a load of pork which he was shipping by flatboat. His account is brief and sketchy, chiefly devoted to complaints at the hazards of steamboats and the crowding of passengers and to apprehensions concerning the safety of his pork. He contracted dysentery at New Orleans and died shortly after his return to Indiana.

[45]

46.

Guide des émigrants Français dans les États de Kentucky et d'Indiana, ou renseignements fidèles sur les États-Unis de l'Amérique Septentrionale en générale et sur les États de Kentucky et Indiana en particulier, indiquant les mesures et précautions à prendre avant de s'embarquer, ainsi que les moyens d'y émigrer agréablement, d'y doubler sa fortune, etc. Paris, Arthur Bertrand, 1834.

> 66 p. 8vo.
> *Other editions:*
> Paris, A. Bertrand, 1835. 55 p. 22½ cm.
> *Location of copy:* Library of Congress.

Promotional literature. Description of the United States in general and Kentucky in particular, especially Louisville. Cost of land, character of occupations, society, business, and other aspects of the city's life.

47. Hall, Captain Basil (1788–1844)

Forty etchings, from sketches made with the camera lucida, in North America, in 1827 and 1828, by Captain Basil Hall . . . Edinburgh, Cadell & co.; [etc., etc., 1829].

> 1 p.l., ii p., 21 l. front. (fold. map) XL plates on 20 l. 30½ cm.
> *Maps:* Folding map of U. S., showing Captain Hall's route.
> *Location of copy:* Duke University Library.

These are sketches made by Captain Hall on his American tour. There are two etchings on the verso of each plate, accompanied by a leaf with descriptive text. Etchings xvii–xxxvi relate to the South.

48. Hall, Captain Basil (1788–1844)

Travels in North America in the years 1827 and 1828. By Captain Basil Hall . . . 3 vols. Edinburgh, printed for Cadell and co.; London, Simpkin and Marshall, 1829.

> Vol. I, vi, 421 p. Vol. II, ii, 432 p.; Vol. III, vii, 436 p. fold. map, fold. tables. 19½ cm.
> *Maps:* Colored map of the United States, showing route.
> *Inclusive dates:* January–May, 1828.
> *Other editions:*
> (1) 2d ed. Edinburgh, printed for Cadell and co.; London, Simpkin and Marshall, 1829.
> (2) 3d ed. Edinburgh, printed for R. Cadell; London, Simpkin and Marshall, 1830.

(3) 2 vols. Philadelphia, Carey, Lea & Carey, 1829. Vol. I, 322 p.; Vol. II, iv, 9–329 p. illus. (map). 21 cm.

(4) Voyage dans les États-Unis de l'Amérique du Nord, et dans le Haut et le Bas-Canada, par le capitaine Basil-Hall . . . 2 vols. Paris, A. Bertrand, 1834. fold map. 21½ cm.

Location of copy: Indiana University.

The Southern phase of Captain Hall's tour lasted from January 31 until about the middle of May, 1828. Accompanied by his wife, their small child, and a nurse, he traveled from Washington by steamer and stage to Richmond and thence by steamer to Norfolk, where he spent two days visiting the navy yard and Fortress Monroe and also made an excursion into the Dismal Swamp. Southward by stage he proceeded through Winton and Fayetteville, North Carolina, and Camden and Columbia, South Carolina, to Charleston. Here he attended the Jockey Club races and the St. Andrew's Society ball, visited the orphan asylum, the workhouse, poorhouse, jail, and a rice mill, and talked freely with a number of citizens. The party continued by private carriage to Savannah, being hospitably entertained at plantation houses along the way; and on to Darien, where a sea-island cotton plantation was observed in some detail. At Darien a light baggage cart was secured, in order to allow more room in the carriage, and in these two equipages the party traveled across the state of Georgia, through the pine barrens and over swollen streams, with nightly comforts to be secured only at rude farmhouses, to Macon and on through Columbus and the Creek country to Montgomery. Here they transferred to a steamboat and proceeded to Mobile and thence to New Orleans, where about two weeks were spent in sightseeing, including a trip to the mouths of the Mississippi. Northward from New Orleans, the trip was continued by steamboat to Louisville and thence, by retracing a part of the route, to St. Louis where the Southern portion of the tour came to an end.

Although Captain Hall was not pleased with the South, it can be scarcely said that, except for his hostility to slavery, he singled out this section of the country for special criticism. Accustomed to a better-disciplined society and bred in the exacting traditions of the British Navy, he found difficulty in adjusting himself to the democratic manners and rude accommodations that he found in the United States, both North and South. Nevertheless, he was a clear and forceful writer, and his work contains many excellent descriptions of places and conditions that came under his observation. Among these are: bad food in North Carolina (III, 115–16); a party of migrants going to Florida (III, 126–29); houses (III, 271–72); Creek Indian ceremonies, including a ball game (III, 289–305); the mouths of the Mississippi (III, 336–40); the currents and methods of navigating the Mississippi (III, 357–68).

49. Hall, James (1793–1868)

Statistics of the West, at the close of the year 1836. By James Hall. Cincinnati, J. A. James & co., 1836.

> xviii, ₍2₎, ₍13₎–284 p. 18 cm.
> *Other editions:*
> (1) Cincinnati, J. A. James & co., 1837.
> *Published also under these titles:*
> (2) Notes on the western states; containing descriptive sketches of their soil, climate, resources, and scenery. By James Hall . . . Philadelphia, H. Hall, 1838. xxiii, ₍13₎–304 p., incl. tables. 18½ cm.
> (3) The West; its soil, surface, and productions. By James Hall. Cincinnati, Derby, Bradley & co., 1848. ₍5₎–260 p. 19½ cm.
> *Location of copy:* Library of Congress.

Includes Tennessee, Kentucky, and parts of Virginia. The author states that he spent many years in the Western states, engaged in active business, traveling extensively, and mingling intimately with the people; and that he proposes to record the results of this experience and of the information gathered personally from the inhabitants. His work deals with topography, natural scenery, prairies, waters, wild animals, agriculture, the public domain, cities, Western steamboats, and descriptions of the Ohio and Mississippi rivers. It should be regarded more as a guidebook than as a travel account, being mainly descriptive and historical.

50. Hall, Margaret (Hunter) "Mrs. Basil Hall" (1799–1876)

The aristocratic journey; being the outspoken letters of Mrs. Basil Hall written during a fourteen months' sojourn in America, 1827–1828; prefaced and edited by Una Pope-Hennessy . . . New York, London, G. P. Putnam's sons, 1931.

> vii, 308 p. front. (port.), plates, facsims. 21½ cm.
> *Illustrations:* Eleven illustrations taken from Hall's *Forty Etchings.*
> *Inclusive dates:* January–May, 1828.
> *Location of copy:* University of North Carolina Library.

Mrs. Hall's itinerary in the South was the same as that of her husband, whom she accompanied on his *Travels in North America*—Richmond, Norfolk, Fayetteville, Columbia, Charleston, Savannah,

Darien, Macon, Columbus, Montgomery, Mobile, New Orleans, and up the Mississippi and Ohio to Louisville. These letters, addressed to her sister, were written artlessly and from the point of view of an elegant lady who was suddenly dropped into a society for which she was not fitted by any past experience to appraise leniently or sympathetically.

Like her husband, she was on principle opposed to the spirit of equality and fraternity that she found in the New World, and was completely out of her bearings in a society unmapped by class distinctions. The South was little better than a wilderness to her prejudiced mind. She was critical of the barbarism of the dancing and the dirtiness of the servants in Charleston, of the rutted tracks and tree stumps over which her conveyance traveled in Alabama, and of the sleepless nights, execrable food, and dreadful taverns which she experienced generally. With all her diffidence, however, she possessed an instinct for minute observation and description, by which she was able to give one of the most complete pictures of men, manners, hostelries, means of travel, and other phases of Southern life to be found in the writing of any tourist of her period. An additional merit of her work arises from the fact that she names many persons and places which in Captain Hall's account (*q.v.*) are described without identification.

51. Hamilton, Thomas (1789–1842)

Men and manners in America. By the author of "Cyril Thornton," etc. . . . Edinburgh, W. Blackwood; ₎etc., etc., pref. 1833₎.

> 2 vols. in 1.: Vol. I, ix, 384 p.; Vol. II, 401 p. front. 19½ cm.
> *Inclusive dates:* February–April, 1831.
> *Other editions:*
>   (1) 2d ed. Edinburgh, ₍etc.₎, W. Blackwood, ₍etc.₎, 1834.
>   (2) 3d ed. Edinburgh, William Blackwood, n.d.
>   (3) New ed., with a portrait of the author, and letters written by him during his journey through the United States . . . Edinburgh and London, W. Blackwood and sons, 1843. xxxvi, 454 p. front. (port.). 17½ cm.
>   (4) Philadelphia, Carey, Lea & Blanchard, 1833. vi, ₍9₎–410 p. 22 cm.
>   (5) American ed. 2 vols. Philadelphia, Carey, Lea & Blanchard, 1833. Vol. I, vi, 9–208 p.; Vol. II, 3–204 p. 18½ cm.
>   (6) Bruxelles, A. Peeters, 1834.
>   (7) Les hommes et les moeurs aux États-Unis d'Amérique, par le colonel Hamilton. Traduit de l'anglais sur la 3ᵉ ed. par le comte D. L. C. . . . Paris, H. Fournier, jeune, 1834. 2 vols. in 1.: Vol. I, xv, 311 p.; Vol. II, 4, 380 p.
>   (8) Leben und Sitten in Nordamerika . . . Aus dem Englischen übersetzt von Franz Bauer. 2 vols. Quedlinburg und Leipzig, G. Basse, 1834. 16½ cm.
>   (9) Die Menschen und die Sitten in den Vereinigten Staaten von Nord-

amerika. 2 vols. in 1. Mannheim, Hoff, 1834. (Translated from the third English edition by L. Hout.).
Location of copy: Duke University Library.

Hamilton traveled from Baltimore to Ellicott Mills on a horse-drawn railroad, thence by stage to Wheeling, and by boat to Cincinnati and Louisville. He then descended the Ohio and Mississippi to New Orleans, crossed Lakes Pontchartrain and Borgne and continued by stage to Mobile, ascended by boat to Montgomery, and proceeded by stage, through Fort Mitchell, Macon, Milledgeville, and Augusta, to Charleston, where he sailed for New York. Among his comments are interesting references to his voyage down the Mississippi, including squatters he observed along the banks, "arks" he saw on the river, and a slave dealer and his merchandise that he encountered aboard the steamboat (pp. 302–308). At New Orleans he made favorable allusions to the Catholic church as he witnessed its ministrations to the poor (pp. 313–14) and expressed himself on the subject of slavery, to which he was quite strongly opposed (pp. 317–22). At Mobile he talked with a Scottish baker, from whom he learned something of the opportunities open to emigrant tradesmen in a Southern city (pp. 328–32). He was very caustic in his account of the hardships of travel which he experienced in Alabama (pp. 335–41), but grateful for the services of a Milledgeville, Georgia, physician in whose care he remained for several days when taken ill.

In general, Hamilton was none too well impressed with the South, as was true of his attitude toward the United States as a whole. He called his work "the conclusions of an independent observer," but admitted that he "may have been influenced by the prejudices natural to an Englishman" (pp. iii, iv). (Citations are from Philadelphia, 1833, edition.)

52. Hayward, John (1781–1862)

A view of the United States; historical, geographical and statistical. November, 1832. By John Hayward . . . New York, J. & W. Day, [c.1832].
cover title, 20 l., incl. tables. 27 x 16½ cm.
Other editions:
(1) 2d ed. . . . New York, Collins & co., [c.1832].
A later edition published under title:
(2) The Columbian traveller, and statistical register. Principally relating to the United States. November, 1833. By John Hayward. [Boston], the author, [1833]. 40 p. 4 maps (incl. front.). 27 cm.
Location of copy: Library of Congress.

A gazetteer, containing a brief description of each state and territory. Statistics based on Census of 1830.

53. Helm, Mrs. Mary (Sherwood) Wightman (b. 1807)

Scraps of early Texas history, by Mrs. Mary S. Helm, who, with her first husband, Elias R. Wightman, founded the city of Matagorda, in 1828–9. Austin, the author, 1884.

1 p.l., iv, 198 p., 1 l.   21 cm.
Inclusive dates: 1828–1829.
Location of copy: Library of Congress.

Contains a brief account of the author's journey from New York down the Ohio and Mississippi to New Orleans and thence by sea to Matagorda Bay, in company with her husband, who was leading a party of sixty immigrants to Austin's colony. Upon reaching Texas, she became a resident of that state, and her work is not further concerned with travel, being mainly a mixture of reminiscences, history, religion, and social life.

54. Heywood, Robert (1786–1868)

A journey to America in 1834, by Robert Heywood . . . ₁Cambridge, Eng.₁ priv. print., 1919.

viii, 112 p.   21 cm.
Edited by Mrs. Mary (Heywood) Haslam.
Inclusive dates: June and July, 1834.
Location of copy: Library of Congress.

The author was an Englishman traveling for the pleasure of seeing the country. South of Washington his itinerary was Mount Vernon, Fredericksburg, Charlottesville, Staunton, and Charleston to Guyandotte, thence by steamboat to Maysville, Kentucky, by stage from Maysville through Paris, Lexington, and Frankfort to Louisville, and thence by steamboat to Cincinnati. The narrative is in the form of a day-to-day account of places visited, hotels and inns, prices, means of conveyance and general conditions. The descriptions are not detailed.

55. Hoffman, Charles Fenno (1806–1884)

A winter in the West. By a New Yorker . . . 2 vols. New York, Harper & brothers, 1835.

Vol. I, 4, 337 p.; Vol. II, 4, 346 p.   18 cm.
Inclusive dates: April–June, 1834.
Other editions:
(1) ₁Second edition₁. 2 vols. New York, Harper & brothers, 1835. Vol. I, 2, 282 p.; Vol. II, 286 p.   18 cm.
(2) A winter in the west; letters descriptive of Chicago and its vicinity in

1833–34 . . . Reprint, with the original and new notes. Chicago, Fergus printing co., 1882. 64 p. 8vo. (No. 20 of "Fergus' historical series").
   (3) A winter in the far West . . . 2 vols. London, R. Bentley, 1835. Vol. I,
xii, 282 p.; Vol. II, xiii, 286 p. 20 cm.
Location of copy: Duke University Library.

On his return from the West, Hoffman bought a horse at Cincinnati and traveled through Lexington and Frankfort, Kentucky; the
Cumberland Gap; Tazewell, Tennessee; Pearisburg and White Sulphur Springs, Virginia, and on to Charlottesville, where his journey
closes. His account of this tour, which is found in Volume II, consists
of a series of letters written, presumably, en route. They are mainly
descriptive of natural scenery, but there are some few accounts of
people whom he met. Among the latter is a good description of a
mountain family in Clay County, Kentucky (pp. 157–61), and a
humorous account of the ravings of a drunken fellow at Tazewell,
Tennessee (pp. 184–87). The author was critical neither of the people
nor of their culture. (Citations are from New York, 1835, edition.)

56. Holley, Mrs. Mary (Austin) (d. 1846)

Texas. Observations, historical, geographical and descriptive, in a series
of letters, written during a visit to Austin's colony, with a view of a per-
manent settlement in that country, in the autumn of 1831. By Mrs. Mary
Austin Holley. With an appendix containing specific answers to certain
questions, relative to colonization in Texas, issued some time since by
the London geographical society. Also, some notice of the recent politi-
cal events in that quarter. Baltimore, Armstrong & Plaskitt, 1833.
   167 p. front. (fold. map). 16½ cm.
   Maps: Folding map of the state of Coahuila and Texas.
   Inclusive dates: October–December, 1831.
   Other editions:
     Baltimore, 1838.
    Also in:
     Holley, Mrs. Mary (Austin). Letters of an early American traveller, Mary
Austin Holley; her life and her works, 1784–1846, by Mattie Austin Hatcher . . .
Dallas, Tex., Southwest press, [c.1933]. pp. 95–210. 23½ cm.
   Location of copy: Library of Congress.

Written by the widow of Horace Holley, president of Transylvania
College, 1818–27, for the purpose of attracting prospective emigrants
to settle in the trans-Sabine Mexican provinces of Coahuila and
Texas. It is not strictly a series of letters, but a book composed in
letter form at Bolivar, the Brazos River plantation of the author's
brother, where she had gone for a visit in the fall of 1831. Letters I–V
(pp. 5–51) relate an account of her trip from New Orleans to Bolivar,

by way of the Gulf of Mexico and up the Brazos River. Letters VI–XII (pp. 51–131) are descriptive of Texas history and geography, including topography, rivers and harbors, climate, soil, towns, natural resources, and Indians. In the preparation of this volume Mrs. Holley had the assistance of her brother and their cousin Stephen F. Austin. Pages 133–67 comprise an appendix of documents relating to Texas.

This was the first book on Texas printed in English (C. W. Raines, *Bibliography of Texas* [Austin, 1896], 116), and it appears to have been a factor of some importance in stimulating homeseekers to locate in that state. It also provided the basic geographical and agricultural information for many other works on Texas published in the United States during the 1830's and 1840's. Among these was the same author's *Texas* (Lexington, Kentucky, J. Clarke & Co., 1836. 17 cm. [v]–viii, 410 p.), which is a different book entirely, containing more history and less description (copy in Duke University Library).

57.

An immigrant of a hundred years ago; a story of someone's ancestor, translated and retold by an old hand. Hattiesburg, Miss., the Book farm, 1941.

[5]–85 p. 23½ cm. (Heartman's historical series, No. 61).
Inclusive dates: 1831–?
Location of copy: Duke University Library.

The author of this account describes himself as a young German peasant who came to the United States in 1831, having fled his native land after an altercation in which he believed that he had killed the seducer of his sister. Landing in Connecticut, he secured employment as a sailor and made a number of voyages south, putting in variously at Norfolk, Baltimore, and New Orleans. Brief descriptions of these places are given, together with accounts of several escapades and adventures of a personal nature, including fights, gambling, and experiences with a New Orleans quadroon woman of easy virtue. There is also an account of a trip up the Mississippi and of employment on a steamboat running between Paducah, Kentucky, and Florence, Alabama, on the Tennessee. After a lengthy ramble through the Northwest and a voyage to Brazil, the author returned to Germany, brought his parents and sister to the United States, and settled with them in Mississippi upon land he had purchased from John McDonogh at New Orleans.

It is impossible to determine the extent to which the account, pre-

sumably a diary originally written in German, has been retouched by
the translator and editor. The manuscript is said to be in the hands
of the author's descendants, who forbade the revelation of his identity
for fear that certain details might reflect upon the honor of their
ancestor.

58. [Ingraham, Joseph Holt (1809–1860)]

The South-West; by a Yankee . . . 2 vols. New-York, Harper & brothers,
1835.

Vol. I, xi, ₍13₎–276 p.; Vol. II, xi, ₍9₎–294 p.   17½ cm.
Inclusive dates: c.1830–1835.
Location of copy: Library of Congress.

Ingraham was a native of Portland, Maine, who arrived in the South
about 1830 to teach languages at Jefferson College, Washington, Mississippi. Here he saw plantations, slaves, masters, and other elements
of a civilization widely different from the social order that he had
known in New England.

The South-West, in which Ingraham recorded his impressions of
this new land, is mainly descriptive. It contains an account of his
voyage from New England to the mouth of the Mississippi, up the
river to New Orleans, and thence, by way of Donaldsonville and
Baton Rouge, to Natchez. In addition, and occupying a much greater
portion of the work, there are detailed descriptions of New Orleans,
including street scenes, churches and cemeteries, theaters, gambling
establishments, the Chalmette battleground, the Pontchartrain railroad, and the legislature; and similar descriptions of Natchez and
its environs. Slavery and plantation economy in Mississippi are extensively treated, the author believing slavery to be a benevolent
system and that interference from the North would be more injurious
than beneficial. Other topics include a deer hunt, Indian mounds,
geological and topographical accounts of Mississippi, and remarks on
the state's various towns, villages, and educational institutions.

Ingraham later settled permanently in the South and became identified with the life of his adopted section. Among his other works
was *The Sunny South: or, The Southerner at Home* (Philadelphia,
1860), a collection of letters originally published in the *Saturday
Courier* in 1853–54.

59. [Irving, Washington (1783–1859)]

A tour on the prairies. By the author of the Sketch book. Philadelphia,
Carey, Lea & Blanchard, 1835.

xv, [17]–274 p. 18½ cm.

Inclusive dates: October–November, 1832.

Other editions:

American:

(1) New York, John W. Lovell company, [1883]. 1 p.l., [7]–137 p. 18½ cm. (Lovell's library, Vol. 6, No. 305).

(2) Edited for school use by George C. Wells, and Joseph B. Thoburn . . . Oklahoma City, Harlow publishing co., 1926. 1 p.l., lvi p., 1 l., 251 p. front., (map). 17 cm. (The Western series of English and American classics).

English:

(3) London, J. Murray, 1835. xiii, 335, [1] p. 21 cm.

(4) London, 1836.

(5) London, 1851.

(6) Tour in the Prairies; and, Abbotsford and Newstead Abbey. By Washington Irving. New edition. London, G. Routledge & co., 1855. 248 p. 12mo.

French:

(7) Voyage dans les prairies à l'ouest des États-Unis. Traduit par A. Sobry. Paris, 1835.

(8) Un Tour dans les prairies à l'ouest des États-Unis; traduit de l'anglais de Washington Irving par Ernest W. Nouvelle édition. Tours, Mame et fils, 1851. 239 p. 12mo.

(9) Tours, Mame et fils, 1865.

German:

(10) Ausflug auf die Prairien zwischen dem Arkansas und Red-river. Stuttgart und Tübingen, J. G. Cotta, 1835. 4, 136 p. 12mo.

(11) Reise durch die Prairien. Aus dem Englischen. Berlin, Veit und comp., 1835.

(12) Eine wanderung in den Prairien. Aus dem Englischen von H. Roberts. Braunschweig, Vieweg, 1835.

Location of copy: Library of Congress.

Irving's Western tour of 1832 was taken in response to the widespread demand for a book on a native subject from his pen after a long preoccupation with European themes, and also to renew a youthful enthusiasm for the frontier. He traveled in the company of Henry L. Ellsworth and Charles J. Latrobe, both of whom also wrote accounts of the tour: Ellsworth in a long letter to his wife, eventually published as *Washington Irving on the Prairie* (New York, 1937), and Latrobe in *The Rambler in North America* (London, 1835).

The party went down the Ohio and up the Mississippi to St. Louis and across the country to Fort Gibson, where they were joined by guides and a detachment of mounted Rangers. The *Tour* began here in early October and ended on November 11, when Irving left the party near the Osage agency on the Verdigris River and proceeded by steamboat down the Arkansas and Mississippi to New Orleans. He continued on through Alabama and Georgia, the Carolinas, and

Virginia, to Washington, but no reference to this journey is made in the *Tour*.

A lover of cities and long a resident of Europe, Irving missed the respectful demeanor of Continental servants on this tour, and he was not at home among the familiarities of the Western woodsmen. But he was courageous on a buffalo hunt or a foraging party, and he enjoyed camping under trees, fording rivers on horseback, and talking with the Indians of the Osage villages. "We send our youth abroad to grow luxurious and effeminate in Europe," he wrote, "but it appears to me that a previous tour on the prairies would be more likely to produce that manliness, simplicity, and self-dependence most in unison with our political institutions" (p. 57).

Irving's aim was "a simple narrative of every day occurrences" (p. viii), and in contrast to Latrobe's garrulous recital of the same journey, his version is a direct and well-written log book of the tour. On the other hand it is unenriched by new data, silent on the political and social future of the area, and, apart from its style, not unique among books on the frontier. It is also lacking in many of the inevitable realities of frontier life, in which Ellsworth's narrative is abundant. (See Stanley T. Williams, *The Life of Washington Irving* [2 vols. New York, Oxford University Press, 1935], II, 38–44, 80–83.)

Irving based the writing of his *Tour on the Prairies* very largely upon "a few leaves out of my memorandum book" (p. viii). This was his journal for 1832, entitled "The Tour through the West," which is published in William P. Trent and George S. Hellman, eds., *The Journals of Washington Irving* (hitherto unpublished) (3 vols., Boston, The Bibliophile Society, 1919), III, 101–86. (Copy in Duke University Library). The journal, dated September 3–November 17, is a bare outline of laconic notes; but it covers more territory than the Tour, in that it includes the trip from Cincinnati to Fort Gibson and from the Osage Agency to a point on the Mississippi below the mouth of the Arkansas.

60.   James, Joshua, and McCrae, Alexander

A journal of a tour in Texas; with observations, &c., by the agents of the Wilmington emigrating society. ₍Wilmington? N. C.₎, printed by T. Loring, 1835.

> 16 p.   25½ cm.   cover title.
> *Inclusive dates:* May–July, 1835.
> *Location of copy:* Library of Congress.

[56]

Joshua James and Alexander Macrae went to Texas as agents of the Wilmington Emigrating Society in 1835. They traveled by sea from Wilmington to New Orleans, thence by steamboat to Natchitoches, and then on horseback to the vicinity of St. Augustine, Texas. On the return trip they came overland from New Orleans, by way of Montgomery, where the account ends.

Upon reaching Texas, they separated and made independent investigations, James reporting his in the "Journal" (pp. 1–12) and Macrae recording his in the "Observations" (pp. 13–16). The two accounts are similar in substance, presenting detailed information on the land and products of Texas. A valuable and rare item.

61. Julius, Nicolaus Heinrich (1783–1862)

Nordamerikas sittliche Zustände. Nach eigenen Anschauungen in den Jahren 1834, 1835 und 1836, von Dr. N. H. Julius . . . 2 vols. Leipzig, F. A. Brockhaus, 1839.

> Vol. I, xxviii, [5]–514 p.; Vol. II, xii, [3]–502 p. fold. plates, fold. map, fold. plans, fold. tables. 21 cm.
> *Maps:* Folding map of North America (Vol. I).
> *Illustrations:* Thirteen folded plans of U. S. prisons.
> *Location of copy:* University of North Carolina Library.

Although the author traveled in the United States and visited the South at least once, this work is not properly a travel account. The first volume relates the history of the United States and describes its government, population, religion, charitable institutions, and other social features. There are short accounts of each state, including the Southern states, but these are based upon reading rather than observation. The second volume is a detailed treatise upon crime and punishment in the United States, making some reference to the South, but here again the author relies mainly upon the study of printed sources.

Dr. Julius was one of a number of Europeans who came to the United States during the 1820's and 1830's to study prison systems. He spent some time at Richmond investigating the prison there, mainly because this institution had been omitted by Beaumont and Tocqueville in their *Du système pénitentiaire,* but he makes no reference to this visit in the above work. (See George W. Pierson, *Tocqueville and Beaumont in America,* 707–708.) Julius had previously published a German translation of *Du système pénitentiaire* under the title of *Amerika's Besserungs-System, und dessen Anwendung auf Europa, mit einem Anhange über Straf-Ansiedelungen und zwei und zwanzig Beilagen* (Berlin, Enslin, 1833).

62. Latrobe, Charles Joseph (1801–1875)

The rambler in North America: MDCCCXXXII–MDCCCXXXIII. By Charles Joseph Latrobe . . . 2 vols. London, R. B. Seeley and W. Burnside, [etc.], 1835.

Vol. I, xi, 321 p.; Vol. II, viii, 336 p. 19 cm.
Inclusive dates: 1832–1834.
Other editions:
(1) New York, Harper & brothers, 1835.
(2) 2d ed. 2 vols. London, R. B. Seeley and W. Burnside, 1836. front. (fold. map). 20 cm.
Location of copy: University of North Carolina Library.

Latrobe came to America in 1832, accompanied by a young Swiss gentleman, Count de Pourtales, whom he was anxious to wean from unsatisfactory attachments at home by allowing him to sow his wild oats on foreign soil. While in the United States, Latrobe and Pourtales made four separate trips into the South.

In June, 1832, they visited Baltimore and Washington and took a short excursion to Harpers Ferry and Point of Rocks. This, like most of Latrobe's travel, was mainly for the purpose of observing the scenery and stimulated no remarks other than descriptive ones (I, 28–36).

While touring New England with Washington Irving later in the year, the three met Henry L. Ellsworth, who was going as an Indian commissioner to what is now Oklahoma, and decided to accompany him to the West. Entering the South at Cincinnati, they went by steamboat to St. Louis and then by land to Fort Gibson. Here they were joined by guides and mounted Rangers, with whom they proceeded to the buffalo country about one hundred miles farther on. The episodes occurring on this expedition, including buffalo hunting and other adventures, are described in somewhat discursive fashion by Latrobe (I, 119–251), whose account parallels closely those written by Irving in *A Tour on the Prairies* (London, 1835) and by Ellsworth in a narrative later published as *Washington Irving on the Prairie* (New York, 1937).

At the conclusion of their prairie tour Latrobe and Pourtales engaged a canoe and with the assistance of two paddlers descended the Arkansas from Fort Gibson to Little Rock, and continued on by steamer to Wheeling, Virginia, where they arrived late in December (I, 252–304).

In the spring of 1833 the two set out from Baltimore for a third tour. By steamer they went to Norfolk and Richmond; by stage through Petersburg, Fayetteville, and Georgetown to Charleston, where their stay was brief because of the ferment over nullification; and on to Savannah and Darien. A sloop was taken to Fernandina, Florida, and southward to the mouth of the St. Johns River, from which the journey was continued by land to St. Augustine, Jacksonville, Tallahassee, and St. Marks. The return trip north was made by stage through Milledgeville, Georgia, Abbeville and Greenville, South Carolina, Flat Rock and Hot Springs, North Carolina, Jonesboro, Tennessee, and Abingdon, Lynchburg, and Richmond to Baltimore. The account of this tour (II, 1–74) consists mainly of descriptive material relating to scenery and wild life, with occasional references to inns and travel facilities. There is a good description of a Florida plantation establishment, with its "hap-hazard and disorderly way of living" (II, 32–34). Casual comments upon slavery advance the view that slaves are spoiled children, less to be pitied than their owners (II, 15–16).

The last experience of these travelers in the South occurred in December, 1833, and January, 1834, when they descended the Mississippi from St. Louis and spent two weeks at New Orleans before sailing for Mexico (II, 328–36).

Latrobe was described by Washington Irving as "a man of a thousand occupations; a botanist, a geologist, a hunter of beetles and butterflies, a musical amateur, a sketcher of no mean pretensions . . . a very indefatigable, if not always a very successful, sportsman" (*A Tour on the Prairies,* 14). Such were the activities he pursued on his tour, and having so many interests, naturally he had little time for social and economic observation and comment.

63. Linn, John J. (b. 1798)

Reminiscences of fifty years in Texas. By John J. Linn. Pub. for the author. New York, D. & J. Sadlier & co., 1883.

> 369 p. plates, 2 port. (incl. front.). 17 cm.
> *Other editions:*
> Austin, Tex., The Steck company, 1935. 3 p.l., 5–369 p. plates, ports. 21½ cm. (Original narratives of Texas history and adventure). "A facsimile reproduction of the original" edition.
> *Location of copy:* Harvard University Library.

The author was born in Ireland and brought to the United States as a child. In 1822 he went to New Orleans, and thence in 1829 to Texas, where he remained for the rest of his life. Pages 1–17 contain a few casual references to his journey from New Orleans to Texas. The remainder deals with accounts of the Alamo, Goliad, San Jacinto, and other places, historical or pseudo-historical in nature; also reprints the journal of Dr. J. H. Barnard, a physician in Fannin's command at Goliad (pp. 148–82). This journal runs from March 10 to May 19, 1836, and appears to have been originally printed in the Goliad *Guard* in 1875.

64. Löwig, Gustav

Die Freistaaten von Nord-Amerika. Beobachtungen und praktische Bemerkungen für auswandernde Deutsche, von Gustav Löwig. Heidelberg und Leipzig, K. Groos, 1833.

> x, 264 p. 18½ cm.
> *Location of copy:* Library of Congress.

A guidebook for German travelers and immigrants in the United States, this account has considerable information on Virginia and the two Carolinas.

65. Ludecus, Eduard

Reise durch die mexikanischen Provinzen Tumalipas, Cohahuila und Texas im Jahre 1834. In Briefen an seine Freunde, von Eduard Ludecus. Leipzig, Joh. Friedr. Hartknoch, 1837.

> xx, 356 p. 21 cm.
> *Inclusive dates:* August to November, 1834.
> *Location of copy:* Library of Congress.

This was one of the first works appearing in German and in Germany with Texas as its main topic. The purpose of Ludecus' trip was to survey a site for a settlement near the Río Grande, not far from the Gulf. The account, which ends at New Orleans, is mainly descriptive of the region through which the author passed.

66. Lundy, Benjamin (1789–1839)

The life, travels and opinions of Benjamin Lundy, including his journeys to Texas and Mexico, with a sketch of contemporary events, and a notice of the revolution in Hayti. Compiled under the direction and on behalf of his children. Philadelphia, William D. Parrish, 1847.

> 2 p.l., [9]–316 p. front. (port.), fold. map. 19½ cm.
> *Maps:* Folding map of Texas and Mexico.
> *Inclusive dates:* 1831–1834.
> *Location of copy:* Duke University Library.

Contains Lundy's journals kept on his second and third journeys to Texas, 1833–34 and 1834–35, in search of suitable places for the colonization of freed slaves (pp. 32–110, 112–86).

On the second trip his route was by steamboat from Cincinnati to Nashville, thence to Memphis and New Orleans, and by sea to Brazoria; on foot to San Felipe; to San Antonio de Bexar, where he worked at his trade of saddler while planning a colonization scheme, August–October, 1833; and to Monclova, where he remained until January, 1834. He returned by way of Aransas Bay and New Orleans and up the Mississippi and Ohio to Cincinnati.

The third journey began at Nashville, from which he went by steamboat to New Orleans, back up the Mississippi and the Red River to Natchitoches; by way of Nacogdoches to Monclova, where he had arranged to apply for two grants of land but failed to secure them; to Matamoras and Victoria, Mexico, where he hoped to get land after failing in Texas; back to Matamoras and thence to New Orleans and up the Mississippi, Ohio, and Cumberland to Nashville.

On each of these tours he kept day-to-day accounts of his itinerary and activities. There are also some excellent descriptions of Texas.

67. Martin, Joseph, ed.

A new and comprehensive gazetteer of Virginia, and the District of Columbia, by Joseph Martin. To which is added a history of Virginia from its first settlement to the year 1754: with an abstract of the principal events from that period to the independence of Virginia . . . by a citizen of Virginia W. H. Brockenbrough. Charlottesville, J. Martin, 1835.

> 636 p. front. (fold. map). 22½ cm.
> *Maps:* Folding map of Virginia.
> *Other editions:*
> (1) Charlottesville, J. Martin, 1836.
> (2) A comprehensive description of Virginia, and the District of Columbia: containing a copious collection of geographical, statistical, political, commercial, religious, moral, and miscellaneous information, chiefly from original sources. By Joseph Martin. To which is added a History of Virginia, from its first settlement to the year 1754, with an abstract of the principal events from that period to the independence of Virginia. By W. H. Brockenbrough . . . Richmond, J. W. Randolph, [183–]. 636 p. 22½ cm.
> *Location of copy:* Library of Congress.

A general description of Virginia and the District of Columbia, followed by information on each county, including towns, villages, and post offices.

68. McCall, George Archibald (1802–1868)

Letters from the frontiers. Written during a period of thirty years' ser-

vice in the army of the United States. By Major General George A. Mc-
Call . . . Philadelphia, J. B. Lippincott & co., 1868.

x, [11]–539 p.   20 cm.
Inclusive dates: c.1822–1850.
Location of copy: Library of Congress.

Immediately after graduating from West Point in 1822, McCall was
assigned to duty at Pensacola and remained in the South almost continuously for the next thirty years. Like army men in general, he
was constantly moving from post to post—Tampa, Memphis, New
Orleans, among the Seminoles and Cherokees, and in Alabama, Arkansas, Texas, and in the Oklahoma country.

These published letters cover a long period and treat many subjects.
In the main they describe such varied activities as establishing military
posts, experiences among the Indians, hunting deer in Florida, shooting grouse in Arkansas, recovering stolen horses, attending balls and
dances, feats of horsemanship, and other diversions of army life. Interspersed among these are some accounts of journeys taken, both
with troops and in going to new assignments, but in such instances
the author appears usually to have regarded himself as a soldier engaged in the performance of his duty rather than as an observer of
new regions and diverse cultures. For these reasons the work should
probably be considered as primarily a military autobiography, describing a collection of experiences in which travel was extensive but
not of primary concern.

69.   McCoy, Isaac (1784–1846)

History of Baptist Indian missions: embracing remarks on the former
and present condition of the aboriginal tribes; their settlement within
the Indian Territory, and their future prospects. By Isaac McCoy . . .
Washington, William H. Morrison; New-York, H. and S. Raynor;
[etc., etc.], 1840.

5 p.l., [3]–611 p.   23½ cm.
Inclusive dates: 1827–1837.
Location of copy: Duke University Library.

Relates principally to the author's experiences in charge of an Indian
mission in Michigan, but also includes brief accounts, apparently
based upon a manuscript journal, of various trips to what is now
Oklahoma in the interest of Indian missions between 1827 and 1837.
Has considerable information on religious life among the Indians,
and some comments upon Indian character and customs.

[62]

70. McKenney, Thomas Lorraine (1785–1859)

Memoirs, official and personal; with sketches of travels among the northern and southern Indians; embracing a war excursion, and descriptions of scenes along the western borders. By Thomas L. M'Kenney ... New York, Paine and Burgess, 1846.

> 2 vols. in 1: Vol. I, viii, ₁17₁–340 p.; Vol. II, vi, ₁9₁–136. front. (port.), plate, facsim. 23½ cm.
> *Illustrations:* Fifteen landscapes and personalities.
> *Inclusive dates:* 1827.
> *Other editions:*
>   2d ed. New York, Paine & Burgess, 1846.
> *Location of copy:* Duke University Library.

Contains an account of a trip in September and October, 1827, taken by McKenney, then in charge of the Bureau of Indian Affairs, to confer with the Chickasaws, Choctaws, and Cherokees with regard to their emigration to the West (I, 142–90). He traveled by steamboat from St. Louis to Memphis, thence overland into northern Mississippi, where he held a council with the Chickasaws, through the Choctaw country, and back to Washington by way of Tuscaloosa, Montgomery, and Augusta. Has a good description of the currents, snags, sawyers, and other obstructions to navigation in the Mississippi River (I, 149–53); also some descriptive material relating to the Indians in general and to some particular chiefs.

71. Mitchell, Elisha (1793–1857)

Diary of a geological tour by Dr. Elisha Mitchell in 1827 and 1828, with introduction and notes by Dr. Kemp P. Battle, LLD. Chapel Hill, ₁N.C.₁, The University of North Carolina, 1905.

> 73, ₁1₁ p. 20½ cm. (The University of North Carolina. James Sprunt historical monograph No. 6).
> *Inclusive dates:* 1827–1828.
> *Location of copy:* Duke University Library.

This book is in the form of letters from Elisha Mitchell to his wife, but evidently was intended to constitute the body of a report or an article for some scientific journal. The 1827 tour included Greensboro, Lexington, Concord, Charlotte, and Lincolnton, North Carolina; the 1828 itinerary was by way of Greensboro, Salem, Wilkesboro, and various other points in the western part of the state. There is also a long letter describing a journey from Raleigh to New Bern, where the author had gone, apparently to preach, in December, 1827.

There is considerable geological information, many references to

[63]

persons visited, and some account of the author's preaching. Primarily of interest for reference to North Carolina family names and descriptions of the geology of the state.

72. Mitchell, Samuel Augustus (1792–1868)

An accompaniment to Mitchell's reference and distance map of the United States; containing an index of all the counties, districts, townships, towns, &c., in the Union; together with an index of the rivers; in which any county, district, township, &c., or river, may be found on the map, without difficulty: also, a general view of the United States, and the several states and territories; with an account of the actual and prospective internal improvements throughout the Union. Philadelphia, Mitchell and Hinman, 1834.

[5]–324 p. 20 cm.
Other editions:
(1) Philadelphia, Mitchell and Hinman, 1835.
(2) Philadelphia, Mitchell and Hinman, 1836. 342 p. 21½ cm.
(3) Philadelphia, Mitchell and Hinman, 1838. 344 p. 21½ cm.
(4) Philadelphia, R. L. Barnes, 1839.
(5) Philadelphia, R. L. Barnes, 1840.
(6) An accompaniment to Mitchell's reference and distance map of the United States: containing an index of the various counties, districts, parishes, townships, towns, etc. and an index of the rivers; together with a geographical description of every state and territory in the Union; also an accurate synopsis of the population in the year 1840, according to the sixth census . . . and a synopsis of the new postage law. Philadelphia, S. A. Mitchell, 1845. 2 p.l., [9]–320, [89]–208, iv p. 23 cm.
Location of copy: Library of Congress.

Contains a general view of each state in the Union, including a short historical sketch, index of towns and rivers, roads and canals, and other statistical information.

73. Mitchell, Samuel Augustus (1792–1868)

A general view of the United States; comprising, also, a description of each individual state and territory in the Union; to which are added, various tabular statements, comprehending aggregates of the population of the United States at different periods, as well as in the year 1840. By S. Augustus Mitchell. Philadelphia, S. A. Mitchell, 1846.

128 p. 23 cm.
Also in:
Remark, Gustav. Die Vereinigten Staaten und die andern Länder Amerikas, enthaltend eine umständlich Beschreibung ihrer physischen, politischen und statistischen Zustände, die Geschichte, Verfassung und Statuten der Vereinigten

Staaten . . . Nach dem englischen Werke von S. Augustus Mitchell. Richmond, Va., Harold and Murray, 1852. pp. 49–179, 294–305. illus. 23½ cm.
Location of copy: Library of Congress.

Statistical information, its character indicated by the title.

74.   Mitchell, Samuel Augustus (1792–1868)

Mitchell's traveller's guide through the United States, containing the principal cities, towns, &c, alphabetically arranged; together with the stage, steamboat, canal, and railroad routes, with the distances, in miles, from place to place. Illustrated with an accurate map of the United States. Philadelphia, Thomas Cowperthwait & co., [c.1836].

78 p.   fold. map.   12½ cm.
Maps: Folding map of the U.S.
Other editions:
(1) Illustrated by [a] . . . map of the United States [by J. H. Young]. Philadelphia, Mitchell & Hinman, 1836. 78 p. fold. map.
(2) Philadelphia, Mitchell & Hinman, 1837. 78 p. fold. map. 13½ cm.
(3) Philadelphia, Hinman & Dutton, 1838. 78 p. fold. map. 13½ cm.
(4) Philadelphia, Thomas, Cowperthwait, & co., [1843]. 78 p. fold. map. 13½ cm.
(5) Mitchell's new traveller's guide through the United States, containing the principal cities, towns, &c. alphabetically arranged; together with the railroad, stage, steamboat and canal routes, with the distances, in miles, from place to place. Illustrated by an accurate map of the United States. Phildelphia, Thomas, Cowperthwait & co., 1849. 128 p. fold. map. 15 cm.
(6) Illustrated by [a] . . . map of the United States [drawn by Ira S. Drake]. Philadelphia, Thomas Cowperthwait & co., 1850 [c.1848]. 118 p. fold. map.
(7) Philadelphia, Thomas, Cowperthwait & co., 1852. 118 p. fold. map. 14½ cm.
(8) Philadelphia, C. Desilver, 1855. xxxii, 124 p., fold. map. 15 cm.
(9) Philadelphia, C. Desilver, 1860. xxxii, 123 p. fold. maps. 15 cm.
(10) Philadelphia, C. Desilver, 1864. xxxii, 123 p. fold. map. 14 cm.
Location of copy: Library of Congress.

A guidebook, the contents of which are indicated by its title.

J. Monroe Thorington's sketch of Mitchell in the *Dictionary of American Biography* (XIII, 61–62) refers to the above work as having been published in 1832, but the 1836 edition is the earliest that I have been able to discover. It was reissued at intervals for about thirty years, among the later editions being: Philadelphia, Mitchell & Hinman, 1837; Philadelphia, Hinman and Dutton, 1838; Philadelphia, Thomas Cowperthwait & Co.; 1843. A somewhat revised and enlarged edition, with a slight change in title, was brought out by Thomas, Cowperthwait & Co. in 1848, and again in 1849 and 1852;

and by Charles Desilver, also at Philadelphia, in 1855, 1860, and 1864.

Mitchell was a prolific compiler and publisher of maps, guides, atlases, and other geographical information, which he constantly sought to keep up to date. For this reason the above editions, all of which may be found in the Library of Congress, cannot be regarded as a complete list of all the appearances of this work.

75. Mitchell, Samuel Augustus (1792–1868)

The principal stage, steam-boat, and canal routes in the United States; with the population of each state, and other statistical information: being an accompaniment to Mitchell's traveller's guide. Philadelphia, Mitchell & Hinman, 1834.

> 96 p. 11½ cm.
> *Location of copy:* Library of Congress.

> Composed entirely of statistics, the nature of which is indicated by the title.

76. Morris, Eastin

The Tennessee gazetteer, or topographical dictionary; containing a description of the several counties, towns, villages, post offices, rivers, creeks, mountains, valleys &c. in the state of Tennessee, alphabetically arranged. To which is prefixed a general description of the state . . . and a condensed history from the earliest settlements down to the . . . convention in . . . 1834. With an appendix, containing a list of the practising attorneys at law in each county; principal officers of the general and state governments; times of holding courts; and other valuable tables. By Eastin Morris. Nashville, W. H. Hunt & co., 1834.

> 4, cxvi, 178 p. 9 l. 17½ cm.
> *Location of copy:* Library of Congress.

> The usual type of gazetteer, its arrangement being indicated in the title. Has 116 pages of history and documents, and the remainder is on cities, counties, and towns.

77. Murat, Achille, Prince (1801–1847)

Esquisse morale et politique des États-Unis de l'Amérique du Nord. Par Achille Murat . . . Paris, Crochard, 1832.

> 2 p.l., xxvii, 389 p. 15 cm.
> *Inclusive dates:* 1826–1832.
> *Other editions:*
> (1) A moral and political sketch of the United States of North America.

By Achille Murat . . . With a note on negro slavery, by Junius Redivivus [pseud. of W. B. Adams]. London, E. Wilson [etc.], 1833. [iii]–xxxix, [1] 402 p. front. (fold. map). 18½ cm.

(2) Second edition. London, Effingham Wilson, 1833. xxxviii, 402 p. 8vo.

(3) America and the Americans. By the late Achille Murat . . . Translated from the French. New York, W. H. Graham, 1849. 2 p.l., vii, [9]–260 p. 18½ cm.

(4) Briefe über den moralischen und politischen Zustand der Vereinigten Staaten von Nord-Amerika. Braunschweig, 1833.

(5) Brieven over de zeden en staatkunde der Vereenigde Staten van Noord-Amerika door Achilles Murat . . . Uit het Fransch . . . 2 vols. Zalt-Bommel, J. Noman en zoon, 1834. 23 cm.

(6) Karakteristik öfver Förenta Staterna. Öfversattn. Af G. Loederus. Stockholm, 1831.

Location of copy: Library of Congress.

Murat, son of the King of Naples and a nephew of Napoleon, came to the United States in 1823 and settled in Florida, where, except for a two-year return to Europe in the early 1830's, he remained for the rest of his life. During 1826–27 he addressed four letters to Count Thibeaudeau, which were published in the *Revue Trimestrielle* (1828) and later in book form as *Lettres sur les États-Unis . . . à un de ses amis d'Europe* (Paris, Hector Bossange, 1830. 15½ cm. [4]–155 p. Copy at Harvard University Library). To these he subsequently added six more letters on the United States, written from London and Brussels during 1831–32, and published the whole as the above described *Esquisse morale et politique.*

Although Murat considered himself an American, he was, certainly at the time of his writing the first four letters, so recent an arrival in this country that his work should be regarded as that of a traveler. As the title would indicate, it is a philosophical account of American institutions, including political parties, the frontier, slavery, Indians, religion, law and justice, the army and navy, finance, manners, fine arts, and literature. No itinerary is mentioned, but it is evident that the author's experiences and contacts had been largely in the South. His sympathies were almost as exclusively Southern as if he had been a native. He considered agriculture as the primal and prevailing interest of the United States, advocated slavery on both practical and metaphysical grounds, and thought Charleston to be the center of all that was polished and superior in American society.

78. Murray, Sir Charles Augustus (1806–1895)

Travels in North America during the years 1834, 1835, & 1836. Including a summer residence with the Pawnee tribe of Indians, in the remote

TRAVELS

IN

NORTH AMERICA

DURING

THE YEARS 1834, 1835, & 1836.

INCLUDING

A SUMMER RESIDENCE WITH THE PAWNEE TRIBE
OF INDIANS,

IN THE REMOTE PRAIRIES OF THE MISSOURI,

AND

A VISIT TO CUBA AND THE AZORE ISLANDS.

BY

THE HON. CHARLES AUGUSTUS MURRAY.

" Le voyager me semble un exercise profitable: l'ame y a une continuelle ex-
ercitation, à remarquer les choses incognües et nouvelles; et je ne sçache pas
meilleure escole à façonner la vie que de luy proposer incessamment la diversité
de tant d'autres fantasies et usances, et luy faire gouter une si perpetuelle varieté
de formes de nostre nature."—*Essais de Montaigne*, liv. 3, chap. ix.

IN TWO VOLUMES.

VOL. I.

LONDON:

RICHARD BENTLEY, NEW BURLINGTON STREET,

𝔓𝔲𝔟𝔩𝔦𝔰𝔥𝔢𝔯 𝔦𝔫 𝔒𝔯𝔡𝔦𝔫𝔞𝔯𝔶 𝔱𝔬 𝔥𝔢𝔯 𝔐𝔞𝔧𝔢𝔰𝔱𝔶.

1839.

[68]

prairies of the Missouri, and a visit to Cuba and the Azore Islands. By the Hon. Charles Augustus Murray. 2 vols. London, R. Bentley, 1839.

Vol. I, xvi, 473 p.; Vol. II, x, 372 p. front. 22 cm.

Inclusive dates: 1834–1836.

Other editions:

(1) 2 vols. New York, Harper & brothers, 1839. Vol. I, xii, [13]–324 p.; Vol. II, vii, [13]–247 p. 18½ cm.

(2) 3d ed. rev.; with a new introduction. London, R. Bentley, 1854.

Location of copy: Duke University Library.

Murray was a grandson of Lord Dunmore and eventually rose to a position of considerable prominence in the British Court. While in the United States, he entered the South on five different occasions.

One of the objects of his visit to the United States being to look after an estate belonging to his family in Virginia, he set out from Washington for Leesburg, late in November, 1834, traveling in a small wagon drawn by two ponies hitched tandem. This novel conveyance was wrecked by the bad roads (I, 85–87), but he continued on to Romney "to arrange some business connected with land in its neighborhood," and remained there for about two weeks, having the land surveyed and hunting, after which he returned to Washington.

In March, 1835, he made a more extensive tour of Virginia, going down the Potomac for about sixty miles by boat and then by stage to Fredericksburg and Richmond; down the James for two visits with Old Virginia families; and to Williamsburg and Norfolk, and again returning to Washington.

Two months later he went westward to Pittsburgh and down the Ohio to Cincinnati and Louisville, making a side trip to Lexington and proceeding from Louisville by boat to St. Louis. At Lexington he met Harriet Martineau at the home of Henry Clay's son-in-law and also visited Clay himself, and met a young German traveler who accompanied him on his excursion among the Indians.

After a summer among the Pawnees he returned to St. Louis and traveled from there to New Orleans by boat, stopping off for a short time in Natchez. Murray remained in New Orleans for two weeks, and toward the close of December he sailed for Havana.

From Havana he returned to the United States in February, 1836, landing at Charleston, where he spent twelve days, and then continued by sea to Norfolk and Baltimore and thence to Washington.

Despite his aristocratic background, Murray looked with favor upon American ways, and he appears to have enjoyed his experiences in the South. The latter, he wrote, afforded many refutations to the charges "of rudeness, so frequently and unjustly brought against

Americans" (I, 87). He was, however, opposed to slavery, which he regarded as "a foul stain upon the honour, humanity, and justice of the United States" (I, 120–25; II, 203–204); and he was critical of certain traits he found among Kentuckians, such as carrying lethal weapons, fighting, gouging, picking teeth with knives, and excessive swaggering and boasting (I, 151–54). (Citations are from New York, 1839, edition.)

79. [Nicklin, Philip Holbrook (1786–1842)]

Letters descriptive of the Virginia springs; the roads leading thereto, and the doings thereat. Collected, corrected, annotated, and edited by Peregrine Prolix [pseud.] . . . Philadelphia, H. S. Tanner, 1835.

> xii, [9]–99 p. front. (fold. map). 15 cm.
> *Maps:* Folded map of Virginia.
> *Inclusive dates:* 1834.
> *Other editions:*
> (1) 2d ed., containing eight more letters. Philadelphia, H. S. Tanner, 1837. 2 p.l., [iii]–x, [11]–248 p. front., fold. map. 16½ cm.
> (2) 3d ed. New York, H. S. Tanner, 1844.
> *Location of copy:* Library of Congress.

The author left Philadelphia in August, 1834, and traveled by boat to Baltimore, by stage to Washington, by boat and stage to Fredericksburg, and on by stage, through Orange Court House, Charlottesville, Staunton, and Rock-Fish Gap, to Warm Springs. He then made a tour of the springs, including visits to White Sulphur, Salt Sulphur, Red Sulphur, Gray Sulphur, the Sweet Springs, and Hot Springs. His return trip was made through Harrisonburg, New Market, Woodstock, Winchester, and Point of Rocks, to Frederick, and thence by rail to Baltimore.

The text is arranged in the form of twelve letters, stated to have appeared originally in the *United States Gazette* and later collected, edited, and published under the above title by one Peregrine Prolix, obviously a pseudonym, very likely for the author. There are brief descriptions of the waters and accommodations at the various springs, and of the inns and travel facilities used both in going to and from the region of the springs, and from one spring to another, together with some information on prices charged. The editor observed that the author has given but a superficial view of the region which he treats; "yet the things he has described are those most interesting to the majority of travellers who skim the surface with a rapidity which does not permit them to penetrate the substance" (p. vii).

Two years later the author made a second excursion to the springs, leaving Philadelphia in July, 1836, and going this time by sea to Norfolk, up the Chesapeake and the James to Richmond, and then by stage through Cumberland Court House, Lynchburg, Lexington, Natural Bridge, and Covington. He revisited the various spas described on his 1834 tour, noting the changes and improvements that had been made in the meantime. The return trip was over the same route as that of the previous visit. The 1836 tour was described in eight additional letters, which were printed along with the original twelve in the second edition.

80.   O'Ferrall, Simon Ansley (d. 1844)

A ramble of six thousand miles through the United States of America. By S. A. Ferrall . . . London, Effingham Wilson, 1832.

> xii, 360 p., incl. front. (facsim.).   21 cm.
> *Inclusive dates:* 1829–1830.
> *Location of copy:* Library of Congress.

O'Ferrall visited the United States "without any definite scientific object, or indeed any motive much more important than a love of novelty." On the Southern phase of his itinerary, he went from Cincinnati to Louisville and down the Ohio and Mississippi to New Orleans, where he spent about a month, and then returned along the same route (pp. 177–249). Most of his comments upon New Orleans relate to its history rather than to his own observations there. Descending and ascending the Mississippi, he described the channel of the river, steamboats, woodcutters, and a sugar plantation; and at Memphis he observed the Chickasaw Indians. The Cherokees and other Indian tribes are discussed at some length (pp. 251–90), but there is no reference to his having visited them. A picturesque description of Kentuckians is given on page 242.

O'Ferrall was skeptical of slavery, but otherwise not critical of the South. "As the Americans always allowed me to act as I thought proper, and even to laugh at such of their habits as I thought singular, I am by no means inclined to take exception to them."

81.   O'Kelly, Patrick

Advice and guide to emigrants, going to the United States of America. By P. O'Kelly . . . Dublin, printed by William Folds, 1834.

> iv, [2], [5]–96, [2] p.   18½ cm.
> *Location of copy:* Library of Congress.

Advice to Irish emigrants, containing information on the various states, their boundaries, chief cities, and products. The author, a devout Roman Catholic, calls attention to the places where that church is strong. He spent six years as a teacher in Louisville and Baltimore previous to 1823, but this experience is treated only casually.

82. Parker, Amos Andrew (b. 1792)

Trip to the West and Texas. Comprising a journey of eight thousand miles, through New-York, Michigan, Illinois, Missouri, Louisiana and Texas, in the autumn and winter of 1834-5. Interspersed with anecdotes, incidents and observations. With a brief sketch of the Texian war. By A. A. Parker. Concord, N. H., White & Fisher, 1835.

> 276 p.   2 plates (incl. front.).   18 cm.
> *Inclusive dates:* 1834–1835.
> *Other editions:*
>   Same title, "with a brief sketch of the Texian war" added. Concord, N. H., W. White; Boston, B. M. Mussey, 1836.   iv, ₁5₁–380 p., incl. plates.   17½ cm.
> *Location of copy:* Duke University Library.

One of the earliest descriptions of Texas in English, by an observing and friendly traveler. Parker went on horseback through Louisiana into Texas, where he arrived late in November, 1834. He remained a month in Texas, touring the country in various directions, especially in the vicinity of St. Augustine, Nacogdoches, and San Felipe. On his return he walked from San Felipe to Columbia and then went to Brazoria, where he took a schooner to New Orleans. He spent four days in New Orleans, from which he continued on to Boston by sea.

The account of his travels in Texas is presented in some detail (pp. 118–35), followed by a general view of that region, with references to the land, crops, game, and advice to travelers and emigrants (pp. 135–74). With regard to slavery he observed that emancipation would be unthinkable as long as the Negroes remained in their existing condition of ignorance, and felt that the North was not sufficiently aware of the problems facing the South in this respect.

83. Pattie, James Ohio (1804?–1849?)

The personal narrative of James O. Pattie, of Kentucky, during an expedition from St. Louis, through the vast regions between that place and the Pacific ocean, and thence back through the city of Mexico to Vera Cruz, during journeyings of six years; in which he and his father, who accompanied him, suffered unheard of hardships and dangers, had various conflicts with the Indians, and were made captives, in which captivity his father died; together with a description of the country, and the various nations through which they passed. Ed. by Timothy Flint. Cincinnati, E. H. Flint, 1833.

> xi, ₁13₁–300 p. 5 plates. 19½ cm.
> *Inclusive dates:* 1830.
> *Other editions:*
> (1) Pattie's Personal narrative of a voyage to the Pacific and in Mexico, June 20, 1824–August 30, 1830. ₁Cleveland, O., The A. H. Clark company, 1905₁. 379 p. 5 plates, facsim. 23½ cm. (In Reuben G. Thwaites [ed.], Early western travels, 1748–1846. Cleveland, 1904–1907. Vol. XVIII).
> (2) . . . The personal narrative of James O. Pattie of Kentucky, edited by Timothy Flint, historical introduction and foot-notes by Milo Milton Quaife . . . Chicago, R. R. Donnelley & sons co., 1930. xliii, 428 p. front., plates. 17½ cm. (The Lakeside classics).
> *Location of copy:* Library of Congress.

This narrative is not concerned with the South except for Pattie's coming up the Mississippi on his return from Mexico in 1830 (pp. 248–51), and this has little reference to anything Southern. According to Henry R. Wagner's *The Plains and the Rockies* (3d. ed., revised by Charles L. Camp, Columbus, O., 1953), the first edition was published in 1831 by John H. Wood, and only a few copies exist. This 1833 imprint "is not exactly a new edition, and is the same book with a different title page, bearing Flint's name instead of that of Wood" (p. 74).

84.   Pavie, Théodore Marie (1811–1896)

Souvenirs atlantiques. Voyage aux États-Unis et au Canada. Par Théodore Pavie. Angers, Impr. de L. Pavie, 1832.

> viii, 550, ₁2₁ p. 20 cm.
> *Inclusive dates:* c.1829–1830.
> *Other editions:*
> (1) Paris, Roret ₁etc.₁ 1833. 2 vols. in 1. Vol. I, viii, 350 p.; Vol. II, 354 p.
> (2) Atlantische Erinnerungen. Reisebilder aus Canada und den Vereinigten Staaten von Nord-Amerika, von Theodor Pavie. Aus dem Französischen . . . Braunschweig, C. Horneyer, 1834. 2 vols. in 1: Vol. I, ₁3₁–274 p.; Vol. II, ₁5₁–275 p. 16 cm.
> *Location of copy:* Library of Congress.

This is an account of a visit to America, said by the author to have been made in his eighteenth year, which would fix the date at about 1829–30. The Southern portion of the tour consists of two phases. On the first of these the author visited Baltimore, Washington, and Annapolis, and then returned to New York by sea, stopping briefly at Norfolk. Later he crossed the mountains and descended the Ohio and Mississippi, stopping at and describing Louisville, Memphis, Natchez, and New Orleans. He also appears to have gone up the Red River to Alexandria and Natchitoches, and to have made a horseback trip into Texas, after which he returned by the same route to New Orleans and sailed for Bordeaux.

Pavie was a thoroughgoing romanticist, weighted down with a profound sense of melancholy. He was strongly influenced by Chateaubriand, whose account of America he was apparently attempting to imitate. With the exception of a few remarks on slavery, which he vigorously opposed, and on woodcutters and other primitives whom he encountered along the Mississippi, he wrote mainly of Indians, forests, camping, bear hunting, prairie fires, and other aspects of nature in what he wistfully calls the wild and savage land where *"j'y ai passé les plus beaux jours de ma jeunesse, au milieu de tout ce que demande en soupirant une jeune tête malade de désirs."* Although he vouches for the authenticity of most of what he described, he admits that some of the incidents were not actually witnessed, but are "probable" and based on facts.

85. Peck, John Mason (1789–1858)

Forty years of pioneer life. Memoir of John Mason Peck, D.D. Edited from his journals and correspondence. By Rufus Babcock. Philadelphia, American Baptist publication society, [1864].

> 360 p. front. (port.), plates. 19½ cm.
> *Inclusive dates:* 1835, 1842.
> *Location of copy:* Library of Congress.

A biography of Peck, but containing numerous excerpts from his journals. Among these are brief accounts of a trip from St. Louis to Richmond and Norfolk in April, 1835 (pp. 260–62), and a journey by way of Nashville and thence down the Cumberland, Ohio, and Mississippi to New Orleans and return in 1842 (pp. 300–302). While at Nashville, Peck made visits to the Hermitage and to churches in Wilson County, Tennessee.

86. Peck, John Mason (1789–1858)

A guide for emigrants, containing sketches of Illinois, Missouri, and the adjacent parts. By J. M. Peck ... Boston, Lincoln and Edwards, 1831.

> 336 p. front. (fold. map). 14½ cm.
> *Other editions:*
> Published under title:
> (1) A new guide for emigrants to the West, containing sketches of Ohio, Indiana, Illinois, Missouri, Michigan, with the territories of Wisconsin and

Arkansas, and the adjacent parts. By J. M. Peck . . . Boston, Gould, Kendall & Lincoln, 1836. vii, ₍ᵥ₎–x, ₍11₎–374 p. 15 cm.

(2) 2d ed. Boston, Gould, Kendall & Lincoln, 1837. xii p., 1 l. ₍15₎–381 p. 16 cm.

(3) Cincinnati, D. Anderson, 1848.
Location of copy: Library of Congress.

A guidebook relating primarily to the West and only incidentally concerned with the South. There is a description of the lower Mississippi Valley (pp. 50–84), but this is taken mainly from the work of Timothy Flint.

87.   Persat, Maurice (1788–1858)

Mémoires du commandant Persat, 1806 à 1844; publiés avec une introduction et des notes par Gustave Schlumberger . . . Paris, Plon-Nourrit et Cie., 1910.

3 p.l., ₍ᵥ₎–xxx, ₍c₎–i, 367 p. facsim. 22 cm.
Inclusive dates: 1825.
Location of copy: Library of Congress.

Persat, a Napoleonic veteran, was in the United States during 1817–19, after which he went to South America and fought under Bolívar against the Spaniards. He returned to the United States in 1824 and remained until 1827. During this second visit he traveled widely through the country, making detailed notes on the cities he visited and on the character, customs, and industries of the inhabitants. His itinerary included the South, in which he traveled in 1825 by boat from Louisville to Smithland, Kentucky, and thence overland to Nashville. In southern Kentucky he encountered a community of polygamists (*les multiplicateurs*), whom he appears to have regarded as Mormons but who were more probably the Shakers at South Union. From Nashville he continued on foot to Natchez and then to New Orleans, joining at the latter point a filibustering expedition, probably connected with the Fredonian Republic. He accompanied the expedition to Texas and then returned to France. The account of his Southern travels (pp. 158–98) is of only incidental importance in his memoirs.

88.   Pike, Albert (1809–1891)

Prose sketches and poems, written in the western country, by Albert Pike. Boston, Light & Horton, 1834.

viii, ₍9₎–200 p. 18½ cm.
Inclusive dates: 1831–1832.
Location of copy: Duke University Library.

[75]

Pike, who had gone to Santa Fé in 1831, joined a trapping expedition into the Comanche country in September, 1832. The party crossed the Staked Plains, entered the present state of Oklahoma, passed through the Cross Timbers, and arrived at Fort Smith in December. They had some associations with the Indians, not altogether friendly, and experienced a number of hardships, but enjoyed some exciting adventures in the form of buffalo hunting and other sports. A day-to-day account of these experiences, which Pike says he wrote entirely from memory, aided by that of one of his companions, appears under the caption "Narrative of a Second Journey in the Prairie," pages 36–80 of the above work. That portion of the tour relating to Oklahoma parallels closely the route taken by Washington Irving in his *Tour on the Prairies,* and for that reason is described in less detail by Pike, who felt that Irving would do it better (p. 78).

Among the members of the party that went into the Comanche country was one Aaron B. Lewis, who had gone on a trading expedition from Fort Towson, Arkansas Territory, to Taos during September, 1831–May, 1832. His adventures on this expedition were related to Pike from memory and described by the latter in a "Narrative of a Journey in the Prairie," pages 9–36 of the *Prose Sketches.*

Both narratives are concerned mainly with adventure and descriptive material. Pike states that such portions "as purport to be true, are actually and truly facts," although he admits that he had polished up the narrative of the uneducated Lewis (p. vii).

89. Pope, William F. (1814–1895)

Early days in Arkansas; being for the most part the personal recollections of an old settler. By Judge William F. Pope. Arranged and ed. by his son Dunbar H. Pope. With an introduction by Hon. Sam W. Williams . . . Little Rock, Ark., F. W. Allsopp, 1895.

330 p. front., plates, ports. 19½ cm.
Inclusive dates: 1832.
Location of copy: Duke University Library.

Contains an account, based upon the author's recollections, of a journey in September, 1832, from Louisville to Little Rock, where he went as secretary to the territorial governor of Arkansas, John Pope (pp. 55–76). The trip was taken on a side-wheel steamer down the Ohio and Mississippi and up the Arkansas River to Arkansas Post, and thence overland to Little Rock. There is a good account of a hurricane that struck the boat just after its entrance to the Mississippi (pp. 58–59), and some descriptive material relating to Arkansas Post.

In matters that can be checked, the author's recollections prove none too reliable, and this criticism may also apply to this travel account.

90. Power, Tyrone (1797–1841)

Impressions of America, during the years 1833, 1834, and 1835. By Tyrone Power ... 2 vols. London, R. Bentley, 1836.

Vol. I, xv, 440 p.; Vol. II, vi, 408 p. fronts. 21 cm.
Inclusive dates: 1834–1835.
Other editions:
  (1) 2 vols. Philadelphia, Carey, Lea & Blanchard, 1836. Vol. I, viii, [13]–262 p.; Vol. II, [3]–219 p. 19 cm.
  (2) 2d American ed. Philadelphia, Carey, Lea & Blanchard, 1836. 2 vols. in 1: Vol. I, [13]–262 p.; Vol. II, [3]–204 p. 17½ cm.
Location of copy: Library of Congress.

Power, an Irish comedian, toured the South twice while on his American visit in 1833–35. In late October, 1834, he traveled by boat from Baltimore to Norfolk and thence, by way of City Point, to Petersburg, from which he returned to New York early in November. Later in the same month he sailed to Charleston, and from there continued on to Savannah and up the Savannah River to Augusta; thence by stage, through Milledgeville, Macon, and Columbus, to Montgomery; and by boat to Mobile and New Orleans. From the latter place he went up the Mississippi to Natchez and returned, paid a second visit to Mobile, and finally sailed from New Orleans for New York in March, 1835.

He was favorably impressed with the South and, quite unlike most foreigners, was not disturbed by slavery (II, 58). He liked Virginia, was well pleased with Savannah, and apparently derived considerable satisfaction from his Southern travel generally. Indeed, he admitted a sort of prejudice in favor of the United States, to which the South was no exception; writing "that the person who, for two years, could be in constant intercourse with a people, to the increase of his fortune, the improvement of his health, and the enlargement of all that is good in his mind, yet feel no partiality in their favor, I pity for coldness more than envy for philosophy" (I, viii). (Citations are from Philadelphia, 1836 edition.)

91. Rafinesque, Constantine Samuel (1783–1840)

A life of travels and researches in North America and south Europe; or, Outlines of the life, travels and researches of C. S. Rafinesque, A.M., Ph.D. ... Containing his travels in North America and the south of

Europe; the Atlantic Ocean, Mediterranean, Sicily, Azores, &c., from 1802 to 1835—with sketches of his scientific and historical researches, &c. . . . Philadelphia, printed for the author by F. Turner, 1836.

> 148 p. 18½ cm.
> *Inclusive dates:* 1819–1825.
> *Other editions:*
>
> (1) A life of travels, by C. S. Rafinesque, being a verbatim and literatim reprint of the original and only edition (Philadelphia, 1836). Foreword by Elmer D. Merrill . . . critical index by Francis W. Pennell . . . [Waltham, Mass., The Chronica botanica co.; New York city, G. E. Stechert and co.; etc., etc., 1944]. [3], 294–360 p. illus. (facsim.), ports. 26 cm. (Chronica botanica, Vol. VIII, No. 2).
> *Location of copy:* Library of Congress.

Chapter V (pp. 60–75) of this work is devoted to Rafinesque's seven-year residence in Lexington, Kentucky, where he served as professor of botany, natural history, and modern languages at Transylvania College, 1819–26. During this period he traveled extensively in Kentucky and Tennessee, gathering botanical data, visiting springs, and searching for archaeological remains. Various itineraries are mentioned, among them being a tour through Bowling Green and Hopkinsville to Clarksville, Tennessee, made in 1823. The accounts of these travels are not always presented consecutively, and the information is meager.

92. Reed, Andrew (1787–1862)

A narrative of the visit to the American churches, by the deputation from the Congregational Union of England and Wales. By Andrew Reed, D.D. and James Matheson, D.D. . . . 2 vols. London, Jackson and Walford, 1835.

> Vol. I, xvii, [3], 498, [1] p.; Vol. II, vii, 526 p. Map, 4 plates. 8vo.
> *Inclusive dates:* 1834.
> *Other editions:*
>
> (1) 2 vols. New-York, Harper & brothers, 1835. Vol. I, xiv, 9–336 p.; Vol. II, vi, 9–362, [1] p. 12mo.
> (2) New-York, Thomas Gage, Jr., 1835. [2], 587–784 p. 8vo.
> (3) 2 vols. London, Jackson and Walford, 1836. Vol. I, xxiv, 371 p.; Vol. II, viii, 400 p.
> (4) Verhaal van het bezoek bij de Amerikaansche Kerken, door de Afgevaardigden van wege de Congregationale Vereeniging van Engeland en Wallis. Uit het Engelsch vertaald door Adr. van Deinse. Rotterdam, 1838.
> *Location of copy:* Duke University Library.

The purpose of the tour was a fraternal visit to the Presbyterian and Congregational bodies in the United States. The section of the book relating to the South was written by Reed, Matheson having remained in the East. Reed entered Kentucky from Cincinnati and went east to Virginia, through Lexington, Kentucky, Charleston, Lexington, Staunton, Charlottesville, Richmond, and Fredericksburg, Virginia, across to the Northern Neck, and on to Baltimore and Philadelphia. On the Northern Neck he attended a camp meeting, with which he was not favorably impressed (I, 203–13). He gives a brief description of the University of Virginia, of Natural Bridge, and a more extended account of Weyer's Cave (I, 167–75). His work is a good analysis of religious conditions in the South by a foreigner.

Volume II contains some observations on slavery, to which the authors were opposed, but not violently (II, 182–204). (Citations are from London, 1836, edition.)

93. [Reynal, Rafael]

Viage por los Estados Unidos del Norte, dedicado a los jovenes mexicanos de ambos secsos . . . Cincinnati, Impreso por E. Deming, 1834.

> 3 p.l., 164 p.   plates.   13½ cm.
> *Illustrations:* Numerous.
> *Inclusive dates:* c.1830.
> *Location of copy:* Library of Congress.

Purports to be a series of letters written by Reynal after making a trip from Mexico by way of New Orleans, up the Mississippi and Ohio to Cincinnati, and thence to Baltimore and New York. Descriptive of the country and the manners of the people, but not definitely ascertained to be based on actual travel.

94. Rich, Obadiah (1783?–1850)

A general view of the United States of America. With an appendix containing the Constitution, the tariff of duties, the laws of patents and copyrights, &c. . . . London, O. Rich, 1833.

> vi, 278 p.   front. (fold. map).   16½ cm.
> *Maps:* Folding map of U. S.
> *Other editions:*
>   Second edition. London, James S. Hodson, 1836.   iv, [2], v–vi, 278 p.   16mo.
> *Location of copy:* Library of Congress.

A general view of the history, geography, and various statistics relating to the United States, followed by similar material for each state, including the Southern states. It appears to have been compiled in England from American almanacs and other sources, and was designed as a book of reference for readers of travel accounts, and perhaps for travelers themselves.

95. Royall, Mrs. Anne (Newport) (1769–1854)

The black book; or, A continuation of travels in the United States . . .
By Mrs. Anne Royall . . . 3 vols. Washington, printed for the author,
1828–29.

> Vol. I, [3]–328 p.; Vol. II, [3]–395 p.; Vol. III, [3]–234 p.   18½ cm.
> *Inclusive dates:* 1827.
> *Other editions:*
>   In two volumes . . . Washington, printed for the author, 1828.   Vol. I, 328,
> [1] p.; Vol. II, 395,[1] p.   12mo.
> *Location of copy:* Library of Congress.

This is a continuation of the *Sketches of history, life and manners
in the United States* and, except for the itineraries, does not differ
materially in character from that book. Three Southern tours are
included in the first volume. These are (1) south from Washington
through Alexandria, Fredericksburg, and Richmond, to Petersburg
(I, 140–63), with descriptions of each city and of the author's experiences there, usually critical: (2) from Petersburg to Norfolk, Portsmouth, Gosport, Old Point Comfort, Fortress Monroe, and back to
Washington (I, 247–66); and (3) from Washington to Harpers
Ferry, Charlestown, Shepherdstown, Hagerstown, Baltimore, and
Annapolis (I, 275–313).

With the exception of a novel published in 1827, this was Mrs.
Royall's second book; and in it she achieved the style that remained
characteristic of her works. She was critical of travel facilities, hotel-
keepers, and their accommodations. Owing to the large amount of
baggage she carried, she was in a state of chronic war with stage
drivers; and she kept a sharp eye on tavern-keepers to see that they
posted their rates and did not overcharge. She was especially hostile
to "missionaries" and distributors of religious tracts, being obsessed
with an idea that such persons, "blue skins" as she called them, were,
along with the British, in a conspiracy, to overthrow the government
and effect a union of church and state in America.

Her husband had been a prominent Mason, and she was assisted
by Masons on several occasions during her travels. These facts made
her a vigorous defender of that order and a violent critic of any
anti-Mason, no matter how excellent his character. It is also probable
that the title *Black Book* may have had some cryptic significance
in this connection.

96. Royall, Mrs. Anne (Newport) (1769–1854)

Letters from Alabama on various subjects: to which is added, an appendix, containing remarks on sundry members of the 20th and 21st Congress, and other high characters, &c., &c. at the seat of government. In one volume. By Anne Royall ... Washington, 1830.

232, 6 p.   22 cm.
Inclusive dates: 1817–1822.
Location of copy: Library of Congress.

Following the death of her wealthy Virginia husband in 1813, Mrs. Royall went, for some undisclosed reason, to Alabama. Here she spent the greater portion of the next ten years, chiefly at St. Stephens, Huntsville, and Melton's Bluff at the head of Muscle Shoals, but also visiting Charleston and New Orleans and making several trips back and forth to Virginia, journeying luxuriously in her own coach and attended by three slaves and a courier. She tarried leisurely at inns along the way, was entertained at the homes of prominent planters, and herself gave elaborate dinners in return. During this period she was often writing to a young Virginia lawyer, identified only as "Matt"—a strange but interesting correspondence, of which fifty letters were published under the above title.

These are the first travels of which Mrs. Royall left an account, although not the first of her travel books to be published. The title is somewhat inaccurate, since of the 160 pages devoted to the letters, only 60 relate to Alabama. The first hundred (pp. 5–104) describe a trip taken in November, 1817–February, 1818, from Cabell Court House, Virginia, through Mount Sterling, Lexington, and Bowling Green, Kentucky, Nashville and Fayetteville, Tennessee, to Huntsville, and Melton's Bluff. The remaining pages (104–65) contain letters dated at Melton's Bluff (December, 1818), Moulton (March, 1819, and April and May, 1821), Courtland (June, 1821), Florence (July, 1821), and Huntsville (January, February, April, and June, 1822).

It is impossible to determine the extent to which these letters were written contemporaneously with the events which they purport to relate. According to the introduction, they were to have appeared much earlier, "but, unfortunately, were lost, and only recovered a few months since." They include, in addition to personal matters and discussions on religion, literature, education, social vices, and crop statistics, a considerable amount of description of the country through which the author traveled, and observations upon towns, inns, conveyances, and persons she met on stages and at other places on her tours. In this work her comments are not so violent as in her other books.

Pages 169–232 comprise an appendix relating to Congress and not concerned with travels.

97. Royall, Mrs. Anne (Newport) (1769–1854)

Mrs. Royall's Southern tour, or, Second series of the Black Book. By Mrs. Anne Royall . . . 3 vols. Washington, 1830–31.

Vol. I, [5]–169, 12 p.; Vol. II [3]–217 p.; Vol. III [3]–246 p. 21½ cm.
Inclusive dates: 1829–1830.
Location of copy: Library of Congress.

This three-volume work deals almost entirely with the South. The first lap of the journey began at Baltimore in November, 1929, and ended in the spring of 1830 (I, 24–169), the itinerary including Norfolk, Petersburg, Richmond, Washington, Alexandria, Warrenton, Winchester, Staunton, Charlottesville, Lynchburg, and Farmville, in Virginia; Greensboro, Hillsboro, Chapel Hill, Raleigh, Fayetteville, and Wilmington, North Carolina, from which she departed by sea to Charleston. The second stage (II, 3–208) began at Charleston and included Camden, Columbia, and Augusta; a boat trip down the river to Savannah and back to Augusta; a stage tour from Augusta, by way of Sparta, Milledgeville, Macon, Columbus, and Fort Mitchell, to Montgomery; and thence by boat to Mobile and New Orleans. From New Orleans she went up the Mississippi to St. Louis, overland to Shawneetown, Illinois, by boat to Smithland and Eddyville, Kentucky, and thence by stage, through Princeton, Hopkinsville, Russellville, and Bowling Green, to Nashville (III, 3–204).

It would be impossible, within any reasonable space, to digest the contents of these three volumes. There is a long section on each city and author visited, describing its history, public buildings, principal citizens, and other items; also the usual criticism which she directed against any person or object falling under her suspicion or arousing her dislike, as suggested in the foregoing comment upon the *Black Book*. Indeed, Mrs. Royall's books do not differ greatly one from another, and the reading of one is sufficient to obtain an insight into their general character.

98. Royall, Mrs. Anne (Newport) (1769–1854)

Sketches of history, life, and manners, in the United States. By a traveller. New-Haven, printed for the author, 1826.

2 p.l., [13]–392 p. front. 18 cm.
Illustrations: Frontispiece (Young ladies' academy at Georgetown, D. C.).
Inclusive dates: 1823–1824.
Location of copy: Library of Congress.

The pleasant existence described by Mrs. Royall in *Letters from Alabama* came to a sudden end in 1823 when, after ten years of litigation, the other heirs in Virginia succeeded in breaking her husband's will, leaving her penniless at the age of fifty-four. Rallying after the first shock of this misfortune, she decided to go to Washington and apply for a pension as the widow of a Revolutionary officer. On horseback she went from St. Stephens to Huntsville, through Tennessee by way of Winchester, McMinnville, Sparta, and Knoxville, to the Virginia Springs, and thence through Staunton and Winchester to Alexandria. In contrast to earlier journeys she now traveled in hardship, frequently indebted to strangers for stage fare, eating scraps thrown from tavern windows, and sleeping where she could.

Upon leaving Alabama, she resolved, with a view to diverting her mind from melancholia, "to note everything during my journey worthy of remark and commit it to writing." Upon reaching Alexandria, late in December, she obtained a room and began the task of arranging her notes into a book. In April of the next year she made a short trip to Richmond, to secure evidence in connection with her pension application, and six weeks later was off through Pennsylvania, New York, and New England to collect further material and solicit advance subscriptions.

The completed volume, published under the above title, set the the pattern of her life for the next five years, during which she traveled almost continuously and issued a total of ten additional volumes. As soon as one volume was off the press, she would load several trunks full of copies on the stage and set out on a tour, selling the books just printed and collecting material for a succeeding one.

Her works, of which the above is typical, were in the nature of guidebooks, containing descriptions of nearly every important village, town, and city in the United States. She usually began with a historical sketch of the place she was describing, followed by full information concerning schools and their curricula; charitable, reformatory, and penal institutions; public buildings and crop and trade statistics; and inns, taverns, and the manners and appearance of the inhabitants. She also included numerous "pen portraits" of the principal citizens of the places she visited. A woman of violent prejudices, her writings were often given to personalities of doubtful taste, and the constant expression of her sympathies and antipathies is frequently tiresome to the reader.

In the above work, pages 13–130 relate to her travels in the South, the remainder being concerned with the middle states and New England.

99. Sánchez, José María (1801?–1834)

Viaje a Texas en 1828–1829; diario del teniente D. José María Sánchez, miembro de la comisión de límites. Introducción por Jorge Flores D. Mexico, 1939.

> 4 p.l., ₁vₗ–xvi, 79, ₁1ₗ p., 2 l. 23½ cm. (Papeles históricos mexicanos, 1).
> *Inclusive dates:* 1828.
> *Other editions:*
> The Texas portion of this diary was translated by Carlos E. Castañeda and published as "A Trip to Texas in 1828," Southwestern historical quarterly, XXIX (April, 1926), 248–88.
> *Location of copy:* Library of Congress.

The author, a lieutenant of artillery, was attached as a draftsman to a commission appointed to fix the boundary between the United States and Mexican Texas. The Texas portion of his diary begins near Laredo in February, 1828, and ends abruptly at Nacogdoches in June of the same year, the itinerary including San Antonio, Gonzales, San Felipe, and various other small settlements. On each of these places there is some comment regarding the habits and character of the people, their resources, and their condition under Mexican rule. The author believed that the Mexican government was not sufficiently aware of the discontent that prevailed among the American settlers in Texas. There is also considerable material, written for the most part in a romantic vein, on the appearance of the country, the watercourses, forests, mosquitoes and other insects, and on the experiences of the expedition.

100. Sealsfield, Charles (1793–1864)

The Americans as they are; described in a tour through the Valley of the Mississippi. By the author of "Austria as it is." London, Hurst, Chance, and co., 1828.

> 2 p.l., vi, ₁4ₗ–218, ₁3ₗ p. 19 cm.
> *Inclusive dates:* 1826.
> (The above title is an English version, abridged, of the author's Die Vereinigten Staaten von Nordamerika nach ihren politischen, religiosen und gesellschaftlichen Verhältnissen betrachtet).
> *Location of copy:* Library of Congress.

This is an English translation of the second volume of Sealsfield's *Die Vereinigten Staaten von Nordamerika nach ihren politischen, religiösen und gesellschaftlichen Verhältnissen betrachtet. Mit einer Reise durch den westlichen Theil von Pennsylvanien, Ohio, Kentucky, Indiana, Illinois, Missouri, Tennessee, das Gebiet Arkansas, Mississippi, und Louisiana. Von C. Sidons, Bürger der Vereinigten*

Staaten von Nordamerika (Stuttgart and Tübingen, J. G. Cotta'schen Buchhandlung, 1827. 18½ cm. 2 vols. in 1; Vol. I, x, 206 p.; Vol. II, ix, 247 p. (Copy at Harvard University Library). The first volume, which is a social and political treatise not concerned with the South, appeared in English as *The United States of North America as They Are* (London, J. Murray, 1827. 21½ cm. xii, 242 p.). Also in a later edition, with same text and collation, published in London by W. Simpkin and R. Marshall, 1828. (Copies of both editions in The New York Public Library.) This was the only occasion upon which Sealsfield used the pseudonym "Sidons."

Sealsfield's itinerary included Cincinnati, Newport, and Louisville, thence by keelboat to Owensboro, from which he made a side trip to the New Harmony colony of Indiana; then back to the Ohio and up that river and the Mississippi to St. Louis, and thence down the Mississippi to New Orleans. He has some good descriptions, such as Kentucky hospitality and violence (pp. 22–27); the keelboat on which he traveled from Louisville to Owensboro (pp. 54–58); the steamboat on which he went from St. Louis to New Orleans (pp. 104–109); and of Palmyra plantation which he visited near Natchez. Since he kept almost entirely to the Ohio and Mississippi rivers, his lengthy descriptions of Tennessee, Louisiana, and other states would seem to have been based more largely upon observations made during an earlier tour than upon this one. He states in the preface that he "has twice seen these countries" and that "truth and practical observation are his chief points."

Sealsfield had traveled through the Southern states and the Mexican province of Texas in the early 1820's, observing the region with the eye of an artist, historian, and ethnographer. He returned to the Southwest again in 1828 and remained until 1832, working as a journalist and apparently engaging in various business enterprises. On the basis of these experiences he later wrote five novels dealing with life in the Southwest, eventually brought together and published under the title *Lebensbilder aus der Westlichen Hemisphere* in vols. IX–XII of his collected works (Stuttgart, 1846) (copies at Harvard University Library). An English translation of the *Lebensbilder* was brought out as *Life in the New World: or Sketches of American Society* (Translated from the German by G. C. Hebbe and James Mackey. New York, J. Winchester, [1842]. 349 p.). A second edition of this translation, with same text and collation, appeared in 1844, with the author's name printed as "Seatsfield."

A more famous work of Sealsfield, also drawn from his experiences in the Southwest, was *Das Kajütenbuch oder nationale Charak-*

teristiken, a vivid picture of Texas and its society in the early days and during the war for Texan independence. This is generally regarded as his masterpiece and was issued in a dozen or more editions, among these being *The Cabin Book; or Sketches of Life in Texas* (Translated from the German by Professor C. F. Mersch. New York, J. Winchester, 1844. iv, 155 p.; and *The Cabin Book; or National Characteristics* (Translated from the German by Sarah Powell. London, Ingram, Cooke and Company, 1852. iv, 296). (Copies of these and various other editions, some under different titles, are in the Library of Congress.)

For further information on Sealsfield's works and the location of copies thereof, see Otto Heller and Theodore H. Leon, *Charles Sealsfield: Bibliography of His Writings Together with a Classified and Annotated Catalog of Literature Relating to His Works and His Life* (Washington University Studies, New Series, Language and Literature, No. 8, St. Louis, 1939. x, 88 p.).

101.   Sherwood, Adiel (1791–1879)

A gazetteer of the state of Georgia. By Rev. Adiel Sherwood, A.M. Charleston, printed by W. Riley, 1827.

iv p., 1 l., ₁7₁–143 p.   15 cm.
Other editions:
    (1) 2d ed. Philadelphia, printed by J. W. Martin and W. K. Boden, 1829. 1 p.l., ₁v₁–vi, ₁2₁, ₁9₁–300 p., 1 l. front. (fold. map), 1 illus., plan.   15 cm.
    (2) A gazetteer of the state of Georgia; embracing a particular description of the counties, towns, villages, rivers, &c., and whatsoever is usual in geographies, and minute statistical works, together with a new map of the state. By Adiel Sherwood. 3d ed., greatly enl. and improved. Washington city, printed by P. Force, 1837. 2 p.l., 344 p.   maps.   19 cm.
    (3) 3d ed., greatly enl. and improved. Washington city, printed by P. Force, 1837. 2 p.l., 356 p.   maps.   18½ cm.   (Reissue of 3d ed., 1837, with addenda [p. 345–56]).
    (4) 4th ed., rev. and cor. Macon, Ga., S. Boykin; Atlanta, J. Richards; ₁etc., etc.₁, 1860. 209 p.   map.
    (5) A gazetteer of the state of Georgia, by Rev. Adiel Sherwood, A.M.; biographical sketch by John B. Clark, M.A., PhD.; foreword by President Spright Dowell, Mercer university. The present edition being a facsimile reprint of the original 1827 publication, with a map of Georgia from the 1829 edition and a portrait of the author. Athens, Ga., The University of Georgia press, 1939. 4 p.l., facsim.: iv. p., 1 l., ₁7₁–143 p. front. (port.), fold. map. 16½ cm
Location of copy: Library of Congress.

Contains a brief description of Georgia in 1827, followed by sentence descriptions of counties, towns, villages, mountains, rivers, creeks, canals, mineral springs, and other geographical points of interest, alphabetically arranged; and an appendix of statistical information.

102. Shillitoe, Thomas (1754–1836)

Journal of the life, labors, and travels of Thomas Shillitoe, in the service of the gospel of Jesus Christ. 2 vols. London, Harvey and Darton, 1839.

Vol I, xvi, 428 p.; Vol. II, iv, 427 p. 1 illus. 22½ cm.
Illustrations: Silhouette of the author.
Inclusive dates: 1828–1829.
Other editions:
(1) The second edition. London, Harvey and Darton, 1839.
(2) Reprinted in The Friends' library, Vol. III, Philadelphia, 1839.
Location of copy: Duke University Library.

The author was a London Quaker who made a fraternal visit to the churches of his faith in the United States about 1826. He was in the South from October, 1828, until March or April, 1829, traveling through Kentucky, North Carolina, and Virginia (II, 349–76). The Southern phase of his account deals almost entirely with religious conditions among the Friends in North Carolina, including his visits to the yearly meeting at New Garden and to monthly meetings at various churches along the Deep and Yadkin rivers. There is a good description of the Moravian community at Salem, where he had some difficulty in securing permission to hold services.

103. Short, Rich

Travels in the United States of America, through the states of New-York, Pennsylvania, Ohio, Michigan Territory, Kentucky, Virginia, Maryland, Columbia, North Carolina, Rhode-Island and Massachusetts; with advice to emigrants. By Rich Short . . . 2 d ed. London, R. Lambert, [183–?].

24 p. 17 cm.
Inclusive dates: 1831–1833.
Location of copy: Library of Congress.

Short, who appears to have been an English laborer, made three trips to the United States in search of work in 1828, 1830, and 1832. On the second of these (pp. 16–19), he was in Kentucky, stopping briefly at Frankfort, but gives no details of his experiences there. On the third trip (pp. 20–24), he went by boat from Washington to Norfolk and, finding no work at the latter city, continued on by land to Elizabeth City and Raleigh. At Raleigh he worked for two weeks, fell sick, and upon his recovery walked to Richmond and on out of the South. He found much trouble in securing employment and more difficulty in getting his pay. His references to the Southern phase of his experiences are brief.

104.   Sims, James Marion (1813–1883)

The story of my life. Edited by his son, H. Marion Sims. New York, D. Appleton and company, 1885.

> 471 p.   19 cm.
> *Inclusive dates:* 1830–1840.
> *Location of copy:* Duke University Library.

Sims moved from South Carolina to Alabama in 1835 and remained until 1853. During this period he took a trip to Philadelphia, served in the army for five weeks during the Seminole War, and visited South Carolina at least once. Only brief allusions are made to these journeys, the main emphasis, in the section dealing with his Alabama years, being upon his experiences as a physician in that state. This includes accounts of the ravages of yellow fever in the 1830's and 1840's and descriptions of Sim's epoch making achievements in the surgery of gynecology.

105.   Smithwick, Noah (1808–1899)

The evolution of a state; or, Recollections of old Texas days, by Noah Smithwick (nonagenarian). Compiled by his daughter Nanna Smithwick Donaldson. Austin, Tex., Gammel book company, [c.1900].

> 5 p l., 9–354 p.   front., illus. (incl. music), ports.   20 cm.
> *Inclusive dates:* 1827.
> *Other editions:*
>   Austin, Tex., The Steck company, 1935.   6 p.l., 9–354 p.   illus., ports.   21 cm. (Original narratives of Texas history and adventure).
> *Location of copy:* Duke University Library.

Contains a brief account of the author's migration from Tennessee to Texas in 1827, down the Ohio and Mississippi to New Orleans, and thence by schooner to DeWitt's colony on Matagorda Bay (pp. 10–19). Thereafter he lived in Texas until 1860, when he left for California on account of Union sentiments. Although he seems to have traveled extensively within the state of Texas, his reminiscences are mainly composed of descriptive material.

106.   Stuart, James (1775–1849)

Three years in North America. By James Stuart, esq. . . . . 2 vols. Edinburgh, printed for R. Cadell; [etc., etc.], 1833.

Vol. I, ix, 495, [1] p.; Vol. II, vi, [2], 580 p.   front. (fold. map).   20 cm.
Inclusive dates: 1829–1830.
Other editions:

(1) 2d ed., rev. . . . Edinburgh, printed for R. Cadell; [etc., etc.], 1833.   2 vols. in 1: Vol. I, xii, 525, [1] p.; Vol. II, viii, 544 p.

(2) From the 2d London ed. 2 vols. New York, J. & J. Harper, 1833.   Vol. I, xii, [13]–334 p.; Vol. II, vii, [9]–337 p.   19 cm.

(3) Third edition, revised. Edinburgh, printed for R. Cadell [etc., etc.], 1833.   2 vols in 1: Vol. I, xii, 525, [1] p.; Vol. II, viii, 544 p.

(4) Drie jaren in Noord Amerika, door James Stuart . . . Gevolgd naar den derden Engelschen druk . . . 3 vols. Gorinchem, J. Noorduyn, 1835. Vol I, xvi, 404 p.; Vol. II, vii, 382 p.; Vol. III, vii, 386 p.
Location of copy: Library of Congress.

After traveling through the East and Canada, Stuart came to Washington in May, 1829, and while there made a brief visit to Mount Vernon (I, 252–53). In February, 1830, he set out upon an extensive tour of the South, going by stage from Baltimore, through Washington, Richmond, Raleigh, Fayetteville, and Georgetown, to Charleston, and thence by steamboat to Savannah and Augusta. Transferring to stage again, he proceeded through Milledgeville, Macon, and Columbus to Montgomery, from which, unlike most travelers of the period, he continued by stage instead of the river to Mobile. He then went by steamboat to New Orleans, up the Mississippi and Ohio to Louisville, and back down the Ohio and up to St. Louis. After an overland journey from St. Louis to Louisville, he again entered Kentucky, going by stage through Lexington, Paris, and Georgetown to Cincinnati, where he ended his Southern travels in May (II, 48–192, 270–73).

Much of Stuart's account of the South was derived from reading rather than observation, particularly from Timothy Flint's *Geography and History of the Western States,* William Darby's *View of the United States,* and François Barbé-Marbois's *History of Louisiana.* At the same time, however, he includes detailed descriptions of the routes along which he passed, noting especially, and usually critically, the travel facilities and hotel and tavern accommodations which he encountered. His lengthy account of the stage trip from Montgomery to Mobile is of special interest (II, 111–23). He was critical of the treatment of slaves, accounts of which are extensively quoted (II, 72–76, 85–86, 132–35).

The book was designed primarily to furnish "such information, geographical and historical, as travellers generally wish to possess respecting a country which they may have occasion to visit, as well as hints which may be of some value to emigrants from Europe to the United States" (I, vii–viii). Stuart's conclusion was that there was less to interest a traveler, and greater difficulty and cost to be encountered in traveling, in the Southern states than in any other parts of the country which he had visited. He was inclined, therefore, "to think that the fatigue and expense of a journey to the South is hardly repaid by the sight of any thing that is not to be found in the Northern states" (II, 304). (Citations are from New York, 1833, edition.)

107. Tanner, Henry Schenck (1786–1858)

The American traveller; or Guide through the United States. Containing brief notices of the several states, cities, principal towns, canals and rail roads, &c. With tables of distances, by stage, canal, and steam boat routes. The whole alphabetically arranged, with direct reference to the accompanying map of roads, canals, and railways of the United States. By H. S. Tanner. Philadelphia, the author, 1834.

>iv, 5–144 p. fold. map, 4 plans. 15 cm.
>*Maps:* Folded map of U. S.; maps of Boston, Philadelphia, New York, and Baltimore.
>*Other editions:*
>(1) 2d ed. by H. S. Tanner. Philadelphia, the author, 1836.
>(2) 3d ed. Philadelphia, the author, 1837.
>(3) 3d ed. Philadelphia, the author, 1838.
>(4) 4th ed. Philadelphia, the author, 1839.
>(5) 5th ed. Philadelphia, 1839.
>(6) 5th ed. New York, published by T. R. Tanner, 1839.
>(7) 6th ed. Philadelphia, published by the author, 1840.
>(8) 7th ed. Philadelphia, H. Tanner, jr.; New York, T. R. Tanner, 1841.
>(9) 8th ed. Philadelphia, H. Tanner, jr.; New York, T. R. Tanner, 1842.
>(10) 9th ed., with several additional routes, and a new map, in which the various routes described in the work, whether by railroad, canal, steamboat, or stage, are represented by appropriate lines. By H. S. Tanner. New York, T. R. Tanner, 1844.
>(11) 10th ed. With several additional routes . . . New-York, pub. at the Map establishment, 1846.
>*Location of copy:* Library of Congress.

Solely a guidebook, the contents of which are indicated by the title page.

108. Tanner, Henry Schenck (1786–1858)

A brief description of the canals and rail roads of the United States: comprehending notices of all the most important works of internal improvement throughout the several states. By H. S. Tanner. Philadelphia, the author, 1834.

iv, ₁5₁–63 p. 2 fold. plates, fold. map on cover. 14 cm.
Maps: Folded map of U. S.
Other editions:
 (1) New York, T. R. Tanner & J. Disturnell, 1840. vii, ₁9₁–272 p. 2 fold. plates, 3 fold. maps. 23 cm.
 (2) New York, T. R. Tanner & J. Disturnell; London, Wiley & Putnam; Paris, Arthur Bertrand, 1840.
 (3) A description of the canals and railroads of the United States, comprehending notices of all the works of internal improvement throughout the several states. New York, T. R. Tanner & J. Disturnell, 1840. 273 p. fold. map, 2 fold. diagrs. 8vo.
Location of copy: Library of Congress.

Arranged by states, with brief description of canals and railroad lines in each state.

109. Tanner, Henry Schenck (1786–1858)

A geographical, historical and statistical view of the central or middle United States; containing accounts of their early settlement; natural features; progress of improvement; form of government; civil divisions and internal improvements ... By H. S. Tanner. Philadelphia, H. Tanner, jr.; New York, T. R. Tanner, 1841.

 v, ₁3₁–524 p. 4 fold. maps. 14½ cm.
Other editions:
 2d ed. By H. S. Tanner. Philadelphia, H. Tanner, jun'r.; New York, T. R. Tanner, 1841.
Location of copy: Library of Congress.

This sketch includes Maryland and Virginia. A detailed guidebook, containing descriptions of cities, towns, villages, public buildings, objects of curiosity, literary, scientific, and other institutions.

110. Tanner, Henry Schenck (1786–1858)

Memoir on the recent surveys, observations, and internal improvements, in the United States, with brief notices of the new counties, towns, villages, canals, and railroads, never before delineated. By H. S. Tanner. Intended to accompany his new map of the United States. Philadelphia, the author, 1829.

 1 p.l., 108 p. 18½ cm.
Other editions:
 2d ed. Philadelphia, the author, 1830.
Location of copy: Library of Congress.

A work designed to accompany Tanner's famous map entitled *United States of America.* This map, issued in 1829, was a work of remarkable accuracy for its time, 64 by 50 inches in size and on the scale of exactly 1:2,000,000, or about 32 miles to the inch—practically twice as detailed as John Melish's map of 1816. Tanner was a trained engraver endowed with a scientific and artistic sense which had already been demonstrated in his *New American Atlas: containing maps of the several states of the North American Union, projected and drawn on a uniform scale from documents found in the public offices of the United States . . . and other original and authentic information* (5 pts., 1818–23). The compilation of the maps for this atlas had given him a mastery of the cartographic sources relating to the United States, and he was further aided in the construction of his 1829 map by the results of a circular letter which he addressed widely inviting information on recent surveys in the recipient's local region.

111. Tocqueville, Alexis Charles Henri Clerel de (1805–1859)

De la démocratie en Amérique. 4 vols. Paris, Charles Gosselin, 1835–1840.

> 2 pts. in 4 vols.; Pt. I, Vol. I, xxiv, 367 p.; Vol. II, 459 p.; Pt. II, Vol. I, 333 p.; Vol. II, 363 p.
>
> *Other editions:*
>   *French (France)*
>   (1) De la démocratie en Amérique. Paris, Charles Gosselin, 1835. 2 vols.
>   (2) 2nd ed. 1835.   2 vols.
>   (3) 4th ed. 1836. 2 vols.
>   (4) 5th ed. 1836. 2 vols.
>   (5) 6th ed. Paris, Charles Gosselin et W. Coquebert, 1838. 2 vols.
>   (6) 7th ed. Paris, Charles Gosselin, 1839. 2 vols.
>   (7) Seconde Partie. Paris, Charles Gosselin, 1840. 2 vols.
>   (8) Paris, Pagnerre, 1835–40. 4 vols.
>   (9) 9th ed. Paris, Charles Gosselin, 1842. 4 vols.
>   (10) 12th ed. Rev., cor., et augum. d'un avertissement et d'un examen comparatif de la démocratie aux Etats-Unis et en Suisse. Paris, Pagnerre, 1848. 4 vols. (Vols. III–IV are of the 5th edition).
>   (11) 13th ed. Rev., cor., et augm. d'un examen comparatif de la démocratie aux États-Unis et en Suisse, et d'un appendice. Paris, Pagnerre, 1850. 2 vols.
>   (12) 14th ed. Revue avec le plus grand soin et augmentée de la preface mise en tête des oeuvres complètes. Paris, Michel Levy Frères, 1864. 3 vols. (Oeuvres complètes d'Alexis de Tocqueville publiés par Madame de Tocqueville, I–III).
>   (13) 15th ed. 1868. 3 vols.
>   (14) 16th ed. 1874. 3 vols.
>   (15) 17th ed. 1888. 3 vols.
>   (16) 1888–1890. 4 vols.
>   (17) Paris, Hatier, 193–?   (Classiques pour tous).
>   *French (Belgium)*
>   (18) De la démocratie en Amérique. Bruxelles, Hauman, 1835. 2 vols.

(19) 4th ed. Bruxelles, Hauman, Cattoir et cie., 1837. 3 vols.

(20) Bruxelles, Hauman, 1840. 3 vols. Part II.

(21) Bruxelles, Hauman, Cattoir, 1837–40. 6 vols. Pts. I and II. (Pt. I is 4th edition).

(22) Bruxelles, Meline, Cans et compagnie, 1840. 2 vols.

(23) Bruxelles, Meline, Cans et compagnie, 1840. 5 vols.

French (United States)

(24) De la démocratie en Amérique. Extraits. Avec une preface par Gilbert Chinard. Princeton, Princeton University Press, 1943.

Danish

(25) Demokratiet i Amerika, efter A. T. af Hother Hage. (*In* Selskabet för Trykkefrihedens rette Brug. Gjengangeren indeholdende Bidrag til den nyeste Tids Historie. Kjöbenhavn, 1844. pp. 141–447).

English (Great Britain)

(26) Democracy in America. Trans. by Henry Reeve. London, Saunders and Otley, 1835. 2 vols.

(27) 2nd ed. 1836. 2 vols.

(28) 3rd ed. 1838. 2 vols.

(29) Part the second. Trans. by Henry Reeve. Vols. III–IV. London, Saunders and Otley, 1840. 2 vols.

(30) Trans. by Henry Reeve. London, Saunders and Otley, 1835–40. 4 vols.

(31) 1838–40. 4 vols.

(32) Trans. by Henry Reeve. A new ed., with introductory notice by the translator. London, Longman, Green, Longman and Roberts, 1862. 2 vols.

(33) 1875. 2 vols.

(34) Trans. by Henry Reeve. New ed., with a biographical notice by the trans. and a preface. London, Longmans, 1889. 2 vols.

English (United States)

(35) Democracy in America. Tr. by Henry Reeve, Esq. With an original preface and notes by John C. Spencer. New York, Dearborn, 1838.

(36) Tr. by Henry Reeve, Esq. With an original preface and notes by John C. Spencer, New York, Adlard and Saunders, 1838. 2 vols.

(37) 2nd American ed. New York, George Adlard, 1838.

(38) 2nd American ed. 1838–40. 2 vols.

(39) 3rd American ed., rev. and cor. 1839.

(40) 3rd American ed., rev. and cor. 1839. 2 vols.

(41) Tr. by Henry Reeve, Esq. With an original preface and notes by John C. Spencer. New York, Langley, 1840. 2 vols.

(42) Part II. Tr. by Henry Reeve, Esq. With an original preface by John C. Spencer. New York, Langley, 1840.

(43) 4th ed., rev. and cor. from the 8th Paris ed. Tr. by Henry Reeve, Esq. With an original preface and notes by John C. Spencer. New York, Langley, 1841. 2 vols.

(44) Vol. I, 4th ed. Tr. by Henry Reeve. With an original preface and notes by John C. Spencer. New York, Langley, 1843.

(45) 4th ed., rev. and cor. from the 8th Paris ed. 1845.

(46) [in relation to political institutions]. Tr. by Henry Reeve. Adapted for the use of schools . . . by John C. Spencer. New York, Langley, 1845. (Part I only).

(47) 6th ed. Part II. 1845.

(48) 1847.

(49) 7th ed., rev. and cor. from the 8th Paris ed. Tr. by Henry Reeve, Esq. With an original preface and notes by John C. Spencer. New York, Walker, 1847.

Location of copy: The New York Public Library.

This great work is too well known to require analysis here. It is not so much a traveler's account as a political and social treatise, but, like Beaumont's *Marie,* it is a product of its author's observations in America, including the South, no less than of his studies in the Constitution, statutes, and other source materials which he gathered in this country and carried back to France for use in his writing. Originally published in 1835, this work has been translated into some nine or ten different languages, including Serbian and Hungarian, and has appeared in a total of at least one hundred editions. The most recent American appearance is *Democracy in America by Alexis de Tocqueville. The Henry Reeve text as revised by Francis Bowen, now further corrected and edited with introduction, editorial notes and bibliography by Phillips Bradley. Foreword by Harold J. Laski* (2 vols. New York, Alfred A. Knopf, 1945. 21½ cm. Vol. I, [v]–cxii, [3]– 434 + xii p.; Vol. II, [v]–xii, [3]–401 + x p.). Volume II, pages 385–89, contains a list of all prevoius editions which have been found in American libraries or are traceable to European libraries through catalogs and correspondence.

For Tocqueville's itinerary in the South, see entry for Gustave Auguste de Beaumont de la Bonnière (No. 13). Tocqueville recorded these experiences in extensive letters and diaries, portions of which were published, with alterations and omissions, by Beaumont in his friend's *Nouvelle correspondence entièrement inédite* and *Mélanges, fragments historiques, et notes sur l'Ancien Régime, la Révolution et l'Empire, voyages—pensées, entièrement inédits,* the sections relating to the Southern tour being pages 89–112 and 289–300, respectively (Vols. VII–VIII of *Oeuvres complètes d'Alexis de Tocqueville* [Paris, Michel Levy Frères, 1864–1867. 9 vols. 21 cm. Copy at Library of Congress]).

A painstaking examination of the original Beaumont and Tocqueville manuscripts has been made by George W. Pierson, who completely reconstructed the route of their American tour and published, in English, lengthy excerpts from their contemporaneous accounts in his monumental *Tocqueville and Beaumont in America* (New York, Oxford University Press, 1938. 23½ cm. xiv, [3]–852 p. front. (port.), 32 illus., end-sheet map showing route of the American tour).

112. Trollope, Mrs. Frances (Milton) (1780–1863)

Domestic manners of the Americans. By Mrs. Trollope . . . 2 vols. London, printed for Whittaker, Treacher & co., 1832.

Vol. I, xi, 336 p.; Vol. II, v, 271 p. fronts., plates. 19 cm.
Inclusive dates: 1827–1831.
Other editions:

(1) London, Whittaker, Treacher, & co.; New-York, reprinted for the booksellers, 1832. ix, [i], [iii]–viii, [25]–325 p. 8 plates (incl. front.). 23½ cm.

(2) Second edition. 2 vols. London, printed for Whittaker, Treacher & co., 1832. Vol. I, xi, 304 p.; Vol. II, vii, 303 p. 24 plates. 12mo.

(3) Third edition. London, printed for Whittaker, Treacher & co., 1832.

(4) Fourth edition. London, printed for Whittaker, Treacher & co., 1832.

(5) Fourth edition. Complete in one volume. London, printed for Whittaker, Treacher & co., 1832.

(6) New York, Harper & brothers, 1838. ix, [25]–325 p.

(7) Fifth edition. London, R. Bentley, 1839. [8], 384 p. front. (port.). 16mo.

(8) New York, H. W. Bell, 1904. 402 p. 18 cm. (The unit books, No. 6).

(9) With an introduction by Michael Sadleir . . . London, G. Routledge and sons, ltd., [1927]. xxx, 398 p. viii plates incl. front. (port.). 22½ cm. (The English library, ed. by J. Isaacs).

(10) Moeurs domestiques des Américains, par Mistress Trollope; ouvrage traduit de l'anglais sur la quatrième édition. . . . 2 vols. Paris, Librairie de Charles Gosselin, 1833. Vol. I, [4], 356, [3] p.; Vol. II, [4], 358, [2] p. 8vo.

(11) Ouvrage traduit de l'anglais sur la quatrième édition. Troisième édition. Paris, 1841. 416 p. 12mo.

(12) Costumbres familiares de los americanos del Norte, Obra escrita en ingles por Mistress Trollope, y traducida por Don Juan Floran . . . 2 vols. Paris, Librerie de Lecointe, 1835. Vol. I, xxiii, 312 p.; Vol. II, [4], 331 p. 16mo.

(13) Zeden Gewoonten en Huisselijk Leven der Noord-Amerikanen, door Mistress Trollope beschreven, na een driejarig Verblijf in de Vereenigde Staten; (gevolgd naar den Vierden Engelschen Druk). In twee deelen . . . 2 vols. Te Haarlem, bij de Wed. A. Loosjes, Pz., 1833. Vol. I, viii, 237, [1] p.; Vol. II, vi, 256 p. 8vo.

(14) Leben und Sitte in Nordamerika geschildert von Mrs. Trollope. Nach der vierten Auflage aus dem Englischen übertragen von Dr. Hermann Franz. Drei Theile. Mit 24 Darstellungen in Steindruck . . . 3 vols. Kiel, Universitäts-Buchhandlung, 1835. Vol. I, x, 238 p.; Vol. II, [6], 202 p.; Vol. III, [6], 264 p. plates. 18mo.

Location of copy: Library of Congress.

Although Mrs. Trollope was one of the most widely known and bitterly criticized of all foreign travelers of her period, her experiences in the South were not an important phase of her American sojourn. Landing at New Orleans in late December, 1827, she went almost immediately up the river to Memphis and thence to Louisville and Cincinnati, reaching the latter place about February 10, 1828. At

Memphis she tarried a few days and went to visit Frances Wright's near-by Nashoba Community, which oppressed her with its unfinished buildings and primitive surroundings. After leaving Cincinnati, the scene of her most violent tirades against the United States, she passed the summer of 1830 in Maryland. Here she observed slavery, especially among the small landed proprietors, and found the slaves not badly treated, although she believed the essence of the system to be bad.

It is not apparent that Mrs. Trollope held any grudge against the South except so far as this region was a part of a nation which she disliked. Her travels in the South were incidental, and her comments upon this phase of her experiences are not important as compared with her reactions to Cincinnati and other portions of the United States.

113. Tudor, Henry

Narrative of a tour in North America; comprising Mexico, the mines of Real del Monte, the United States, and the British colonies: together with an excursion to the island of Cuba. In a series of letters, written in the years 1831–2. By Henry Tudor . . . 2 vols. London, J. Duncan, 1834.

Vol. I, xix, 468 p.; Vol. II, x, 548 p.
Inclusive dates: 1831–1832.
Location of copy: Duke University Library.

Tudor's voyage across the Atlantic "was undertaken for the purpose of re-establishing a state of health somewhat impaired, as also of visiting the only quarter of the globe which the writer had not seen; and in order to behold, among the wonders of the New World, the magnificent Cataract of Niagara." In the South he traveled from Washington by way of Fredericksburg and Lexington, Kentucky, to the Ohio River, and thence by way of Louisville to New Orleans, which he reached late in December, 1831. After about ten days in the latter city, he departed for Cuba and Mexico, but returned in May, 1832, and ascended the Mississippi and Ohio to Cincinnati. His comments include observations upon soil exhaustion in Virginia (I, 450–53), good descriptions of Weyer's Cave and Natural Bridge (I, 458–64; II, 1–6), a lengthy criticism of the "Kentucky manners" of a stage passenger he encountered in western Virginia (II, 13–20), and an account of his trip down the Mississippi and of the city of New Orleans, including a slave auction which he witnessed there (II, 56–71). With regard to slavery he admitted that the British were originally responsible for its existence in the United States, but he blamed the latter country for continuing it. Yet he did not favor indiscriminate emancipation without preparatory steps being taken (II, 71–75).

114.

A visit to Texas: being the journal of a traveller through those parts most interesting to American settlers. With descriptions of scenery, habits, &c., &c. New York, Goodrich & Wiley, 1834.

> iv, [9]–264, [4] p. front. (fold. map), 4 plates. 19½ cm.
> *Inclusive dates:* 1831.
> *Other editions:*
> (1) 2d ed. With an appendix, containing a sketch of the late war. New York, Van Nostrand and Dwight; Mobile, Woodruff, Fiske, and McGuire, 1836. xi, 262 p. 14½ cm.
> *Location of copy:* Library of Congress.

The author, having previously come from the North, went by boat from New Orleans to Brazoria, took part in a hunting expedition in the vicinity of the latter town, made a trip from Brazoria by way of Harrisburg to Anahuac, took an excursion down Galveston Bay, and then visited San Felipe. He was victimized by vendors of "Texas land script," which he found to be entirely worthless upon arriving in Texas. A very rare book, containing fine descriptions of natural scenery, prairies, some natural history, and an account of political conditions. Authorship has been attributed to Colonel Morris and to Dr. M. Fiske.

115. **Wied-Neuwied, Maximilian Alexander Philipp, Prinz von (1782–1867)**

Travels in the interior of North America. By Maximilian prince of Wied . . . Tr. from the German, by H. Evans Lloyd. To accompany the original series of eighty-one elaborately-coloured plates . . . London, Ackermann and co., 1843.

> x, [2], 520 p. illus. 30 cm. (Accompanied by volume of plates).
> *Maps:* Folded map of U. S. showing Maximilian's route.
> *Illustrations:* Numerous.
> *Inclusive dates:* 1832–1833.
> *Other editions:*
> (1) Originally published in German as: Reise in das innere Nord-Amerika in den Jahren 1832 bis 1834; von Maximilian Prinz zu Wied . . . 2 vols. Coblenz J. Hoelscher, 1839–41. Vol. I, xvi, 653, [1] p.; Vol. II, xxii, [2], 687, [1] p. illus. 32 cm. (With atlas).
> (2) Voyage dans l'intérieur de l'Amérique du Nord, exécuté pendant les

années 1832, 1833 et 1834, par le prince Maximilien de Wied-Neuwied. Ouvrage accompagné d'un atlas de 80 planches environ, format demi-colombier, dessinées sur les lieux par m. Charles Bodmer . . . 3 vols. Paris, A. Bertrand, 1840–43. Vol. I, 383 p.; Vol. II, 487 p.; Vol. III, 407 p. illus., plates, fold. map, plan. 23½ cm. (And atlas, 61½ x 46 cm.).

(3) . . . Maximilian, prince of Wied's Travels in the interior of North America, 1832–1834. 3 vols. Cleveland, O., The A. H. Clark company, 1906. plates, facsim. 24½ cm. (And atlas of 81 plates, incl. ports., fold. map, 53 cm.). (In Reuben G. Thwaites [ed.], Early western travels, 1748–1846. Cleveland, 1904–1907. Vols. XXII–XXIV). There is an atlas volume that contains illustrations of Indians drawn by the Swedish illustrator Bödmer.

(4) . . . Travels into the interior of North America. ₍Leipzig, Schmidt & Guenther, 192–?₎. 2 portfolios of 81 plates (incl. ports.). 51 x 66 cm. (Vol. II: 34 x 42 cm.). (Reprints of rare Americana, II, published by Schmidt & Guenther, Leipzig).

(5) . . . Unter den Rothäuten, Leipzig, F. A. Brockhaus, 1924. 159, ₍1₎ p. front. (port.), illus. (incl. map), plates. 19 cm. (Reisen und Abenteuer 29). [This last edition is an abridgement. The scientific part has for the most part been omitted.]
Location of copy: The New York Public Library.

Relates to the South only slightly. The author descended the Ohio from Wheeling to Mount Vernon, Indiana, stopping for a part of one day at Louisville, in October, 1832 (pp. 69–73). There is a brief description of his experiences in Louisville. After spending the winter at New Harmony, Indiana, he returned to Mount Vernon and traveled thence by steamboat down the Ohio and up the Mississippi to St. Louis (pp. 94–97). Otherwise not concerned with the South.

116. Williams, James (b. 1805)

Narrative of James Williams. An American slave; who was for several years a driver on a cotton plantation in Alabama . . . New-York, the American anti-slavery society, 1838.

xxiii, ₍25₎–108 p. front. (port.) 15½ cm.
Inclusive dates: 1833–1837.
Other editions:
(1) ₍Boston, Massachusetts anti-slavery society, 1838₎. 8 p. 32 x 24 cm. (Abolitionist's library. No. 3).
(2) Second edition. New York, published by the American Anti-slavery society, 1838. 108 p. 18mo.
(3) New York, published by the American Anti-slavery society; Boston, Isaac Knapp, 1838.
(4) Also issued as No. 6 of the *"Anti-slavery Examiner,"* New York, 1838.
Location of copy: Duke University Library.

The author, a Virginia slave, was carried by his master to Greene County, Alabama, in 1833 and left there, by trick, as a driver. In

1837 he escaped and made his way to Pennsylvania, through the Creek Indian country, Washington and Augusta, Georgia, Halifax, and Richmond, Virginia, and the state of Maryland. The main emphasis is upon Williams' experiences on the Alabama plantation, at which time he could scarcely be called a traveler, but there is a brief account of his trip from Virginia (pp. 37–39) and a more extended description of his flight from Alabama to Pennsylvania (pp. 83–99).

The Library of Congress card states that this work was "written by J. G. Whittier from the verbal narrative of Williams."

117. Woodman, David, jr.

Guide to Texas emigrants. By David Woodman, jr. Boston, printed by M. Hawes, 1835.

> vi, [13]–192 p. front. (fold. map), plates. 18 cm.
> *Maps:* One: folded map of Texas.
> *Illustrations:* One: buffalo hunt.
> *Location of copy:* Library of Congress.

A compendium of facts, official reports, speeches, letters, and other materials, compiled and issued as promotional literature for the Galveston Bay and Texas Land Company.

118. Zavala, Lorenzo de (1788–1836)

Viage a los Estados-Unidos del Norte de America, por D. Lorenzo de Zavala. Paris, Impr. de Decourchant, 1834.

> 2 p.l., vii, 374 p. 20½ cm.
> *Inclusive dates:* May–June, 1830.
> *Other editions:*
> Viaje á los Estados-Unidos del Norte de America por D. Lorenzo de Zavala . . . Con una noticia sobre su vida y escritos, por D. Justo Sierra. Mérida de Yucatán, Imprenta de Castillo y Compania, 1846. 57, 382, [5] p. 8vo.
> *Location of copy:* Duke University Library.

Zavala was a Mexican republican who fled his country upon the usurpation of Santa Anna, later settling in Texas, where he cooperated with Austin in preparing for the struggle for independence and was elected to the office of vice-president. The American tour described in this volume began at New Orleans in May, 1830, and continued up the river, with brief stops at Baton Rouge, Natchez, Memphis, and Louisville, to Cincinnati, where the Southern phase ended in June of the same year. The remaining and greater portion of the work relates to the Eastern states and Canada. There are short accounts of the places visited and a description of the steamboat voyage up the Mississippi and Ohio, accompanied by quotations and paraphrases from Barbé-Marbois, Timothy Flint, James Stuart, and Mrs. Trollope. The author's purpose was to furnish useful information on American manners, customs, politics, and institutions to the people of Mexico. On the whole he was not displeased with the South, but was critical of the racial discriminations he saw practiced in New Orleans, and of the excesses of camp-meetings, one of which he appears to have observed in Tennessee.

PART II

A Decade of Nationalism, 1836–1845

INTRODUCTION

A PHRENOLOGIST, a teacher of penmanship, a blind Methodist preacher, a free Negro, a police officer, and a "professor of mesmerism and psycography" were among the more than one hundred men and ten women who visited the South within the years 1836–1845 and wrote books about their travels. About one-fifth of these were clergymen or leaders of church-sponsored reform movements. Nearly a dozen were military men, and almost as many were professors or college presidents. There were about half a dozen each of scientists, businessmen, actors, and professional men of letters. Lawyers, doctors, diplomats, politicians, and artists also traveled and wrote, but in smaller numbers. Some of these travelers took only passing notice of the South in a very few pages, while others filled several volumes with accounts of what they had seen there. Besides these travel accounts, twenty-three guidebooks and gazetteers containing information useful to travelers in the South were published during this decade.

The large quantity of this travel literature, with books appearing at the rate of one a month, suggests that there was a lively interest in the South at this time. Some of the books were printed almost simultaneously on both sides of the Atlantic, and some were republished in second and third editions. This curiosity about the South in the 1830's and 1840's was no new thing, for the South had already been extensively explored and frequently described in previous years. What is noteworthy is its continuance in such vigorous form. True enough, many of the new generation of travelers, like their predecessors, dealt with such subjects as the exploration of frontier areas, natural phenomena, religious and moral conditions, and information useful to the emigrant or the land speculator. But the travelers of the 1830's and 1840's also wrote about subjects that had received little or no attention in earlier years. The Seminole War and the Texan Revolution took men into new places and provided new experiences to be related. Descriptions of steamboats and railroads filled many pages. These innovations in transportation not

[103]

only gave the travelers something new to write about, but allowed them to move over the South with greater ease and speed.

Politics and slavery received much attention because of events outside the South—the Reform Movement in England and the abolition crusade in the North. Perhaps it is worth remarking that those who came to the South for the purpose of investigating the controversial subjects of slavery and democracy usually had their minds made up before they arrived. Most of their generalizations could have been written before they left home. Scarcely any of those who were primarily interested in slavery wrote about it with the wisdom and objectivity of Sir Charles Lyell, who came to America to study geology. In writing about American politics, the British travelers usually reflected their views about English society and politics, nearly all of them displaying either a Whiggish or a Tory point of view. None of the travelers penned a useful description of American local government, and few of them wrote wisely about national politics. However, valuable descriptions of American public men, especially of Clay, Webster, Jackson, and Calhoun, can be found in some of their pages.

Of the travel books that give at least some attention to the South in the late thirties and early forties, about two-fifths were written by Americans. Only a few of the American travelers in the South were Southerners, and for the most part they wrote only of local excursions. Another two-fifths were British, chiefly English, but some of them were Scottish and a few were Irish. The other travelers were either Frenchmen or Germans, with a sprinkling of Austrians, Italians, and Mexicans. The length of time spent in the South by these writers ranged from a decade or more in several instances to the brief visits of scarcely two weeks paid by Robert Barclay Allardice and Charles Dickens. In fact, there is some question as to whether several of the authors ever set foot in the South.

The individual interests of the travelers led them to different places. Seventeen of them were primarily concerned with Texas, and nearly half a hundred more spent most or all of their time on the frontier. A dozen or so traveled chiefly in the lower South, and nearly twice as many dipped into the South no farther than Baltimore and Washington, with perhaps an excursion into Virginia. Sixteen took the long tour southward to Charleston across to New Orleans, up the Mississippi River, and then back to the East. A few of the sixteen made this trip in reverse direction.

It would be difficult to say which are the best known of those who traveled in the South between 1836 and 1845, but the names of Charles Dickens, Harriet Martineau, Fanny Kemble, James Silk Buckingham, and Captain Frederick Marryat immediately come to mind. Of these, Martineau is the most informative and reliable. Marryat is almost useless. Several of the less known travelers are far ahead of some of their more famous contemporaries in the quality of their reporting. William Thompson, a Scottish weaver, Clara von Gerstner of Vienna, Philip Henry Gosse, an English naturalist, George Rogers, a Universalist preacher, Ludwig de Wette, a German physician, George Lewis, a Scottish clergyman, Bishop Henry Benjamin Whipple, and Francis, Comte de Castlenau, notable for his superb illustrations, are outstanding for their careful description of out-of-the-way places and unusual customs.

The travelers, some serious and some frivolous, came to investigate slavery and democracy, to fight Indians and Mexicans, to get fertile land, to regain health, to follow their professions, for the sheer fun and adventure of traveling, and for a variety of other reasons. Many of them drew broad conclusions and ventured sweeping generalizations about Southern life and institutions; but what are of chief value to the serious student and of most interest to the casual reader are their firsthand accounts of particular places, persons, and episodes. Fortunately, many of the records made by travelers of this period are rich in detailed and authentic description.

No attempt has been made to include in this listing the publications of early state geological surveys. Most of the geologists traveled, and a few of their reports include interesting bits of travel experiences. An introduction to this literature is provided in "State Geological Surveys in the Old South," in David K. Jackson, editor, *American Studies in Honor of William Kenneth Boyd* (Durham, N. C., 1940).

CHARLES S. SYDNOR

A Decade of Nationalism, 1836–1845

119.　Aimard, Gustave (*pseud.* of Oliver Gloux) (1818–1883)
Les Trappeurs de l'Arkansas. Paris, Arthème Fayard, Editeur, n.d.

　　ii, 408 p.　19 cm.
　　Inclusive dates: Approximately 1835–1845; 1850 and later.
　　Other editions:
　　　　(1) Paris, Amyot, 1858. xii, 455 p.　8vo.
　　　　(2) Loyal heart; or, the trappers of Arkansas. Translated by William Robson. London, G. Routledge & co., 1858.　xvi, 294 p.　8vo.
　　　　(3) Cinquième edition. Paris, MDCCCLIX.　xii, 455 p.　12mo.
　　　　(4) London, J. A. Bergen, 186–?　1 p.l., 337 p.　16mo.
　　　　(5) [Translated by Sir F. C. L. Wraxall]. London, Ward & Lock, 1864. 337 p.　8vo.
　　　　(6) 4 vols. [Paris], Amyot, [1867?]. illus.　29 cm.
　　　　(7) Revised and edited by Percy B. St. John. London, George Vickers, 1876.　128 p.　8vo.
　　　　(8) London, J. & R. Maxwell, [1879].
　　　　(9) London, Ward, Lock & Tyler, 1879?　iv, 337 p.　12mo. (Tales of Indian life and adventure, No. 9).
　　　　(10) Loyal heart; or, the trappers of Arkansas. N. Y., Beadle & Adams, 1879. 24 p.　illus.　folio. (Beadle's dime library, No. 62).
　　　　(11) Rev. and enl. by Percy B. St. John. New York, J. W. Lovell, company, [1878].　128 p.　18½ cm.
　　　　(12) 18 éd. Paris, E. Dentu, 1894.　xii, 455 p.　19 cm.
　　　　(13) Edited by M. Ninet. London, 1896.　112 p.　8 vo.　(Blackie's Modern French texts).
　　　　(14) Edited by B. Helliwell . . . London, Oxford university press, H. Milford, 1935.　64 p.　16½ cm.
　　Location of copy: Duke University Library.

This novel was the first great success of Oliver Gloux, who is usually known by his pen name, Gustave Aimard. Its scene is laid along the boundary of Arkansas and Oklahoma; the story begins in January, 1817, but it is based on what the author learned during his first visit to America from about 1835 to 1845. He returned about 1850.

Aimard has been called the French Fenimore Cooper. His novels about the United States, Mexico, and South America appeared from 1848 to 1875 in such great numbers "that he became more than a mere author and rose to the dimensions of an industry." (Frank Monaghan, *French Travellers in the United States, 1765–1932*). At one time his publisher was promising a new novel each month.

A good many of his scenes are laid along the western frontier of the Old South. Aimard knew the country of which he wrote. His descriptions of geography, flora, fauna, customs, and ceremonies are usually correct and sometimes detailed.

Monaghan, cited above, contains the best available list of titles and editions of Aimard and a brief appraisal of him. A longer essay about this prolific writer is by Virgil L. Jones, "Gustave Aimard," *Southwest Review,* Vol. XV (1930), pp. 452–68.

120.   Aitken, W.

A journey up the Mississippi River, from its mouth to Nauvoo, the city of the Latter Day Saints. Ashton-under-Lyne, ᵢEnglandᵢ, printed by John Williamson, ᵢ1845?ᵢ.

> 56 p. 21 cm.
> *Inclusive dates:* November 5, 1842, to ? In South, November, 1842.
> *Other editions:*
>   Micklethwaite, Ashton-under-Lyne, ᵢ1845?ᵢ.
> *Location of copy:* Yale University Library.

Although the title page of this rare pamphlet is undated, its preface is dated February 8, 1845, at Ashton-under-Lyne, England, whither the author had presumably returned after his trip to America. Aitken was not pleased with America; he was especially hostile to slavery and Mormonism. The first dozen pages recount a sojourn of two days in New Orleans and a trip of fourteen days' duration up the Mississippi River to St. Louis.

121.   Allardice, Robert Barclay (1779–1854)

Agricultural tour in the United States and Upper Canada, with miscellaneous notices. By Captain Barclay of Ury. Edinburgh and London, W. Blackwood & sons, 1842.

> 1 p.l., ᵢvᵢ–xxiii, 181 p. 20 cm.
> *Inclusive dates:* May to July, 1841.
> *Location of copy:* Duke University Library.

Allardice, who was generally known as Captain Barclay, was sixty-two years old when he came to America to compare the agricultural prospects of Canada and the United States. He had previously held a commission in the British Army, interested himself in agricultural improvement and cattle breeding, failed to establish his claim to an earldom, and become famous for his powers of endurance, especially as a pedestrian. His American tour included twelve days in the

[107]

slave states. He entered Virginia at Wheeling (now West Virginia) and traveled through "Haggerston" and Frederick, Maryland, to Baltimore and thence to Washington and Richmond. Besides commenting on his experiences on the road, he described Mount Vernon, his introduction to President Tyler, his impressions of slavery, and several farms which he had hurriedly inspected. A sketch of his life is to be found in the *Dictionary of National Biography*.

122.   Arese, Francesco, Conte (1805–1881)

A trip to the prairies and in the interior of North America (1837–1838). Travel notes by Count Francesco Arese, now first translated from the original French by Andrew Evans. New York, the Harbor press, 1934.

> 3 p.l., [v]–xxiv p., 1 l., 217 p., 1 l.   fold. map.   19 cm.
> *Maps:* One: showing Arese's route.
> *Inclusive dates:* 1837–1838.
> *Other editions:*
>   Arese's travel notes, written in French, were first published in the last hundred pages of Romualdo Bonfadini, *Vita di Francesco Arese con documenti inediti.* Torino, Roma, 1894.
> *Location of copy:* Duke University Library.

When Louis Napoleon, who was later to become Napoleon III, was exiled to America early in the year 1837, his Italian friend Count Francesco Arese crossed the Atlantic to be with him; and after Louis Napoleon sailed for Europe on June 8, Arese remained to undertake an adventurous journey into the Indian country between the Missouri River and the Great Lakes. He was no stranger to travel and adventure, for his thirty-two years had included revolutionary activities in Italy and two years of service in the French Foreign Legion in Algeria. His journey westward was through the upper South. He left New York on June 11, 1837; from Baltimore he traveled by railway to Harpers Ferry and returned to Washington by canalboat; his journey across Virginia was through Fredricksburg, Charlottesville, Lexington (where he joined in the celebration of the Fourth of July), to the Virginia springs, and to Kanawha Valley. From there he proceeded westward by boat, but he interrupted this trip by a brief visit to Lexington, Kentucky. The last paragraph of his frank and urbane comments on travel experiences, scenery, and manners contains the tantalizing statement that after returning through the Great Lakes to New York, "I visited Florida, Alabama, Louisiana . . . I went to Georgia, crossed South and North Carolina, and returned to New York after seven months' absence." Of this journey we have no record.

123.   Bacourt, Adolphe Fourier de (1801–1865)

Souvenirs d'un diplomate: lettres intimes sur l'Amérique. Paris, Calmann Lévy, 1882.

> 2 p.l., xiii, 399 p. 18 cm.
> *Inclusive dates:* May 24, 1840, to July 25, 1842. In the South, parts of these years.
> *Other editions:*
>   Souvenirs of a diplomat. Private letters from America during the administrations of Presidents Van Buren, Harrison, and Tyler, by the chevalier de Bacourt, minister from France, with a memoir of the author by the Comtesse de Mirabeau. Tr. from the French. New York, H. Holt and company, 1885. 1 p.l., 297 p. 18½ cm.
> *Location of copy:* Library of Congress.

Bacourt was the French minister of the United States from 1840 to 1842, and his hostile and prejudiced impressions of America and American society are conveyed in these private and candid letters. Since he spent most of the time in Washington, his description of that city and its people is extensive. His travels to other parts of the United States include brief excursions to Alexandria, Mount Vernon, Harpers Ferry, and the Falls of the Potomac, and he includes a description of Baltimore.

124.   Baldwin, Joseph Glover (1815–1864)

The flush times of Alabama and Mississippi. A series of sketches. By Joseph G. Baldwin. New York, [etc.], D. Appleton and company, 1853.

> x, 330 p. front. (port.), 3 plates. 19 cm.
> *Illustrations:* Frontispiece and three other drawings of semifictional characters.
> *Inclusive dates:* March, 1836, and following.
> *Other editions:*
>   (1) 9th thousand. New York, [etc.], D. Appleton & co., 1854.
>   (2) 2d ed. New York, London, D. Appleton & co., 1854.
>   (3) 7th ed. New York, 1854.
>   (4) 11th thousand. New York, [etc.], D. Appleton & co., 1856.
>   (5) 11th thousand. New York, 1858.
>   (6) 11th thousand. San Francisco, S. Whitney & co., 1876.
>   (7) 11th thousand. San Francisco, Bancroft-Whitney co., 1887.
>   (8) 11th thousand. San Francisco, Bancroft-Whitney co., 1899.
>   (9) Americus, Ga., Americus book co., [1908].
> *Location of copy:* Duke University Library.

There is a small amount of information on pages 47–50 about Baldwin's trip from the Shenandoah Valley to Mississippi in March, 1836. However, the primary reason for including this work in a travel bibliography is the fact that it is a burlesque description of pioneer life in Alabama and Mississippi as it appeared to a young lawyer who had recently arrived from Virginia. A sketch of Baldwin's life is published in the *Dictionary of American Biography*.

Since the first appearance of this work in New York in 1853, there have been many editions. The latest recorded in the Library of Congress Catalog was published in Americus, Georgia, in 1908.

125. [Ballentine, George (b. 1812?)]

Autobiography of an English soldier in the United States army. Comprising observations and adventures in the States and Mexico. New York, Stringer & Townsend, 1853.

> xii, [9]–288 p. front., plate. 19 cm.
> *Illustrations:* Frontispiece: "The Soldier in Mexico."
> *Inclusive dates:* August, 1845, to August, 1848.
> *Other editions:*
> (1) 2 vols. London, Hurst and Blackett, 1853. 19½ cm.
> (2) The Mexican war, by an English soldier. Comprising incidents and adventures in the United States and Mexico with the American army. New York, W. A. Townsend & company, 1860. xii, [9]–288 p. front. 19½ cm.
> *Location of copy:* University of North Carolina Library.

According to statements made in this book, its author was a Scotch weaver who had served for a time in the British army before he came to America in the summer of 1845. Unable to find employment at the loom, he enlisted in the United States Army, served through the Mexican War, and then wrote a plain-spoken account of his experiences. Before being ordered to Mexico, his company was stationed in Florida—at Pensacola Bay during October, 1845, and from then until the end of the following year, at Tampa. Some thirty-five pages of the book are devoted to descriptions of garrison life at these two points and of the surrounding country.

126. [Barinetti, Carlo]

A voyage to Mexico and Havana; including some general observations on the United States. By an Italian. New York, printed for the author by C. Vinton, 1841.

> x, 139 p. 20 x 11½ cm.
> *Inclusive dates:* About 1840. In South, somewhat earlier.
> *Location of copy:* Duke University Library.

The main object of this work was to describe a journey from New Orleans to Mexico and Cuba during the period from January to May "last." The book was copyrighted in 1841 by Charles Barinetti in the District of Louisiana. The Italian author had been a teacher of French in Cincinnati and Kentucky, and he claimed to have traveled in Tennessee and other slave states. His comments on the United States contain little detail, and Barinetti was not wise enough for his generalizations to have much value. His remarks about the South, which are mostly favorable, related chiefly to slavery and lawlessness.

127. Barr, Captain James

A correct and authentic narrative of the Indian war in Florida, with a description of Maj. Dade's massacre, and an account of the extreme suffering, for want of provisions, of the army—having been obliged to eat horses' and dogs' flesh, &c., &c. By Capt. James Barr. New York, J. Narine, printer, 1836.

> 32 p. 16 cm.
> *Inclusive dates:* February to May, 1836. In South, same.
> *Other editions:*
>   New York, 1834. 32 p. 16 cm.
> *Location of copy:* Library of Congress.

A simple, unembellished account, written mostly as a diary, of the experiences of the author and of the Louisiana volunteers to which he was attached in the Seminole War. The author was stationed at Tampa Bay during a large part of his three months in Florida.

128.

Beers' Carolinas and Georgia almanac, for the year of our Lord 1823: Being the third after Bissextile, or Leap Year, and (till July 4th,) the 47th of American Independence. Calculated for the Horizon and Meridian of Columbia, S. C. and will serve for all the adjacent parts, and also for North-Carolina and Georgia. Charleston, S. C., S. Babcock & co., [etc., etc.], [1822?].

> 19 l. (?). 19½ cm.
> *Location of copy:* The New York Public Library.

In addition to the almanac and the lists of federal officers, this work contains information about civil and military officers in South Carolina, North Carolina, and Georgia, together with a small amount of other information. Copies of editions for 1836 and 1842 are reported extant. The *Beers' Almanacs,* calculated by Andrew Beers, began to appear at Hartford, Connecticut, in the 1780's.

129. Benson, Henry Clark (b. 1815)

Life among the Choctaw Indians, and sketches of the South-west. By Henry C. Benson, A.M. . . . With an introduction by Rev. T. A. Morris

. . . Cincinnati, pub. by L. Swormstedt & A. Poe, for the Methodist
Episcopal church, 1860.

> 314 p. 19½ cm.
> *Inclusive dates:* March, 1843, to May 12, 1845.
> *Location of copy:* Library of Congress.

Benson was a Methodist teacher and minister at Fort Coffee Academy
on the Arkansas River from March, 1843, to May, 1845. The academy
was for the instruction of Choctaw Indian boys. Besides describing life
at the institution, Benson comments at length on Indian customs and
on the country through which he traveled as an itinerant minister.
He was an accurate observer, and he accepted the hardships of frontier life and the difficulties of his work without complaint. He was
distinctly hostile to slavery. He left Fort Coffee Academy in 1845 because of the schism in the Methodist church.

   This book was written from notes and memory during the winter
of 1858–59 at Placerville, California, where winter storms kept Benson from following his usual missionary labors.

130.   Besançon, L. A.

Besançon's annual register of the state of Mississippi, for the year 1838.
Compiled from original documents—being a full exhibit of all the
tabular and statistical information which it was possible to obtain from
authentic sources. Vol. I. Natchez, L. A. Besançon, 1838.

> [6]–232 p., and 11 p. of advertisements. front. (map). 19½ cm.
> *Maps:* One large folded map: "Besançon's Map of Mississippi, 1838. N. Cur-
> rier's Lith. New York."
> *Location of copy:* Library of Congress.

This book contains an almanac, the constitutions of the United States
and Mississippi, data about federal and state offices and officeholders,
descriptions of each of the counties of Mississippi and lists of county
officers, the Mississippi census of 1837, returns of state elections in
July and November, 1837, and lists of newspapers and periodicals, of
churches and clergymen, and of railroads and banks. Besançon was
editor and publisher of the *Mississippi Free Trader and Natchez Gazette.* "Vol. I" appears on the title page, and subsequent editions are
promised in the preface, but the National Union Catalog mentions
only the 1838 edition.

131.   Biggs, Joseph

To America in thirty-nine days before steamships crossed the Atlantic.

[Extracts from a diary. Selected by Maude A. Biggs]. Idbury, Village press, 1926.

> 26 p. 19½ cm.
> *Inclusive dates:* May, 1837, to ?.
> *Other editions:*
> 2d ed. Idbury, Kingham, Oxford, the Village press, 1927.
> *Location of copy:* Duke University Library.

These are extracts from the diary of a businessman of Leicester and London covering his hurried trip to America during the Panic of 1837. Two pages are devoted to Baltimore, Washington, Mount Vernon, and the subject of slavery.

It is curious that a copy of the first edition, published in 1926, should be so difficult to locate.

132. Bonnell, George William

Topographical description of Texas. To which is added an account of the Indian tribes. By Geo. W. Bonnell. Austin, Clark, Wing & Brown, 1840.

> viii, [7]–150 p. 14½ cm.
> *Location of copy:* Library of Congress.

This volume contains a description of bays, rivers, soil, climate, towns, and settlements of Texas in 1840. The author was apparently a resident, not a transient visitor, in Texas. He presents the area in glowing terms, obviously with the idea of promoting immigration. He also summarized the governmental system. Bonnell was apparently one of the public printers (p. iv) of the Republic of Texas.

In the preface Bonnell says he intends to publish an enlarged edition of this work, with a map, in 1841, but there is no evidence of later publication.

133. Bronson, Francis S.

Bronson's travelers' directory, from New-York to New-Orleans, embracing all the most important routes, with a condensed outline of the country through which they pass. By Francis S. Bronson. La Grange, Ga., printed at the American star office, 1845.

> 32 p. 14½ cm.
> *Other editions:*
> New York, printed by J. F. Trow and company, 1845. 64 p. 12½ cm.
> *Location of copy:* Library of Congress.

Two routes are described from New York to New Orleans: the "Mississippi Route" (New York, Pittsburgh, and down the Ohio and Mississippi rivers); and the eastern route (Baltimore, Weldon, Wilmington, Charleston, Augusta, Montgomery, Mobile, and New Orleans). Means and costs of transportation and approximate time required are given, as well as the names of hotels and newspapers in the chief towns along the routes. Two routes across Texas are described.

134. Buckingham, James Silk (1786–1855)

The slave states of America. By J. S. Buckingham, esq. . . . 2 vols. London, Paris, Fisher, son & co. [1842].

Vol. I, xvi, 587 p.; Vol. II, ix, 600 p. fronts., plates. 22 cm.

Illustrations: Eight steel engravings: a frontispiece and three others in each vol. Two deal with slave-trading scenes; most of the others show scenes in Southern cities.

Inclusive dates: September, 1837, to 1840. In South, chiefly, January to August, 1839.

Other editions:

2 vols. London, Paris, Fisher, son & co., [1842]. Vol. I, 9 l., 487 p. (*misprint for* 587); Vol. II, 6 l., 588 p. 8 steel engravings.

Location of copy: Duke University Library.

James Silk Buckingham, world traveler and English reformer, regarded himself as singularly well qualified to write an accurate and impartial appraisal of the United States (*America, Historical, Statistic, and Descriptive.* 3 vols. London, [1841], I, p. 9). First, his experiences as a world traveler ought to have enabled him "to view things with a more catholic spirit of impartiality" (*America,* I, pp. 6–7). Furthermore, he believed that his mission to America in the interests of temperance, education, benevolence, and peace had brought him into association with all classes of society—with the "intellectual" class through his lectures and with "the middle and inferior classes" through the philanthropic aspects of his work (*America,* I, p. 4). Finally, he was of the opinion that he had covered "a greater number of states and territories than had ever before been traversed, and [had made] a more thorough examination of each than had yet been made, by any single traveller, European or American . . ." (*America,* I, p. 5).

It is true that his tour of the United States was extensive. Leaving London in September, 1837, he spent the autumn of that year in New York. In the early months of 1838 he made prolonged trips to Baltimore and Washington (*America,* I, pp. 268–474), returning to New York in May. Remaining in the North until January, 1839, he then sailed for Charleston, South Carolina, to begin an eight months' tour of the South, which is described in his two-volume work entitled *The*

Slave States of America (London [1842]). Spending three weeks at Charleston and two weeks at Savannah, Buckingham proceeded through Georgia via Augusta, Macon, and Columbus, and through Alabama to New Orleans. There he stayed one month, and after an excursion up the Mississippi to Natchez, he retraced his steps from New Orleans to Charleston. Following a trip to Columbia, South Carolina, and North Georgia, Buckingham traveled through North Carolina and Tennessee to Virginia, where he visited the White Sulphur Springs, Monticello, Richmond, Norfolk, and Alexandria. In January, 1840, after touring New England for a second time, the Englishman and his family set forth for a trip to the West, which is narrated in three volumes entitled *The Eastern and Western States of America* (London [1842]). On this trip Buckingham touched Baltimore (II, pp. 95–133), Fredericktown and Harpers Ferry (II, pp. 134–52), Wheeling (II, pp. 252–64), Maysville and Lexington (II, pp. 434–536), Frankfort and Louisville (III, pp. 1–35), and St. Louis (III, pp. 77–148). He returned to New York after a voyage up the Mississippi River and around the Great Lakes.

Buckingham contributes less information than might be expected from the extensiveness of his travels and the lengthiness of his eight-volume account. To avoid being labeled a prejudiced observer he loaded his works with quotations from American newspapers and magazines. He also presents considerable historical and statistical data accumulated in the course of his researches in local archives and in personal conversations. There is hardly an aspect of American society on which Buckingham does not make some personal comment. Slavery, manners, and morals are most frequently mentioned. There is considerable interest and emphasis on the humanitarian and reform movements. For a brief account of Buckingham as an apostle of temperance in America, see Ralph E. Turner, *James Silk Buckingham* (London, 1934), Chapter VI, which includes a summary of the subject's opinions on American society.

135. Büttner, Johann Gottfried

Die Vereinigten Staaten von Nord-Amerika. Mein Aufenthalt und meine Reisen in denselben, vom Jahre 1834 bis 1841. Von Dr. J. G. Büttner . . . 2 vols. Hamburg, M. Geber, 1844.

Vol. I, 6 p., viii, 440 p.; Vol. II, 2 p., 450 p. fold. table. 21 cm.
Illustrations: At end of Vol. II is a folded statistical table giving area, capital, and population of each state.
Inclusive dates: September, 1834, to January 5, 1841. In South, 1835 (?).

Other editions:
2 vols. Hamburg, Schuberth & company, 1847.   Vol. I, vi, 440 p.; Vol. II, 450 p.
1 table.   folio.
Location of copy: Library of Congress.

Büttner landed at Baltimore, went to Wheeling, and down the Ohio
River to St. Louis. His other travels were in Ohio, New York, and
New England. His itinerary is not recorded with chronological con-
tinuity, but he seems to have made a trip down the Mississippi River
early in his sojourn in America. His description of this river and of
Louisville, Kentucky, are his chief contributions to Southern travel
literature.

The author was a minister of the German Reformed church. He
served as pastor of a congregation of that church in Osnaburg, Ohio,
and of the German Evangelical church in Massillon, Ohio. As might
be expected, his book reflects his great interest in the ecclesiastical
condition of the German population of America. He also gives much
space to religious and public education, summarizing the school systems of all the states, but most of what he writes about American
education is not based on personal observation.

136.   Burke, William

The mineral springs of Western Virginia: with remarks on their use,
and the diseases to which they are applicable. New York, Wiley and
Putnam, 1842.

394 p.   16½ cm.
Maps: Frontispiece folded map: "Map of routes & distances to the Mineral
Springs of Western Virginia."
Other editions:
(1) The 2d ed., rev., cor. and enl. To which are added a notice of the Fau-
quier White Sulphur Springs, and a chapter on taverns, also a review of a pamphlet published by Dr. J. J. Moorman . . . New York, Wiley and Putnam, 1846.
394 p.   front. (fold. map).   16½ cm.
(2) A new work. Richmond, Va., Morris & brother, 1851. 2 p.l., 348 p.
front. (fold. map).   19½ cm.
(3) 2d ed., improved and enl. Richmond, Va., Ritchies & Dunnavant, 1853.
2 p.l., 376 p.   front. (fold. map).   20 cm.
Location of copy: Army Medical Library.

Burke was a physician who apparently resided in western Virginia.
Descriptions of scenery and climate alternate with medical discussion
and directions on beneficial ways to use mineral waters. The author
gives analyses of the waters of various springs, describes accommodations at them, and includes numerous "testimonial" letters of persons
claiming to have been benefited or cured. Burke says he is the owner

of Red Sulphur Springs, which he purchased in 1832. Hence, he devotes much space to his description of it.

137. Carlisle, George William Frederick Howard, Seventh Earl of (1802–1864)

Travels in America. The poetry of Pope. Two lectures delivered to the Leeds Mechanics' Institution and Literary Society, December 5th and 6th, 1850. By the Right Honorable the Earl of Carlisle, (Lord Morpeth). New York, G. P. Putnam, 1851.

> 135 p. 18½ cm.
> *Inclusive dates:* 1841–1842.
> *Other editions:*
> (1) London, 1850. 44 p. quarto.
> (2) Two lectures, on the poetry of Pope, and on his own travels in America . . . Eighth thousand. London, Simpkin, Marshall, & co., [etc., etc.], 1851. 44 p. 21½ cm.
> *Location of copy:* Duke University Library.

In contrast to many visitors to America, the Earl of Carlisle traveled extensively and wrote briefly about his transatlantic experiences. This famous Whig politician entered twenty-two of the twenty-six states. Early in the year 1842 he traversed the South Atlantic states from Baltimore to Charleston. Then, after several weeks in Cuba, he went to New Orleans where he stayed at the St. Charles Hotel, traveled up to Kentucky where he was the guest of Henry Clay at "Ashland," and visited the White Sulphur Springs before the opening of the season. There is more of opinion and of generalization than of description in his lecture on America.

138. Castelnau, Francis, Comte de (1812–1880)

Vues et souvenirs de l'Amérique du Nord, par Francis de Castelnau . . . Paris, A. Bertrand, 1842.

> viii, 165, [2] p. 35 plates (part col.). 31 cm.
> *Illustrations:* 35 plates, some of them colored. They are extremely good, and Castelnau states in the preface that he made most of the sketches for them. Thirteen of the plates contain scenes in Georgia, Alabama, and Florida, chiefly the latter.
> *Inclusive dates:* 1837–1839.
> *Other editions:*
> Paris, A. Bertrand, 1852. viii, 168 p. 35 plates.
> *Location of copy:* Library of Congress.

In his general discussion of American life and customs, Castelnau treats each topic from the standpoints of white man, Negro, and

[117]

Indian. This book also contains essays on various sections of the United States, among which is an "Essai sur les Seminoles de la Floride" which describes the country as well as the life and customs of the Indians. With only slight variations, the "Essai sur les Seminoles de la Floride" was published in Société de Géographie de Paris, *Bulletin,* Series 2, Vol. XVII, pp. 392–403 (Paris, 1842). Two other contributions by Castelnau appeared in the *Bulletin.* In Ser. 2, Vol. XVIII, pp. 241–59 (Paris, 1842), is his "Notes sur deux Itinéraires de Charleston à Tallahassee (Floride)," which is a full and interesting account of a journey in the winter of 1837–38 by railroad, carriage, horseback, and steamboat; it includes descriptions of terrain, flora and fauna, settlements, towns, and Indians. One phase of this trip was an exploration of the Wakulla River. This episode was the basis of his "Note sur la source de la rivière de Wakulla dans la Floride" and its prefatory "Extrait d'une lettre de M. le comte de Castelnau à M. le baron de Walckenaer" which was published in the *Bulletin,* Ser. 2, Vol. XI, pp. 240–47 (Paris, 1839). One other contribution by this author deserves notice, namely, his "Essai sur Floride du Milieu," in *Nouvelles Annales des Voyages et des Sciences Géographiques,* Vols. XCIX–C (Ser. 4, Vols. XV–XVI), pp. 129–208 (Paris, 1843).

Castelnau was an experienced naturalist and traveler. His observations are full, detailed, and apparently accurate, and they have a touch lacking in those of less trained observers.

139. Castro, Henry (1786–1865)

Le Texas. [Anvers, 1845].

> 38 p., 1 l.   24 cm.
> *Inclusive dates:* 1841, 1844 (years in which author says he visited Texas).
> *Other editions:*
> (1) Anvers, 1845.   24 p.   plate, plan.
> (2) Anvers, 1845.   43 p.
> (3) Le Texas en 1845. Castroville, colonie fondée par Henry Castro, le 1er septembre 1844 sur la rivière Medina, 24 milles ouest de San Antonio de Bexar. [Anvers, 1845].   43 p.
> *Location of copy:* Library of Congress.

Pages 7–16 contain a summary of Texas history and some mention of natural resources, rivers, soil, boundaries, towns, crops, and the financial condition of the government. Pages 17–38, entitled "Mon Procès," are Castro's diatribe against the Strasbourg court which interfered with the carrying out of his colonization scheme on the Medina River in Texas.

140. Caswall, Henry (1810–1870)

America, and the American church. By the Rev. Henry Caswall . . . London, printed for J. G. & F. Rivington, 1839.

xviii, 1 l., 368 p. front., 3 plates, fold. map. 20 cm.

Maps: One: "America (U. S.) divided into Dioceses."

Illustrations: Four: frontispiece, "Methodist Camp-Meeting in Kentucky at Night"; "Log-house in Ohio"; "Ruins of the First Church Erected in America," Jamestown; "Episcopal Log-Church (in the woods) near Gambier," Ohio.

Inclusive dates: September, 1828, to 1842.

Other editions:
(1) London, 1849.
(2) 2d ed. London, J. and C. Mozley, 1851. xii, 400, [2] p. 21 cm.

Location of copy: Duke University Library.

Caswall came to America in 1828 to teach at Kenyon College in Ohio; he moved to Lexington, Kentucky, in May, 1834, to teach in the theological seminary that was being established by the Episcopal diocese of Kentucky; he went to Indiana two or three years later; and in 1842 he returned to England. His *America, and the American Church,* the second edition, deals with these experiences. In 1853 he was in America once more, this time as a delegate of the Society for the Propagation of the Gospel in Foreign Parts, and the next year he brought forth *The Western World Revisited* (Oxford and London). He also wrote about the Mormons in a volume entitled *The American Church and the American Union* (London, 1861). Caswall was a sensible and judicious observer whose interests were chiefly in religion and education.

141. Catlin, George (1796–1872)

Letters and notes on the manners, customs, and condition of the North American Indians. By Geo. Catlin. Written during eight years' travel amongst the wildest tribes of Indians in North America. In 1832, 33, 34, 35, 36, 37, 38, and 39 . . . 2 vols. London, pub. by the author; printed by Tosswill and Myers, 1841.

Vol. I, viii, 264 p.; Vol. II, viii, 266 p. Vol. I, front., plates, ports., 2 maps (1 fold.). 25½ cm.

Maps: Three: location of Indian tribes in 1833, Indian frontier in 1840, and route of the Mandans to the place of their extinction.

Illustrations: 312 plates according to title page. (Actually 309 plates).

Inclusive dates: 1832–1839. In South, 1838 and earlier.

Other editions:
(1) New-York, Wiley and Putnam, 1841.
(2) 2d ed. New-York, Wiley and Putnam, 1842.
(3) 3d ed. New-York, Wiley and Putnam, 1844.

(4) 4th ed. 1843.

(5) Illustrations of the manners, customs, and condition of the North American Indians . . . 5th ed. London, H. G. Bohn, 1845.

(6) 6th ed. 1846.

(7) 7th ed. London, H. G. Bohn, 1848.

(8) 8th ed. London, H. G. Bohn, 1851.

(9) 9th ed. London, H. G. Bohn, 1857.

(10) Philadelphia, Willis P. Hazard, 1857.

(11) 10th ed. 1866.

(12) London, Chatto & Windus, 1876.

(13) Catlin's Indians. Being a . . . series of letters and notes on the manners, customs, and condition of the North American Indians. Two vols. in one . . . Philadelphia, Hubbard brothers, 1891.

(14) North American Indians; being letters and notes on their manners, customs, and conditions . . . Edinburgh, J. Grant, 1903.

(15) Philadelphia, Leary, Stuart and company, 1913.

(16) Edinburgh, J. Grant, 1926.

(17) Die Indianer Nord-Amerikas und die während eines achtjährigen Aufenthalts unter den wildesten ihrer Stämme erlebten abenteuer und Schicksale von G. Catlin. Nach der fünften englischen Ausgabe Deutsch herausgegeben von Dr. Heinrich Berghaus . . . Mit 24 vom Verfasser nach der Natur entworfenen Gemälden. 2 Ausg. Brüssel, [etc.], C. Muquardt, 1851. x p., 1 l., 382 p. incl. plates. 23 plates (1 col.). 26½ cm.

Location of copy: First edition not seen; collation from Wagner. Most of the editions are represented in the Library of Congress.

This important work does not contain much information about the South, for Catlin preferred to study and paint the Far Western Indians who had been least affected by white civilization. He spent two winters on the Florida and Texas coasts, but he wrote nothing about them except brief descriptions of Pensacola and the Perdido River. He visited Fort Moultrie, South Carolina, in 1838 to see 250 Indians who had been captured in Florida. He painted several of them, including the famous Seminole Chieftain Osceola shortly before his death. In the West, Catlin visited the Cherokee, Creek, and Choctaw Indians soon after they had crossed the Mississippi River, and he included some of their legends and a fine description of a Choctaw ball game, with illustrative plates of the game and of Indian personalities.

142.   Champlin, James (b. 1821)

Early biography, travels and adventures of Rev. James Champlin, who was born blind; with a description of the different countries through which he has traveled in America, and of the different institutions, etc., visited by him; also an appendix, which contains extracts from addresses delivered by him upon several occasions. Written by himself. 2d ed., rev. Columbus, O., [C. Scott's power press, 1842].

206 p. 18½ cm.
Inclusive dates: 1837–1842? In South, the same.
Other editions:
   Columbus, O., 1842. 192 p.
Location of copy: Duke University Library.

Champlin was no more than twenty-one years old when he published
this autobiography with the principal object of instructing "the young
in mind." He had already been licensed as a "public exhorter" in the
Methodist church, and his work is full of religious admonition and of
warnings against evil companions. His travels were from the home
of his parents, who lived first near Knoxville and then in middle
Tennessee. About the year 1837 he went to Lexington, Kentucky, with
the hope, that proved to be in vain, that Dr. Benjamin Dudley could
give sight to his eyes. He traveled over parts of east and middle Tennessee on preaching tours; and he made a trip to Boston, going across
Virginia to Norfolk and then by water and returning through the
Erie Canal and across Ohio and Kentucky. As would be expected,
Champlin's comments on people are better than his descriptions of
places. The chief value of the book is its reflection of the treatment
and experiences of a blind traveler.

143.   Claiborne, John Francis Hamtranck (1809–1884)
A trip through the Piney Woods.

First published in 1841–1842 in the newspaper Natchez free trader and gazette.
Inclusive dates: July, 1841.
Other editions:
   In Mississippi historical society publications, Vol. IX, pp. 487–538. Oxford,
   Miss., ₁etc.₁, The society, 1906. 22½–25 cm.
Location of copy: Duke University Library.

In the summer of 1841 the Mississippi politician, newspaper editor, and
historian J. F. H. Claiborne engaged in a political campaign eastward
from Natchez in the poorer part of Mississippi that was known as
the piney woods. At its conclusion he described his trip in a series of
sketches that were published in the form described above. "A Trip
Through the Piney Woods" is entertaining and anecdotal, and it
includes fanciful stories and historical digressions as well as detailed
sketches of a region that was rarely mentioned by other travelers.

144.   Clark, John Alonzo (1801–1843)
Gleanings by the way; by Rev. John A. Clark . . . Philadelphia, W. J. & J. K. Simon; New York, R. Carter, 1842.

[121]

v, [7]–352 p. 19½ cm.
Inclusive dates: 1837–1840.
Location of copy: Davidson College Library.

Most of this book consists of excerpts from a journal kept on vacation trips by the rector of St. Andrew's Episcopal Church, Philadelphia. Clark was in Kentucky in June, 1837. His published record of these days contains stories about Indian warfare, opinions about slavery and about the character of Kentuckians, and a detailed description of a funeral.

145. Cohen, Myer M.

Notices of Florida and the campaigns. By M. M. Cohen (an officer of the left wing). Charleston, S. C., Burges & Honour; New-York, B. B. Hussey, 1836.

240 p. front. (fold. map), plate. 18 cm.
Maps: One, folded: "Map of Florida according to the latest authorities . . . Corrected and improved from data furnished by M. M. Cohen." Engraved by Wm. Keenan.
Illustrations: One: "Oseola or Powell. Drawn, engraved & printed by W. Keenan."
Inclusive dates: January to May, 1836. In South, the same.
Location of copy: Duke University Library.

This book came out quickly after the conclusion of an expedition against the Seminole Indians early in the year 1836, in which the author had served with the South Carolina volunteers as an officer. In the first 105 pages he sketches the history of Florida and circumstances behind the conflict in which he participated. In the rest of the book, which is entitled the "Author's Journal," he tells of the raising of the volunteer contingent in Charleston, their transportation to St. Augustine, their march through the Indian country across to Tampa and back again, and their return to Charleston. This journal is both a history of the expedition and a record of Cohen's personal experiences. It is a revealing account of hardships, courage, high spirits, inefficiency, and military ignorance. It contains descriptions of St. Augustine, the interior of Florida, and the Indians, including a careful description of two dead Indians and phrenological analyses of their skulls.

146. Collyer, Robert H.

Lights and shadows of American life. Boston, Redding & co., etc. [1844?].

40 p. 25 cm.

Illustrations: One: Drawing of a man's head, presumably Robert H. Collyer, done by F. E. Worcester, on the front of the paper jacket.
Inclusive dates: June, 1836, to September, 1843?
Other editions:
    Boston, Brainard & co. ₁1843?₁.
Location of copy: Boston Athenaeum.

This self-styled "Professor of Mesmerism and Psycography" claimed to "have lived long at the South—in Maryland, Virginia, Kentucky, and in most of the slaveholding states," but this brief record of his tour in the United States contains nothing about the South except a short and pontifical opinion on the subject of slavery. Collyer also wrote pamphlets about phrenology and hypnotism.

147.   Combe, George (1788–1858)

Notes on the United States of North America, during a phrenological visit in 1838–9–40. By George Combe . . . 2 vols. Philadelphia, Carey & Hart, 1841.

Vol. I, xvi, 374 p.; Vol. II, 405 p.   illus.   20 cm.
Illustrations: Several drawings of heads, explaining Combe's beliefs about phrenology.
Inclusive dates: September, 1838, to June, 1840.
Other editions:
    3 vols., Edinburgh, Maclachlan, Stewart, & company, ₁etc., etc.₁, 1841.   illus., fold. map.   19½ cm.
Location of copy: Duke University Library.

Only a dozen pages in the latter part of Volume II deal with the South, and these contain scarcely any useful information. They recount a trip from Baltimore to Kentucky and Cincinnati in April, 1840, by Combe, a Scotsman, who was regarded as "the world's outstanding phrenologist" at the time of his visit to the United States, *American Historical Review,* Vol. XXXIX, 73–78; see also the *Dictionary of National Biography.* Combe was the author of a number of other works, some of which went through many editions.

148.   [Croghan, John]

Rambles in the Mammoth Cave, during the year 1844, by a visitor. Louisville, Ky., Morton & Griswold, 1845.

xii, ₁9₁–101 p.   6 plates, fold. map.   17½ cm.
Maps: One, folded: "Map of the Explored Parts of the Mammoth Cave of Ky. By Stephen Bishop, One of the Guides. Published by Morton & Griswold, Louisville, Ky., 1845."
Illustrations: Six scenes in the cave, lithographed, like the map, by Bauer & Teschemacker of Louisville.
Location of copy: Library of Congress.

Written as an account of a trip through Mammoth Cave, this work is clearly designed to attract visitors to it. It contains substantial information about the interior of the cave together with directions about the routes to it from neighboring towns. The anonymity of the author may be explained by the probability that he owned the cave he was praising (p. 53).

149. Daubeny, Charles Giles Bridle (1795–1867)

Journal of a tour through the United States, and in Canada, made during the years 1837–38, by Charles Daubney . . . Oxford, printed by T. Combe, printer to the University . . . for private circulation only, 1843.

vi, 231 p. fold. map. 18 cm.
Maps: One, folded: "Map of the United States and of the Canadas."
Inclusive dates: July 27, 1837, to July 10, 1838. In South, January to June, 1838.
Location of copy: Library of Congress.

The British naturalist Daubeny came to America to study its botanical and geological features. He was tolerant of physical inconveniences and of American ways of life, noting with good humor that he emptied his portmanteau of abolitionist writings before entering Virginia. He traveled in the North until the last days of the year 1837. During January, 1838, he traveled from Baltimore to Charleston, S. C. February was spent in Cuba. Re-entering the United States at New Orleans, he went by boat and horseback to Pittsburgh, with a side excursion into Kentucky, and then turned southward again for a tour of the Virginia springs. This record is in the form of a diary; it is well written and interesting, but it has no unusual value.

The sketch of Daubeny in the *Dictionary of National Biography* refers to his *Notes of a Tour in North America* (privately printed, 1838), but no copy has been located.

150. Davidson, Robert (1808–1876)

An excursion to the Mammoth cave and the barrens of Kentucky. With some notices of the early settlement of the state. By the Rev. R. Davidson. Philadelphia, Thomas, Cowperthwait, and co., 1840.

ix p., 1 l., [13]–148 p. 14½ cm.
Inclusive dates: October, 1836. In South, the same.
Other editions:
Lexington, Ky., A. T. Skillman & son, 1840.
Location of copy: Library of Congress.

Davidson was a graduate of Princeton, a Presbyterian minister, and the president of Transylvania University. This volume consists of two addresses. The first is entitled: "An Excursion to the Mammoth Cave and the Barrens of Kentucky. Read before the Society of Adelphi of Transylvania University, January 16, 1840." It describes a journey made in October, 1836, through Henderson, Hopkinsville, Elkton, Russellville, Shakertown, and Bowling Green, to Mammoth Cave. Davidson was a close and careful observer, and his descriptions of these towns and of the cave are of considerable value. The second portion of the volume, which begins on page 82, does not concern travel. It is entitled: "Some Notices of the Early History of Kentucky. Read before the Transylvania Institute, December 17, 1838; and since Read by Request before the Kentucky Historical Society of Louisville."

151. Dickens, Charles (1812–1870)

American notes for general circulation. By Charles Dickens . . . 2 vols. London, Chapman and Hall, 1842.

Vol. I, x [wrongly numbered xvi], 308 p.; Vol. II, vii, 306 p. 20½ cm.
Inclusive dates: January to June, 1842.
Other editions:
(1) New York, Harper & brothers, 1842. 92 p. 24 cm.
(2) 1st American ed. New York, Wilson & company, 1842. 47, [1] p. 28½ cm. (Brother Jonathan. Extra number. Nov. 7, 1842).
(3) Paris, Galignani, 1842.
(4) Paris, Baudry, Stassin et Xavier, Amyot, Truchy, 1842.
(5) Leipzig, B. Tauchnitz, 1842.
(6) With a frontispiece by C. Stanfield, R. A. London, Chapman and Hall, 1850.
(7) Philadelphia, T. B. Peterson & Brothers, 1859.
(8) London, Chapman & Hall, 1861.
(9) New York, Hurd & Houghton, 1867. 335 p.
(10) Boston, Ticknor and Fields, 1867. 4 p.l., [7]–126 p. front., plates. 21½ cm.
(11) New York, John W. Lovell company, [1883]. 8 p.l., p. 585–826. 18½ cm. (Lovell's library, Vol. V, No. 210).
(12) London, Chapman and Hall, 1884. 96 p.
(13) New York, G. Munroe, [c.1885]. 181 p. 18½ cm. (The Seaside library. Pocket ed., [No. 447]).
(14) Uitstapje naar Noord-Amerika, van Ch. Dickens. Uit het Engelsch. Met eene plaat. Amsterdam, C. F. Stemler, 1842. 1 p.l., 441 p. front. 23½ cm.
(15) Nieuwe Diep, C. Bakker Bz., 1842.
(16) American notes and pictures from Italy, by Charles Dickens. A reprint of the first editions, with the illustrations, and an introduction, biographical and bibliographical, by Charles Dickens the younger. London and New York, Macmillan and co., 1893. xvii, [1] p., 1 l., 379, [1] p. 19½ cm.
(17) London, J. M. Dent & co.; New York, E. P. Dutton & co., [1907]. xxii p., 1 l., 430 p. 17½ cm. (Everyman's library).

(18) With 8 illustrations by Maurice Stone . . . London, Chapman & Hall, ltd.; New York, C. Scribner's sons, 1910. xiii p., 2 l., 517, ₁1₁ p. 8 plates (incl. front.) 22 cm. (The centenary edition of the works of Charles Dickens in 36 volumes).

(19) London & Toronto, J. M. Dent & sons, ltd.; New York, E. P. Dutton & co., ₁1926₁. xxii p., 1 l., 430 p. 17½ cm. (Everyman's library. Fiction, No. 290).

(20) People's edition. London, Chapman and Hall, ₁n.d.₁. 298 p.

(21) Pictures from Italy. And American notes for general circulation. By Charles Dickens . . . London, Chapman and Hall, 1862. vii p., 1 l., 437 p. front., plates. 19½ cm. (Library ed., Vol. XVII).

(22) 2 vols. New York, Hurd and Houghton, 1866. front., port. 18 cm. (In his Works. Household ed. New York, 1866-).

(23) With illustrations by Marcus Stone. New York, G. W. Carleton & co.; London, Chapman & Hall, 1874. 416 p. front., plates. 19 cm. (Works of Charles Dickens. "Carleton's new illustrated edition." Vol. XVII).

(24) New York, Hurd and Houghton, 1877. xxxii, 437 p. front. (port.), 9 plates. 19½ cm. (Works. New illustrated library ed., Vol. XV).

(25) Pictures from Italy, sketches by Boz, and American notes. By Charles Dickens. Illustrated by Thomas Nast and Arthur B. Frost. New York, Harper & brothers, 1877. 383 p., incl. front., illus. 2 plates. 25½ cm.

Location of copy: The first edition is described in *Catalogue of an Exhibition of the Works of Charles Dickens,* with an Introduction by Royal Cortissoz (New York, The Grolier Club, 1913).

Charles Dickens' tour in the United States included a fortnight in Baltimore, Washington, and Richmond in the month of March, 1842. Some of his experiences in these cities and an entertaining account of his trip by stage to Fredericksburg, Virginia, are recounted in his *American Notes for General Circulation.* His chapter on slavery was influential, for it stirred the hatred of British liberals against slavery, and it was a source of inspiration for Longfellow's *Poems on Slavery;* but it was not based on Dickens' observation. Most of it was taken from Theodore D. Weld, *American Slavery as It is: Testimony of a Thousand Witnesses* (New York, 1839), according to Louise H. Johnson in *American Literature,* Vol. XIV (1943), pp. 427-30.

152.   Didimus, Henry (Durrell, Edward H.)

New Orleans as I found it. By H. Didimus . . . New York, Harper & brothers, 1845.

125 p.   23 cm.
Inclusive dates: Winter of 1835-1836. In South, the same.
Location of copy: Duke University Library.

The author's dedication claims that these are "sketches of some of the incidents of my first visit to New Orleans, in the winter of 1835-36." It contains some information about places and things in New

Orleans, told in a gossipy, informal fashion; but most of the pages are filled with incidents and tales. On page 69 the author launches into the story of a character called "Oceanus" which continues to the end of the book. Didimus' facile pen makes scant information cover many pages.

153.   Ellet, Mrs. Elizabeth Fries Lummis (1818–1877)
Rambles about the country. New York, Harper & brothers, 1847.

> 257 p.   15 cm.
> *Inclusive dates:* Late 1830's. In South, the same.
> *Other editions:*
>   This work was copyrighted in 1840 by Marsh, Capen, Lyon, and Webb of Boston, who published it as Vol. IX of the School Library . . . Juvenile series. An 1854 edition was published in New York.
> *Location of copy:* The New York Public Library.

Rambles about the Country was written for children. The children of that day must have been hard pressed for something to read to account for this book's going through several editions. It consists of laboriously enthusiastic descriptions of incidents and places, many of them in the South Atlantic states. Among them are "A Southern Winter," "A Visit to Albemarle Sound," "Fall of Tallulah," and "The Santee River and Swamp." The writer may be presumed to have seen some of the things she describes, for she lived in the South from the middle 1830's until 1849 while her husband was a professor in South Carolina College. Some sections of the book were contributed by others.

154.   Ewbank, Thomas (1792–1870)
Life in Brazil; or a journal of a visit to the land of the cocoa and the palm. With an appendix, containing illustrations of ancient South American arts in recently discovered implements and products of domestic industry, and works in stone, pottery, gold, silver, bronze &c., by Thomas Ewbank . . . New York, Harper & brothers, 1856.

> xvi, [17]–469 p.   illus.   23½ cm.
> *Illustrations:* "Over one hundred illustrations," but none dealing with the South.
> *Inclusive dates:* 1845–1848. In South, December, 1845.
> *Location of copy:* Duke University Library.

The author, who was United States commissioner of patents from 1849 to 1852, was a man of broad and keen intellectual interests. Only the first eight pages of the present work deal with travel in the South, but this small quantity is excellent. It describes Ewbank's trip from

New York to Richmond, the city of Richmond, and the bark on which he set sail for Brazil. He crowds in brief notes about a Virginia country store and about slaves. A sketch of Ewbank's life is in the *Dictionary of American Biography*.

155. Falconer, Thomas (1805–1882)

Letters and notes on the Texan Santa Fe expedition, 1841–1842, by Thomas Falconer, with an introduction and notes by F. W. Hodge. New York city, Dauber & Pine bookshops, inc., 1930.

159 p., incl. front. (port.). 25 cm.
Illustrations: Frontispiece: Portrait of Thomas Falconer.
Inclusive dates: 1840–1842. In South, 1841.
Location of copy: Duke University Library.

This volume affords convenient access to some of Falconer's writings which are relatively inaccessible in their original form. One of these is his "Notes of a Journal through Texas and New Mexico, in the Years 1841 and 1842," which was first published in the *Journal of the Royal Geographical Society of London,* Vol. XIII, Part 2 (1844), pp. 199–226. The first part of the notes tells of his travels through Galveston, Houston, San Antonio, and Austin from March to June, 1841; the rest of it recounts his experiences on the plains and his capture and eventual release by the Mexicans. Of somewhat less interest to the student of Southern travel is the rare pamphlet, an original of which is in the University of Texas Library, entitled, *Expedition to Santa Fé. An Account of Its Journey from Texas through Mexico, with Particulars of Its Capture. By Thomas Falconer* (New Orleans, published by Lumsden, Kendall & Co., Office of the Picayune, 1842). Hodge's compilation presents several other documents from Falconer's pen together with a bibliography of his writings and a day by day record of his American itinerary.

156. Fawcett, Jos. W.

Journal of Jos. W. Fawcett (Diary of his trip down the Ohio and Mississippi rivers to the Gulf of Mexico and up the Atlantic coast to Boston) with an introduction by Eugene Rigney. Chillicothe, Ohio, David K. Webb, 1944.

59 p. 14 cm.
Inclusive dates: February to April, 1840.
Location of copy: University of Kentucky Library.

This Wheeling, Virginia, lad went south to see the sights before he died with tuberculosis. Going aboard the *Monongahela* at 9:00 in the morning, on February 25, he looked back tearfully at his home with the thought he would never see it again. Down the river the steamer went, bringing into view the famous landmarks on both sides of the Ohio. Maysville, Ripley, North Bend, former home of General Harrison, Cincinnati, Louisville, Memphis, Natchez, and New Orleans all fascinated the sick traveler. At Natchez he spat blood but was determined to go on.

Fawcett was a good observer, and he wrote vividly of the sights before the boat. Eleven days in New Orleans gave him a chance to savor life in that romantic city. Even Dr. Robert J. Breckinridge's stern Presbyterian sermon seemed to fit into Joe Fawcett's concept of romance. The value of this journal lies in its description of travel on both a river steamer and a coastal sailing vessel en route to Boston. The picture of New Orleans is vivid and revealing.

157. Field, Joseph E.

Three years in Texas. Including a view of the Texan revolution, and an account of the principal battles, together with descriptions of the soil, commercial and agricultural advantages, &c. By Dr. Joseph E. Field, one of the few survivors of Fanning's command. Greenfield, Mass., J. Jones; Boston, A. Tompkins, 1836.

iv, [5]–47 p. 20½ cm.
Inclusive dates: 1834? to May, 1836.
Other editions:
(1) Tarrytown, N. Y., reprinted, W. Abbatt, 1925. (In the magazine of history, with notes and queries. Tarrytown, N. Y., 1925. 26½ cm. Extra number. No. 108 [Vol. XXVII, No. 4], p. [5]–42).
(2) Austin, Texas, The Steck company, 1935. 2 p.l., [iii]–iv, 5–59 p. 22 cm. (Original narratives of Texas history and adventure).
(3) Texas. A view of the Texas Revolution, an account of the principal battles, and geographical, historical and other important information. By Dr. Joseph E. Field . . . Springfield, Mass., Justin Jones, 1836. 47 p.
Location of copy: Yale University Library.

The text of this rare work falls short of the expectations created by its title. Its value as a work of travel consists chiefly in Field's narrative of several encounters between Texans and Mexicans in which he was a participant. His misspelling of Fannin's name occurs in the text as well as in the title.

158. [Flagg, Edmund (1815–1890)]

The far West: or, a tour beyond the mountains. Embracing outlines of western life and scenery; sketches of the prairies, rivers, ancient mounds, early settlements of the French, etc. . . . 2 vols. New-York, Harper & brothers, 1838.

> Vol. I, xvi, 14–263 p.; Vol. II, xi, 241 p. 18½ cm.
> *Inclusive dates:* June, 1836, to October, 1837. In South, June, 1836.
> *Other editions:*
> Flagg's The far West, 1836–1837 . . . (In Reuben Gold Thwaites, [ed.],
> Early western travels, 1748–1846. Cleveland, O., 1904–1907. Vol. XXVI, p.
> [21]–370; Vol. XXVII, p. [13]–121. fold. map). 24½ cm.
> *Location of copy:* Library of Congress.

This work originally appeared in the Louisville *Journal* as a series of sketches of a trip that Flagg made in Illinois and Missouri. The only part of it that relates to the South is the rather literary account in the early pages of the work of his journey down the Ohio River in June, 1836. In these pages he wrote chiefly about the scenery along the river, about steamboats, and about the Louisville water front.

159. Fournel, Henri Jérome Marie (1799–1876)

Coup d'oeil historique et statistique sur le Téxas. Paris, Delloye, 1841.

> 57 p. fold. map. 25½ cm.
> *Maps:* One folded map at end of volume: "Carte du Texas, Extraite de la Grande Carte du Mexique par A. Brué Géographe du Roi; Revue, corrigée et considerablement augmentée, d'après des documens récens et des renseignemens fournais par M. le Docteur Fc. Leclerc."
> *Location of copy:* Library of Congress.

This work is regarded as a gazetteer or guide rather than a travel account because of the nature of its content and because the author states that it is based chiefly on Chester Newell, *Account of Texas* (New York, 1838), and on data gained from conversations with General James Hamilton while he was in Paris on behalf of the Republic of Texas. However, Fournel, a French mining engineer, is said to have made a visit to Texas (Larousse, *Grande Dictionnaire Universel de XIXe Siècle,* VIII), and some of his observations may have been incorporated.

160. Fuller, James Cannings

"Extract of a letter from James Cannings Fuller to Joseph Sturge."

> In Sturge, Joseph. A visit to the United States in 1841; by Joseph Sturge . . .
> Boston, D. S. King, 1842. Appendix I., p. lxxii–lxxxv.
> *Inclusive dates:* July to September, 1841.
> *Location of copy:* Duke University Library.

A detailed account of the experiences and observations of an outspoken Quaker abolitionist who traveled from New York State to

Harrodsburg, Kentucky, to buy a family of slaves who had once belonged to Mrs. Gerrit Smith. She and her husband, wishing to set them free, sent Fuller to Kentucky to purchase them. Besides fulfilling this mission, he turned his trip into a vigorous crusade against slavery in Kentucky and against "colorophobia" in the North.

161. Gaillardet, Frédéric (1808–1882)

L'aristocratie en Amérique, par Frédéric Gaillardet . . . Paris, E. Dentu, 1883.

> 2 p.l., 375 p. 18½ cm.
>
> *Inclusive dates:* 1837 and intermittently for many years thereafter. In South, 1837.
>
> *Location of copy:* Library of Congress.

According to Frank Monaghan, *French Travellers in the United States, 1765–1932* (New York, 1933), p. 44, Gaillardet "came to New Orleans in 1837 with two brothers and while travelling in the Mississippi Valley and Texas he frequently wrote to the Parisian newspapers." However, his *L'Aristocratie en Amérique,* which was published the year after his death, does not contain much about the South except a brief account of New Orleans and of his voyage up the Mississippi River, episodes of Texas history, and several tales and legends.

162. Gelline, P. L.

Journal de mer d'un voyage à la Nouvelle Orléans, capitale de la Louisiane; départ et retour à bord des trois mâts le Severn et le Chateaubriand, du 2 Octobre 1841 au 21 Février 1842. Par P. L. Gelline. Paris, l'auteur, 1842.

> 40 p. 8vo.

Frank Monaghan, *French Travellers,* p. 44, lists this travel account and says that a copy is in the Bibliothèque Nationale. In a letter of July 3, 1946, Monaghan informed the compiler that he found one other copy in Brussels but that none had been located in an American library. The Union Catalog at Library of Congress shows no American copy.

The only chance to examine this work seemed to be to secure a photostat from the Bibliothèque Nationale. In September, 1946, the attempt was made through the Duke University Library. The Bibliothèque Nationale answered that it does not possess the work.

163. Gerstäcker, Friedrich Wilhelm Christian (1816–1872)

Wild sports in the far West. By Frederick Gerstaecker. Tr. from the

German. With tinted illustrations, by Harrison Weir. London, New York, G. Routledge & co., 1854.

> xi, 396 p. front., plates. 18½ cm.
>
> *Illustrations:* "Eight crayon drawings, executed in oil colors, from designs by Harrison Weir." All show hunting scenes, and they are presumably entirely imaginative. The original of "The Captured Buffalo" lived in a barnyard rather than on the plains.
>
> *Inclusive dates:* Spring, 1837, to 1843? In South, 1838–1843?
>
> *Other editions:*
>
> (1) London, Routledge, 1854. 314 p.
> (2) New ed. London, 1856.
> (3) London, 1862.
> (4) Boston, 1866.
>
> *Location of copy:* Duke University Library.

Unlike most travelers of his day, this young German hurried out of the more civilized parts of the United States and lived for several years on the frontier. After landing at New York and seeing a few sights in the North, he turned westward to the Mississippi Valley. He visited various places up and down the river from Cincinnati to New Orleans, but chiefly he roamed over the less settled parts of Arkansas. Part of the time he lived with frontier farmers who preferred hunting and cattle raising to agriculture, but at frequent intervals his restless disposition took him into the wilderness for weeks or months, trusting to his gun for food. Hunting adventures occupy much of his narrative. He tells of killing deer, turkeys, bear, panthers, and wolves, and he recounts many hairbreadth escapes such as his fight far back in a narrow cave with a wounded bear. Along with this high adventure, he does not forget the hardships of heat and cold, rain, swamps, hunger, mosquitoes, and ague. He also describes life among the pioneer settlers—their home life, agricultural practices, and manners, and such social occasions as house raisings, debating societies, and Fourth of July celebrations. As a description of pioneer life and as a collection of hunting stories, Gerstäcker's *Wild Sports* ranks high.

In 1844, shortly after returning home, Gerstäcker brought out the first of his many volumes, *Streif- und Jagdzüge durch die Vereinigten Staaten Nord-Amerikas (Der Grosse Brockhaus)*, and upon this is based *Wild Sports in the Far West*. London editions of *Wild Sports* appeared in 1854 and 1862, and there was another Boston edition in 1866. Among his other works there are two novels that relate to the South: *The Regulators of Arkansas* and *The Pirates of the Mississippi*. Each appeared in several editions, first appearing in German as early as 1846 and 1848 respectively.

164. Gerstner, Clara (von Epplen-Härtenstein) von

Beschreibung einer Reise durch die Vereinigten Staaten von Nord-America in den Jahren 1838 bis 1840. In Gesellschaft des Ritters Franz Anton von Gerstner unternommen, von Clara von Gerstner, geb. von Epplen-Härtenstein. Leipzig, J. C. Hinrichs, 1842.

> xii, 456 p. 16½ cm.
> *Inclusive dates:* October, 1838, to May, 1840. In South, March to June, 1839.
> *Location of copy:* Historical Society of Pennsylvania.

While not a great travel work, this is distinctly a good one. Its author was the wife of Franz von Gerstner (*q.v.*), and her book is in the nature of a journal of their experiences during the trip on which her husband was assembling data for his treatise on transportation. In fact, she presents many valuable details about travel, including data on its cost, that cannot be found in Franz von Gerstner's work. From her we learn that they spent four months in New England and the Middle States, traveled through the chief South Atlantic cities to Charleston, thence overland to Mobile and New Orleans, up the Mississippi to Kentucky, and on to Philadelphia where her husband died. Clara von Gerstner's observations reflect a wholesome interest in life, a curiosity for detail, and a willingness to accept inconveniences without undue complaint. She devoted about 150 pages to the South.

165. Gerstner, Franz Anton, Ritter von (1793–1840)

Die innern Communicationen der Vereinigten Staaten von Nord-amerika. Von Franz Anton Ritter von Gerstner . . . Nach dessen Tode aufgesetzt, redigiet und hrsg. von L. Klein . . . 2 vols. Wien, L. Forster's Artistische Anstalt, 1842–43.

> Vol. I, viii, 376 p.; Vol. II, [iv], 339 p. xxxiv (i.e., 35) fold. plates. 27½ cm.
> *Maps:* One. In the back of Vol. I there is an excellent folded map, dated 1842, showing canals and railroads in the United States.
> *Illustrations:* Thirty-four folded plates (15 in the back of Vol. I; 19 in the back of Vol. II), showing details of construction of American railroads, particularly roadbeds, varieties of rails, switches, bridges, culverts, hoists, and snowplows. Plates 29–34 contain data about railroads in the South.
> *Inclusive dates:* November, 1838, to November, 1839.
> *Location of copy:* Library of Congress.

After serving as professor of mathematics in the Vienna Polytechnic Institute, Gerstner became a pioneer builder of railroads in Europe and a student of railroad construction. From 1834 to 1837 he was engaged in building the first Russian railroad. The following year he came to America, and in November he began a twelve months' tour in the United States. He died in Philadelphia in 1840. The data he had collected was edited and published in the work described above by Ludwig von Klein, who had worked with Gerstner in Europe and had accompanied him on his American trip. Except for the brief statement in Klein's introduction to the effect that Gerstner traveled on the leading railroads and the most important canals, this work contains no information about the journey. It is, rather, a technical description of American railroads and canals, and of its kind it is one of the best works of its period.

166. Gilman, Mrs. Caroline [Howard] (1794–1888)

The poetry of travelling in the United States. By Caroline Gilman. With additional sketches, by a few friends; and a week among autographs, by Rev. S. Gilman . . . New York, S. Colman, 1838.

> 5 p.l., 430 p.   18 cm.
> *Inclusive dates:* 1835–1836, and possibly other years. In South, the same.
> *Location of copy:* Duke University Library.

Mrs. Gilman was a native of Boston, but she had lived for many years at Charleston before she wrote this book to attract "both the Northern and Southern reader." She and her husband, who was a pastor of the Unitarian Church, were among the leaders of Charleston literary life. The first half of *The Poetry of Travelling* contains her "Notes of a Northern Excursion" which began in April, 1836, and she devotes a few sentimental pages to Norfolk, Mount Vernon, Washington, and Baltimore as she was making her progress toward New England. The rest of the book which is related to the South is a medley of sketches by Mrs. Gilman, of poems, and of contributions by various persons. Most of them are unsigned, and only one is dated. Three of them contain travel material: "Sketches from Buncombe, N. C.," by Anna Maria Wells; "Letters from Georgia," the first of which is dated January, 1835; and "Extracts from a Private Journal Kept on a Tour from Charleston to New York; by Four Friends." This is the best travel writing in the book, and the only piece of much significance. The trip was by carriage and stage to the Virginia springs and Lexington, and thence up the Shenandoah Valley and through Harpers Ferry and Baltimore to New York.

167. Godley, John Robert (1814–1861)

Letters from America. By John Robert Godley . . . 2 vols. London, J. Murray, 1844.

Vol. I, xxiii, 272 p.; Vol. II, viii, 243 p.   20 cm.
Inclusive dates: July to November, 1842.
Location of copy: University of Kentucky.

After traveling extensively in New England, Canada, and New York in July, August, and October, 1842, Godley made a hurried trip in November to Baltimore, Washington, Richmond, and Charlottesville. Fifty pages of his *Letters from America* are devoted to this southern excursion. These pages contain some description, but they chiefly contain essays on subjects suggested by what he saw. Most of the Baltimore chapter is devoted to Roman Catholicism in America and to the activities of the Maryland Colonization Society, slavery occupied his thoughts at Richmond and on a Virginia plantation, and American education and democracy were suggested by his visits to the University of Virginia and "Monticello." This serious-minded young Irishman saw much in the South and elsewhere in America that he disliked, for he was Tory in politics and a staunch Anglican, but he lived up to the purpose stated in his preface of avoiding the "declamatory vituperation or satirical bitterness" of some of the British travelers. A brief sketch of his life is in the *Dictionary of National Biography*.

168.   Goodmane, W. F.

Seven years in America; or, a contrast of British America, namely Canada, New Brunswick, Prince Edward Island, Nova Scotia, Cape Breton, and Newfoundland, with the United States and Texas, shewing the superiority of the former over the latter, for the British emigrant. By W. F. Goodmane . . . London, R. Jones, 1845.

32 p.   21½ cm.
Location of copy: University of Minnesota.

The only parts of this pamphlet that deal with the South are two pages about slavery and one about Texas, and these are worthless. Indeed, there is no evidence that this professor of penmanship was ever in the South except his statement that his residence of seven years in the United States was "passed almost equally in each division of the Union."

169.   Gosse, Philip Henry (1810–1888)

Letters from Alabama, (U.S.) chiefly relating to natural history. By Philip Henry Gosse, F.R.S. London, Morgan and Chase, 1859.

xii, 306 p.   illus.   16 cm.

[135]

Illustrations: The numerous drawings are presumably by the author. They include: deer shooting at night, a wild-turkey trap, the tiny village of Pleasant Hill, a steamboat loading cotton, and many drawings of Alabama flora and fauna.
Inclusive dates: May to December, 1838.
Location of copy: Duke University Library.

Gosse's dominant interest in natural history was evident during his youth in England and during the eleven years that he spent in Newfoundland and Canada before coming to Alabama in May, 1838. There, in Dallas County, he conducted a school for the sons of several planters. He returned to England after eight months to continue his zoological investigations, to write many books, and to win enough recognition to be elected a fellow of the Royal Society. His book, *Letters from Alabama,* was not published until 1859; however, this volume was based at least in part on a diary Gosse had kept while he was in Alabama. The postures of the birds in some of his drawings resemble the postures of Audubon's birds. While Gosse gives most space to descriptions of flora and fauna, he treats a number of phases of life in the interior of Alabama. The book is especially rich in hunting stories. The chief merit of *Letters from Alabama* derives from the fact that Gosse lived for some months in a region that was seldom seen by travelers. A sketch of his life is in the *Dictionary of National Biography.*

170.   Grattan, Thomas Colley (1792–1864)

Civilized America. By Thomas Colley Grattan ... 2 vols. London, Bradbury and Evans, 1859.

Vol. I, xix, 444 p.; Vol. II, vii, 517, [1] p. 2 maps (1 fold.). 22 cm.
Maps: Two, both in Vol. I: folded frontispiece, "Civilized America" and "Map of Boundary Lines" relating to the northeastern boundary dispute.
Inclusive dates: Summer, 1839, to summer, 1846.
Other editions:
   2d ed. London, Bradbury and Evans, 1859.
Location of copy: Duke University Library.

For a period of seven years, Grattan, who was an Irish author of some note, served as British consul at Boston. During this time he made several trips to Washington, usually to witness Presidential inaugurations, he visited in Richmond and at plantation homes in Maryland and Virginia, and he became acquainted with many Southerners at Newport, Rhode Island, and elsewhere in the North. Although he did not write about his American experiences until some years after their termination, he mentions having many notebooks and other private papers before him while he was writing. His *Civilized America* is regarded as one of the best of the commentaries on the United States by a British traveler. The chapter on slavery contains little firsthand information, but some of his other comments on the South are obviously based on personal observations. A sketch of his life is in the *Dictionary of National Biography*.

171.   Gray, William F. (d. 1841)

From Virginia to Texas, 1835. Diary of Col. Wm. F. Gray giving details of his journey to Texas and return in 1835–1836 and second journey to Texas in 1837, with preface by A. C. Gray; printed for the information of his descendants . . . Houston, Tex., Gray Dillaye & co., printers, 1909.

> viii, 230 p. 23½ cm.
> *Inclusive dates:* Oct. 6, 1835 to July 12, 1838. In South, the same.
> *Location of copy:* Library of Congress.

Gray's account of the incidents of his journey is spontaneous, informal, and quite detailed. According to the preface, he went to Texas to speculate in land. His first journey was made down the Ohio and Mississippi rivers; the second, overland to Montgomery, Ala., and thence by boat to Texas. There is some description of scenery but more of fellow passengers, incidents, accommodations, plans, and business dealings. Gray was a resident of Fredericksburg, Va. He was in Texas at the time of the Alamo, and his record reflects the confusion subsequent to that disaster. The record of his second journey, covering pages 194–230, is much briefer. Gray then settled in Texas and held various posts under the Texas government until he died April 16, 1841. On his first trip he spent nearly a month viewing Mississippi lands.

172.   Gregg, Josiah (1806–1850)

Diary & letters of Josiah Gregg: Southwestern enterprises, 1840–1847. Edited by Maurice Garland Fulton, with an introduction by Paul Horgan. Norman, University of Oklahoma press, 1941–44.

> xvii, 413 p. front., 1 illus., plates, ports., maps (part fold.), facsims.   23 cm.
> (American exploration and travel. No. 7).
> *Maps:* Seven, mostly dealing with the West and Mexico. Of interest to Southern travel is the folded "Map showing the route of the Arkansas Regiment from Shreveport, La., to San Antonio de Bexar, Texas," drawn by Gregg.
> *Illustrations:* Frontispiece portrait of Gregg. None of the other illustrations shows places in the South.

Inclusive dates: 1840–1847. In South, chiefly, June, 1841, to June, 1842; May to October, 1846.
Location of copy: Library of Congress.

Gregg spent much of his life traveling in the Southwest. From 1831 to 1839 he engaged in the Santa Fé trade, and out of the information gained in this experience he wrote the important work, *Commerce of the Prairies; Or the Journal of a Santa Fe Trader* (2 vols., New York, 1844, and many later editions. Also printed in Reuben Gold Thwaites, *Early Western Travels*). Its only contribution to the South is a little information about the Arkansas and Texas termini of the trade.

The *Diary & Letters* contains an excellent account of a trip from June, 1841, to June, 1842, from Jackson County, Missouri, through Arkansas and Louisiana to Texas, where he visited Houston, Austin, and other towns, and returned from Bastrop over the old San Antonio and Nacogdoches Road to Van Buren, Arkansas. His descriptions of towns, soil, vegetation, and crops are detailed and careful, and he records events that he witnessed, such as the inauguration of General Sam Houston as president of the Republic of Texas. Beginning in May, 1846, Gregg retraced much of this route with the Arkansas Volunteers. In October the expedition crossed the Río Grande, and the remainder of the volume is devoted to its experiences in Mexico.

In 1944 another volume of the *Diary & Letters* was published by the University of Oklahoma Press with the subtitle: *Excursions in Mexico & California, 1847–1850.* The only material relating to travel in the South is brief notes of a trip up and down the Mississippi River in June and August, 1837, and a twelve-page description of the country about Shreveport, Louisiana.

173. Grund, Francis Joseph (1805–1863)

The Americans in their moral, social, and political relations. By Francis J. Grund. 2 vols. London, Longman, Rees, Orme, Brown, Green & Longman, 1837.

Vol. I, viii, 365 p.; Vol. II, iv, 418 p.   20½ cm.
Inclusive dates: A period of years prior to December, 1836.
Other editions:
    (1) From the London edition of Longman . . . Two volumes in one. Boston, Marsh, Capen and Lyon, 1837.   1 p.l., [9]–423 p.   19½ cm.
    (2) Die Americaner in ihren moralischen, politischen und gesellschaftlichen verhältnissen. Von Francis P. [!] Grund. In's deutsche übersetzt vom verfasser. Stuttgart und Tübingen, Cotta, 1837.   4 p.l., 444 p.   22 cm.
Location of copy: Duke University Library.

This work is not a diary of travel experiences but is a generalized discussion of American customs, institutions, and characteristics. The German author claims to have "resided in America many years" (I, p. v) and to have "lived in several slaveholding states in North and South America" (II, p. 287). Chapter iv of Volume II is one of the best analyses of the slavery problem in the United States written during the 1830's by a traveler. In contrast to the serious, philosophical tone of this work is the gossipy but somewhat penetrating comments in *Aristocracy in America. From the Sketch-book of a German Nobleman* (2 vols., London, Richard Bentley, 1839). Grund may have written this work, although he claims to have edited the manuscript of an anonymous German nobleman. It contains valuable sketches of national political celebrities and of Washington society during Jackson's second administration. German editions of *The Americans* . . . and of *Aristocracy in America* . . . appeared in the same years as the English editions. Each was in two volumes, and both were published at Stuttgart and Tübingen.

174. Gurney, Joseph John (1788–1847)

A journey in North America, described in familiar letters to Amelia Opie. By Joseph John Gurney . . . Norwich, ₁Eng.₁, printed for private circulation, by J. Fletcher, 1841.

> 1 p.l., 414 p., 1 l. 22 cm.
> *Inclusive dates:* July, 1837, to August, 1840.
> *Location of copy:* Haverford College Library.

Gurney was a prominent English Quaker who came to America to visit meetings of Friends and to preach the gospel of Christ. The emphasis in his book is upon these activities and upon his efforts for the abolition of slavery. His travels in the South included a trip in the winter of 1837 and 1838 from the Ohio River through western Virginia and North Carolina to the coast and thence upward through Richmond to Washington, a subsequent trip from Baltimore to Harpers Ferry and Winchester, and a visit in April, 1840, to Savannah and Charleston. At Washington he talked to a number of men in public life, including Calhoun and Clay. Judging that Clay was friendly to emancipation, he secured his permission to address to him a volume entitled, *Familiar Letters to Henry Clay of Kentucky, Describing a Winter in the West Indies* (New York, 1840), in which Gurney endeavored to show the happy results of emancipation in the British West Indies.

[139]

175. Hall, Frederick (1780–1843)

Letters from the East and from the West. By Frederick Hall ... Washington city, F. Taylor and W. M. Morrison; Baltimore, F. Lucas, jr.; [etc., etc., 1840].

xi, 168 p. 23 cm.
Inclusive dates: May to October, 1837; July to August, 1838.
Location of copy: University of Kentucky.

The author was a member of several learned societies, a former professor in Middlebury College, Vermont, and a former president of Mount Hope College, Maryland. His letters from the East describe a tour in the Connecticut Valley in July and August, 1838, and these letters were first published in the *National Intelligencer*. His letters from the West cover a journey that began in May, 1837. He went westward over the National Road and down the Ohio River to Louisville, and from this point the book becomes of more interest to the student of Southern history. From Louisville his route was through Lexington and Harrodsburg (with a side trip to Mammoth Cave) to Nashville, Tennessee, where he remained until July 6. He then left by boat for Indiana. Here the narrative ends, although Hall probably did not reach Baltimore until October. His chief interest was in geology and mineralogy. Besides, he described scenery and unimportant incidents of travel, and he commented on the state of religion with many pious and pat moralizations. He was the author of several other brief works about mineralogy, travel, and religion.

176. Harris, Lewis Birdsall (1816–1893)

Journal of Lewis Birdsall Harris, 1836–1842: Personal history for my sons.

In Southwestern historical quarterly, Vol. XXV (1921–22). Austin, Texas, Texas state historical association. p. 63–71, 131–146, 185–197. 23 cm.
Inclusive dates: 1836–1849.
Location of copy: Duke University Library.

This is an unadorned but exciting account of the activities of a resourceful and determined young man who went from New York state to Texas in his twentieth year. The record includes scanty notes of his steamboat trip down the Mississippi River, two pages about what he saw and did in New Orleans, and much information about Texas in the perilous days of the Revolution. It also includes descriptions of several journeys in Texas before Harris left for California in the gold rush. Some of this record was extracted from a diary, and the rest was written in later years from memory.

177.   [Harris, N. Sayre] Protestant Episcopal church in the U. S. A. Board of missions, Domestic committee.

Journal of a tour in the "Indian Territory," performed by order of the Domestic Committee of the Board of Missions of the Protestant Episcopal Church in the spring of 1844, by their secretary and general agent. [N. S. Harris, added in pencil to title page of Library of Congress copy.] New-York, published for the Domestic committee of the Board of missions by Daniel Dana, jr., 1844.

> 2 p.l., 74 p. front., 3 maps (2 fold.).   22 cm.
>
> *Maps:* 3 maps: "Outline Map of Indian Localities in 1833"; "Aboriginal America East of the Mississippi"; and "U. States Indian Frontier in 1840. Shewing the Positions of the Tribes that have been removed west of the Mississippi."
>
> *Inclusive dates:* February to April, 1844. In South, the same.
>
> *Location of copy:* Library of Congress (Rare Book Division).

N. Sayre Harris, secretary of the Protestant Episcopal Board of Missions, made this tour to ascertain the status of mission work among the Indians and to discover opportunities for its expansion. His itinerary was from New York to Charleston, Columbia, Camden, Savannah, Montgomery, Mobile, New Orleans, and by boat to the Indian territory in western Arkansas. From there he traveled northward by horseback to Fort Leavenworth. In the towns he visited churchmen. He made frequent and apparently careful comments on soil and weather, flora and fauna, and, of course, on mission schools and progress of the Indians, and prospects of promoting mission work among them. He visited missions of all denominations. Slightly more than half of the booklet describes his journey; the remainder is an appendix summarizing the status, population, progress, and general history of the Indian tribes.

This work is catalogued in the Library of Congress under "Protestant Episcopal Church in the U.S.A. Board of Missions, Domestic Committee."

178.   Haskel, Daniel (1784–1848)

A complete descriptive and statistical gazetteer of the United States of America, containing a particular description of the states, territories, counties, districts, parishes, cities, towns, and villages—mountains, rivers, lakes, canals, and railroads; with an abstract of the census and statistics for 1840, exhibiting a complete view of the agricultural, commercial, manufacturing, and literary condition and resources of the country. By Daniel Haskel and J[ohn] Calvin Smith. New York, Sherman & Smith, 1843.

752 p.   22 cm.
Other editions:
   (1) Reissued in 1844 and 1845.
   (2) New York, 1847.   754 p.   23½ cm.
   (3) New York, 1850.   770 p.   23½ cm.
Location of copy: University of Kentucky.

The large amount of material in this gazetteer, much of which was taken from the census of 1840, is arranged alphabetically under place names and in a few instances under topics. It was reissued with little change in 1844, 1845, and 1850 by the same publisher. It serves as a quick means of securing a few facts about many points in the South as well as in the rest of the United States. Haskel was a former president of the University of Vermont (*National Cyclopaedia of American Biography,* II, p. 40). Smith published a number of guides and maps.

179.   Hitchcock, Ethan Allen (1790–1870)

Fifty years in camp and field, diary of Major-General Ethan Allen Hitchcock, U.S.A.; ed. by W. A. Croffut, Ph.D. New York and London, G. P. Putnam's sons, 1909.

   xv, 514 p.   front. (port.).   24 cm.
   Illustrations: One: Frontispiece photograph of Hitchcock.
   Inclusive dates: In South, intermittently 1817 to 1849?
   Other editions:
      Also in:
      A traveler in Indian territory; the journal of Ethan Allen Hitchcock; late major-general in the United States army, edited and annotated by Grant Foreman. Cedar Rapids, Ia., the Torch press, 1930.   270 p.   front., plates, ports., fold. map.   25 cm.
   Location of copy: Duke University Library.

This volume consists in large part of quotations from the voluminous diaries of General Hitchcock. In the course of his military career he was stationed in the South and traveled through parts of the South several times, but most of his comments on these experiences are brief. However, he wrote at some length about his participation in the Seminole War from January to March, 1836, and again in 1842. His sympathies were with the Indians.

   In the fall of 1841, Hitchcock was sent to the Indian Territory to investigate alleged frauds practiced by government agents and army officers upon the Five Civilized Tribes. His report to the Secretary of War created a sensation. His day by day account of this mission is briefly exploited in the book described above; it is printed *in extenso* in *A Traveler in Indian Territory: The Journal of Ethan Allen Hitchcock, Late Major-General in the United States Army.*

180. Höhne, Friedrich

Wahn und Ueberzeugung. Reise des Kupferschmiede-Meisters Friedrich Höhne in Weimar über Bremen nach Nordamerika und Texas in den Jahren, 1839, 1840, und 1841. Wahrhafte und ergreifende Schilderungen der Bremer Seelen-Transportiungen, der Schicksale deutscher Auswanderer, vor, bei und nach der Ueberfahrt; Reisescenen zu Wasser und zu Lande und ausführliche Rathschläge für Ansiedler im Bezug auf den Charakter, die Sitten und konstitutionellen Verhältnisse der Amerikaner, ihren Handel und Gewerbe. Zum Nutz und Frommen deutscher Auswanderer von ihm selbst gesammelt und zusammengestellt. Nebst seiner Rückreise über England und Frankreich. Weimar, bei Wilhelm Hoffmann, 1844.

vi, 435 p. 15 cm.

Illustrations: Eight: Frontispiece scene of New York harbor; scene on an unnamed river, showing a steamer almost surrounded by threatening snags; and six line drawings, one showing the Ohio River at Louisville.

Inclusive dates: June, 1839, to February, 1841. In South, December, 1839, to June, 1840.

Location of copy: Yale University Library.

After visiting New York, Niagara Falls, and Cincinnati, Höhne traveled down the Mississippi River to New Orleans at the end of the year 1839. He remained a short time in that city, somewhat longer in Texas, and then returned to New Orleans in time to embark in March, 1840, for Baltimore. There he observed the convention of young Whigs on May 4, 1840. He visited Washington, D.C., before returning northward and thence to Europe. Much of Höhne's descriptions of rivers, cities, and states closely resembles the gazetteers of that day; but if he used them to pad his work, he was not slavish in copying place names, for he frequently used such spellings as "Hauston", Texas, and "Viksburgh", Mississippi.

181. Holweck, Frederick George (b. 1856)

The beginnings of the church in Little Rock.

In the Catholic Historical Review, Vol. VI (1920). Washington, D. C., The Catholic University of America. p. 156–171. 23 cm.

Inclusive dates: 1832–1840.

Location of copy: Duke University Library.

This article contains a number of letters from Catholic priests in

Arkansas to the Bishop of St. Louis. One of the priests, Rev. Peter Donnelly, was Irish; Rev. Annemond Dupuy and several others were French. None of them remained in Arkansas more than a few years. The letters throw light on religious conditions in this area, especially at Little Rock, between the years 1832 and 1840. The originals are "in the archives of the chancery office at St. Louis."

182.   Houstoun, Mrs. Matilda Charlotte (Jesse) Fraser (1815?–1892)

Texas and the Gulf of Mexico; or, yachting in the New World: by Mrs. Houstoun . . . 2 vols. London, J. Murray, 1844.

> fronts., plates, ports. 20 cm.
> *Illustrations:* Lithograph frontispiece of "Antonio Lopez de Santa Anna"; and three pen sketches: the yacht "Dolphin" and two Negroes.
> *Inclusive dates:* September, 1843, to May, 1844.
> *Other editions:*
>> Philadelphia, G. B. Zieber & co., 1845.   xii, ₁13₁–288 p., incl. front. (port.), illus., plates. 15 cm.   (The home and traveller's library, No. 1).
>> *Also in:*
>> Smith's Weekly Volume. A Select Circulating Library for Town and Country, containing the best popular literature. Philadelphia, L. P. Smith, 1845–46. Vol. I, p. 99–112, 115–128, 131–140.
> *Location of copy:* Harvard University Library.

Mrs. Houstoun and her husband sailed from England in September, 1843, in the yacht *Dolphin* with the primary purpose of improving her health. They reached New Orleans in December, and from then until March they sailed the Gulf Coast and alternately visited New Orleans and Texas. Three years later she spent another winter in America and then wrote a second book, *q. v.,* entitled *Hesperos: or, Travels in the West* (2 vols., 19½ cm., London, John W. Parker, 1850). This time she landed at Boston, and after spending several weeks in the East she traveled through Washington and Harpers Ferry to Cincinnati and thence down the Mississippi River to New Orleans which she reached in December. Again she visited her friends in Texas and then retraced her course, returning to England about the month of April. Her father was Edward Jesse, a popular writer of natural history and a friend of the Duke of Clarence, afterwards William IV, and of other persons of high rank. This background may account for the condescension which crops out in her writing. Her books are sprightly though superficial. She managed to see and do much while in America, and she wrote entertainingly about persons, scenery, and manners and about the fishing and hunting excursions of her husband.

183. Hunt, Richard S.

Guide to the Republic of Texas: consisting of a brief outline of the history of its settlement; a general view of the surface of the country; its climate, soil, productions; rivers, counties, towns, and internal improvements; the colonization and land laws; list of courts and judicial officers; tariff and ports of entry &c. Accompanied by a new and correct map. By Richard S. Hunt and Jesse F. Randel . . . New York, J. H. Colton, 1839.

> 63, [1] p. fold. map. 15½ cm.
> *Maps:* Folded map (colored): "A new map of Texas, with the contiguous American & Mexican states," By J. H. Young, Philadelphia, published by S. Augustus Mitchell, 1835.
> *Other editions:*
> (1) A new guide to Texas . . . New York, Sherman & Smith, 1845. 62, [1] p. fold. map. 15 cm.
> (2) New York, Sherman & Smith, 1846.
> *Location of copy:* Library of Congress.

Intended as a source of information for emigrants to Texas, the contents of this small volume are accurately stated in the title.

Sabin shows later editions, published in New York in 1844 and 1846.

The Duke Library contains an 1845 edition published by Sherman & Smith of New York with the title: *A New Guide to Texas: Consisting of a Brief Outline of the History of Its Settlement, and the Colonization and Land Laws; a General View of the Surface of the Country; Its Climate, Soil, Productions, etc. with a Particular Description of the Counties, Cities, and Towns* ([63], 15 cm.). This edition differs from that of 1839 in its improved, colored, folded map: "Map of Texas, Compiled from Surveys on Record in the General Land Office of the Republic, by Richard S. Hunt and Jesse F. Randel. Published by Sherman & Smith, New York, 1845."

184. Ikin, Arthur

Texas: its history, topography, agriculture, commerce, and general statistics. To which is added, a copy of the treaty of commerce entered into by the Republic of Texas and Great Britain. Designed for the use of the British merchant, and as a guide to emigrants. By Arthur Ikin, Texian consul . . . London, Sherwood, Gilbert, and Piper, 1841.

> vii, [1], 100 p. front. (fold. map). 14 cm.

Maps: One, folded: "Map of Texas," drawn by A. Ikin.
Illustrations: Title-page vignette, "The Alamo."
Location of copy: Yale University Library.

Within its small compass this was an informative guide, designed to encourage British emigration to Texas. The author defended his spelling of "Texian" in the title on the ground that such was the spelling used by the government of Texas in public acts and treaties. As for sources, the introduction states that "the materials ... were chiefly obtained in Texas, where the writer has extensively travelled . . . ."

185. Irving, John Beaufain (1800–1881)

A day on Cooper river. By John B. Irving, M.D. Charleston, ₁S.C.₁, printed by A. E. Miller, 1842.

> 2 p.l., 83 p.   19 cm.
> *Inclusive dates:* Summer, 1842.
> *Other editions:*
> Enlarged and edited by Louise Cheves Stoney: published under the auspices of the St. John's hunting club . . . 2d ed. Columbia, S. C., press of the R. L. Bryan company, 1932. xv, 220 p., 1 l. front. (port.), fold. map. 23½ cm.
> *Location of copy:* Duke University Library.

When the rice fields of low-country South Carolina were ripening toward the harvest of 1842, Dr. J. B. Irving made several trips to the head of steamboat navigation on the western branch of the Cooper River on a steamer which left Charleston at 5:00 each Tuesday morning and returned on the evening of the same day. He had known this river and the rice estates on its borders since his youth. With his memory stirred by familiar scenes, he prepared a series of articles for the *Charleston Courier* and then republished them with corrections and additions in the present booklet. Besides description, this work is rich in local history.

186. [James, Thomas Horton]

Rambles in the United States and Canada during the year 1845, with a short account of Oregon. By Rubio [*pseud.*]. London, John Ollivier, 1846.

> viii, 259 p.   front.   19½ cm.
> *Inclusive dates:* 1845. In South, probably in May and June.
> *Other editions:*
> 2d ed. London, John Ollivier, 1847.
> *Location of copy:* Library of Congress.

The only association of this British traveler with the South was a trip down the Ohio River. He was opposed to liquor and slavery; he regarded Americans as ignorant and their cities as filthy. His gazetteer-like descriptions of the Southern states are not based on personal observation.

187. Kemble, Frances Anne (1809–1893)

Journal of a residence on a Georgian plantation in 1838–1839. By Frances Anne Kemble . . . London, Longman, Green, Longman, Roberts, & Green, 1863.

4 p.l., 434 p. 18½ cm.
Inclusive dates: Winter of 1838–1839. In South, the same.
Other editions:
  (1) New York, Harper & brothers, 1863. 337 p. 19 cm.
  (2) New York, Harper & brothers, 1864.
Location of copy: Duke University Library.

Coming directly from her triumphs at Covent Garden, the famed English tragedienne, Fanny (Frances Anne) Kemble considered her first trip to "that dreadful America" in 1832 as banishment. She stayed four years, however, and married Pierce M. Butler in Philadelphia in 1834. Her experiences in the United States, prior to this marriage, are related in her *Journal* (2 vols., Philadelphia, 1835; also a 2 vol. London ed. of the same year). *Records of a Girlhood* (New York, 1879), consisting of letters from Fanny Kemble to her friends abroad with later annotations, supplements the *Journal*. Her trips southward during her first sojourn in America were to Baltimore and Washington, the first being in January, 1833. Her reception at the White House and her unfavorable impressions of the national capital, as well as a sketch of Baltimore, are given in the *Journal* (II, pp. 68–105) and *Records of a Girlhood*.

After returning to England for ten months, the actress made her second trip to the New World in 1837; and in December, 1838, she and her two small children began a thousand-mile trip from Philadelphia to her husband's plantation in Georgia. The letters of Kemble in *Records of Later Life* (2 vols., London, 1882) give a graphic account of this journey (I, pp. 170–218). Proceeding to Baltimore by railroad, she boarded a boat for Portsmouth, Virginia; thence to Weldon and Wilmington, North Carolina, by train and stagecoach; the remainder of the trip to Charleston and Savannah was by steamer. Accustomed to luxury and convenience, the English actress found the southward trip a torturous ordeal; she dwells at length on the inconveniences and inadequacies of accommodations encountered, and there are disdainful references to the landscape and towns en route.

Having arrived at the Butler plantation on the Sea Islands of Georgia, Kemble was in for a most unhappy sojourn there during the winter and spring of 1838–39. She had a profound antipathy for slavery before this visit, but her firsthand experiences with the "peculiar institution" intensified her prejudice, a prejudice which was further complicated by growing difficulties with her slaveowning husband. The actress, however, possessed an intense curiosity about the subject, and she kept a day by day account of what she saw of the Negroes in Georgia. Her *Journal of a Residence on a Georgian Plantation in 1838–1839* was put in the form of letters addressed to a New England friend, Elizabeth Dwight Sedgwick, but it was not published until the middle of the Civil War. It was then printed, according to Kemble, to counteract the pro-Southern sentiments of the English aristocracy. This book portrays the mistreatment of the unfortunate blacks and describes in minute detail the clothing, medical care, illiteracy, diseases, food, religious life, and difficulties of the slaves, especially those of the Negro women. Interspersed with bitter comments on slavery are excellent word pictures of the natural life and scenery of Georgia.

The English writer Harriet Martineau, who saw much of Kemble in the United States, read the proof sheets of Kemble's *Journal* and was so shocked by certain passages that the actress consented to cancel thirty pages of it. Although Martineau (*Autobiography*, I, pp. 275–76) admired her talent, she felt that there was a "radical unreality" about Kemble's words and deeds; in a striking analysis Martineau said that Kemble was "wasted and tortured by want of discipline, principle and self-knowledge."

A recent biographer, Leota S. Driver, in her *Fanny Kemble* (Chapel Hill, 1933), gives an almost antithetical analysis when she says that Kemble "refused to compromise with anything which she conceived to be wrong. To her, integrity was a virtue beyond comparison. Her beliefs, her ideas, her personality were sacred" (p. xiii). When Driver analyzes Kemble from a temperamental standpoint, however, her comments substantiate Martineau's analysis, for Driver characterizes the actress as "impulsive, self-willed, and individualistic." Margaret Armstrong's *Fanny Kemble, A Passionate Victorian* (New York, 1938) does little more than paraphrase the material given in Kemble's works. Her biography is less interpretative than Driver's. A brief, but sympathetic, treatment of Kemble's experiences in the South is also given by Dorothie Bobbé, *Fanny Kemble* (New York, 1931), pp. 121–46. Another summary account is to be found in Una Pope-Hennessy, *Three English Women in America* (London, 1929), pp. 184–208.

[148]

188. Kendall, George Wilkins (1809–1867)

Narrative of the Texan Santa Fé expedition, comprising a description of a tour through Texas, and across the great southwestern prairies, the Comanche and Caygüa hunting-grounds, with an account of the sufferings from want of food, losses from hostile Indians, and final capture of the Texans, and their march, as prisoners, to the city of Mexico . . . By Geo. Wilkins Kendall . . . 2 vols. New-York, Harper and brothers, 1844.

Vol. I, xii, 405 p.; Vol. II, xii, 406 p.   20½ cm.

Maps: One, folded, in front of Vol. I: "Texas and part of Mexico & the United States, showing the route of the first Santa Fe expedition." Drawn and engraved by W. Kemble, N. Y.

Illustrations: Five plates, including a frontispiece in each volume. All of the scenes are in the West or in Mexico. The preface contains a statement about the sources of the illustrations and the map.

Inclusive dates: May, 1841, to May, 1842. In South, May to June, 1841.

Other editions:

(1) London, Wiley & Putnam, 1844.

(2) ₁London, Sherwood, Gilbert, and Piper₁, etc.; Bristol, Office of the great western advertiser and chronicle, ₁1845?₁. iv, 599 p. 17 cm.

(3) Narrative of an expedition across the great southwestern prairies, from Texas to Santa Fé . . . 2 vols. London, D. Bogue, 1845. fronts., fold. map. 18 cm.

(4) 6th edition. 2 vols. New York, Harper & brothers, 1847. map, plates. 12mo.

(5) A new edition. London, Henry Washbourne, 1847. iv, 599 p. 8vo.

(6) 6th ed. 2 vols. New York, Harper and brothers, 1850. fronts., plates, map. 19½ cm.

(7) 7th ed. 2 vols. N. Y., 1856. Vol. I, ₁18₁, 452; Vol. II, ₁14₁, 11–442. map, 5 plates. (Best edition, contains two extra chapters, which are portions of Falconer's diary).

(8) Historical introduction by Milo Milton Quaife . . . Chicago, R. R. Donnelley & sons co., 1929. xxxiv, 585 p. front., fold. map, facsim. 17½ cm. (The Lakeside classics).

(9) 2 vols. Austin, Tex., the Steck company, 1935. plates, fold. map. 22 cm. (Original narratives or Texas history and adventure).

Location of copy: Library of Congress.

Four years after the establishment of the New Orleans *Picayune,* Kendall, one of its founders, sailed for Texas. He arrived on May 19, 1841, and spent the following month at Galveston, Houston, San Antonio, and Austin. Some sixty pages are devoted to the experiences of this month. Part of this time Kendall was accompanied by the English traveler Thomas Falconer (*q.v.*). Kendall then joined an expedition bound for Santa Fé, but most of its members were captured and taken to Mexico. After spending a time in prison, he regained his freedom and returned to New Orleans one year after he had left it.

Kendall in his preface charged Captain Frederick Marryat (*q.v.*) with having stolen some of his sketches from the *Picayune*, where they first appeared, and having incorporated them in *The Travels and Adventures of Monsieur Violet.*

For a life of Kendall, see Fayette Copeland, *Kendall of the Picayune* (Norman, Oklahoma, 1943). Kendall's *Narrative* was extremely popular in its day and deservedly so, for his experiences were exciting, and Kendall knew how to write. Unfortunately, Copeland makes no attempt to resolve the confusion in bibliographical works concerning the various editions of the *Narrative,* although he throws some light on Falconer's assistance to Kendall, especially in the preparation of an additional chapter for the seventh edition.

189. Kennedy, William (1799–1871)

Texas: the rise, progress, and prospects of the Republic of Texas . . . By William Kennedy, esq. . . . 2 vols. London, R. Hastings, 1841.

Vol. I, lii, 378 p.; Vol. II, vi, 548 p. maps (2 fold.). 22 cm.

Maps: Four, all in Vol. I: a large frontispiece map of Texas, chart of Matagorda Bay, plan of Aransas Bay, and map of Texas, indicating the Empresario system.

Inclusive dates: June, 1838, to the fall of 1839.

Other editions:

(1) Second edition. London, R. Hastings, 1841.

(2) New York, Benjamin and Young; Boston, sold by Redding & co.; ₍etc., etc.₎, 1844. x, 118 p. 20½ cm. (Reprinted from Vol. I, Book 1 of the author's Texas . . . London, 1840).

(3) New York, W. Jackson; Boston, sold by Redding & co.; ₍etc., etc.₎, 1844. 1 p.l., 118 p. 20½ cm. (Reprinted, with introduction omitted, from Vol. I, Book 1, of the author's Texas: the rise . . . London, 1841).

(4) William Kennedy's Geographie, Naturgeschichte und Topographie von Texas. Aus dem Englischen von Otto von Czarnoswky . . . Frankfurt am Main, J. D. Sauerländer, 1845. 212 p. fold. map. 22 cm.

(5) 2. verm. aufl. Mit einer Karte von Texas. Frankfurt am Main, J. D. Sauerländer, 1846. 180 p. fold. map. 21 cm.

Location of copy: University of North Carolina Library.

According to the *Dictionary of National Biography,* Kennedy was an Irish "poet and miscellaneous writer." His American experiences began with service in Canada under the command of the Earl of Durham during the latter half of the year 1838. That over, he spent a short time in Washington and then followed the coast to Texas, which he reached near the end of April, 1839. Two months later he started homeward, going up the Mississippi River and embarking at Baltimore. His two-volume work on Texas was written to enlighten Englishmen about the potential values of that country. It opens with forty pages of "Personal Narrative, and Introductory Remarks," which recount Kennedy's travels and some incidents along the way; the rest of the work is a substantial history and description of Texas derived chiefly from documents that he collected on his journey. Kennedy returned to Galveston to serve as British consul from 1841 to 1847.

The first volume, somewhat altered, was published in New York (Benjamin and Young) and Boston (Redding & Co.) in 1844 under the title: *Texas: Its Geography, Natural History and Topography.*

190. Lang, John Dunmore (1799–1878)

Religion and education in America; with notices of the state and prospects of American unitarianism, popery, and African colonization. By John Dunmore Lang . . . London, T. Ward and co., 1840.

> viii, 474 p. 16½ cm.
> *Inclusive dates:* Early months of 1840?
> *Location of copy:* Library of Congress.

Lang was born in Scotland, educated at the University of Glasgow, and ordained a minister in the Presbyterian church. In 1823 he emigrated to Australia and in time became a vigorous and uncompromising leader in ecclesiastical and political affairs (*Dictionary of National Biography*). When this book was written, he was senior minister of the Presbyterian church in New South Wales and principal of the Australian College. He came to the United States to interest Americans in the support of missionary work in Australia and in other British colonies in the southern hemisphere. He traveled through the seaboard states from Massachusetts to South Carolina; the Southern part of his itinerary included Baltimore, Fredericksburg, Richmond, Petersburg, Wilmington, and Charleston. He describes these towns and the countryside with emphasis on ecclesiastical affairs; he discusses the faculty, equipment, and endowment of two Presbyterian seminaries in the South, the Union Theological Seminary in Virginia and the Theological Seminary of Columbia, South Carolina; and he defends the voluntary system of church support as opposed to an ecclesiastical establishment. His itinerary is not dated; but he began to write this book in June, 1840, upon leaving the United States, and his tour probably did not occupy more than a few months.

[151]

191.   Lang, John Dunmore (1799–1878)

Report of a visit to some of the tribes of Indians, located west of the
Mississippi River. By John D. Lang and Samuel Taylor, jr. Providence,
printed by Knowles and Vose, 1843.

> 47 p.   21½ cm.
> *Inclusive dates:* September to December, 1842.
> *Other editions:*
>   New-York, press of M. Day & co., 1843.   34 p.   22 cm.
> *Location of copy:* Library of Congress. Bound in vol. entitled: Miscellaneous
> pamphlets, Vol. XIX, No. 7.

This is a report by Lang and Taylor to the New England and New
York Yearly Meetings of Friends about what they had learned of
religious conditions among some of the Indian tribes. A few pages
record their visit, toward the end of their trip, to the Cherokee, Creek,
and Choctaw tribes.

192.   Lardner, Dionysius (1793–1859)

Railway economy; a treatise on the new art of transport, its management, prospects, and relations, commercial, financial, and social, with
an exposition of the practical results of the railways in operation in
the United Kingdom, on the continent, and in America. By Dionysius
Lardner . . . New York, Harper & brothers, 1850.

> xxiii, [25]–442 p.   20 cm.
> *Inclusive dates:* Early 1840's.
> *Other editions:*
>   (1) London, Taylor, Walton and Maberly, 1850.   xxiii, 528 p., 1 l.,   19 cm.
>   (2) New York, Harper & brothers, 1856.
> *Location of copy:* Duke University Library.

Having been assessed 8,000 francs damages in an action for seduction,
Lardner, an Irishman, left for America in the early 1840's under something of a cloud. He was a versatile, lucid, and prolific writer on
scientific subjects; he was also a popular lecturer and is said to have
realized 40,000 francs from lectures in the United States. He wrote
little about his American experiences, which terminated about the
year 1845, but his treatise on *Railway Economy* includes a valuable
chapter on "Inland Transport in the United States." In it Lardner
claims to have traveled nearly twenty thousand miles by railroad in
the United States and to have found "the highest refinements of the
art of locomotion" even in so remote a place as "the back woods of
Mississippi" (pp. 328, 337). His biography is sketched in the *Dictionary of National Biography*.

193. Leclerc, Frédéric

Le Texas et sa révolution. Paris, impr. de H. Fournier et Cie., 1840.

104 p. map. 22 cm.

Maps: Folded map, entitled: "Carte du Texas Extraite de la grande Carte du Mexico Par A. Brue, géographe du Roi, revue, corrigée et considerablement augmentée, d'après des documens récens et des renseignemens fournis par M. le Docteur Fc. Leclerc."

Inclusive dates: 1838. In South, 1838.

Other editions:
In Revue des deux mondes. Paris, 1840. Ser. 4, Vol. XXI, p. 605–639; Vol. XXII, p. 220–253.

Location of copy: The New York Public Library.

Most of this work is a history of Texas; about a third is a description of its soil, crops, rivers, towns, and facilities for travel. How much of all this Leclerc saw with his own eyes cannot be determined; but it is at least clear that during the first six months of the year 1838 he visited Galveston Island, the mouth of the Colorado River, and Houston, and he traveled by steamboat some distance up the San Jacinto River. His impressions were altogether favorable, and he urged the French government to recognize the young republic. While the work is devoted entirely to Texas, the author mentions being in Cincinnati in June and July, 1837, and seeing immense fields of cotton *"sur la route de MontGomery (sic) à Charleston, dans l'Alabama et la Georgie."*

194. Levinge, Sir Richard George Augustus, Seventh Baronet (1811–1884)

Echoes from the backwoods; or, sketches of transatlantic life. By Captain R. G. A. Levinge . . . 2 vols. London, H. Colburn, 1846.

Vol. I, xvi, 293 p.; Vol. II, v, 258 p. 6 plates (incl. fronts.). 20½ cm.

Illustrations: Frontispiece and two other plates in each volume. All are hunting scenes or scenes of nature.

Inclusive dates: 1845. In South, 1845.

Other editions:
(1) London, George Routledge, 1847.
(2) London, J. & D. A. Darling, 1849. 2 vols. in 1.
(3) New edition, with illustrations. London, 1859.
(4) London, George Routledge and sons, 1860.

Location of copy: Library of Congress.

Data on the South can be found in the section of this work entitled: "Race through the United States" (II, pp. 4–67), which describes a trip down the Ohio and Mississippi rivers, and from New Orleans through Mobile and Pensacola to Charleston, where Levinge embarked for the North. He was critical of much that he found, especially the rude accommodations and the boastfulness of Americans. His comments on natural features and vegetation are superior in quality and accuracy to his observations about people.

195. Lewis, George, of Ormiston

Impressions of America and the American churches; from journal of the Rev. G. Lewis . . . Edinburgh, W. P. Kennedy; [etc., etc.], 1845.

viii, 432 p. 20½ cm.
Inclusive dates: February to July, 1844.
Location of copy: Duke University Library.

George Lewis, a Scotch Presbyterian minister, came to the United States as a member of a deputation sent by the Free Church of Scotland. Landing at Boston in February, 1844, he reached Washington early in March; thence he proceeded to Charleston and Columbia in South Carolina, Savannah and Augusta in Georgia, Montgomery and Mobile in Alabama, and on to New Orleans. After some days in New Orleans he went by river steamboat to St. Louis, stopping only at Natchez. He was at Louisville, Kentucky, for ten days in May attending the General Assembly of the Presbyterian Church, and then traveled in the North and in Canada until he sailed for England on July 1.

Lewis' account of the southern part of his American tour occupies about one-half of his book, and it reflects his interest in the Presbyterian church and religion in general, education, slavery, and the condition of American workmen and of emigrant Scotsmen. He included statistics taken from various compilations and recounts stories picked up along his route. But mostly he tells what he himself saw and experienced, and within the limits set by his interests he is one of the more informative as well as one of the more reliable and unprejudiced of the travelers.

196. Löwenstern, Isidore (1815–1858 or 1859)

Les États-Unis et la Havane; souvenirs d'un voyageur par m. Isidore Löwenstern . . . Paris, [etc.], A. Bertrand, [etc.], 1842.

xii, 372 p. 21 cm.
Inclusive dates: July, 1837, to January, 1838. In South, December, 1837, to January, 1838.
Location of copy: Library of Congress.

As part of a journey around the world, Löwenstern, an Austrian, traveled over parts of the United States. He landed at New York on

September 8, 1837, traveled northward, then as far south as Washington, D. C., where he turned west and went down the Mississippi River to New Orleans. On his way down he visited a cotton plantation in Arkansas. He was at New Orleans from December 20, 1837, to January 10, 1838, when he sailed for Havana. He was critical of American accommodations, particularly the food, but he was favorably impressed by Philadelphia and New Orleans, which he described in some detail. He was hostile to slavery, and he was inclined to judge America by European standards.

197. Logan James, Advocate, of Edinburgh

Notes of a journey through Canada, the United States of America, and the West Indies . . . Edinburgh, [etc.], Fraser and co., 1838.

xii, 259 p. front. (fold. map). 20½ cm.

Maps: One(folded frontispiece): "Map of Canada, United States of America & West Indies Shewing Mr. Logan's Route (in red) through those countries in 1836."

Inclusive dates: May, 1836, to June, 1837. In South, October, 1836, to February, 1837.

Location of copy: Library of Congress.

The emphasis in this travel work is upon information that might prove useful to emigrants. After traveling in Canada and visiting his brother there, Logan came to St. Louis, and, in October, 1836, he worked his way up the Ohio River loading wood and pig iron on a steamer.

A few weeks later he traveled from Baltimore to New Orleans, passing through Richmond, Columbia, Augusta, Montgomery, and other fall-line towns, and in February he left New Orleans for Cuba. His writing is compounded of descriptions of the places he visited, stories of his personal experiences, and discussions in general terms of morals, customs, and manners. Logan seems to be sincere, but neither discerning nor acute, in his observations.

198. Long, (Mrs.) Calista Rossa (Cralle) (1809?–1840)

Journal of Calista Cralle Long; a diary record of a forty-two day journey, Campbell co., Va., to Union co., Ky., Dec., 1836–Jan., 1837. Fayetteville, West Virginia, privately printed by Armistead Rosser Long, 1940.

cover title, 1 l., 17 (i.e., 19) p. 23 cm.

Inclusive dates: December 4, 1836–January 12, 1837. In South, the same.

Other editions:

("First printed in the Fayette Tribune-Democrat, August, 1940").

Location of copy: The New York Public Library.

This is a short, but good, record kept by a young woman who was one of a party of some forty persons who left Virginia for Kentucky in "the hope of being transplanted into a richer, kinder soil." The journey was rough, but the diarist records pleasant as well as unpleasant scenes and incidents.

199. Lyell, Sir Charles, Baronet (1797–1875)

Travels in North America; with geological observations on the United States, Canada, and Nova Scotia. By Charles Lyell . . . 2 vols. London, J. Murray, 1845.

Vol. I, [xv], 316 p.; Vol. II, viii, 272 p. col. fronts., illus., plates (part fold.), maps (part fold.), facsims. 20 cm.

Maps: Two, both colored: As frontispiece of Vol. II, a large, folded "Geological Map of the United States, Canada, &c.," and in Vol. I, there is a one-page "Map of the Niagara District."

Illustrations: Five which together with the two maps are known as plates. Several of these illustrations are colored; some cover a single page and others are folded; none show Southern scenes. The most ambitious is the folded frontispiece of Vol. I: "Birds-Eye View of the Falls of Niagara & Adjacent Country, Coloured Geologically." In addition to the seven plates, a number of drawings of geological sections are scattered through the two volumes. None pertain to the South.

Inclusive dates: First trip, August, 1841, to August, 1842. In South, December, 1841, to January, 1842. Second trip, September, 1845, to June, 1846. In South, December, 1845, to April, 1846.

Other editions:

(1) 2d ed. London, J. Murray, 1855.

(2) Travels in North America, in the years 1841–2 . . . New-York, Wiley and Putnam, 1845. 2 vols. in 1. illus., plate. 20 cm.

(3) New York, Wiley and Putnam, 1845. 2 vols. in 1. 5 plates (part fold., incl. col. front., Vol. I), 2 maps (incl. front., Vol. II). 19½ cm.

(4) New York, J. Wiley, 1852. 2 vols. in 1. illus., plate. 20 cm.

(5) Travels in North America, in the years 1841–2 . . . Without the larger plates . . . New York, Wiley & Halsted, 1856. 2 vols. in 1. illus., plate. 20½ cm.

(6) Lyell's travels in North America in the years 1841–2; abridged and ed. by John P. Cushing . . . New York, C. E. Merrill co., [c.1909]. 172 p. 17 cm. (Maynard's English classic series).

(7) Charles Lyell's Reisen in Nordamerika, mit Beobachtungen über die geognostischen Verhältnisse der Vereinigten Staaten, von Canada und Neu-Schottland. Deutsch von Dr. Emil Th. Wolff . . . Halle, C. Graeger, 1846. xii, 395, [1] p. front. (fold. map), plates (partly fold.). 22 cm.

Location of copy: Duke University Library.

Lyell came to America in August, 1841, to continue his investigations in geology and to give lectures on this subject in Boston. His fame was attested by the fact that his audiences averaged three thousand persons. His first field trips were made in the North and in Canada. On December 13, 1841, he was in Baltimore. From there he traveled through Richmond, Norfolk, the Dismal Swamp, and Charleston to Augusta, returning to Maryland near the end of January, 1842. In April and May he made a trip to Cincinnati, visiting Frederick, Harpers Ferry, Hagerstown, and Wheeling. In August he returned to England. While busying himself with the task of working the data he had collected into scientific papers, the idea occurred to him, as he explained in a lengthy and thoughtful letter to the historian George Ticknor, of writing an account of his American travels that would reflect his experiences and impressions as well as his geological discoveries. In the two-volume work that was the result of this decision, some ninety pages are devoted to his travels in the South.

Lyell's powers of close, accurate observation, coupled with his judicious temper, render his works on America among the best of his generation. He planned his main route and numerous side trips with care. The presence of his wife enabled him to check his observations and judgments by hers, and she was able to give him some information that he otherwise would have missed. Instead of trying to draw his data together in essays on various subjects, he usually put it down as he found it, frequently adding brief interpretative comments. Among the things that interested him in the South were geology, soil erosion, steamboats and other means of transportation, public opinion—especially on British-American relations—business, morality, social classes, and customs and etiquette. More than most travelers, he was able to see slavery as a matter of race relations as well as of servitude, and he compared the status of the Negro in the North with that of the Negro in the South.

The *Life, Letters and Journals of Sir Charles Lyell, Bart ... Edited by his Sister-in-Law, Mrs. Lyell* (2 vols., John Murray, London, 1881) publishes material that adds somewhat to our knowledge of Lyell's impressions of the South, and it contains the important letter to Ticknor mentioned above (II, pp. 66–71).

200. Lyford, William Gilman (1784–1852)

The Western address directory: containing the cards of merchants, manufacturers, and other business men, in Pittsburgh, (Pa.) (Wheeling, (Va.) Zanesville, (O.) (Portsmouth, (O.) Dayton, (O.) Cincinnati, (O.) Madison, (Ind.) Louisville, (K.) St. Louis, (Mo.) together with historical, topographical & statistical sketches, (for the year 1837,) of those cities, and towns in the Mississippi Valley. Intended as a guide to travellers. To which is added, alphabetically arranged, a list of the steam-boats on the Western waters. By W. G. Lyford. Baltimore, printed by J. Robinson, 1837.

> 468 p. 17½ cm.
> *Inclusive dates:* November 16, 1836, to March 20, 1837.
> *Location of copy:* Yale University Library.

> This work is a curious combination of several things: a traveler's guide to the Western cities, advertisements of businessmen in those cities, and a sketchy record of Lyford's journey, which began and ended at Baltimore, in search of the materials to make this book. The book is strung together in the form of letters.

201. Macready, William Charles (1793–1873)

The diaries of William Charles Macready, 1833–1851, edited by William Toynbee ... with forty-nine portraits ... 2 vols. London, Chapman and Hall, Ltd., 1912.

> Vol. I, xvi, 512 p.; Vol. II, vi, 543 p. fronts., ports. 23½ cm.
> *Illustrations:* 49 portraits: of Macready, his relatives, and his associates.
> *Inclusive dates:* American trip, September, 1843, to November, 1844. In South, January to March, 1844.
> *Other editions:*
>   *First published under title:*
>   Macready's reminiscences, and selections from his diaries and letters. Edited by Sir F. Pollock, Bart. 2 vols. London, Macmillan and co., 1875. 8vo.
>   New edition. London, 1876.
> *Location of copy:* Yale University Library.

> Of the several trips made to America by the English tragedian William Charles Macready, the record is most satisfactory for his tour that began in September, 1843. He spent the first three months of 1844 in the South, playing in Charleston, Mobile, and New Orleans (*Diaries,* II, pp. 245–67). While his diary naturally deals much with rehearsals, performances, and other theatrical matters, Macready met persons of importance, and he commented on slavery, dueling, and inconveniences of travel. His most enjoyable experience was a gin mint julep which he tried in New Orleans "by way of experiment" (II, p. 267). Before accepting this diary seriously, the reader should familiarize himself with the character of its author. His writing is strongly colored by his temperament.

202. Maissin, Eugène

Notes et documents sur l'expédition Française au Mexique ... suivi d'un aperçu général sur l'État actuel du Texas ...

In Blanchard, P. San-Juan de Ulùa, ou Relation de l'expédition française au Mexique, sous les ordres de M. le contre-amiral Baudin; par MM. P. Blanchard et A. Dauzats. Suivi de notes et documents et d'un aperçu général sur l'état actuel du Texas, par M. E. Maissin . . . Paris, Gide, 1839   illus., plate. p. 445–591.   28 cm.

Illustrations: Plates and illustrations all relate to Mexico; none to the South.
Inclusive dates: May, July, 1839. In South, the same.
Location of copy: Library of Congress.

There are fifteen "Notes and Documents." In Note XIII, Maissin describes a visit to Texas from May 2 to 14, 1839 (pp. 522–72). He came from Vera Cruz, describes Galveston, and narrates a journey to Houston. He wrote of these matters two days after leaving Texas, while at sea. He then summarized the history and government of Texas and discussed its geography, rivers, towns (especially Galveston and Houston), climate, customs, slavery, cotton, land office, commerce, population, military establishments, and religion.

In Note XIV, entitled "La Havane, Pensacola" (pp. 581–87), Maissin gives a brief description of Pensacola Bay, the fortifications and the town, which his ship visited on July 1, 1839.

203.   Manford, Erasmus

Twenty-five years in the West. By Erasmus Manford. Chicago, E. Manford, 1867.

2 p.l., [3]–359 p.   19 cm.
Inclusive dates: None given, but his journey South was apparently in 1836.
Location of copy: Library of Congress.

Pages 45–54 cover Manford's journey down the Ohio and Mississippi rivers to New Orleans, thence to Texas, and then on foot from Matagorda Bay to Houston. Manford intended to settle in Texas but changed his mind after arriving. He was a Universalist minister, and he was horrified by the moral laxities of frontier life. He returned by boat from Galveston to New Orleans and to Leavenworth, Indiana. He gives very few dates, not even that of his birth, but the last of his autobiography is dated October, 1866. The entire volume appears to have been written largely from memory. The author's account of his Southern journey describes personal incidents and hardships.

204.   Marryat, Captain Frederick (1792–1848)

A diary in America, with remarks on its institutions. By Capt. Marryat . . . 3 vols. London, Longman, Orme, Brown, Green & Longmans, 1839.

First series, first edition:
Vol. I, [4], 321 p.; Vol. II, [4], 319 p.; Vol. III, [4], 311, [1] p.   19½ cm.
Inclusive dates: May, 1837, through 1838.
Other editions:
    (1) 2 vols. Philadelphia, Carey & Hart, 1839.   19½ cm.
    (2) In Waldie's select circulating library . . . Philadelphia, 1833–42. Vol.
XIV (1839), p. 194–225.   29 cm.
    (3) 2 vols. Paris, Baudry, 1839. 8vo.
    (4) New-York, W. H. Colyer, 1839.   263 p.   19½ cm.
    (5) New York, Harper & brothers, 1839.   247 p.   12mo.
    (6) New York, D. Appleton & co., 1839.   263 p.   12mo.
Location of copy: Duke University Library.

A diary in America, with remarks on its institutions. Part second. By Capt. Marryat . . . 3 vols. London, Longman, Orme, Brown, Green & Longmans, 1839.

[Second series], first edition:
Vol. I, [4], 304 p.; Vol. II, [4], 293 p.; Vol. III, [4], 362 p.   fold. maps.
19½ cm.
Maps: Two, folded, in Vol. II: Frontispiece, "Portion of Middle Florida, shewing the seat of hostilities between Seminole Indians, and United States," and "Aboriginal America."
Inclusive dates: May, 1837, through 1838.
Other editions:
    (1) London, Longman, Orme, Brown, Green & Longmans, 1840.
    (2) Philadelphia, T. K. and P. G. Collins, 1840.   [2], 300 p.   12mo.
Location of copy: Duke University Library.

Before coming to America, Captain Marryat had served with distinction in the British Navy and had written several popular novels. The six-volume work on America which he published soon after his return to England was filled with facile and caustic criticisms of American institutions and customs. Its reception in the United States was wrathful, and it was censured at length in the *Edinburgh Review,* Vol. LXX, pp. 123–49. The first volume and most of the second give a running account of Marryat's travels and observations. This part of the work is entitled "Diary," and in it he describes society at the Virginia springs and some of the things he saw in Kentucky, especially cattle and mule fairs at Lexington. There is no evidence in the "Diary" or in the rest of the work, which is entitled "Remarks," that he traveled south of Lexington and the Virginia springs. Although the Remarks" include chapters on "Slavery," "The Mississippi," and other topics of Southern interest, they hardly deserve to be regarded as the record of a traveler because they are compiled from the books of previous travelers, various documents, hearsay stories, and Marryat's prejudices. Nevertheless, he tells some good stories and copies a few documents that may be used with caution.

205. Martineau, Harriet (1802–1876)

Retrospect of western travel. By Harriet Martineau . . . 2 vols. London, Saunders and Otley; New York, sold by Harper & brothers, 1838.

> Vol. I, [6], 13–276 p.; Vol. II, 239 p. 18½ cm.
>
> *Inclusive dates:* September, 1834, to August, 1836. In South, December, 1834, to July, 1835.
>
> *Other editions:*
> 3 vols. London, Saunders and Otley, 1838. Vol. I, vi [2], 318 p.; Vol. II, [6], 292 p.; Vol. III, [6], 293 p. 20½ cm.
>
> *Location of copy:* Duke University Library.

The eminent English writer and humanitarian Harriet Martineau landed in New York on September 19, 1834, with a mind that she felt was "as nearly as possible unprejudiced about America, with a strong disposition to admire democratic institutions, but an entire ignorance how far the people of the United States lived up to, or fell below, their own theory." In her *Autobiography* (2 vols., Boston, 1877), she asserts that it was at the suggestion of Lord Henley that she crossed the Atlantic to find out how Americans had succeeded in incorporating the principles of justice and mercy in their treatment of "the least happy classes of society." The bulk of her findings are presented in *Society in America* (3 vols., London, 1837; 2 vols., New York, 1837). On the whole, she was favorably impressed by what she saw in the new republic.

Society in America is a synthesis and an interpretation of Martineau's impressions organized in topical fashion with the subject matter divided into four major parts: politics, economy, civilization, and religion. The author's own criticism of this organization is pertinent: "The fundamental fault of the book . . . [is] its metaphysical framework, and . . . abstract treatment of what must necessarily be a concrete subject." (*Autobiography,* I, p. 405.) She does, however, illustrate her generalizations and interpretations with a number of specific incidents drawn from her two-year stay in America.

Miss Martineau spent six months in the South. Her Southern journeyings included a three-week stay in Baltimore and five weeks in Washington, where she visited the Supreme Court and Congress and met the leading figures of the day: Henry Clay, Daniel Webster, Chief Justice Marshall, and President Jackson. After stops at Charlottesville and Richmond, she spent two weeks in Charleston, ten days in Columbia, three days in Augusta, two weeks in Montgomery, and ten days in New Orleans. The return route northward was by steamer up the Mississippi River, with a visit to Mammoth Cave and a three-week sojourn at Lexington, Kentucky; after seeing the White Sulphur Springs and Natural Bridge of Virginia, she returned to New York.

Although most of the references to her experiences on this Southern trip are scattered through *Society in America,* there are several detailed passages: the description of her trip from Cincinnati to the Hot Springs of Virginia (I, pp. 176-93); her experiences as the guest of a wealthy Kentucky landowner (I, pp. 201-205); and her journey from Columbus, Georgia, to Montgomery, Alabama (I, pp. 212-31). There are also discussions of agriculture (I, pp. 299-307) and of the means of transportation in the South (II, pp. 2-11). An outspoken opponent of slavery, Martineau devotes much space to this question (I, pp. 347-95); in a chapter entitled "Morals of Slavery" (II pp. 106-36), she commends the slaveholders for instances of mercy, indulgence, and patience to the Negroes but wholeheartedly condemns the system as being essentially unjust.

A later work by this author, *Retrospect of Western Travel* (2 vols., London and New York, 1838), was allegedly written at the request of her readers who wanted more of the "personal narrative and of the lighter characteristics of men, and incidents of travel" than were given in *Society in America.* A considerable portion of *Retrospect* is devoted to the author's travels in the South. It describes her tour of Washington and Mount Vernon, her interview with Madison at his estate Montpelier, and her visit to the University of Virginia where she was hailed as the first British visitor (I, pp. 143-68, 185-208). She depicts "Country Life in the South" (I, pp. 208-23) and "City Life in the South" with especial reference to Charleston, South Carolina (I, pp. 224-41); and another attack on slavery is made in "Restless Slaves" (I, pp. 242-54). After a chapter on New Orleans (I, pp. 254-76), Miss Martineau sketches her trip back to Virginia partly by steamboat up the Mississippi and Ohio rivers (II, pp. 5-68).

In using Miss Martineau's works, several factors that may have affected her interpretations should be borne in mind. First, she was handicapped by her deafness, although she doubted that the accuracy of the information obtained was endangered since she used "a trumpet of remarkable fidelity." Secondly, previous to her American tour she had committed herself to the position that slavery was indefensible from an economic, social, and moral point of view. Finally, she thought she must be wary of what she heard and saw, because she believed that the "whole conduct and conversation of my southern entertainers showed an expectation of seeing in print all that was then passing."

206.   Martinez, Caro Ramón

Verdadera idea de la primera campaña de Tejas y sucesos ocurridos despues de la acción de San Jacinto, por D. Ramón Martinez Caro. México, impr. de Santiago Perez a cargo de A. Sojo, 1837.

vii, 162 p.   20 cm.
Inclusive dates: June, 1836, to August, 1837.
Location of copy: Library of Congress.

"The author was Santa Anna's private secretary. The book contains Santa Anna's report to the secretary of war and marine, never published entire in English, and many other interesting documents on Texas," says Raines in the *Texas Bibliography*, page 44.

Pages 1–69 contain the author's account of the campaign, and it deals chiefly with troop movements and actions with only enough description of the country to clarify the military narrative. Among the places mentioned are New Orleans, New Washington, Matamoras, Galveston, San Jacinto, San Luis Potosí, and Harrisburg. The narrative is continued on pages 139–58. Pages 73–138 contain letters, treaties, and other documents that pertain to the narrative.

207.   Mather, James

Two lectures, delivered at Newcastle-upon-Tyne, on the Constitutions and Republican institutions of the United States, including the legislative and executive powers, Representatives, Senate, State legislatures and governors, the suffrage, ballot, law, education, religion, newspapers, slavery, &c. &c., from data procured on a visit to that country. By James Mather . . . Newcastle-upon-Tyne, H. Gibb, 1840.

x, 90, [2] p.   18 cm.
Inclusive dates: 1840 or earlier. In South, the same.
Location of copy: Library of Congress.

These *Lectures* are not a travel account, but a general discussion of the United States, chiefly of its political organization. The author apparently visited Maryland and Virginia. The chapter on slavery shows a decided antislavery point of view, but even so, Mather considered the Negroes the happiest element of the population. He favored compensated emancipation.

208.   Maxwell, Archibald Montgomery

A run through the United States, during the autumn of 1840. By Lieut.-
Col. A. M. Maxwell, K. H. 2 vols. London, H. Colburn, 1841.

> Vol. I, xx, ₁1₁, 310 p.; Vol. II, xii, 261 p.   front. (port.).   19½ cm.
> *Illustrations:* Two: Major General Sir John Harvey (frontispiece of Vol. I)
> and General Winfield Scott (frontispiece of Vol. II).
> *Inclusive dates:* August to October, 1840.
> *Location of copy:* New York State Library (Albany).

In February, 1839, Lieutenant Colonel Maxwell, a Scotsman, was
placed in charge of British forces on the New Brunswick side of the
disputed frontier during the Aroostook War. After order had been
restored, he made a seven weeks' tour in the United States, beginning
at Boston on August 22, 1940. During the first five days in October
he visited Baltimore, Washington, Alexandria, and Mount Vernon;
and he wrote fifty pages about the crowded railroad train from Baltimore to Washington, the lovely scenery and the miserable road to
Mount Vernon, the appearance of the towns, the high prices charged
by hackney coachmen, social life in Washington, and a church service
at Alexandria. His tone is condescending but good-natured.

209.   McCalla, William Latta

Adventures in Texas, chiefly in the spring and summer of 1840; with
a discussion of comparative character, political, religious and moral;
accompanied by an appendix, containing an humble attempt to aid in
establishing and conducting literary and ecclesiastical institutions, by
W. L. McCalla . . . With consistency and prosperity, upon the good old
foundation of the favour of God Our Saviour. Philadelphia, printed for
the author, 1841.

> 8, ₁13₁–199 p.   15 cm.
> *Inclusive dates:* Spring and summer, 1840. In South, the same.
> *Location of copy:* Library of Congress.

About a third of this book recounts the author's experiences as he
wandered widely and rather aimlessly over Texas. McCalla was a
conservative and argumentative Presbyterian preacher who spent
much of his life in Pennsylvania. He devotes most of this book to
defending his religious opinions and to answering some of the critics
of Texan morals and manners.

210.

Mémoire présenté à Son Éminence le cardinal Fransoni préfet de la propagande par les ordres du souverain pontife, dans lequel l'expose l'état de mon diocèse en 1810, et celui où il est en 1836. ɪN.p., n.d.ɪ.

12 p. 28½ cm. (Photostatic reproduction).
Inclusive dates: 1810–1836. In South, the same.
Location of copy: The New York Public Library.

This pamphlet mentions the author's trip from Paris to Bardstown, Kentucky, and it briefly sketches his travels and ecclesiastical labors in Kentucky and neighboring regions within the dates given in his title. The concluding page presents a tabular comparison of the strength of the Roman Catholic church in the Diocese of Kentucky in 1810 and 1836.

Bound with the photostat of this pamphlet there is a photostat of a recent letter, suggesting that the pamphlet was probably printed in France in 1836.

211. **Merlin, Maria de las Mercedes (Jaruco), Comtesse de (1789–1852)**

La Havane par madame la comtesse Merlin . . . 3 vols. Paris, Librairie d'Amyot, 1844.

Vol. I, v, 366 p.; Vol. II, 431 p.; Vol. III, 488 p.   20 cm.
Inclusive dates: April to July, 1840. In South, May, 1840.
Other editions:
    (1) 5 vols. Bruxelles, Hauman, 1844.   8vo.
    (2) Viaje á la Habana por la condesa de Merlin, precedido de una biografía de esta ilustre Cubana por la señorita d.ª Gertrudis Gómez de Avellaneda. Madrid, Impr. de la sociedad literaria tipografía, 1844.   xvi, 109, ɪ2ɪ p. 22½ cm. (Tr. from the French).
    (3) Habana, ɪLibrería Cervantesɪ, 1922. 204 p. port. 19½ cm.
Location of copy: Duke University.

Less than twenty pages of Volume I contain the comments of this Havana-born Frenchwoman on Baltimore and Washington, where she spent several days in May, 1840; and she commented on too many things from too brief an experience for any of her comments about these two cities to have much value.

212. **Moore, Francis, Jr.**

Map and description of Texas, containing sketches of its history, geology, geography and statistics: with concise statements, relative to the soil, climate, productions, facilities of transportation, population of the country; and some brief remarks upon the character and customs of its inhabitants. By Francis Moore, Jr., editor of the Telegraph and Texas register. Philadelphia, H. Tanner junr.; New York, Tanner & D[i]sturnell, 1840.

> 143 p., 1 l. 8 plates (incl. front.), fold. map. 14½ cm.
> *Maps:* One, folded: "New map of Texas . . . by J. H. Young. Philadelphia: published by S. Augustus Mitchell. 1835."
> *Illustrations:* Eight full-page engravings: Front., "Ruins of the Alamo"; most of the others show missions. Two bear the words: "Sketched by W. Bissett."
> *Other editions:*
>   Description of Texas, containing sketches of its history, geology, geography and statistics . . . 2d ed. New York, T. R. Tanner, 1884. v, [5]–143 p. 16mo.
> *Location of copy:* Library of Congress.

This work is based mostly upon the author's observations during several years' residence in Texas. More than two-thirds of the pages are devoted to sketches of the various counties.

The second edition (T. R. Tanner, New York, 1844) does not deserve to be called another edition. It is a page by page reproduction of the first, in which the author did not take the trouble to correct the errors listed on the errata sheet of the first and did not even include that sheet. Neither does the second edition include any of the plates or the map of the first.

The folded map at the end of the first edition is missing from the Library of Congress copy, and nowhere else has a copy been found with the map in place. The Map Division of the Library of Congress contains the map described above. It is probably the missing map.

213. Moore, George (1806–1876)

Journal of a voyage across the Atlantic: with notes on Canada & the United States; and return to Great Britain, in 1844, by George Moore, esq. London, printed for private circulation, 1845.

> 4 p.l., 96 p. 18½ cm.
> *Inclusive dates:* August 17 to November 14, 1844.
> *Location of copy:* Library of Congress.

Moore was a prominent English businessman and philanthropist. His observations about America are mostly elementary and superficial except for comments on business methods. He traveled southward only as far as Baltimore and Washington.

214. Morris, Thomas Asbury, Bishop (1794–1874)

Miscellany: consisting of essays, biographical sketches and notes of travel. By Rev. T. A. Morris, D.D., one of the Bishops of the Methodist Episcopal Church. Cincinnati, published by L. Swormstedt & J. H.

Power, for the Methodist Episcopal Church, at the Western book concern, 1852.

390 p. front. (port.). 18½ cm.
Illustrations: Frontispiece picture of "Rev. Thomas A. Morris, one of the Bishops of the Methodist Episcopal Church."
Inclusive dates: 1826–1849. In South, chiefly, 1841–1842.
Other editions:
    Cincinnati, published by L. Swormstedt & A. Poe, for the Methodist Episcopal church, 1854.
Location of copy: Duke University Library.

Most of the materials in this book first appeared in various church papers. In the "Notes of Travel" there is a bit of information about the author's experiences as an itinerant Methodist preacher in Kentucky about the year 1826 and a brief account of a journey from Cincinnati to the Tennessee, Arkansas, Mississippi, and Alabama conferences in 1836. A more substantial contribution to Southern travel literature is the record, in the form of letters, of a trip from St. Louis to Texas, which began in October, 1841. Morris and several other Methodist preachers traveled in a covered wagon and a buggy, and his account of this journey naturally tells much about Methodist meetinghouses, schools, and conferences as well as the accommodations and experiences met with on the road. Morris' return journey began at Houston in January, 1842; he traveled by boat to New Orleans, where this series of letters is concluded.

215.   Newell, Chester

History of the Revolution in Texas, particularly of the War of 1835 & '36; together with the latest geographical, topographical, and statistical accounts of the country, from the most authentic sources. Also, an appendix. By the Rev. C. Newell. New-York, Wiley & Putnam, 1838.

2 p.l., ₍vii₎–x, 215 p. front. (fold. map). 19 cm.
Maps: One, folded: "Texas, 1838," lithographed by Baker, 8 Wall St., New York.
Inclusive dates: 1837–1838. In South, the same.
Other editions:
    Austin, the Steck Company, 1935. 4 p.l., ₍vii₎–x, 215 p. front. (fold. map). 21 cm. (Original narratives of Texas history and adventure. (A facsimile reproduction of the original).
Location of copy: Library of Congress.

According to the note "To the Reader," Newell's "work is the result of a twelvemonth's residence in Texas, whither the Author repaired in the Spring of 1837, for the benefit of his health." Although Newell presumably saw much, he wrote scarcely any part of this book as a firsthand observer. Instead, he presented his work in the form of an impersonal compendium of useful information, divided almost equally between history and description. This is one of the best, as well as one of the earliest, works published about Texas while it was a republic.

216.

The North American tourist. New York, A. T. Goodrich, [1839].

ix, 506 p. front., plate, fold. maps. 14½ cm.

Maps: Eight small folded maps, the following relating to the South: "Baltimore, Annapolis and adjacent country," "District of Columbia," and "Charleston and adjacent country." Three larger folded maps at the end of the volume, none relating exclusively to the South but containing some data about it.

Illustrations: Five plates, one of which includes a view of Harpers Ferry.

Location of copy: Library of Congress.

This traveler's guide gives information about routes, means of transportation, hotel facilities, cities, scenic features, and the extent of railroad lines. Pages 398–488 cover the South. Much of the information is organized about the main routes including, in the South, the "Grand Interior Route" from Baltimore to Wheeling and the "Main Southern Inland Route" from Baltimore to Montgomery, Alabama.

217.   Northup, Solomon (b. 1808)

... Twelve years a slave. Narrative of Solomon Northup, a citizen of New-York, kidnapped in Washington City in 1841, and rescued in 1853, from a cotton plantation near the Red River, in Louisiana. Auburn, Derby and Miller; Buffalo, Derby, Orton and Mulligan; etc., etc., 1853.

xvi, [17],–336 p. front., plate. 19½ cm.

Illustrations: Seven drawings, most of them imaginative, by N. Orr of New York, including a frontispiece "Portrait of Solomon in his plantation suit," and the musical score of the slave song, "Roaring River."

Inclusive dates: April, 1841, to January, 1853.

Other editions:

(1) Edited by D. Wilson. London, 1853.

(2) Auburn, 1854.

(3) New edition. Auburn, 1855.

(4) New York, C. M. Saxton, 1859.

(5) Twelve years a slave: the thrilling story of a free colored man, kidnapped in Washington in 1841, sold into slavery, and after twelve years' bondage, reclaimed by state authority from a cotton plantation in Louisiana. By S. Northup. Philadelphia, J. E. Potter and company 18—.

Published also under this title:

A freeman in bondage; or, twelve years a slave. (Companion story to "Uncle Tom's cabin.") A true tale of slavery days. By Solomon Northup. Philadelphia, Columbian publishing company, 1890. (Columbian library, No. 6).

Location of copy: Duke University Library.

The "Editor's Preface" indicates that this book was written by David Wilson of Whitehall, New York, as the story was told to him by Solomon Northup. While the whole book is a record of a twelve-year sojourn in the South by an unwilling traveler, the narrative of the transportation of the kidnapped free Negro from Washington, D. C., to Louisiana and of his movements inside Louisiana is especially pertinent to travel literature. The chief value of this book lies in the fact that whereas many travelers described the enforced movement of slaves in coffles and by boat, Northup was among the few who left a record of what it was like to be one of the slaves who was being compelled to travel about the South. The main defect in the work is the uncertainty about Wilson's contribution; one gets the impression that he was not content to write the narrative exactly as Northup told it to him.

218. O'Brien, Andrew Leary

The journal of Andrew Leary O'Brien; including an account of the origin of Andrew College, Cuthbert, Georgia. Foreword and notes by Annette McDonald Suarez . . . Athens, Georgia, the University of Georgia press, 1946.

> 1 p.l., vii–xiii, 76 p. front., illus. (facsims.). 23½ cm.
> *Illustrations:* Three: Frontispiece, drawing of "Andrew Female College as built in 1854," and two facsimile reproductions of pages in O'Brien's journal.
> *Inclusive dates:* April, 1837, to 1859. In South, December, 1839–1859.
> *Location of copy:* Duke University Library.

O'Brien landed at New York in June, 1837, shortly before his twenty-second birthday. Behind him were County Cork and Irish parents of small means who had wanted him to enter the Catholic priesthood. With a view to carrying out their wishes, he entered Chambly College in Lower Canada. When political riots closed that institution in November, he found work as a stonemason in New York and Pennsylvania. He came to Charleston, South Carolina, in December, 1839, but soon left for Augusta. A minor incident on the way turned him to schoolteaching, and he continued to teach in South Carolina, Georgia, and Florida until 1859, when this record ends. In 1845 he became a member of the Methodist Episcopal church. O'Brien wrote chiefly about his life as a pedagogue, but he also commented on politics, family events, assistance to relatives who followed him to America, a trip to Florida, and other things. He fitted into the life of the South too well to leave a first-rate travel account, for he seldom wrote like a stranger looking at society from the outside.

While the record here published is in chronological form, it is not a contemporary diary. Instead, O'Brien compiled it for his children from his "note books and books of acct."

219.   Oliver, William

Eight months in Illinois; with information to emigrants. By William Oliver . . . Newcastle-upon-Tyne, printed by W. A. Mitchell, and sold by E. & T. Bruce, ₍etc.₎, 1843.

> 3 p.l., iv, 141, ₍1₎ p.   20 cm.
> *Inclusive dates:* December, 1841, to September, 1842.
> *Other editions:*
>   Chicago, Walter M. Hill, 1924.   260 p.   20 cm.
> *Location of copy:* Duke University Library.

Oliver did not go farther south than to touch at some of the towns on the lower bank of the Ohio River. Hence, his excellent account contains little about the South except comments on the tension created when the subject of slavery was introduced into conversation, his impressions of a Southern planter, the merits of Kentucky rifles, and a tavern brawl in which two "Kentucks" were involved, one of whom was "as ugly a fellow as I ever saw."

220.   Orr, Jehu Amaziah

A trip from Houston to Jackson, Miss., in 1845. By J. A. Orr.

> In Mississippi historical society publications, Vol. IX (1906). Oxford, printed for the Society.   p. 173–178.
> *Inclusive dates:* Summer, 1845.
> *Location of copy:* Duke University Library.

These are an old and distinguished man's recollections of a trip made when he was seventeen years old to attend the state convention of the Democratic party, which met at Jackson, Mississippi, on July 5, 1845. The brief record has modest value as a commentary on the economic depression and on political conditions. A sketch of Orr's life is in the *Dictionary of American Biography*.

221.   Page, Frederic Benjamin

Prairiedom; rambles and scrambles in Texas or New Estrémadura. By a Suthron . . . New York, Paine & Burgess, 1845.

> 2 p.l., ₍iii₎–vi p., 1 l., ₍11₎–166 p.   front. (fold. map).   17½ cm.
> *Maps:* Folded map of "Mexico" with an inset map of "Texas."
> *Other editions:*
>   Second edition. New York, Paine & Burgess, 1846.
> *Location of copy:* The New York Public Library.

Although the author includes some of his experiences on the road, this work is organized as a description of Texas rather than as a traveler's log. His tone is favorable, and it may be significant that his last chapter is a description of "Salinilla Springs." His descriptions of towns, scenes, and travel routes have minor value. The introductory "Advertisement" is dated October, 1845, and the text refers to the "re-annexion" of Texas as an accomplished deed.

222.   Pencil, Mark [*pseud.*]

White Sulphur papers; or, life at the springs of western Virginia. By Mark Pencil, esq. New-York, S. Colman, 1839.

xi, [13]–166 p.   19 cm.
Location of copy: Library of Congress.

This is partly a guidebook, partly promotional literature, and partly "fine" writing; for the author believed that "information . . . is generally best received when it comes in a pleasing form." The small amount of factual information is heavily interspersed with romantic descriptions of life at the springs.

223.   Peters, John

John Peters' diary of 1838–1841, ed. by Margaret L. Brown.

In Mississippi valley historical review, Vol. XXI (1935). Cedar Rapids, Iowa, Mississippi valley historical association. p. 529–542. 25½ cm.
Inclusive dates: November, 1838, to March, 1841.
Location of copy: Duke University Library.

John Peters, born at Fishkill, New York, in 1812, became a dry-goods merchant in Brooklyn. Driven out of business by the panic of 1837, he secured employment in a mercantile firm at Vicksburg, Mississippi. The diary which he kept at that place deals chiefly with business conditions during the depression.

224.   [Playfair, Hugo] R. N. [*pseud.?*]

The Playfair papers, or; brother Jonathan, the smartest nation in all creation . . . 3 vols. London, Saunders and Otley, 1841.

Vol. I, iv, 311 p.; Vol. II, 311 p.; Vol. III, 336 p.   fronts., 5 plates (part col.). 21 cm.
Illustrations: Vol. I, frontispiece (plate), double title-page with one illustration, three colored plates; Vol. II, four colored plates; Vol. III, two colored plates.
Inclusive dates: About 1840.

Other editions:

Brother Jonathan, the smartest nation in all creation. By Hugo Playfair. 3 vols. London, Saunders and Otley, 1844. Vol. I, iv, 311 p.; Vol. II, [2], 339 p.; Vol. III, [2], 311 p. 9 plates by Robert Cruikshank.

Originally issued in monthly parts, under following title:

Brother Jonathan: or the "smartest nation in all creation." Sketches of American life and manners, selected from the papers of Mr. Hugo Playfair, late an Officer in the Royal Navy of England. Edited by Paul Paterson . . . London, 1840–41.

Location of copy: Library of Congress.

A superficial record, containing much dialogue and trivial incident. The author looks on all Americans as vulgar, ignorant, boasting, and ungrammatical. Most of the plates are caricatures of American scenes and life. Volume II, pages 17–28 and 83–206, describes Baltimore and Washington, with some attention to prominent persons at the capital. The remainder of the work is devoted to the East and Canada. The author is decidedly hostile to slavery, and gives (II, pp. 54–82) a number of instances of miscegenation in Virginia.

The Library of Congress Catalog card contains the following note: "Originally issued in monthly parts, 1840–41, under title: Brother Jonathan: or the 'Smartest nation in all creation.'

225. Potter, Woodburne

The war in Florida: being an exposition of its causes, and an accurate history of the campaigns of Generals Clinch, Gaines, and Scott . . . By a Late Staff Officer. Baltimore, Lewis and Coleman, 1836.

viii, 184 p. front. (fold. map), fold. plans. 19½ cm.

Maps: One, folded: "A map of the seat of war in Florida, 1836." An unusually good map of this area.

Illustrations: Two folded plans: "Battle and Massacre ground of Major Dade and Command Dec. 28th, 1835" and "Camp Izard on the Ouithlacoochee River Feb. 29, 1836."

Inclusive dates: January to April, 1836. In South, the same.

Location of copy: Yale University Library.

This is one of the better works produced by the participants in the Seminole War of 1836. It is almost equally divided between the "Exposition of Its Causes" and the "History of the Campaigns." In writing of the campaigns, the author does not trace his own movements in detail or give intimate personal touches. On the other hand, he seems to be careful to keep his facts straight, and he describes with much care several events that he witnessed.

226. [Putnam, George W.]

Four months with Charles Dickens. During his first visit to America (in 1842). By his secretary.

> In Atlantic monthly, Vol. XXVI (1870). Boston, Fields, Osgood & co. p. 476–482, 591–599. 23 cm.
> *Inclusive dates:* January to June, 1842.
> *Location of copy:* Duke University Library.

This account, published anonymously soon after Dickens' death, treats the Southern part of the journey briefly and adds but little to what Dickens wrote in his *American Notes.*

227. Raumer, Friedrich Ludwig Georg von (1781–1873)

America and the American people. By Frederick von Raumer . . . Tr. from the German, by William W. Turner. New-York, J. & H. G. Langley, 1846.

> 512 p. fold. table. 22½ cm.
> *Inclusive dates:* April to September (?), 1844.
> *Other editions:*
> *First published in German as:*
> (1) Die Vereinigten Staaten von Nordamerika. Von Friedrich von Raumer . . . 2 vols. Leipzig, F. A. Brockhaus, 1845. Vol. I, xxiv, 552, [1] p.; Vol. II, xii, 540, [1] p. map, 4 fold. tables. 17½ cm.
> (2) Die Vereinigten Staaten von Nordamerika, von Friedrich von Raumer . . . Philadelphia, J. H. Schwacke und comp., 1846. 2 pts. in 1 vol. fold. table. 23 cm.
> (3) De Vereenigde Staten van Noord-Amerika, door F. von Raumer, naar de nieuwste bronnen en berigten bijen omgewerkt . . . 2 vols. Te Deventer, bij A. Ter Gunne, 1849. Vol. I, xii, 324 p.; Vol. II, [6], 344 p. fold. table. 23 cm.
> *Location of copy:* Duke University Library.

Having occupied the chair of history in the University of Berlin for twenty-five years and having written authoritatively in several fields of history, Baron von Raumer was one of the most scholarly visitors to the United States in the 1840's. His *America* is obviously the work of an experienced historian who was chiefly interested in politics and education. The main body of the work consists of a history of the United States and essays on phases of American life worked up from printed sources with a few of von Raumer's firsthand observations thrown in (e. g., pp. 117, 123). The last ninety pages contain "Extracts from Letters Written during My Tour," with dates ranging from April 22 to September 29, 1844. Those dated in May and early June describe two visits to Baltimore and Washington and an intervening trip to Charleston and Columbia, South Carolina. He spent the last week in June in Kentucky. For an extended sketch of von Raumer's life, see *Allgemeine Deutsche Biographie.*

228.   Regan, John

The emigrant's guide to the western states of America; or, backwoods and prairies: containing a complete statement of the advantages and capacities of the prairie lands—full instructions for emigrants in fitting out; and in selecting, purchasing, and settling on, sic land—with particulars of farming and other business operations, etc., etc. By John Regan ... 2d ed., rev. and enl. Edinburgh, Oliver & Boyd; etc., etc., 1852.

> vii, [6], [9]–408 p.   front., 4 illus.   17 cm.
> *Illustrations:* Four: Frontispiece, "Backwoods Village," "A Prairie," "Backwoods Log House," "Clearing."
> *Inclusive dates:* March, 1842, to 1852.
> *Other editions:*
>   *First edition published in:*
>   Edinburgh, [1842].
> *Location of copy:* Knox College Library.

An intelligent, lively, and circumstantial account of life in Illinois by a former teacher of Ayrshire who had emigrated to America and who was seeking to encourage other Britishers to do likewise. Only a few pages relate to the South. They recount Regan's experiences, which were in no way remarkable, at New Orleans and on the Mississippi River when he was entering the United States in late April and early May, 1842.

229.   Richards, Thomas Addison (1820–1890)

Tallulah and Jocassee; or, romances of Southern landscape, and other tales. By T. Addison Richards. Charleston, S. C., Walker, Richards & co., 1852.

> 2 p.l., 255 p.   19 cm.
> *Inclusive dates:* Early 1840's.
> *Location of copy:* Duke University Library.

Thomas Addison Richards gained the reputation of being one of the best landscape painters of his time. His career began in Georgia and South Carolina, where he lived for a time before moving to the North about the year 1845. *The Orion,* edited by his brother William Carey Richards *(q.v.),* contained "the first efforts of his pencil" (II, p. 251). These were mostly scenes of rivers and mountains, though they include Madison Springs (a Georgia summer resort) and several Charleston, South Carolina, views. For most of these illustrations Richards did the plate work as well as the drawing. He also drew the thirteen illustrations of *Georgia Illustrated in a Series of Views,* but he did not engrave all of these. About half of them were of public buildings, the rest were landscapes. He wrote descriptions to accompany some of the drawings in these two works. He also wrote local-color fiction for *The Orion,* and some of it was reprinted in *Tallulah and Jocassee; or, Romances of Southern Landscape, and Other Tales* (Charleston, 1852). The following year this book was brought out in Philadelphia with a new title-page (*Summer Stories of the South*) and a different binding, but the sheets seem to have been the unsold remainder of the Charleston edition. One of the sketches in this book is entitled: "The Travellers' Club; or Lights and Shadows of Locomotion."

230.   Richards, William Carey (1818–1892)

Georgia illustrated in a series of views, embracing natural scenery and public edifices, engraved on steel by Rawdon, Wright, Hatch and Smillie, from sketches made expressly for this work, by T. Addison Richards. Accompanied by historical and topographical sketches, by our own writers. Edited by William C. Richards . . . Stereotype ed. Penfield, Ga., W. & W. C. Richards, 1842.

> 3 p.l., 44 p.   12 plates.   26½ cm.
> *Inclusive dates:* Early 1840's.
> *Other editions:*
>   Originally published in parts, January to November, 1841.
> *Location of copy:* Duke University Library.

William Carey Richards came to America in 1831 with his father, William Richards, who was an English Baptist minister. In 1835 the family moved to South Carolina and soon afterward to Penfield, Georgia. There William Carey edited the work mentioned above. He himself contributed descriptions of "The Rock Mountain," "The Falls of Tallulah," "The Falls of Towaliga," and "The Lover's Leap." He also established and edited one of the better literary periodicals of the South in this day, namely, *The Orion: A Monthly Magazine of Literature, Science, and Art.* The first number appeared in March, 1842, at Penfield; it was moved to Charleston in March, 1844, and died with the August issue, before the completion of the fourth volume. Richards wrote some of the material in *The Orion;* among it was his "Notes of a Month's Tour on the Sea Board" (I, pp. 186–91), which was a brief and informal account of a steamboat trip from

Savannah, Georgia, to Jacksonville, Florida. A trip into the up-country of Georgia and South Carolina furnished him with material for another short contribution entitled: "Notes of a Summer Tour" (II, pp. 181–85).

231. Ries, Julius

Schilderungen des Treibens im Leben und Handel in den Vereinigten Staaten und Havana, gesammelt auf Reisen in den Jahren 1838 und 1839. Von Julius Ries. Berlin, Selbstverlag des Verfassers, 1840.

> x, 236, [2] p. 20½ cm.
> *Inclusive dates:* 1838–1839. In South, 1839.
> *Location of copy:* Library of Congress.

Ries's itinerary was from New York to Havana, to New Orleans, thence up the Mississippi and Ohio rivers to Philadelphia and New York. He describes points of interest in New Orleans, but he is chiefly interested in business, trade, and finance. He comments on steam-boats and other river craft, and he compares the scenery on the Mississippi River with that on various German rivers. Louisville is given brief comment. The last two chapters deal with trends in British and American trade and contain comments on American life, based chiefly, however, on his observations in New York City.

232. [Rogers, Rev. George]

Memoranda of the experience, labors, and travels of a Universalist preacher. Written by himself. Cincinnati, J. A. Gurley, 1845.

> 400 p. 19½ cm.
> *Inclusive dates:* December, 1836, to April, 1844.
> *Location of copy:* Duke University Library.

Born a Philadelphian and reared an Episcopalian, Rogers changed his abode and his theology and became an itinerant Universalist preacher. In December, 1834, he moved with his family to the Ohio Valley; and in quick succession he settled at Cincinnati as the pastor of a Universalist congregation, became assistant editor of the *Sentinel and Star in the West,* resigned his pastorate, and resumed the life of an itinerant preacher, with occasional visits to his family in Cincinnati. During the next ten years he traveled widely in the West, the South, and the Northeast, eking out a living from the contributions of those who heard his discourses and from the sale of religious books, some of which he had written. His first Southern tour began in December, 1836. By April of the following year he had traveled more than 1,400 miles by horseback in Kentucky and Tennessee and in the northern parts of Alabama and Mississippi, where Joseph G. Baldwin was then writing the sketches that were to compose *The Flush Times of Alabama and Mississippi*. By 1844, Rogers had made more than half a dozen tours through these states and southward as far as New Orleans. His account of these travels has great value, for he gave exact statements about persons and places, and he traveled on the backroads to out-of-the-way hamlets as well as on steamboats to the larger cities. Besides recounting the varied responses to his preaching, he found space for comments on Indians and slaves, poor people and planters, preachers, taverns, steamboat explosions, and many other things that he saw or experienced.

233. Salzbacher, Joseph (1790–1867)

Meine Reise nach Nord-Amerika im Jahre 1842. Mit statistischen Bemerkungen über die Zustände der katholischen Kirche bis auf die neueste Zeit. Von Dr. Joseph Salzbacher, Domkapitular zu St. Stephan in Wien. Mit einer geographischen Karte der katholischen Diöcesen und deren Missionsorte in Nord-Amerika. Der Ertrag ist zum Besten der deutsch - katholischen Missionen von Nord - Amerika gewidmet. Wien, In Commission bei Wimmer, Schmidt & Leo, 1845.

> viii p., 2 l., 479, [1] p., 1 l., xii p. fold. map. 22 cm.
> *Maps:* One folded map with colored boundaries, entitled: "Karte der katholischen Diöcesen und deren Missionen in Nordamerika nach den neuesten geographischen Angaben zusamengestellt und herausgegeben von Dr. Joseph Salzbacher . . . 1845."
> *Inclusive dates:* 1842. In South, 1842.
> *Location of copy:* Duke University Library.

Salzbacher's itinerary was from New York southward through Baltimore and Richmond to Charleston, South Carolina; westward to Pittsburgh, Louisville, and St. Louis; and thence to Detroit, Buffalo, Albany, and back to New York. He gives some description of his travel experiences and of the cities he visited. His chief interest was in the Catholic church, although he includes some information about other religious sects, charitable institutions, and literary and cultural organizations. His comments on Catholic activities at Mobile, New Orleans, Natchez, and Nashville are apparently not based on actual visits to those places.

234. Scherpf, G. A.

Entstehungsgeschichte und gegenwärtiger Zustand des neuen, unabhängigen, amerikanischen Staates Texas. Ein Beitrag zur Geschichte, Statistik und Geographie dieses Jahrhunderts. Im Lande selbst gesammelt von G. A. Scherpf. Mit zwei Karten ... Augsburg, Matth. Rieger, 1841.

> vi p., 1 l., 154 p. maps. 20½ cm.
> *Maps:* Two folded maps at end: "Karte von Texas entworfen nach den Vermessungen welche in den Acten der General-Land-Office der Republic liegen bis zum Jahr 1839 von Richard S. Hunt & Jesse Randel. Augsburg, 1841" and "Karte vom Rio Grande und dem West Land am Stillen Ocean."
> *Location of copy:* Library of Congress.

The first fifty pages deal with colonization and the Texan Revolution. The remainder describe government, climate, products, rivers, harbors, cities, trade, and finance; and the book concludes with a meteorological table showing temperature, wind, and weather from March to September (1839 ?).

235.   Silliman, Augustus Ely (1807–1884)

A gallop among American scenery; or, sketches of American scenes and military adventure, by Augustus E. Silliman. New-York, D. Appleton & co., 1843.

> 4 p.l., 267 p. illus. 18½ cm.
> *Illustrations:* Title vignette; tailpiece vignette (p. 231).
> *Inclusive dates:* Before 1843.
> *Other editions:*
>   New York, A. S. Barnes & co., 1881. 340 p. 16mo.
> *Location of copy:* Library of Congress.

The author was a prominent New York financier (*National Cyclopaedia of American Biography,* VI, p. 231) and a nephew of the distinguished Benjamin Silliman, Sr., of Yale University. His book is a curious potpourri of sketches, some dealing with incidents of the Revolutionary War and of the War of 1812 and some dealing with travel experiences. Southern topics treated include a plantation on the Potomac and Mount Vernon. This material should be used only with caution, for the author states that his work is "tinged by the imagination." Sketches are undated, but extracts of letters in the appendix are dated January 15, 1841, and February 16, 1843.

236.   Simms, William Gilmore (1806–1870)

The geography of South Carolina; being a companion to the history of that state by William Gilmore Simms. Compiled from the latest and best authorities, and designed for the instruction of the young. Charleston, Babcock & co., 1843.

viii, [9]–192 p., incl. tables. 17 cm.
Location of copy: Library of Congress.

Although planned for school use, even to the point of being supplied with questions to be asked of pupils, this little book might well have served as a guide for travelers to South Carolina. Most of the book consists of descriptions of the geography, climate, resources, economic activities, and towns of the several districts of the state.

237.

Sketch of the Seminole War, and sketches during a campaign. By a Lieutenant, of the Left Wing. Charleston, [S. C.], Dan J. Dowling, sold by J. P. Beile and W. H. Berrett, etc., 1836.

iv p., 1 l., 311 [1] p. 19 cm.
Inclusive dates: February to April, 1836. In South, the same.
Location of copy: Duke University Library.

The unknown author states that the first part of his work, the "Sketch of the Seminole War," is mostly "the result of the tedious labor of compilation." The rest of it, which begins on page 111 and is entitled "Sketches during a Campaign," recounts his experiences in an expedition which left Charleston, S. C., on February 10, 1836, for Florida, where it fought mosquitoes, rain, swamps, measles, and Seminoles until the end of April. The writing is of uneven quality, but some of it is sprightly. The book contains a little information about sugar plantations and much about Florida botany.

This work has been attributed to Meyer M. Cohen, author of *Notices of Florida and the Campaigns,* but the evidence is unconvincing. Nevertheless, the two books have much in common.

238.

Sketch of Western Virginia; for the use of British settlers in that country . . . London, E. Bull, 1837.

vi p., 1 l., 117, [1], 6 p. fold. map. 17 cm.
Maps: One folded, colored map: "Map of the counties of Monongalia, Tyler, Harrison, Wood, Lewis & Randolph, the North Western portion of Virginia, one of the United States of North America, shewing the situations of lands for sale by private contract."
Location of copy: Library of Congress.

The avowed purpose of this little work, probably written by an Englishman, was to induce British emigration to western Virginia, and the tone of the work is therefore favorable. It describes the mineral resources, climate, fauna, population, political institutions, internal improvements, and agricultural practices of this section. An appendix contains descriptions of these counties as given in Joseph Martin, *A New and Comprehensive Gazetteer of Virginia* ... (Charlottesville, Va., 1835).

239.   Smith, J. Gray

A brief historical, statistical and descriptive review of East Tennessee, United States of America: developing its immense agricultural, mining, and manufacturing advantages, with remarks to emigrants. Accompanied with a map & lithographed sketch of a Tennessee farm, mansion house, and buildings. By J. Gray Smith, a naturalized citizen of the United States of America. London, J. Leath, 1842.

> xii, 71 p.   front. (fold. map), fold. plate.   21 cm.
> *Maps:* One large, folded map: "Map of East Tennessee, forming the eastern portion of Tennessee, one of the United States of North America."
> *Illustrations:* One, folded: "View of Mossy Creek Farm, Jefferson County Tennessee, U. S. America." The map and the view are both by J. R. Robbins.
> *Other editions:*
>   London, C. Mitchell, 1843.   24 p.   8vo.
> *Location of copy:* The New York Public Library.

The foreword, dated at London on July 21, 1842, advocates British emigration to America. The author claims to have resided some years in the valley of east Tennessee, but his work tells none of his own experiences. Instead, he describes east Tennessee, includes numerous statistics, lists the types of occupations that would insure ready employment, gives advice to prospective emigrants, and concludes with an eleven-page quotation from J. S. Buckingham's description of the region.

240.   Smith, Solomon Franklin (1801–1869)

The theatrical journey-work and anecdotal recollections of Sol. Smith, comedian, attorney at law, etc., etc. Comprising a sketch of the second seven years of his professional life; together with sketches of adventure in after years; with a portrait of the author ... Philadelphia, T. B. Peterson, [c. 1854].

> 1 p.l., 7–254 p.   front. (port.).   18½ cm.
> *Illustrations:* One: Frontispiece portrait of the author.
> *Inclusive dates:* In South, intermittently, 1823–1853.
> *Location of copy:* Duke University Library.

Of the three books written by Sol Smith, the one listed above is richest in material about travel in the South. An earlier volume, *The*

Theatrical Apprenticeship and Anecdotical Recollections . . . A Sketch of the First Seven Years of His Professional Life . . . (Philadelphia, 1846, and later editions), recounts the first twenty-six years of his life and his first seven years on the stage. Besides making brief reference to wandering to Louisville and Nashville, he tells in some detail of a theatrical tour through Kentucky in 1826 and 1827.

The Theatrical Journey-Work covers the years 1827 to 1835 when Smith traveled widely over the South and played in virtually every town of importance in the lower Mississippi Valley, Alabama, and Georgia. Since he traveled as actor and manager, Smith naturally wrote mostly about the stage, but he includes much information, chiefly in the form of ludicrous or dramatic incidents, about steamboats and stages, inns and taverns, and the customs and attitudes of the people.

241.   Solms-Braunfels, Karl, Fürst zu (1812–1875)

Texas, 1844–1845, by Carl, prince of Solms-Braunfels; translated from the German. Houston, Tex., the Anson Jones press, 1936.

7 p.l., 141, [3] p., incl. front. (port.), illus. (incl. plates). 28 cm.

Maps: Two maps reproduced as end sheets: "Map of the north-western part of Texas, received from the general Land Office in 1845" and "Karte von Texas entworfen nach den Vermessungen der General-Land-Office der Republic," from originals published at Frankfurt a.M. by J. D. Sauerländer. Plans of Friedrichsburg and New Braunfels, reproduced from the original German edition. Also an envelope pasted in the back of the copy examined contains ten plates and maps relating to the Texas War of Independence.

Illustrations: A portrait of the author and three landscapes showing settlements made in Texas by German immigrants.

Inclusive dates: May, 1844, to July, 1845.

Other editions:

   First published in Frankfurt am Main, under following title:

   Texas. Geschildert in Beziehung auf seine geographischen, socialen und übrigen Verhältnisse mit besonderer Rücksicht auf die deutsche Colonisation. Ein Handbuch für Auswanderer nach Texas. Seinen deutschen Landsleuten gewidmet von Carl, Prinzen zu Solms-Braunfels. Nebst zwei Karten von Texas. Frankfurt am Main, Johann David Sauerländers Verlag, 1846. x, 134 p. 2 fold. maps. 8vo.

Location of copy: Duke University Library.

Prince Solms-Braunfels left Germany in the middle of May, 1844, landed at Boston, and after traveling down the Mississippi River, reached Galveston, Texas, on July 1. He came as commissioner general of the Association for the Protection of German Immigrants in Texas, which had been organized to sponsor the establishment of a German colony in Texas. He left in May, 1845, and returned to Germany in July.

[181]

This work contains such information as the author thought would be useful to German immigrants. While it is not cast in the form of a travel narrative, some of it is evidently based on the observations and experiences of Solms-Braunfels.

242. Steele, Mrs. Eliza R.

A summer journey in the West. By Mrs. Steele . . . New York, J. S. Taylor and co., 1841.

> 3 p.l., [13]–278 p. 18½ cm.
> *Illustrations:* One: Vignette of railroad train on the half-title page.
> *Inclusive dates:* June 14 to July 27, 1840.
> *Location of copy:* University of Kentucky Library.

The parts of this book which deal with the South are the records of a steamboat trip up the Ohio River between July 16 and 23, 1840, and of a brief stay in Baltimore. The author was then returning toward New York after a tour in the West. This section of the book is of scant value; it relates inconsequential incidents of travel, it comments on the scenery along the Ohio, and it briefly describes Louisville and Wheeling. Little is known of the author, except that she wrote *Heroines of Sacred History* (New York, 1841).

243. Stewart, Catherine

New homes in the West. By Catherine Stewart . . . Nashville, Cameron and Fall, 1843.

> iv, [5]–198 p. 17½ cm.
> *Inclusive dates:* 1830–1842. In South, late 1830's?
> *Location of copy:* Library of Congress.

The author was enthusiastic over the beauties and opportunities of the West; her descriptions of scenery are unusually effective. The itinerary was chiefly through Michigan, Illinois, and Wisconsin. One of the letters was written from the vicinity of Nashville, Tennessee, perhaps between 1836 and 1839, but there is almost nothing in the book about Tennessee or other parts of the South. Four pages are devoted to slavery.

244. Stiff, Edward

The Texan emigrant: being a narration of the adventures of the author in Texas, and a description of the soil, climate, productions, minerals, towns, bays, harbors, rivers, institutions, and manners and customs of the inhabitants of that country; together with the principal incidents of fifteen years revolution in Mexico; and embracing a condensed statement of interesting events in Texas, from the first European settlement in 1692, down to the year 1840. By Col. Edward Stiff. Cincinnati, G. Conclin, 1840.

v, [7]–367 p. front. (fold. map), 1 illus. 19½ cm.
Maps: One: Folded map of Texas, colored to show land grants.
Illustrations: Two: "View of Galveston City and Bay" and "Battle of San Jacinto." Both crude.
Inclusive dates: 1838. In South, the same.
Other editions:
　Reissued, anonymously, in 1847, with some additions under title:
　(1) A new history of Texas; being a narration of the adventures of the author in Texas, and a description of the soil, climate, productions, minerals, towns, bays, harbors, rivers, institutions, and manners and customs of the inhabitants of that country; together with the principal incidents of fifteen years revolution in Mexico; and embracing a condensed statement of interesting events in Texas, from the first European settlement in 1692, down to the present time; and a history of the Mexican war, including accounts of the battles of Palo Alto, Resaca de la Palma, the taking of Monterey, the battle of Buena Vista, with a list of the killed and wounded, the capture of Vera Cruz, and the battle of Cerro Gordo. Cincinnati, G. Conclin, 1847. 244, [74], 17 p., incl. front., illus. 23 cm.
　(2) Cincinnati, G. Conclin, c.1847. 3 p.l., [9]–336, [8] p. front., illus. 23 cm.
　(3) Cincinnati, published by George Conclin, 1847. 320, [16] p., incl. front. 8vo.
　(4) Cincinnati, published by George Conclin, 1847. 246, [74], 14, [1] p., incl. front. 8vo.
Location of copy: Duke University Library.

Interspersed through the rambling amalgam of history and description that constitutes most of this book are reports of a few of the experiences of this Virginia-born emigrant to Texas. He was at Galveston in the spring of 1838; in September and October of the same year he was a police officer in Houston. In addition to brief descriptions of these places, Stiff tells a little about his travels in more sparsely settled areas but without giving his route or dates. The book has little merit.

245.　Sturge, Joseph (1793–1859)

A visit to the United States in 1841; by Joseph Sturge. Boston, Dexter S. King, 1842.

235, xciii p. 18½ cm.
Inclusive dates: April to July, 1841.
Other editions:
　London, Hamilton, Adams, and co., 1842. viii, [2], 192 p. 8vo.
Location of copy: Duke University Library.

Joseph Sturge, a prominent Quaker of Birmingham, England, came to the United States in 1841 to work for the abolition of slavery and the promotion of international peace. For nearly four months he traveled in the Middle and New England states, attending meetings, writing letters, and counseling with men of like mind. The poet Whittier accompanied him part of the time. Sturge did not enter the South except to spend a few days in Baltimore in April and a few days in Washington and Alexandria in June. In the latter town he visited the establishments of several slave traders, describing what he saw with considerable care. Disturbed lest Joseph John Gurney *(q.v.)* had injured the antislavery cause by presenting Henry Clay as being a friend of emancipation, Sturge gathered evidence to show that he was proslavery. To the student of Southern history the chief value of Sturge's *Visit to the United States* consists in his account of antislavery activities in the North. Among the appendices there is a record of a trip into Kentucky by James Cannings Fuller *(q.v.)*.

246.   Tasistro, Louis Fitzgerald

Random shots and Southern breezes, containing critical remarks on the Southern states and Southern institutions, with semi-serious observations on men and manners. By Louis Fitzgerald Tasistro . . . 2 vols. New-York, Harper & brothers, 1842.

> Vol. I, xi, 274 p.; Vol. II, vii, 230 p. 19 cm.
> *Inclusive dates:* November, 1840, to July, 1841.
> *Location of copy:* Duke University Library.

According to Tasistro's own statements, he was a fellow countryman of the famous Irish actor Tyrone Power, and he had once been a soldier; according to George C. D. Odell *(Annals of the New York Stage,* IV, p. 352), he was "a gentleman" of New York "known from his social position and from his newspaper affiliations" when he was suddenly introduced to the stage on January 28, 1840. Meeting with scant success in that city, he undertook a Southern tour in the following winter which must have added little if anything to his reputation. He went by boat to New Orleans which he reached in November, 1840, and he remained there until the end of the following March except for brief excursions to Mobile, Vicksburg, and Natchez. His northward journey was through Montgomery, Augusta, Savannah, Charleston, Richmond, Fredericksburg, and Washington, which he reached in June, 1841.

The character of Tasistro's two-volume account of his Southern tour is suggested by the first word in its title. It is full of sophomoric digressions on literature, drama, architecture, and philosophy. Nevertheless, it contains some fairly good descriptive passages, especially about New Orleans society and scenes.

247. Texan emigration and land company

Emigration to Texas. Texas:—being a prospectus of the advantages offered to emigrants by the Texan emigration and land company. London, published by Richardson, Cornhill, [1843].

> 24 p. front. (fold. map). 20 cm.
> *Maps:* One, folded: "Map of Texas. Comprising the grant of the Texan emigration and land-company, 1843." Lithographed by J. M. Johnson, London.
> *Location of copy:* The New York Public Library.

There is nothing subtle about this attempt of the promoters of the Texan Emigration and Land Company to secure settlers. In addition to glowing and general claims about the advantages offered to emigrants, brief statements extolling Texas are quoted from the writings of various men.

248.

Texas in 1840, or, the emigrant's guide to the new republic; being the result of observations, enquiry, and travel in that beautiful country. By an emigrant, late of the United States. With an introduction by the Rev. A. B. Lawrence . . . New York, W. W. Allen, 1840.

> 2 p.l., vii–xxii, [23]–275 p. 19 cm.
> *Illustrations:* One: Frontispiece, hand-colored view of "City of Austin the New Capital of Texas in January 1, 1840." Drawn by Edward Hall; lithographed by J. Lowe.
> *Other editions:*
> A history of Texas, or, the emigrant's guide to the new republic, by a resident emigrant, late from the United States . . . With a brief introduction by the Rev. A. B. Lawrence . . . New York, Nafis & Cornish, 1844. xxii, [23]–275 p. col. front. 19½ x 11½ cm.
> *Location of copy:* Yale University Library.

This is one of the better descriptions of Texas for the use of emigrants. It treats the usual subjects: climate, geography, natural resources, relations with Indians and Mexicans, the state of society, settlements, crops, and wild life, including descriptions of red bugs and ticks. The author states that he came to Texas near the close of the year 1839 and that he gathered much of the information for this book by numerous short trips to farmhouses and villages as well as to larger towns. He published most of his journal of his travels during January, 1840.

249.   Thomson, William

A tradesman's travels, in the United States and Canada, in the years 1840, 41, & 42. By William Thomson, Stonehaven. Edinburgh: Oliver & Boyd, etc., etc., 1842.

> viii, 228 p.   18½ cm.
> *Inclusive dates:* August, 1840, to May, 1842.
> *Location of copy:* University of Kentucky Library.

This "humble tradesman," as Thomson described himself, was a Scotch weaver of woolen goods who came to South Carolina in the late summer of 1840 to seek relief from "a pulmonary disease" and to visit his two brothers at Beaufort. In February, finding his health improved, he went to the upcountry of South Carolina and Georgia and lived for seven weeks among the farmers, planters, and cotton mills of that region. Soon afterward he journeyed northward to Canada and then down the Mississippi Valley to New Orleans where he spent the first seven days in March, 1842, "visiting the battle ground and everything about the city that did not cost money to get a sight of." He returned to Beaufort by boat and soon afterward sailed for home.

It was Thomson's aim to collect information about working people, and to offer "minute information" rather than "general description." He earned his living as he traveled, he sought inexpensive accommodations, and sometimes he "thumbed a ride" with farmers. There is scarcely another traveler who tells as much as Thomson about the life of laboring people: their food, profanity, forms of salutation, boardinghouses and travel accommodations, methods of washing clothes, and the attitude of the gentleman toward the laborer. While not uncritical, Thomson was favorably impressed by his American experience. Among the valuable sections of this sane and informative work are the chapter on slavery and the description of cotton and woolen mills, including several in South Carolina and Georgia.

250.   Tixier, Victor (1815–1885)

Tixier's travels on the Osage prairies, edited by John Francis McDermott, translated from the French by Albert J. Salvan. Norman, University of Oklahoma press, 1940.

> xv, 309, ₁1₁ p. front., plates, ports., fold. maps. 23 cm. (American exploration and travel, ₁No. 4₁).
> *Maps:* Two, both folded: The Lower Mississippi showing points visited by Tixier and Tixier's route through the Osage country. Both drawn by R. G. Underwood.

Illustrations: Eight: Photographs of paintings of Tixier and two of his white companions, four sketches of Indians by Tixier, and Tixier's notation of an Osage air.

Inclusive dates: November, 1839, to October, 1840.

Other editions:

  First published as:

  Voyage aux prairies osages, Louisiane et Missouri, 1839–40, par Victor Tixier . . . Clermont-Ferrand, Perol; Paris, Roret, 1844. 260, ₁4₁ p. front. (port.), 4 plates (incl. music). 23½ cm.

Location of copy: Duke University Library.

Soon after passing his medical examination in Paris, Tixier sailed for America with James De Berty Trudeau, a schoolmate who was a native of Louisiana. They reached Balise lighthouse at the mouth of the Mississippi on January 25, 1840, and Tixier remained in Louisiana until May, when he left for the country of the Osage Indians. Sixty-five pages of this translation of his *Travels* are devoted to his sojourn in Louisiana. Curiously, he says almost nothing about the city of New Orleans, but he more than compensates by dealing with matters that most of the travelers to Louisiana touched but lightly if at all: the Mississippi River below New Orleans, plantation life in Louisiana especially on the Acadian Coast, and hunting and sight-seeing expeditions into the bayous, the cypress forests, and the *prairie tremblante.* Tixier is notably free from the prejudices and preconceptions that colored the writings of many travelers in his period.

251. Urrea, José

Diary of the military operations of the division which under the command of General José Urrea campaigned in Texas. Translated and printed on pages 204–283 of the Mexican side of the Texan Revolution ₁1836₁, by the chief Mexican participants . . . Translated with notes by Carlos E. Castañeda. Dallas, Texas, P. L. Turner company, c.1928.

  vii, 391 p. 24 cm.

Maps: Two: End papers. One a facsimile, the other a redrawing, of part of a map of Texas compiled by Stephen F. Austin and published by H. S. Tanner & co., Philadelphia, showing land grants in Texas and route of the Mexican army.

Illustrations: Facsimiles of five title-pages and of Colonel Fannin's capitulation.

Inclusive dates: January to June, 1836.

Other editions:

  First published as:

  Diario de las operaciónes militares de la división que al mando del general José Urrea hizo la campaña de Tejas. Publicado su autor, con algunas observaciónes para vindicarse ante sus conciudadanos. Victoria de Durango, impr. del gobierno a cargo de M. Gonzalez, 1838. 136 p. 20½ cm.

Location of copy: Duke University Library.

Urrea's diary is mostly in the form of a day by day account of the expedition of his army into Texas and back again. It was evidently revised before it was published in 1838. The document has some of the qualities of a military travel account; but it is primarily a piece of polemical writing, designed to defend his military record and to attack his critics.

Included in Castañeda's *The Mexican Side of the Texas Revolution* are documents from the pens of four other Mexican participants. They, however, are even less informative about conditions in Texas than Urrea.

252. Waylen, Edward

Ecclesiastical reminiscences of the United States. By the Rev. Edward Waylen . . . New-York, Wiley and Putnam, 1846.

> xv, 501 p. 22 cm.
> *Inclusive dates:* June, 1834, to June, 1845.
> *Other editions:*
> London, W. Straker, 1846. xv, [1], 542 p. front., plates, ports., fold. facsim. 23 cm.
> *Location of copy:* Duke University Library.

This is a rambling and rather pointless account of Waylen's eleven years in the United States. It is chiefly valuable for the information it contains about churches, especially the Episcopal church. The author was the rector of Christ Church in Rockville, Maryland, during his last year in America.

253. Wette, Ludwig de

Reise in den Vereinigten Staaten und Canada im Jahr 1837. Von L. de Wette, Dr. med. Leipzig, Weidmann, 1838.

> xiv, 364 p. 19½ cm.
> *Inclusive dates:* July, 1836, to October, 1837.
> *Other editions:*
> Reis in de Vereenigde Staten en Canada, in 1837. Door L. de Wette, dr. med. Uit het Hoogduitsch . . . 2 vols. Zalt-Bommel, J. Noman en zoon, 1839. front. 23 cm.
> *Location of copy:* University of Michigan.

Ludwig de Wette, a young physician of Basel, Switzerland, was the son of a Protestant theologian and university professor (for a sketch of the father's life, see *Allgemeine Deutsche Biographie,* V, pp. 101–105) whose political liberalism had brought hardship upon the family. In consequence, Ludwig's half brother, Karl Beck, emigrated to

America in the year 1824 (see Charles Beck in the *Dictionary of American Biography*). Ludwig de Wette's tour in America began with a visit to this half brother who had become professor of Latin in Harvard College. After this visit, and after traveling in the East, Ludwig began his extended Southern tour. Late in February, 1837, he reached Baltimore. By early June he had traveled southward to Georgia, thence to New Orleans, up the Mississippi River to Kentucky, across western Virginia to Natural Bridge, up the Shenandoah Valley to Harpers Ferry, and back to Baltimore. His main interests during this three months' journey were in medical schools and health conditions, botany, slavery, cities, the culture of the staple crops, politics, and prisons. His careful and judicious observations about this tour in the South occupy about half the pages of this book.

254. Whipple, Henry Benjamin, Bishop (1822–1901)

Bishop Whipple's Southern Diary, 1843–1844, edited with an introduction by Lester B. Shippee. London, H. Milford, Oxford University press; Minneapolis, the University of Minnesota press, [c.1937].

4 p.l., xi–xxvii, 208 p. plates, ports. 23½ cm.
Illustrations: Eight: Two portraits of Whipple, and 6 reproductions of contemporary prints, including "New Orleans and vicinity, 1863," "Cathedral of St. Louis and Jackson Square, New Orleans, 1858," and "View of Vicksburg, Mississippi, 1855."
Inclusive dates: October, 1843, to May, 1844. In South, the same.
Location of copy: Duke University Library.

The observant eye, the humanitarian instincts, and the critical but unprejudiced mind of the writer combine to make this one of the best travel accounts of its period. In later years Whipple became an Episcopal bishop and attained fame and honor for his efforts to secure fair treatment for the Indians. When he wrote this diary he was a young husband and father from upstate New York who was seeking to improve his health by spending a winter in the South. He came by boat to Savannah, and spent five months near the Gulf Coast, especially at St. Marys, Georgia, Mobile, and New Orleans. His descriptions of the appearance and life of these towns, and of Washington, D. C., which he visited after traveling up the Mississippi and Ohio rivers, comprise a large part of the diary. Instead of using almanacs and guidebooks, he depended mostly on his own eyes and ears; and besides describing the outward appearance of places he was interested in regional characteristics and local customs, including the colloquialisms of the common people.

255. Williams, John Lee

The territory of Florida: or sketches of the topography, civil and natural history, of the country, the climate, and the Indian tribes, from the first discovery to the present time, with a map, views, etc. By John Lee Williams. New York, A. T. Goodrich, 1837.

> vi, 304 p. front. (port.). 22 cm.
>
> *Maps:* One: "Map of Florida by J. Lee Williams, 1837." Large, folded map with notations of kind and quality of land.
>
> *Illustrations:* Three lithographs: frontispiece portrait of Oseola, "St. John's River & Volusia on the Right Bank," and "Fort Mellon, Lake Monroe."
>
> *Inclusive dates:* Sometime before 1837.
>
> *Location of copy:* Duke University Library.

The preface states that the author traveled over much of Florida in preparing to write this book, but none of the content is cast in the form of a travel record; hence, one cannot be sure what parts of the work reflect the personal observations of Williams. He had earlier published *A View of West Florida, Embracing Its Geography, Topography, etc. With an Appendix, Treating of Its Antiquities, Land Titles, and Canals* ... (Philadelphia, 1827).

256. Willis, Nathaniel Parker (1806–1867)

American scenery; or, land, lake, and river illustrations of transatlantic nature. From drawings by W. H. Bartlett engraved in the first style of the art, by R. Wallis, J. Cousen, Willmore, Brandard, Adlard, Richardson, etc. 2 vols. The literary department by N. P. Willis, Esq. London, George Virtue, 1840.

> Vol. I, iv, [2], xii, 140 p.; Vol. II, iv, 106 p. fronts., plates, map. 27 cm.
>
> *Maps:* One in the front of Vol. I, showing the northeastern part of the United States. "Places in the neighbourhood of which the views have been taken" are marked.
>
> *Illustrations:* Sixty-seven in Vol. I (one is a portrait of Bartlett, another is a vignette on the engraved title-page, and the rest are engravings of American scenes that have been drawn by Bartlett); fifty-four in Vol. II (one is a vignette on the engraved title-page, the others are American scenes by Bartlett). Natural Bridge is the most southern point illustrated in the two volumes; there are fourteen scenes of places in Maryland and Virginia.
>
> *Inclusive dates:* 1836–1838.
>
> *Other editions:*
>
> L'Amérique pittoresque, ou, vues des terres, des lacs et des fleuves des États-Unis d'Amérique. Ouvrage enrichi de gravures faites sur les dessins de m. W. H. Bartlett, et exécutées avec le plus grand soin par R. Wallis, J. Cousen . . . &c. La partie littéraire par N. P. Willis. Traduit de l'anglais par L. de Bauclas . . . Londres, G. Virtue, [etc., etc.], 1840.
>
> *Location of copy:* Library of Congress.

According to the *Dictionary of National Biography*, Bartlett (1809–54) was a "topographical draughtsman" who traveled widely. His landscape and scenic drawings were published in many works. In the years 1836–38 and 1851–52 he made four voyages to the United States and Canada, and his drawings for *American Scenery* were made on the earlier of these trips. These are contained in *The Art-Journal* (London), a new series, Vol. I (January, 1855), pp. 24–26.

Willis is known to have been in Washington in February and March, 1837, and he traveled with Bartlett to some of the other places that are illustrated in this handsome work. The best source of information on Nathaniel Parker Willis is Henry A. Beers, *Nathaniel Parker Willis* (Boston, 1885). However, the two pages that Willis wrote to accompany each engraving bear little or no resemblance to the writings of a traveler; they seem to have been written in his study.

257.

A winter in the West Indies and Florida; containing general observations upon modes of travelling, manners and customs, climates and productions, with a particular description of St. Croix, Trinidad de Cuba, Havana, Key West, and St. Augustine, as places of resort for Northern invalids. By an invalid. New York, Wiley and Putnam, 1839.

xi, [13]–199 p.   19 cm.
Inclusive dates: December, 1838, to April, 1839. In South, March to April, 1839.
Location of copy: Yale University Library.

This unknown author seems to have been a resident of New York. His journey southward was made in the hope of arresting a case of tuberculosis. Having met with some success, he wrote this unusual travelers' guide which was designed to be of service to others in like circumstances. His descriptions of Key West and St. Augustine are useful, and so likewise is his narrative of his journeys to and from these Florida towns.

258.   Wood, Samuel

Letters from the United States. By the Rev. S. Wood . . . [London, printed by G. Smallfield, 1837].

11 p.   8vo.
Inclusive dates: July 15, 1836, to 1837. In South, July, 1836.
Other editions:
From the *Christian Reformer*. London, 1838.   27 p.   21 cm.

[191]

Location of copy: Library of Congress (Rare Book Division). Bound in vol. entitled: Controversial and miscellaneous pamphlets.

The letters begin on a steamboat on the Ohio River between Cincinnati and Louisville, and describe the river, boat, towns, and countryside. The author arrived at St. Louis about July 18, and here his brief contact with the South was concluded. His subsequent route took him to Buffalo, N. Y., and to Philadelphia, where he wrote a letter dated April 21, 1837. In August he was in London. He admired the energy of Americans but had a low opinion of the government of the United States and of American culture.

259. Wrede, Friedrich W. von

Lebensbilder aus den Vereinigten Staaten von Nordamerika und Texas, gesammelt von Fr. W. v. Wrede . . . In der Fortsetzung nach Tagebüchern und mündlichen Mittheilungen bearbeitet von E. D. Cassel, Selbstverlag, 1844.

1 p.l., iv, 160, [2], iii-v, 161–324 p. 21½ cm.
Inclusive dates: September, 1835, to August, 1844. In South at frequent intervals throughout these years.
Location of copy: Library of Congress.

The text of this volume is in the form of letters describing the author's travels. He left Bremerhaven on October 14, 1835, and he wrote his first American letter from New Orleans on January 7, 1836. His itinerary included New Orleans, Natchitoches, Baton Rouge, Natchez, St. Louis, various points in Illinois and Missouri, a return to New Orleans, and a trip to Texas; in 1842 he visited New York and then traveled down the Ohio to Cincinnati and down the Mississippi to New Orleans. He returned to Germany in September, 1844. He describes most of the places he visited, with some attention to customs, people, climate, vegetation, animal life, and especially steamboats. He is apparently a person of education and a careful observer. He says that his sojourn in America was the fulfillment of a lifelong ambition.

The curious collation is explained by a note on the Library of Congress card: "Issued in 2 parts. The table following t.-p. gives contents to p. 160 only. 'Vorwort,' signed Emil Drescher, and continuation of the table of contents, with one page repeated, are inserted before p. 161."

260. Wyatt, William N. (1805–1868)

Wyatt's travel diary, 1836, with comment by Mrs. Addie Evans Wynn and W. A. Evans (grandchildren of W. N. Wyatt). The maps used were obtained from the Library of Congress . . . Chicago, priv. print., 1930.

78, [2] p. front. (port.), 2 fold. maps. 19½ cm.
Maps: Two: "Part of Map of Arkansas, by H. S. Tanner, 1836" and "Part of Map of Arkansas, by H. S. Tanner, 1841."
Illustrations: Frontispiece portrait of William N. Wyatt.
Inclusive dates: November 9 to December 25, 1836.
Location of copy: University of North Carolina Library.

During the last weeks of the year 1836, Wyatt, a native of South Carolina, and his cousin James F. Gaines made an extended land-hunting tour over the state of Arkansas, traveling about a thousand miles by horseback. The trip began at Gaines' home near Memphis, Tennessee, it reached almost to the western boundary of Arkansas, and it was concluded at its starting point. The diary is a detailed record of points visited, of conditions of roads, of expenses, and of those things which attracted the attention of an alert young farmer and merchant: the quality and lay of the land, the location and prospects of the towns, the character of the population, and such natural resources as water power and salt wells. Wyatt's diary occupies nineteen pages; the rest of this book consists of notes and comments by the editors.

261. Wyse, Francis

America, its realities and resources: comprising important details connected with the present social, agricultural, commercial, and financial state of the country, its political laws and customs, together with a review of the policy of the United States that led to the War of 1812, and Peace of 1814—the "Right of search," the Texas and Oregon questions, etc., etc., by Francis Wyse . . . 3 vols. London, T. C. Newby, 1846.

Vol. I, iv, 494 p.; Vol. II, 440 p.; Vol. III, 389, lxxviii p. 22 cm.
Location of copy: Library of Congress.

This large work contains much information on many topics that might be of interest to prospective emigrants from England to America. The early part of Vol. II discusses slavery in practice and in politics, the abolition movement, and difficulties of abolishing slavery. Volume III contains descriptions of each of the states, pages 254–366 being devoted to the Southern states. Under each there is a discussion of natural resources, climate, rivers, towns, history, diseases, area, population, government, and general subjects.

PART III

The Slavery South at Noontide, 1846–1852

INTRODUCTION

A T LEAST one hundred and fifty travelers recorded their observations and impressions of their journeys through the South from 1846–52. There were possibly even more who visited and wrote about the region during those years, but their books have not been located. These published works reflect a mounting interest in the South on the part of both Americans and foreigners who journeyed through the region at mid-century.

In the main, this accelerated traveler interest was heightened by such recent developments as the political upheavals of 1848 in Europe, the increase in information, sometimes highly colored, about the "matchless opportunities" for economic and democratic betterment in America, the Mexican War, and the Texas question. Discovery of gold in California, improved transportation facilities, the rising tide of sectional consciousness combined with the curiosity and zeal about slavery brought scores of visitors from outside the South who wished to observe slavery at close range. Others not so sensitive to these basic economic and social issues came to enjoy the lavish appointments of American hotels, to see the Indians, and to travel on the much publicized "floating palaces" on the Western rivers.

The possible routes of entry and the extent of the trip to be taken through the South offered a considerable variety of choice to the traveler, depending upon his means and available time. Some visitors, limited to a few days, did little more than skirt the South. Others stopped at one or two bordering cities. In some instances this hasty view, supplemented by information gained from conversations en route and the reading of earlier published travel accounts, provided the prospective recorders with the documentation needed to write with an air of authority about all aspects of Southern society.

On the other hand, there were a few travelers such as Mrs. Sarah Maury, who spent much of one year, and Solon Robinson, two years, wandering through many parts of the South. A few remained in America for several years before recording their experiences. Attempting to estimate the average length of time spent by travelers in the South is virtually impossible because of the incomplete information given concerning a considerable number of their itineraries. Yet it appears that one to two months was about the usual amount of time taken by a substantial number of the more important visitors. The Pulszky's and Sir Edward Sullivan spent six weeks, Lady Stuart-Wortley three weeks, and Charles Olliffe two months. Sir Charles Lyell, on his second visit, and Alexander Mackay were en route four and five months, respectively.

At least forty travelers, most of whom gave substantial evidence of having traveled extensively through the South, such as Dureau, Captain Flack, Griesinger, Menzel, Milliroux, and Revoil, either indicated no itinerary or intentionally concealed their routes from the reader. Others of the same group merely identified a few of the widely separated localities visited without indicating any chronological pattern. Five or more of this number appeared to have limited their visit to a single city such as Charleston, Louisville, or New Orleans. There are six or eight who may have never set foot on Southern soil, even though they wrote at some length and at times rather convincingly about the South and slavery.

Like most modern travelers who take the regular tours, a majority of the Southern visitors around 1850 naturally followed the main routes, utilizing water and rail transportation whenever possible in preference to stagecoaches. Rarely did they wander far off into the interior where accommodations, if not altogether lacking, were limited. Yet many of those who did venture away from the main stream made some of the most significant contributions to the travel literature of the period. Travelers in this category were Abbé Domenech, Moritz Busch, Charles Lanman, Julius Fröbel, Charles Lyell, Charles Olliffe, Karl Scherzer, Solon Robinson, and Moritz Wagner.

Forty-one of the travelers entered the South by way of Washington and followed the route of the "grand tour" along the eastern seaboard states of Georgia, across Alabama to Mobile and New Orleans, and then up the Mississippi and Ohio rivers to Louisville and Pittsburgh. At least fifteen of this number completed the circle. The others returned by land and water to Washington or other Eastern ports from the various cities along the southeastern coast, or they proceeded to Havana and other foreign destinations from Charleston, Mobile, or New Orleans. Among those who completed the "tour" were Lyell, Mackay, Maury, Tolmer, and Wagner. Some of those who dipped into the South for visits of varying length were the American author William Cullen Bryant, the English divine Jabez Burns, the French pianist Henri Herz, and the British physician John Shaw.

Not many of the travelers completed the entire "grand tour" in reverse order by going down the Ohio and Mississippi rivers to New Orleans and then across the Gulf states and north to Washington. Three important visitors who did this were Samuel Ludvigh, Charles Olliffe, and the Pulszkys. A few, including Bayard Taylor, famous *New York Tribune* correspondent, entered the South at New Orleans and proceeded north to Washington along the usual eastern route.

There were not many observers who extended their travels through the southeastern states to Florida. In 1850 the future "sunshine state," located off the main route, was definitely not a tourist attraction. Charles Olliffe, Charles Lanman, and Solon Robinson, however, spent profitable time there and wrote at some length about their visits.

At least forty-four of the total number saw the South on a one-way or round-trip passage on the Ohio and Mississippi rivers beginning at Pittsburgh, Cincinnati, and the various points along the Upper Mississippi, St. Louis, or New Orleans. Such travelers as Audubon, Baird, Banvard, Devol, Eyma, and Fröbel, together with Henry Lewis, Peyton, Sarmiento, Edward Smith, and Lady Stuart-Wortley, belong in this category. Booty, Brentano, Busch, Caswall, Koch, Löher, and ten others moved along the Ohio River and dipped into Kentucky or Tennessee from the Ohio and Mississippi by boat or stagecoach. At least thirty-four travelers recorded their impressions of various places and persons of interest in Kentucky such as Mammoth Cave, the health springs, Porter, the Kentucky giant at Louisville, and "Ashland" and its owner Henry Clay.

Several nationalities were represented among the one hundred and fifty travelers. Sixty-six were Americans, forty-nine of whom came from the Northern states and seventeen from the Southern. Virginians dominated the latter group. There were forty-three from England and two from Scotland. Next in number were the Germans with twenty-eight; there were twenty-three Frenchmen, two Hungarians, and one each from Argentina, Austria, Holland, Norway, Sweden, and Switzerland.

Even though the Americans who journeyed in the Southern states at this time were more numerous, their collective significance was less than that of some of the foreign groups. No native American set out with the intention of giving a comprehensive picture of the South. It was not until the collecting and editing of Robinson's letters and reports in 1936 that the scope of his contribution was better comprehended; and Lanman's many books must be considered collectively to see the wide range of his work, since the individual accounts relate only to a rather limited area. Several clergymen, an actor or two, a few abolitionists, and two professional gamblers appear to have visited many of the Southern communities, but they stressed professional interests and were often not too objective in their observations.

The accounts of the forty-five Britishers range from the childish impressions of an anonymous twelve-year-old young lady to the sharply etched and understanding observations of the famous geologist Sir Charles Lyell. They include such extremes in reporting as the insignificant and hackneyed descriptions of a conglomeration of events by Charles Casey to the objective observations and remarkably accurate predictions of another outstanding recorder of the American scene, the Scottish-born Canadian journalist Alexander Mackay.

A number of Englishmen, as was true of some in the other groups, arrived with preconceived prejudices against America or wrote condescendingly about aspects of the American scene. "Spitology," "colorophobia," and slavery in the South were their favorite targets. Yet a check shows that almost half of the total number of English travelers who came to America either favored much of what they found in the South, or on leaving they moderated their earlier opinions, especially in regard to the "peculiar institution." In this group were Robert Baird, James Booty, Henry Caswall, Marianne Finch, and Mrs. Matilda Houstoun, together with Professor Philip Kelland, Charles Lyell, Alexander Mackay, Mrs. Sarah Mytton Maury, Robert Playfair, Lady Stuart-Wortley, and Hugh Tremenheere.

Many names among the twenty-eight German travelers who recorded their impressions of the South merit more than a passing notice. Especially outstanding are Viktor Bracht, who settled in Texas; Moritz Busch, who later became Bismarck's confidant; Julius Fröbel, editor and diplomat; Karl Griesinger; Franz von Löher; and Gottfried Menzel. In the same category are the Austrian-born Samuel Ludvigh, who later became a most important editor among the Germans in this country, and the two famous scientists, world travelers, and explorers, Dr. Karl Scherzer and Dr. Moritz Wagner. All of them gave painstaking attention to meticulous detail. Their generally objective observations of the many things in the South that interested prospective German immigrants make important contributions to travel literature. Although basically opposed to slavery, most, with the exception of Griesinger, seemed not to allow bias to distort their impressions. Many German visitors wished to counteract the excessive optimism concerning American emigration. Virtually each observer was a self-appointed committee of one to investigate accurately and report faithfully on the opportunities in America. Their findings were often summarized in the concluding chapter of their books. As a group, their professional training and characteristic thoroughness contributed to the superior quality of the German travel accounts.

The twenty-three French observers probably represented a greater variety of professional interests than did the German visitors. Among the seven or eight of importance were the hard-riding and at times straight-shooting missionary in Texas, Abbé Domenech; the pianist Herz; the sportsman Revoil; the university professor Marmier, who later became a member of the French Academy; the editor Eyma; and the two authors Dureau and Olliffe. The latter, whose *Scènes Américaines* is an unusually solid account, is one of the few French travelers who identifies his itinerary and who discusses his impressions in detail. Most of the Frenchmen resorted to sweeping generalizations and broad conclusions with their itineraries either completely concealed or sufficiently confused so the reader could determine neither the route nor the time of travel. In general, the French travelers were moderate in their criticisms of the South. Their accounts, at times both racy and humorous, indicated a sympathetic understanding of much of Southern life.

Additional significant foreign appraisers of the South were the Pulszkys, who accompanied Louis Kossuth on his visit to America, and the famous Swiss scientist Leo Lesquereux, also a victim of the upheaval of 1848.

Many professions were represented by the travelers. Those that could be identified were twenty-eight writers and editors, twenty-one clergymen, ten scientists, seven physicians, four sportsmen, and four artists, including the panoramists with their one- to three-mile-long rolls of scenes from the Mississippi River. In addition, there were school-teachers, actors, musicians, gamblers, book agents, a carpenter, a seam-stress, and a beautician. Twenty-two of the travelers were attracted to Texas. At least five more of them served in the Mexican War. A few former slaves and abolitionist agents were in the total number.

Rarely did the travelers comment effectively on the national politi-cal issues of the period. The events of the year 1850 in the American political picture appeared to have had little if any significant meaning to the visitors, though a great many of them commented on the devisive effects of slavery.

A final category includes a score of immigrant guidebooks com-piled often by self-appointed immigrant advisers. Eleven of these were American, five were German, three English, and two French.

ROBERT G. LUNDE
University of Kentucky

262. Almbert, Alfred d' (1813–1887)

Flânerie parisienne aux États-Unis, par Alfred d'Almbert. Paris, Librairie Théâtrale, 1856.

> 2 p.l., 278 p., 1 l. 16 cm.
> *Location of copy:* University of Pennsylvania Library.

This Frenchman did not visit the South, but in a brief comment on slavery he discusses the region. His remarks on slavery state the most elementary facts, including some comments upon the economics of the instituiton. D'Almbert's other observations are of a general nature so far as they might relate to the South. He wished to dispel his countrymen's conception of a prosperous, happy, and democratic America.

263.

America compared with England. The respective social effects of the American and English systems of government and legislation; and the mission of democracy. London, Effingham Wilson, Royal Exchange, 1848.

> xxiv, 289 p. 18 cm.
> *Inclusive dates:* 1820–1846.
> *Location of copy:* Newberry Library.

Although not a travel book, this work has a place in a travel bibliography, for the unknown writer in Chapters XXII and XXIII presents extensive testimony about America taken from a number of the important travel accounts of the 1820's to the 1840's. Among those whose works were included were De Tocqueville, Mrs. Trollope, Cyril Thornton (Captain Hamilton), Captain Marryat, Charles Dickens, Charles Lyell, Harriet Martineau, J. Stuart, and J. S. Buckingham. The book, as indicated by the title, compares English and American institutions.

264. Andree, Karl [Theodor] (1808–1875)

Geographische Wanderungen von Karl Andree. 2 vols. Dresden, Rudolf Kuntze, 1859.

Vol. I., viii, 336 p.; Vol. II, 1 l., 358 p. 19 cm.
Location of copy: University of Kentucky Library.

The preface of this two-volume work suggests that Andree secured much of his information about America from the many signed and anonymous contributions to the several German newspapers and the geographical journals which he edited in Mainz, Karlsruhe, Köln, Bremen, and Dresden. Volume I gives sketches of the states of New York, Illinois, California, and Kentucky, while Volume II discusses the Mormons, the West, and Captain Marcy's expedition along the Red River in Texas. His works were quite well known, for frequent references to them appear in the accounts of other travelers of the period. But no evidence could be found that Andree actually traveled in America.

265.   Andree, Karl [Theodor] (1808–1875)

Nord-Amerika in geographischen und geschichtlichen Umrissen; mit besonderer Berücksichtigung der Eingeborenen und der indianischen Alterthümer, der Einwanderung und der Ansiedelungen, des Ackerbaues, der Gewerbe, der Schiffahrt und des Handels, von Dr. Karl Andree. Braunschweig, G. Westermann, 1854.

xiii, 810 p.   25 cm.
Other editions:
Braunschweig, G. Westermann, 1851.   xiii, 810 p.   25 cm.
Location of copy: Wisconsin Historical Association.

There appears to be nothing in this work to indicate that this German geographer, writer, and editor ever traveled in America. Yet the detailed title of the book suggests that he had more than a superficial knowledge of this country. This information appears to have come from his newspaper work, reading of travel books, and geographical reports. Andree's general treatment of the usual historical and descriptive material is interspersed with chapters relating to each of the states. He described in some detail the emigration and settlement of Germans in this country as well as their professional and occupational opportunities.

The above is the second edition. The first edition was published in 1851 with the same title and collation.

266.   Andrew, James Osgood (1794–1871)

Miscellanies: comprising letters, essays, and addresses; to which is added a biographical sketch of Mrs. Ann Amelia Andrew. By James Osgood Andrew. Louisville, Morton and Griswold, 1854.

viii, 321 p.   19 cm.
Inclusive dates: 1843–1849.
Location of copy: University of Kentucky Library.

Bishop Andrew of the Methodist Episcopal church in the South began preaching in 1832. For at least twenty-five years he preached and attended conferences chiefly in Kentucky, Tennessee, Missouri, Arkansas, and Texas. His letters, first appearing in the *Southern Christian Advocate,* cover only a six-year period of his ministry. About two-thirds of the work describes the incidents of travel to and from his appointments. Rarely does he comment on anything not directly associated with his religious activities.

He was especially interested in the religious efforts among the many Indian tribes of this area. His description of the German immigrants in the Texas conference, especially West Texas, is of value.

267.   Assollant, Jean Baptiste Alfred (1827–1886)

Scènes de la vie des États-Unis: Acacia. Les butterfly. Une fantaisie américaine. Paris: Hachette, 1859.

362 p., 1 l., 18 cm.
Inclusive dates: 1852–1853.
Location of copy: Newberry Library.

The title page of this book bears the notation that it is "a railroad book," and it sold in France for two francs. There are three parts: "Acacia," "Les Butterfly," and "Une Fantaisie Américaine." Certainly Assollant knew something about America. He was able to describe the various religious sects in the country and to give something of their differing points of view. He also understood the various social crosscurrents. Yankees, abolitionists, and the missionaries receive attention. Even though some of his comments are severe, he was, in general, favorable to America.

The text of the book is written in the form of a cheap novel. One of the characters is a Kentuckian, and the scene of "Acacia" is the fanciful community of Oakburg, Kentucky, which is described as "the most beautiful in all the valley of the Kentucky, and perhaps of all the world. Its houses are large and commodious, are built of wood and brick and resemble indifferently Greek temples, of byzantine churches, of stables, of the gothic churches, and of the 'comptoirs' of Windsor Castle."

Louisville, Kentucky, is almost the only specific place mentioned. From the quotation above, Assollant was obviously speaking of the Blue Grass area of Kentucky. Internal evidence indicates that the author was a Swedenborgian missionary turned traveler and author. In order to conceal his facts, he hid behind a fictional style. The book is useful only in indicating the kind of reaction that Frenchmen of the mid-nineteenth century had toward American institutions.

268. Audubon, John Woodhouse (1812–1862)

Audubon's western journal: 1849–1850; being the ms. record of a trip from New York to Texas, and an overland journey through Mexico and Arizona to the gold-fields of California, by John W. Audubon, with biographical memoir by his daughter, Maria R. Audubon; introduction, notes, and index by Frank Heywood Hodder . . . with folded map, portrait, and original drawings. Cleveland, Arthur H. Clark company, 1906.

> 249 p. front. (port.), 5 plates, fold. map. 24 cm.
> *Illustrations:* Frontispiece, portrait, and five plates of Mexican and Californian scenes.
> *Maps:* Map illustrating Audubon's western journal.
> *Inclusive dates:* February 8, 1849, to May, 1850.
> *Location of copy:* University of Kentucky Library.

It is sufficient to note for this study that Audubon, son of the famous ornithologist, spent four hours at Louisville on his trip down the Ohio River to join Colonel Henry L. Webb at Cairo. After sailing down the Mississippi for four days, the expedition arrived at New Orleans, where they took on more supplies. Then the party sailed for Brazos where they began the overland trek to Brownsville en route to California. Audubon noted the "rolling of bowling-alleys and the cannoning of billiard balls" in the otherwise drab Western outpost of Brownsville.

269. Baird, Robert (1798–1836)

Impressions and experiences of the West Indies and North America in 1849 by Robert Baird. Philadelphia, Lea and Blanchard, 1850.

> 354 p. 19½ cm.
> *Inclusive dates:* January 1, 1849, to July, 1849.
> *Other editions:*
> (1) 2 vols. Edinburgh, 1850.
> (2) London, 1850.
> *Location of copy:* Yale University Library.

Few travelers of this period were more objective in recording their impressions of America than this Englishman. He realized that a single trip up the Mississippi and Ohio rivers from Cuba, via New Orleans and Cincinnati, en route to Canada and the East did not afford sufficient time or opportunity for the forming of "general conclusions on questions lying . . . far below the surface of society." Yet it is unfortunate that Robert Baird did not visit more of the South. His chapter on the river journey gives an excellent picture of "the crevasse at New Orleans," river steamboats, and other river craft. He revealed an understanding of human nature in his evaluation of Americans and Englishmen with intrusive and offensive manners.

Although opposed to slavery, he was conscious of the realities of the problem, and this made him most critical of the "inconsiderate zeal of the abolitionists." This subject was one of three which the author discussed in a final chapter summarizing his impressions of America.

Some confusion and error is apparent concerning the identity of the author. *The British Museum Catalogue of Printed Books, 1881–1900* (Ann Arbor, 1946) lists the work among the numerous writings of the famous New York Presbyterian clergyman and traveler of the same name. (See the *Dictionary of American Biography*.) By coincidence the British traveler and the American clergyman have identical necrologies.

270. Baker, William Mumford

The life and labours of the Rev. Daniel Baker, D.D., pastor and evangelist. Prepared by his son, Rev. William M. Baker, pastor of the Presbyterian church, Austin, Texas. Philadelphia, William S. and Alfred Martien, 1858.

> 1 p.l., [7]–573 p. front. (port.).
> *Illustrations:* Autographed engraving of "Dan. Baker" by A. H. Ritchie.
> *Inclusive dates:* 1791–1857.
> *Location of copy:* University of Kentucky Library.

Much of Daniel Baker's life of travel—as a Presbyterian minister (1825–83), evangelist, author, and agent and president of Austin (Tex.) College (1853–57)—over most of the South and parts of the East is recorded in this important work. He held pastorates in Savannah, Frankfort (Ky.), Tuscaloosa, Memphis, and several Louisiana and Texas communities. He raised over $100,000 for Austin College in six tours "out of the state." (See the *Dictionary of American Biography* for a sketch of his life.)

His journals, from which Baker wrote an unpublished autobiography for the use of his children, together with letters and supplementary information were used by his son in writing this book. Baker was an accurate observer, but most of his observations related directly or indirectly to his ardor for "souls" and securing contributions for his college. His frequent comments on his salary and the sums raised by him testify to his "persuasive eloquence" and to the interest manifested at that time in a denominational college.

He owned no slaves, yet he believed that "the relation of master and slave was recognized in the Bible, and that ecclesiastical bodies [had] no right to legislate upon the subject."

271. [Banvard, John (1815–1891)]

Description of Banvard's panorama of the Mississippi river, painted on three miles of canvas: exhibiting a view of country 1200 miles in length extending from the mouth of the Missouri river to the city of New Orleans; being by far the largest picture ever executed by man. Boston, John Putnam, 1847.

> 48 p. 21 cm.
>
> *Inclusive dates:* Probably 1840–1846.
>
> *Other editions:*
>
> (1) Description of Banvard's panorama of the Mississippi and Missouri rivers, extensively known as the "three-mile painting," exhibiting a view of country over 3000 miles in length, extending from the mouth of the Yellowstone to the city of New Orleans. London, W. J. Golbourn, 1848 and 1849. 48 p.
>
> (2) Description of Banvard's geographical painting of the Mississippi river, extensively known as the "three mile picture," with new additions of the naval and military operations on that river, exhibiting a view of country 1500 miles in length from the mouth of the Missouri to the Balize. New York, Bigelow, printer, 1862. 38 p.
>
> *Location of copy:* University of Kentucky Library.

This is a series of tributes and testimonials concerning the panorama, a short biographical sketch of the artist, and his description of his work. John Banvard was "actuated by a patriotic and honorable ambition that America should produce the largest painting in the world." He realized his aim with a work three miles long on "upright revolving cylinders." The artist's generalized sketch of the river is of little importance.

A much longer painting including the Missouri River was described in the pamphlet published in 1849 (copy in the Library of Congress). See the *Dictionary of American Biography* for a sketch of Banvard's life.

272. Bartlett, John Russell (1805–1886)

Personal narrative of explorations and incidents in Texas, New Mexico, California, Sonora, and Chihuahua, connected with the United States and Mexican boundary commission, during the years 1850, '51, '52, and '53. By John Russell Bartlett, United States commissioner during that period. 2 vols. New York and London, D. Appleton & Company, 1854.

> Vol. I, xxii, 506 p.; Vol. II, xvii, 624 p. fold. fronts., illus., plates, fold. map. 22 cm.
> *Illustrations:* Folding frontispieces and 110 woodcuts and lithographs of border scenes.
> *Inclusive dates:* August, 1850, to January, 1853.
> *Other editions:*
> (1) 3 vols. New York, 1854.
> (2) New York and London, D. Appleton and Company, 1856. 2 vols. in 1. fold. fronts., illus., fold. map. 23½ cm.
> *Published also under this title:*
> American exploring expedition: a personal narrative. London, George Routledge & Company, 1854.
> *Location of copy:* Cleveland Public Library.

The author was appointed by President Zachary Taylor in 1850 to run the boundary line between Mexico and the United States under the terms of the Treaty of Guadalupe Hidalgo. Born in Rhode Island, John Russell Bartlett, an antiquarian and bibliographer (see the *Dictionary of American Biography*), served more than two years on this assignment. His account of the expedition is a valuable addition to the travel literature of Texas, for the work not only gives a personal narrative of the boundary expedition, but it describes in detail the topography, geology, and natural history of the region. Bartlett states in his preface: "I have endeavored to make it particular and accurate, in order that my book may become a useful guide to emigrants and other travelers." He realized the importance of a guide for the many parties emigrating to the gold fields of California by way of Texas and for those in the future who would be prospecting for the mineral deposits already known to exist in the mountains of Texas, New Mexico, and northern Mexico.

The two volumes are divided into six divisions, each describing a part of the journey. Bearing directly on Southern travel are the first and part of the second division (I, pp. 1–182) and parts of the sixth division (II, pp. 381–404, 513–85), which deal with the route through southern Texas to and from the Pacific Ocean.

Leaving New York in August, 1850, the party of 105 men plus an escort of 85 U. S. Infantrymen sailed for Texas by way of New Orleans, arriving there on August 31. Bartlett's narrative consists of the almost day by day entries en route from Indianola to San Antonio, Fredericksburg, and El Paso to San Diego and the return to El Paso and Corpus Christi on January 1, 1853. Bartlett returned to

Washington by way of New Orleans, Louisville, Cleveland, Albany, and New York.

Chapters on "Results of the Labors of the Boundary Commission," "Notes on the Natural History," "Adaptation of the Country for a Railway" (not the least important purpose of the expedition), and "Remarks on the Introduction of Camels as a Means of Transportation" and appendices of official instructions conclude the volume. Bartlett's early work in ethnology, his ability in careful observation, and his literary style all contribute to the excellence of this work.

273.   Baumbach, [Ludwig Carl Wilhelm] von (1799–1883)
Briefe aus den Vereinigten Staaten von Nordamerika in die Heimath, mit besonderer Rücksicht auf deutsche Auswanderer, von Ludwig Carl Wilhelm Baumbach. Cassel, Theodore Fischer, 1851.

> iv, 192 p.   double front.   16½ cm.
> *Illustrations:* Frontispiece: Lithograph of farm of publisher in Cassel.
> *Inclusive dates:* 1850–1851.
> *Other editions:*
>   Neue Briefe aus den Vereinigten Staaten von Nord-amerika in dis Heimath, mit besonderer Rücksicht auf deutsche Auswanderer, von Ludwig von Baumbach. Cassel, T. Fischer, 1856.   xiv, 333, [2] p.   18½ cm.
> *Location of copy:* University of Pennsylvania Library.

Baumbach arrived in New York and remained in northern Ohio for more than a year. His eleven letters covered a period from October, 1850, to February, 1851. He apparently did not travel in the South, but he recommended east Tennessee and the Northwestern states as the areas best suited for German immigrants (p. 29). He discussed slavery in his seventh letter, acknowledging the influence of the writings of Carl Ludwig Fleischmann on his own views.

274.   Beste, John Richard (1806–1885)
The Wabash: or adventures of an English gentleman's family in the interior of America. 2 vols. London, Hearst and Blackett, 1855.

> Vol. I, viii, 329 p.; Vol. II, viii, 352 p.   front., illus.   20 cm.
> *Inclusive dates:* June 2 to November, 1851.
> *Location of copy:* University of Kentucky Library.

This is a singularly unique two-volume travel account by the family of the wealthy English gentleman John Richard Beste, who together with his wife and twelve children—ages two to nineteen—left France in the spring of 1851 to spend the summer and autumn in the United States. They appeared to be investigating emigration prospects and immigration opportunities for their numerous offspring. Three of the sons were to remain in this country.

The family arrived in New York and journeyed along the Great Lakes and across the state of Ohio to Cincinnati. Although cholera prevented their visiting Mammoth Cave and other parts of Kentucky, they traveled down the Ohio River for a short distance. They had much to write about slavery. Beste "loathed the institution," but he favored a form of compensated emancipation. Much of the second volume centers attention around the time spent in a settlement on the Wabash River, but Chapter XI summarizes the family's general impressions of America. These in the main were interesting and quite favorable.

275. Beyer, Edward

Cyclorama. Reisebilder von Bremen nach New-York und durch die Vereinigten Staaten zurück nach Hamburg, gemalt nach der Natur und erläutert von Edward Beyer. Meiszen, published by the author, n.d.

    62 p., 1 l. 17½ cm.
    Inclusive dates: 1859–?
    Location of copy: Cleveland Public Library.

The writer of this brief account, a pamphlet bound in book form, may have arrived in New York from Bremen sometime in 1859. He visited cities and places of interest in the East before leaving for Cincinnati via Harpers Ferry. Beyer was entranced with the natural beauty of the latter region. He made special mention of a near-by German family noted for its longevity—the father was one hundred and twenty-seven, the mother one hundred and nineteen years of age, and a daughter and son were ninety-four and ninety years of age, respectively (p. 39). He retraced his route by river steamer to Point Pleasant and then dipped into the South through Virginia to North Carolina before returning to New York and Hamburg. His brief comments on the various Virginia springs, a salt pond high in the mountains, and the fisheries on Albemarle Sound were of some interest, but the book is little more than a travel itinerary.

Neither Sabin nor the Library of Congress Catalog list the work.

276. Beyer, Moritz (1807–1854)

Das Auswanderungsbuch; oder, Führer und Rathgeber bei der Auswanderung nach Nordamerika und Australien, mit Berücksichtigung von Texas und Kalifornien, in Bezug auf Ueberfahrt, Ankunft und Ansiedelung nebst einer vollständigen Schilderung des geographischen, politischen und geselligen Zustandes jener Länder und genauer Erörterung aller bei der Auswanderung zu berücksichtigenden Punkte; grossentheils nach eigener Auffassung während eines zweijährigen Aufenthalts in Amerika. Herausgeben von Moritz Beyer, vorm. Ock. Insp. und Prof. der Landwirthschaft. Mit einem Holzschnitt. Leipzig, Baumgartner's Buchhandlung, 1846.

> xii, 236 p. front. 17½ cm.
> *Illustrations:* Frontispiece: Woodcut *"Log-Haus."*
> *Inclusive dates:* 1836?–1846.
> *Location of copy:* Illinois State Historical Library.

Moritz Beyer and Louis Koch, after a two-year residence in the United States in the 1830's, collaborated in writing the travel account *Amerikanische Reisen* (Leipzig, 1839-41). A new edition of that work appeared in 1850. The present guidebook for German emigrants was based on these earlier experiences and observations together with statistics compiled by Dudley Mann and Frances Grund, and it was published in 1846. The book, as indicated by the involved title, follows the usual pattern of German travel guides with more descriptive information concerning the real problems confronting immigrants and less space given to transportation schedules. Yet this work is not as comprehensive as the volume by George von Ross, *Des Auswanderers Handbuch* (Elberfeld, 1851).

277. Booty, James Horatio

Three months in Canada and the United States. By James Horatio Booty. London, privately printed by author at his residence, 1862.

> 2 p.l., 94 p. 21 cm.
> *Inclusive dates:* May 18 to July 23, 1859.
> *Location of copy:* Library of Congress.

Here is a brief but delightful account of a British traveler's three-month tour in the early summer of 1859 through parts of Canada and the United States. Arriving in New York from Liverpool, Booty visited Washington, Mr. Vernon, and Harpers Ferry and then, instead of the usual river trip, traveled by rail to Cincinnati. He dipped into the South from Louisville, by stage to Nashville and by steamboat on the Cumberland River to St. Louis, before returning to New York via Springfield (Mo.), Chicago, Cleveland, Niagara Falls, Montreal, Quebec, and Boston.

He described in detail a packing plant in Cincinnati, the wonders of Mammoth Cave, and that "national peculiarity"—the American hotel, especially the Burnet House in Cincinnati. He noted the poor figures of American women, described an exciting river-boat race tragedy, and concluded that the abusive treatment of slaves by masters was the exception.

His interesting pictures of American life are interspersed with anecdotes of frontier humor (pp. 45–46). It is unfortunate that Booty did not comment on all phases of the American scene in 1859, especially the rising political tensions. He concluded his account with three brief essays on American hotels, railways, and waterways.

278. Bracht, Viktor (1819–1886)

Texas im Jahre 1848. Nach mehrjährigen Beobachtungen dargestellt von Viktor Bracht . . . Mit vershiedenartigen Zugaben, Auszügen aus Briefen. Elberfeld U. Iserlohn, J. Bädeker, 1849.

> xii, p., 1 l., 322 p. illus., plate. 18 cm. (Added t.p.: Neueste Länderkunde mit besonderer Beziehung auf deutsche Auswanderung und Colonisation. 1. bd.).
>
> *Illustrations:* Photograph of the Bracht family and plate of "some early San Antonio scenes."
>
> *Inclusive dates:* In Texas, June 19, 1845, to November 11, 1848.
>
> *Other editions:*
> Texas in 1848 by Viktor Bracht, translated from the German by Charles Frank Schmidt . . . San Antonio, Naylor Printing Co., [1931]. xxiv, 1 l., 223 p. 2 plates (incl. ports.). 22 cm.
>
> *Location of copy:* Translation in University of Texas Library.

. The volume examined is a translation from the original work, *Texas im Jahre 1848. Nach mehrjährigen Beobachtungen dargestellt von Viktor Bracht . . . Mit verschiedenartigen Zugaben, Auszügen aus Briefen* (Elberfeld, 1849) (copy in the Library of Congress).

The book is divided into the following parts: I, "Contributions for a more accurate understanding of present conditions of Texas pertaining to topography, statistics, and natural history"; II, "Reports about European colonies in Texas. Opinions about emigration, suggestions and practical and useful information for German Emigrants to Texas"; and III, "Excerpts from letters to relatives and friends during a sojourn of three years in Texas." The first section gives general information concerning Texas boundaries, size, soil, topography, climate, resources, population, social conditions, and communications. The second part discusses the Irish, German, French, and other settlements and gives forthright advice and warnings to prospective German emigrants concerning routes, costs, needed equipment, first crops, suitable building material, land values, and favorable settlement sites. The last part includes excerpts from some twenty letters

[213]

evidently written by Bracht during his three years in Texas to friends and relatives, most of whom were in Germany. These letters constitute an important and interesting part of the book.

Bracht, born in Düsseldorf, Germany, first came to New Braunfels in 1845 to look after the interests of the German colonists. He remained there as a successful agent and merchant until 1855 when he moved to San Antonio. Later he moved to Rockport, where he was a customs inspector and postmaster. Ever an enthusiastic and optimistic promoter for West Texas, he was careful to picture to the prospective immigrants the disagreeable as well as the favorable aspects of that territory and the other parts of the state.

This work, written while visiting in Germany in 1848 to interest settlers, is an important contribution to the early history of Texas. The author was a very sharp observer. He was honest and forthright in describing his firsthand impressions gained from extensive travels over all parts of the state. He did not hesitate to expose the dangers and evils or to laud the virtues of life in the region. Bracht came from an aristocratic family, but he was generally in favor of the democracy of the Texas frontier.

In the last chapter, entitled "A Final Word To the Readers," he stresses the advantages of German emigration and attacks many of the earlier travel books written about Texas.

279.   Brentano, Carl August von

Bilder auf einer Reise nach Amerika 1852. Gezeichnet von Carl August von Brentano. Mit einer Vorrede von dem ehemaligen königlich bayerischen Licealprofessor Heinrich Ruszwurm, nun Pfarrer in Schwarzach. Augsburg, B. Schmid'sche Berlagsbuchhandlung, 1855.

> xx, 148 p.   17 cm.
> *Inclusive dates:* July 8, 1852 to ?, 1852.
> *Location of copy:* Newberry Library.

Brentano left Augsburg and arrived in New York in July, 1852. He traveled in the East and as far south as Baltimore and Cincinnati. His particular interest appeared to center in the religious life and institutions in the United States, especially those of the Catholic population. He favored the quiet of the American Sabbath in contrast to the German observance of the day. He discussed slavery with much emotion, and he criticized those members of the Catholic clergy who kept slaves as servants and did not emancipate them.

The particular feature of this book for travel was the appendix which listed the many rules and regulations of the Bremen *Hand-*

lungshaus Lüdering & Comp, one of the transportation agencies for immigrants to various parts of America.

280. Bryant, William Cullen (1794–1878)

Letters of a traveller; or, notes of things seen in Europe and America. By William Cullen Bryant. New York, G. P. Putnam, 1850.

442 p. illus. 20½ cm.
Illustrations: Engraved title page. Thirteen illustrations: Steel engravings of scenes about the world. None in the South. (Third edition).
Inclusive dates: 1834–1850. In South, March 1 to April 28, 1843, and March and April, 1849.
Other editions:
　(1) London, 1850.
　(2) Second edition: New York, G. P. Putnam, 1850. 442 p. 19½ cm.
　(3) Third edition. New York, Putnam, 1851. 2 p.l., ₍3₎–422 p. front., plates. 21 cm. (Added t.p., engraved: The picturesque souvenir).
Location of copy: Chicago Historical Society.

This work is the republished third edition of *Letters of a traveller; or, notes of things seen in Europe and America* (New York, 1851). The first and second editions appeared in 1850. The book consists of the fifty-three letters written at various times during the "European, Western and Southern wanderings" of the distinguished poet-editor William Cullen Bryant. Most of the letters first appeared in the columns of the New York *Evening Post,* the important news organ edited by Bryant for almost half a century.

Seven of the letters (pp. 69–127) were written while on a two-month tour from Washington to St. Augustine in March and April, 1843, while three of the letters (pp. 336–55) describe his return visit over some of the same route six years later. These letters attempt to present no general conclusions regarding the South. Instead, they present sharply etched sketches of interesting and ofttimes humorous aspects of travel and life. The description of a corn shucking in South Carolina, the cities of Savannah and St. Augustine, and a visit to a cotton mill are of particular interest.

281. Burke, Emily P.

Reminiscences of Georgia. By Emily P. Burke. ₍Oberlin, O.₎, J. M. Fitch, 1850.

viii, 252 p. front. (port.). 17 cm.
Illustrations: Frontispiece: steel engraved, autographed portrait of author.
Inclusive dates: Probably 1839–1849.
Location of copy: Western Reserve University Library.

Emily Burke, one of the host of New England schoolteachers who taught in the South during this period, made at least two journeys from New York to Savannah, the first probably in the late 1830's and the second in the 1840's (p. 86), to teach for several years in various institutions throughout Georgia. In 1850 she published her *Reminiscences of Georgia,* containing some thirty letters which described in a simple, forthright, though emotional and sentimental, manner, many of the social and economic customs of the everyday lives of the people with whom she was associated.

She taught and visited in many parts of the state, especially in Savannah, on large coastal plantations, in the north of Georgia, and in the interior of the state. Except for her abhorrence of slavery, she expressed a genuine attachment for her many pleasant associations and experiences. Her description of Savannah (pp. 15–75), Georgia plantations (pp. 102–32, 220–34), a camp meeting, and education in Georgia (pp. 195–204) contribute to an understanding of Georgia society in the 1840's. Her sharply etched pictures in miniature of hospitals, a plantation kitchen, runaway slaves, plowing on a large plantation, and a quilting party give some of the detailed information that comes from intimate association and observation not noted in most of the travel accounts.

282.   Burns, Jabez

Notes of a tour in the United States and Canada, in the summer and autumn of 1847, by Jabez Burns, D.D. London, Houlston and Stoneman, 1848.

> vi, [9]–180 p.   15½ cm.
> *Inclusive dates:* August 18 to November 1, 1847. In South, a few days in September.
> *Location of copy:* Enoch Pratt Free Library, Baltimore Public Library.

Dr. Burns (see the *Dictionary of National Biography*), nonconformist divine, author of numerous religious works, public speaker, and temperance and antislavery reformer, visited the United States as "one of two delegates from the general Baptist Association of England to the triennial conference of the Freewill Baptists of the United States" meeting at Sutton, Vermont. Even though his travels in the South were limited to a trip from Washington to Cumberland, Maryland, by way of Harpers Ferry, he had much to say about slavery from his observations and conversations in Maryland, Virginia, and the Northeastern states. To him the dominant discords in American life were "colorophobia," prejudice against the Negro race in the North and slavery in its "foulest form in the South," and "spitology . . . [which rendered] every visible thing foul by the nauseous juice. . . ."

283. Busch, Moritz (1821–1899)
Wanderungen zwischen Hudson und Mississippi, 1851 und 1852. 2 vols. Stuttgart und Tübingen. J. G. Cotta'scher, 1854.

Vol. I, 1, 390 p.; Vol. II, 1, 381 p. 21½ cm.
Inclusive dates: August, 1851, to spring (?), 1852.
Location of copy: University of Kentucky Library.

When Moritz Busch left Germany in 1851, disappointed with the events of 1848, he already had an editorial and literary reputation through his German translations of works by Dickens and Thackeray. But he gained his greatest distinction years later as Bismarck's chief publicist, confidant, and inseparable companion and as the editor of an issue of the Iron Chancellor's letters and papers.

Busch, though trained in philosophy and theology with a Ph.D. from Leipzig—which in part may explain his marked attention to such American religious groups as Shakers, Dunkards, Methodists, and Mormons—was keenly interested yet critical of American political and social institutions. He arrived in New York in August, 1851, and spent several months there and in Ohio, Kentucky, Missouri, and Illinois, traveling by rail and river steamer to and from St. Louis by way of Cumberland, Columbus, and Cincinnati. He returned to Germany in 1852, quite disillusioned with much in America, and in 1854 published the two-volume account of his travels. Although most of the two volumes center on his observations in and around the cities of New York, Cincinnati, and St. Louis, the last 150 pages of Volume I have particular significance for travel through parts of Kentucky and along its Ohio River border.

Chapter VIII describes Busch's three-week side trip by horse and wagon late in November, 1851, from Cincinnati through northern Kentucky to Cynthiana, Millersburg, Owingsville, Flemingsburg, and Maysville (I, pp. 287–346). Detailed comments on institutions, interspersed with descriptive and historical narrative, together with interesting incidents en route, enrich the account of this region. His description of Henry Clay's stop at the "elegant" Thormorton's Inn near Millersburg on the statesman's last trip to the nation's capital and Busch's extended visit with Major Sudduth, wealthy owner of some "hundred and twenty five thousand acres" near the Licking River, highlighted this dip into Kentucky. Next followed his return trip to St. Louis by river steamer, which afforded more details of some of the communities along the Kentucky shore than are to be found in most of the other travel books of the forties and fifties.

In his effort to better interpret the Negro slave for his German readers, Busch did important spadework in a hitherto virtually overlooked significant source, the Negro spiritual, by translating and analyzing some thirteen of these folk songs (I, pp. 250–80). This chapter alone places Busch far in the vanguard of other observers and students of this important phase of the American scene. He appears to have imitated the pattern of his countrymen J. G. Herder and the Grimm brothers in their search for the source of a national German culture in the *volk,* and in so doing Busch anticipated by almost a century similar studies by future students of American folklore.

Another significant chapter in Volume II, entitled "Sons of St. Tammany," is about as intensive a discussion of the American political party system to 1850 as given by any of the foreign travelers in this period (II, pp. 291–369). Busch concluded his impressions of America in a final chapter by calling attention to what he considered to be the four characteristic qualities of Americans. They evidence his closer association with the North and East than with the South and are as follows: "hostility to all authority," "a certain philosophical attitude which expresses itself through questioning and searching for final causes and general ideas," "extraordinary intensity in life and endeavor," and "an exaggerated love for material things . . . which . . . sets money above the value of the human."

Although his travels in the South were limited and his impressions in the main reflected a critical attitude toward America, his scholarly training, wide experience, understanding, and attention to detail make Busch an important observer. He was to become one of the most distinguished of the many Germans who visited America in the mid-century.

284. Casey, Charles

Two years on the farm of Uncle Sam. With sketches of his location, nephews, and prospects. London, Richard Bentley, 1852.

> 1 p.l., ₍v₎–ix, 311 p.   20 cm.
> *Inclusive dates:* May 28, 1848, to 1852 (?).
> *Location of copy:* University of Kentucky Library.

There is little of value for travel literature of the South to be gleaned from this hackneyed, conglomerate description of events by the English traveler Charles Casey. No regular route of travel can be discerned in the organization of his chapters. There is evidence of his having passed over some of the same territory on more than one trip. His descriptions of river travel are interesting, but he commented on little else in the South except New Orleans. On the whole the work is superficial. Arriving in this country with an extreme aversion to slavery, Casey later moderated his criticism of the system.

285.   Caswall, Henry, Rev., M.A., Vicar of Fegheldean (1810–1870)

The Western world revisited. Oxford, John Henry Parker, 1854.
> xvi, 351 p.   16½ cm.
> *Inclusive dates:* September to December, 1853. In South, November 10–12, 1853.
> *Other editions:*
>   The Western world revisited. Oxford and London, John Henry Parker, 1854.
>   xvi, 351 p.   16½ cm.
> *Location of copy:* Library of Congress.

Caswall, prominent Anglican clergyman, first visited America in 1828. Afterwards he made at least four or five trips to Canada and the United States. (See Caswall, *America and the American Church,* London, 1839). Invited to attend the Episcopal Board of Missions meeting in New York in October, 1853, he again traveled through parts of Canada and the United States. Even though his travel in the South was limited to a quick trip by river from Cincinnati to Carrollton, Kentucky, and a brief stay in Washington, D. C., he had discussed the problems of the South with many Southern clergymen at the New York meeting.

He noted many improvements over his previous visits. He described a distillery at Carrollton and commented on the profits made from fattening hogs on the distilled mash. He was not critical of slavery, for he thought the conditions of the Negroes the equal of that of many of the English laborers. Englishmen, he felt, ought to be the last to "reproach the Americans on account of slavery."

286.   [A Child of the Sun, *pseud.*]

The summer-land: a southern story. By a child of the sun. New York, D. Appleton and company, 1855.
> 264 p.   19 cm.
> *Inclusive dates:* 1850's?
> *Location of copy:* University of Kentucky.

This work, in the form of an autobiographical novel, can hardly be considered a travel book; rather it is an idealized and highly colored sentimental picture of planter life by one who was much interested in that class. The anonymous author was a Southerner who traveled extensively "over his native land," taking notes from which he later drew his character sketches.

287. Clapp, Theodore (1792–1866)

Autobiographical sketches and recollections, during a thirty-five years' residence in New Orleans. By Theodore Clapp. Boston, Phillips, Sampson & company, 1857.

> viii, 419 p., 1 l. front. (port.). 20 cm.
> *Illustrations:* Frontispiece: Engraving of T. Clapp by S. A. Schoff.
> *Inclusive dates:* 1821–1856. In South, 1821–1856?
> *Other editions:*
> (1) 2d ed. Boston, Phillips, Sampson & company, 1858. viii, 419 p. front. (port.). 20 cm.
> (2) 4th ed. Boston, Phillips, Sampson & company, 1859. viii, 419 p. 20 cm.
> *Location of copy:* University of Kentucky Library.

For thirty-five years Clapp, a prominent Massachusetts-born clergyman, had ministered to his parish in New Orleans before he retired to Louisville, Kentucky. After graduating from Yale in 1814, he completed his theological training at Andover Seminary and came to Lexington, Kentucky, where he served for a time before going to New Orleans in 1821. His autobiography is a narrative of his ministerial activities, an introduction to many of the prominent preachers of the day, and a description of the numerous cholera and yellow-fever epidemics that threatened the Crescent City during his stay of thirty-five years. His intimate pictures of this phase of New Orleans life, though at times overdrawn, bring into focus the terrible conditions during the epidemics of 1833, 1837, and 1853.

The above is a fourth edition.

288. Clarke, Lewis Garrard

Narratives of the sufferings of Lewis Clarke, during a captivity of more than twenty-five years, among the Algerines of Kentucky, one of the so called Christian states of North America. Dictated by himself. Boston, D. H. Ela, printer, 1845.

> viii, [9]–108 p., incl. front. (port.). 23 cm.
> *Illustrations:* Engravings of each of the authors (1846 edition).
> *Inclusive dates:* 1815–1845.
> *Other editions:*
> Narratives of the sufferings of Lewis and Milton Clarke, sons of a soldier of the revolution, during a captivity of more than twenty years among the slave-

holders of Kentucky, one of the so called Christian states of North America. Dictated by themselves. Boston, B. Marsh, 1846. 144 p. 2 port. (incl. front.). 18 cm.
Location of copy: University of Kentucky Library.

The two brothers, Lewis Clarke (1812–1897) and Milton Clarke (1817?–1901), former slaves from Kentucky whose maternal grandfather was a slaveholder, record their fugitive experiences in the interest of the antislavery movement. References to prominent persons in Kentucky such as Cassius M. Clay give the book some added interest. First published in 1845 as the *Narrative of Lewis Clarke,* the above edition describes the experiences of both brothers. Additional antislavery material is included in the book, which, in general, differs little from other works of this kind.

289.   [Cobb, Charles, comp.]

American railway guide, and pocket companion, for the United States; containing correct tables, time of starting from all stations, distances, fares, etc. on all railway lines in the United States; together with a complete railway map. Also many stage lines running in connection with railroads. Subscription per annum, $1; single numbers, 12 1-2 cts; wholesale price, $7 per 100. New York, Dinsmore, 1850.

133 p.   (22 p. of advertisements).   15 cm.
Location of copy: Duke University Library.

According to the editor's extravagant statement, "this work [which was to be published every month] was commenced in April, 1850 ... and, the traveling public can attest that in all that relates to their use and convenience, no work of a similar description has more faithfully, fully and completely kept 'time' with the great movements of the age." Although much the same as many of the American guidebooks, this one lists some thirty Southern railroads and has an alphabetical listing of the ocean and river steamboats, together with their captains and distances. The editor states that "our circulation varies from 8,000 to 23,000, the former being the lowest winter issue and the latter the average for season of travel." Only Sabin listed this title.

290.   Coke, Henry J[ohn] (1827–1916)

A ride over the Rocky mountains to Oregon and California. With a glance at some of the tropical islands, including the West Indies and the Sandwich Isles. By the Hon. Henry J. Coke. London, Richard Bentley, 1852.

x, 388 p., [2] p, incl. front. (port.). 22 cm.
Illustrations: Engraving of the Hon. Henry J. Coke by Hattmandel and Walton.
Inclusive dates: December 18, 1849, to June, 1851. In South, March, 1850.
Location of copy: University of Kentucky Library.

The Honorable Henry J. Coke, brother of the Earl of Leicester, touched at Charleston, South Carolina, on a trip from Havana to New York before leaving for St. Louis en route to California. In an autobiographical study, *Trades of a Rolling Stone* (London, 1905, 2nd edition), Coke again refers to his stopping at Charleston. The books have no value for Southern travel.

291.   [Colton, Joseph Hutchins (1800–1893)]

Colton's traveler and tourist's guide-book through the United States of America and the Canadas: containing the routes and distances on the great lines of travel by railroads, canals, stageroads, and steamboats; together with descriptions of the several states, and of the principal cities, towns, and villages in each. Accompanied with a large and accurate map. New York, published by J. H. Colton, 1856.

> 1 p.l., v–xiv, 250 p.   2 maps (incl. front.).   15½ cm.
> *Maps:* Frontispiece: Railroad routes between New York, Philadelphia, Baltimore, and Washington. Large folding map of United States in 1850.
> *Other editions:*
>   (1) Colton's traveler and tourist's route-book through the United States of America and the Canadas: containing the routes and distances on the great lines of travel, by railroads, stage-roads, canals, lakes and rivers. New York, J. H. Colton and Co., 1854.   1 p.l., v–xi, 13–134 p. fold. map.   15½ cm.
>   (2) Colton's traveler and tourist's guide-book through the United States of America containing brief descriptions of each, with the routes and distances on the great line of travel. Compiled by Richard S. Fisher. New York, J. H. Colton and Company, 1857.   xix, [21]–354 p. fold. map.   15½ cm.
> *Location of copy:* Wisconsin Historical Society.

The title is self-explanatory. A section on travel information for the Southern Atlantic states (pp. 88–119) and one on the Southwestern States (pp. 120–51) include the usual description of each of the states —the distances by water, rail, or stage and other pertinent facts. Kentucky is listed in the section of Northwestern States (pp. 166–70). The above is the 1856 edition.

292.   Considerant, Victor [1808–1893]

Au Texas. Paris, À La Librairie Phalansterienne, 1854.

> 1 l., 1–194 p.   21½ cm.
> *Maps:* United States and Texas.
> *Inclusive dates:* 1852–1853.

Other editions:

Au Texas, par Victor Considerant. 2. éd. contenant 1° Rapport à mes amis; 2° Bases et statuts de la Société de colonisation européo-américaine au Texas; 3° . . . Les bases d'un premier establissement sociétaire . . . Bruxells, Société de colonisation; [etc.], 1855. 3 p.l., [3]–344 p. fold. map, tables (part fold.). 18½ cm.

Location of copy: Wisconsin State Historical Library.

Considerant, prolific socialist writer and successor to the mantle of Fourier, says in his brief preface that he had not intended that the contents of this book should be published. He wrote that he regarded it more as an appendix to his reports. The author, a communist of the Fourier brand, was forced to flee from France in 1849 and from Belgium a year later. His journey to the United States in 1852 seems to have been primarily for the purpose of locating the site for a colony. Financed in part by Albert Brisbane, Considerant intended to set up a socialist community in Texas. (See Monaghan.)

He entered the South by way of the Ohio River, and his description of this stream is intriguing. Considerant proved to be a good observer. More than three-fourths of the book is devoted to Texas. Not only does he give a careful and full description of that state, but he also gives a considerable amount of American history in his book. Considerant wrote with the prospective Latin immigrant in mind, and much of his material is of a comparative nature. This is a useful travel account and is an unusually full one to have come from a Latin visitor. It does not have the sting that many of the hypercritical accounts of this period contained.

Considerant's settlement some miles from Dallas, Texas, failed after a few years, and he then moved to San Antonio where he lived until 1869, when he returned to Paris.

293. Cooke, Philip St. George (1809–1895), Whiting, William Henry Chase (1824–1865), and Aubry, François Xavier

Exploring Southwestern trails, 1846–1854, by Philip [St. George] Cooke, William Henry Chase Whiting [and] François Aubry; edited by Ralph P. Bieber . . . in collaboration with Averam B. Bender. Glendale, California, Arthur H. Clark company, 1938.

> 383 p., 1 l., incl. front., plates, ports., fold. map. 23½ cm.
> *Maps:* Map showing trails explored by Philip St. G. Cooke, William H. C. Whiting, and François X. Aubry from 1846–1854.
> *Illustrations:* Photographs of Philip St. George Cooke, Church of San Xavier

del Boc about 1854, William Henry Chase Whiting, Plaza and Church of El Paso Del Norte about 1852, and François Xavier Aubry.
Inclusive dates: October 13, 1846, to August 16, 1854.
Location of copy: University of Kentucky Library.

The two manuscript journals of Philip St. George Cooke and William Henry C. Whiting, officers of the U. S. Army, and the diaries of François X. Aubry, civilian trader and adventurer, edited for this volume, describe the surveying of the trails which became the routes for the overland migration into the Southwest. Each of these men traveled extensively in and about Texas, and each described with varying degree of detail the advantages and disadvantages of the region and the routes explored. Whiting's report of his expedition from San Antonio to El Paso and his return (February to May, 1849) to "ascertain if there be a practicable and convenient route for military and commercial purposes" appears to be the most significant for Southern travel. Its contribution is confirmed by the many "California-bound argonauts" in 1849, the overland mail and stagecoaches of a later day, and the trains of the Southern Pacific system today, all of which follow much of Whiting's route.

Cooke's journal of the march of the Mormon battalion in 1846–47, which he commanded, and Aubry's diaries of 1853–54 center attention on the trails from Santa Fé to California. Cooke, a Virginian, and Whiting, a Mississippian, were to have distinguished records in the Civil War, the former in the Union Army, while the latter, "one of the most able engineers in the Confederate service," was wounded in North Carolina in 1865 and died a few weeks later at Fort Columbus on Governor's Island, New York.

294. Creuzbaur, Robert

Route from the Gulf of Mexico and the Lower Mississippi Valley. Austin, Texas and New York, H. Long and Brother and Robert Creuzbaur, 1849.

1–40 p.   maps, tables.   19 cm.
Maps: Six maps of routes to California. Tables of distances.
Inclusive dates: 1849.
Location of copy: Newberry Library.

This rare little book is made up largely of excerpts from the descriptions of travel routes in the Southwest and California. There are selections from Frémont's *Journal*, Captain S. R. Henry's *Journal*, W. H. Emory's *Notes*, P. St. George Cooke, and Dr. John S. Ford. One of the most interesting sections in the book is that giving instructions to travelers concerning equipment. Its specific value as a Southern travel book lies in its description of the route across Texas.

295. Davies, Ebenezer (1808–1882)

American scenes—and Christian slavery: a recent tour of four thousand miles in the United States by Ebenezer Davies ... London, J. Snow, 1849.

> xii, 324 p. 19 cm.
> *Inclusive dates:* January to April, 1848? In South, January to February, 1848.
> *Other editions:*
> London, J. Freeman, 1853.
> *Location of copy:* Cleveland Public Library.

His wife's ill health, resulting from her long residence in British Guiana, caused Ebenezer Davies, "British abolitionist" and minister of a mission church in Berbice for the London Society, to journey for some months through the United States. During a two-week stay in New Orleans, followed by a trip up the river to Pittsburgh, Davies made a point of recording in the thirty-seven letters that make up this travel book (fifteen of which relate directly to the South) his very critical observations on American slavery. He made frequent note of advertisements for slave sales, runaway slaves, the details of slave auctions, and the prices paid for slaves. He condemned the churches, the clergy, and the federal government for their support of the system.

296. Dawson, Nicholas

Narrative of Nicholas "Cheyenne" Dawson (overland to California in '41 and '49, and Texas in '51) with an introduction by Charles L. Camp and colored drawings by Arvilla Parker. San Francisco, Grabhorn press, 1933.

> 6 p.l., 100 p., 4 l. col. illus. 25 cm.
> *Illustrations:* Colored scenes of California.
> *Inclusive dates:* 1841–1851. In South, 1851 (?).
> *Other editions:*
> California in '41, Texas in '51. Memoirs, by Nicholas Dawson. [Austin?, Tex., n.d.]. 119 p. front., port. 17½ cm.
> *Location of copy:* University of California.

Although much of the narrative in this reprint of the rare item of Americana, *California in 41, Texas in 51. Memoirs, by Nicholas Dawson,* focuses on the author's hazardous wagon-crossing of the Rocky Mountains in 1841 with that first valiant band of settlers and his later experiences in the California gold rush, one brief section (pp. 80–84) describes a trip from Arkansas to Texas in 1851. His unadorned but graphic picture of the Texas prairies in that year merits a note in the travel literature of the American Southwest. According to the introductory statement, Dawson, familiarly called "Cheyenne" Dawson, wrote the account some fifty years after the events and intended the edition of fifty copies which appeared in 1901 to be limited to members of his family. This explains in part the infrequent mention of the work by writers on Western history.

297.   Devol, George H. (b. 1829)

Forty years a gambler on the Mississippi. New York, Henry Holt and Company, 1926.

> 3 p.l., 3–288 p.   18½ cm.
> *Inclusive dates:* 1839–1870's.
> *Other editions:*
> Forty years a gambler on the Mississippi, by George H. Devol. 1st ed. Cincinnati, Devol and Haines, 1887.   viii, 9–300 p.   front. (port.), 4 plates.   22 cm.
> *Location of copy:* University of Michigan Library.

"A cabin boy in 1839 [at the age of ten]; could steal cards and cheat the boys at eleven; stack a deck at fourteen; bested soldiers on the Rio Grande during the Mexican War; won hundreds of thousands from paymasters, cotton buyers, defaulters and thieves. . . ." This in brief described the career of George Devol, notorious gambler, whose autobiography written in 1887 is an interesting but rambling and disconnected narrative of his forty years of living by his wits, often by his fists, and "old Betsy Jane," his pistol, on river steamers, railroads, and gambling emporiums throughout the length and breadth of the Mississippi Valley.

Rarely did he comment on anything not directly associated with his vocation. His description of the Wilson Rangers, a cavalry company of New Orleans gamblers who attempted to defend that city against General Butler in 1862, contributes little to military history, but it is interesting reading (pp. 123–29).

Devol identifies the river steamers and their captains as well as the many towns and cities in which he operated.

298.   Dewees, William B.

Letters from an early settler of Texas. By W. B. Dewees. Comp. by Cara Cardelle [*pseud.*]. Louisville, Ky., Morton & Griswold, 1852.

> viii, [9]–312 p.   20 cm.
> *Inclusive dates:* 1818–1852.

Other editions:
(1) Louisville, Hall & brothers, printers, 1854.
(2) ₍2d ed.₎. Louisville, Ky., ₍New Albany Tribune print.₎, 1858. viii, ₍9₎–312 p. 18 cm.
Location of copy: University of Kentucky Library.

The preface states that the compiler, Cara Cardelle, pseudonym for Emaretta C. Kimball, chanced to find among a friend's papers a large stack of Texas letters with much information on the events of Texas history from 1819–1852. The letters were written by William B. Dewees to a friend in Kentucky. Securing the permission of Dewees, they were published in 1852. Although more of a history than a travel work, the thirty-one letters, written over a period of about thirty-three years, are unembellished pictures of the journey to Texas, personal incidents, and facts and events in Texas development.

299. Diehl, Louis

Meine Schicksale und Erlebnisse in Nordamerika, nebst einem Anhang: die Licht- und Schattenseite der Neuen Welt. Darmstadt, C. F. Will, 1851.

vi, 96 p. 23 cm.
Inclusive dates: Probably between 1848–1853 (three months).
Location of copy: Newberry Library.

"Shadows in the New World" or "Misfortune in America" would be fitting titles for this prejudiced but in part interesting account of Diehl's "three long months" in the United States sometime between 1848–1853. He had become disillusioned by his unfortunate experiences in New Orleans, St. Louis, Cincinnati, and on the river steamboats, and he intended this book as a warning to prospective German emigrants that all was not *glanzend* in the New World.

Diehl described the "bad climate" and the darker side of slavery as seen in New Orleans and then proceeded up the river to St. Louis, where he survived a cholera epidemic, mosquitoes, and the "million dollar fire." The latter ended his brief business venture in that city. He was favorably impressed with much that he saw in Cincinnati, only to be the victim of a fire that destroyed the vessel and all his belongings while returning from that city to New Orleans. After witnessing another terrible steamboat explosion which was fatal to some two hundred persons, he decided to return to Germany, only to encounter storms en route which almost wrecked the ship.

General information concerning the geography, resources, and trade, interspersed with chapters discussing other "shadows," such as lynchings, laxity of justice, and "morasses and swamps," make up the last half of the book.

300.　Disturnell [John] (1801–1877)

Disturnell's American and European railway and steamship guide, giving the arrangements on all the great lines of travel through the United States and Canada, across the Atlantic Ocean, and throughout Central Europe. Also containing a brief description of the principal places in England, France, etc. New York, published by Disturnell, 1853.

> 208 p.　front., illus., fold. map.　15 cm.
> *Maps:* Folding map of railways in Central Europe (1853).
> *Illustrations:* Frontispiece: View of the Crystal Palace.
> *Other editions:*
>   1854 edition.　122 p., incl. front., illus., fold. map.　15½ cm.
> *Location of copy:* Library of Congress.

John Disturnell, book dealer, librarian of Cooper Union, and compiler of guidebooks, post office directories, and politicians' manuals, was born in New York. Anticipating the popular demand for travel information during the forties and fifties, he provided the public with travel guides for points in America and abroad, giving information on railroad and steamboat routes, distances, fares, hotels, cities, resorts, and places of interest. The Library of Congress Catalog lists thirty-two titles of guidebooks compiled by Disturnell. For a complete sketch of his life, see the *Dictionary of American Biography.*
　This guidebook was republished in 1854 with the same title.

301.　[Disturnell, John, (publisher) (1801–1877)]

Springs, water-falls, sea-bathing resorts, and mountain scenery of the United States and Canada; giving an analysis of the principal mineral springs with a brief description of the most fashionable watering-places, mountain resorts, etc., with illustrations. New York, J. Disturnell, 1855.

> xii, [13]–227, 12 p.　15 cm.
> *Illustrations:* Several illustrations (none in the South).
> *Location of copy:* University of Kentucky Library.

A brief but well-organized and concise listing, with appropriate descriptions, of the important resorts and places of popular scenic interest throughout Canada and the United States. Included are thirty-five pages of resorts and scenic spots in the South.

302.   Dix, John (1800?–1865)

Transatlantic tracings; or, sketches of persons and scenes in America. By the author of Lions; living and dead; ... London, W. Tweedie, 1853.

xii, 337 p.   front., engr. t.p. in addition.   17 cm.
Illustrations: Frontispiece: Engraving of Harriet B. Stowe.
Inclusive dates: 1846–1852?
Location of copy: Miami University Library.

John R. Dix was born in Bristol and for some years was a practicing surgeon in that city (see the *Dictionary of National Biography*). In 1846 he was in America, and in 1853 he wrote one of his many books. It was a collection of sketches of contemporary American literati, chiefly from New England, together with typical scenes in American life. One chapter of the work, entitled "Southern Sketches—Glances at Negro Life," based at least on one visit to Richmond, Virginia, and its environs, quite superficially discusses aspects of Negro moral and religious life. Dix does, however, give an interesting picture of a Negro funeral (pp. 229–43).

303.   Dixon, James (1788–1871)

Personal narrative of a tour through a part of the United States and Canada: with notices of the history and institutions of Methodism in America. New York, Lane & Scott, 1849.

431 p.   front. (port.).   18½ cm.
Illustrations: Engraving by F. E. Jones, from painting by W. Gush, of James Dixon, D.D.
Inclusive dates: April 8, 1848, to July, 1848.
Other editions:
   Second edition. 1849.
Location of copy: University of Kentucky Library.

In order to "make the Methodist body in England acquainted with the state and progress of their system of religion in the United States," James Dixon, eminent Wesleyan clergyman and president of the Conference of Canada, made a three months' tour of America. His actual observations on the South included in a chapter in the first part of this book, entitled "Personal Narrative," were based on a trip from Washington to Harpers Ferry and a later voyage down the Ohio River to Cincinnati together with frequent contacts with Southern clergymen and reliance on excerpts from American works on Methodism. Dixon was critical of slavery.

The most significant part of this book for Southern travel is the last section (pp. 309–431) on the territorial progress of the Methodist church, which includes a statistical survey of a sort of the various Southern conferences.

A second edition of the work appeared in 1849. See the *Dictionary of National Biography* for a detailed biographical sketch of the author.

304. Domenech, Abbé Em. (1826–1886)

Journal d'un missionaire au Texas et au Mexique, par l'abbé E. Domenech, 1846–1852. Paris, Gaume frères, 1857.

[v]–xii, 477 p. front. (fold. map). 21 cm.
Maps: Frontispiece: Folding map of Texas, illustrating the missions and journeys of Abbé Domenech in Texas.
Inclusive dates: March, 1846, to September, 1852.
Other editions:
   Missionary adventures in Texas and Mexico. A personal narrative of six years' sojourn in those regions. By the Abbé Domenech. Translated from the French under the author's superintendence. London, Longman, Brown, Green, Longmans, and Roberts, 1858. xv, 366 p. front. (fold. map). 22 cm.
Location of copy: Library of Congress.

Five years after returning to France because of "shattered health" from his six years of missionary life on the Texas frontier, Abbé Domenech, prolific writer on Mexico, Indians, and religion and later a protégé of Emperor Napoleon III, published the account of his experiences, hoping to stimulate missionary activity in America. Coming to St. Louis by way of New Orleans in 1846, in response to an urgent appeal for missionaries to work in the "wilds of Texas," he spent two years in the former city completing his theological course. Assigned to the new and extensive mission about Castroville, Texas, the Abbé journeyed there in 1848, passing through New Orleans, Galveston, Houston, Austin, Braunfels, and San Antonio. He labored at his post for two years, suffering the horrors of famine, fatigue, floods, heat, cholera, "serpents, panthers, and Indians." In order to raise funds for a stone church in 1849, he revisited New Orleans and the lower Mississippi River towns, soliciting gifts which enabled him to carry out that project by Easter, 1850, for a total cost of 130 francs.

Shortly thereafter, he left for France and Italy via New Orleans, Cincinnati, Lake Erie, and New York to interest Pope Pius IX in the Texas missions. Returning over the same route to New Orleans on May 5, 1851, he was then transferred to a new mission at Brownsville, Texas, to minister to the widely scattered settlers along the Río Grande. Broken in health, he returned to France in October, 1852.

The considerable interval of time between the experiencing and the recording of the events in no way dulls the vivid descriptions in his self-styled "racy and authentic accounts." At times he was guilty of gross exaggeration and inaccuracies. So often did he report himself in a "dying state" that the reader wonders at his many feats of reported physical courage and survival. Yet the Abbé reveals the self-abnegation and the patient perseverance of the missionaries on the hazardous Texas frontier. The work is not lacking in interest and humor.

Abbé Domenech accompanied Napoleon's expedition to Mexico in 1861 as the almoner and chaplain to Emperor Maximilian. In 1882–83 he revisited America. Concerning the then famous controversy that raged over Domenech's publication of the work *Manuscript Pictographique Américain* (Paris, 1860) and his defense of that work in his published pamphlet *La Vérité sur le Livre des Sauvages* (Paris, 1861), see *An Essay towards an Indian bibliography. Being a Catalogue of Books, Relating to the History, Antiquities, Languages, Customs, Religion, Wars, Literature, and Origin of the American Indians, in the Library of Thomas W. Field* (New York, 1873) (pp. 104–105). For a biographical sketch of Abbé Domenech, see *The Catholic Encyclopedia*, V, p. 102.

305. Domenech, Abbé Em. (1825 or 6–1886)

Seven years' residence in the great deserts of North America, by the Abbé Em. Domenech apostolical missionary: canon of Montpellier; member of the Pontifical Academy Tiberina and of the Geographical and Ethnographical Societies of France, etc. Illustrated with fifty-eight woodcuts by A. Joliet, three plates of ancient Indian music, and a map showing the actual situation of the Indian tribes and the country described by the author. 2 vols. London, Longman, Green, Longman, and Roberts, 1860.

> Vol. I, xiii, 445 p. front., map, col. plates; Vol. II, xii, 465 p. front., plates. 21½ cm.
>
> *Maps:* Vol. I: Large folding map of United States, showing reported route of travel among Indian tribes.
>
> *Illustrations:* Numerous woodcuts and plates of scenery, Indians, and material related to Indian life.
>
> *Inclusive dates:* March, 1846, to September, 1852.
>
> *Location of copy:* University of Kentucky Library.

This work is based on the travels described in Abbé Domenech's earlier book published in 1858 together with materials collected from every available source. The important part of this work has been described as "a category of the Indian Tribes of North America, and some short vocabularies of some of their languages." It includes descriptions of Indians in Texas and Louisiana. There is no reference to personal observations, and the evidence of his travels in Texas in his earlier work, *Missionary Adventures in Texas and Mexico* (London, 1858), raises the question of how much of the route indicated on the map (Vol. I) was actually covered. See Thomas W. Field, *An essay toward an Indian Bibliography* (New York, 1873), pp. 104–105.

306. Duncan, Mrs. Mary (Grey) Lundie

America as I found it. By the mother of Mary Lundie Duncan. New York, Robert Carter & Brothers, 1852.

> 2 p.l., ₁v₁–viii, p. 1 l., ₁11₁–440 p., 12 p. 16½ cm.
> *Illustrations:* Frontispiece: Engraved portrait of author by A. H. Ritchie.
> *Inclusive dates:* Probably 1850–1851.
> *Other editions:*
>   America as I found it. By the author of A memoir of Mary Lundie Duncan. London, J. Nesbst and Co., 1852. 1 p.l., ₁v₁–xii, 380 p. 17 cm.
> *Location of copy:* University of Kentucky Library.

Mrs. Duncan traveled through much of the East, but there is little in her account suggesting the length of time spent or the route taken, nor is there any evidence that she ever crossed the Potomac River into Virginia. She discusses a wide range of subjects of social and humanitarian import, such as education, churches, weddings, funerals, and prisons, in a wordy, rambling, and impersonal fashion that makes for interesting social history. She had much to say about slavery and the colonization society (pp. 215–82). Her solution for the problem of the "American African" was to "give up to the whole race a state for themselves, at the South, and leave them to erect a standard of freedom there . . ." (p. 281). She described an "effervescence of enthusiasm" for Henry Clay on one occasion in Washington when "hundreds upon hundreds" of excited women attempted to embrace the "man of the day" (p. 405). Since Mrs. Duncan apparently did not travel south of Washington, her work has only indirect significance for Southern travel.

307. Dureau, Jean Baptiste

Les États-Unis en 1850. Notes et souvenirs. Paris, L'auteur, 1891.

> iv, 540 p. 18½ cm.
> *Inclusive dates:* 1850–1851.
> *Location of copy:* University of Michigan.

Here is a good contemporary French account of an extended visit in the United States. The book was not published until 1891; the manuscript lay untouched for forty years. Thus the account was apparently written soon after the author's return to France. Dureau said in his preface that he set out to discover the simple, down-to-earth patterns of American life. He was not concerned with theories and learned discussions but with the everyday affairs of the new nation. His language is simple and clear, and his concepts are good.

Like most French travelers, Dureau kept his own itinerary sufficiently confused to prevent a specific statement of where he went or where he was at a given time. He followed the practice of his countrymen of commenting upon what he saw in a general way and then making what he said applicable to a whole institution or region. This is especially true of the rather long section on slavery and the Mississippi Valley. In these chapters he discussed such topics as race relations, plantations, steamboating, camp meetings, and American women. No Frenchman could get his perspective without bringing the history of what he was viewing up to date.

It is clear that Dureau was in the South, and his material is good. For instance, he gives a close picture of the intemperance of the Southern people. Their drinking astonished him, and so did sleeping with them two abed.

308. Ellet, Mrs. Elizabeth Fries (Lummis) (1818–1877)
Summer rambles in the West. New-York, J. C. Riker, 1853.

viii, 268 p. 18½ cm.
Inclusive dates: June to October or November, 1852.
Location of copy: University of Kentucky Library.

The New-York-born author Mrs. Ellet, who lived during the forties in Columbia, South Carolina, where her husband was professor of chemistry at South Carolina College, spent the summer and fall of 1852 traveling about the old Northwest (see the *Dictionary of American Biography*). There is no mention of any part of her trip to or from Kentucky, but she concludes the above account of her journey with a brief but interesting and enthusiastic chapter describing her trip through Mammoth Cave. She wished to provoke curiosity among her readers "to see for themselves" its many attractions.

309. [By an Englishman]
Information for emigrants: in three parts. I—North America. II—New

South Wales, Port Phillip, Cooksland, South Australia, and New Zealand. III—The Cape of Good Hope, Algoa Bay, and Port Natal; also, a view of Canada, etc. comprising an impartial account of the present state, prospects, and capabilities of each; their principal settlements; and the advantages they present to different classes of settlers; together with much useful information on all matters essential to the intending emigrant. London, Kent and Richards, 1848.

48, 52, 52 p. 16½ cm.
Location of copy: Wisconsin State Historical Society.

The first forty-eight-page section of this three-part, brief compendium of information for emigrants deals especially with the valleys of the Ohio and Mississippi rivers. It describes their soils, climate, productions, and routes of travel from New York and gives other useful information. Each part is paged separately. It describes the difficulties and the opportunities but warns that in America, "riches and independence are not to be obtained without steady and patient efforts." Although not a travel account, the book has marginal value.

310. Etourneau, M.

Livret-guide de l'émigrant, du négociant et du touriste dans les États-Unis d'Amérique et au Canada, contenant les renseignements les plus exacts, pris sur les lieux mêmes sur ces contrées indispensables aux personnes qui veulent s'y rendre ou acquérir les connaissances nécessaires à leur genre d'affaires. Paris, A. Petit-Pierre, 1855.

2 p.l., 211, [1] p. 15 cm.
Location of copy: Library of Congress.

French interest in America provoked many self-appointed emigrant advisers to prepare notes on the United States. This was true in the case of M. Etourneau. He gives a detailed account of American geography, social customs, modes of travel, and resources. Although the book is general in its approach to the American scene, it does give considerable attention to New Orleans. In this section the author describes the economic and social life of the place and gives his Latin readers the information which he knows will appeal to them.

The value of this book is not sectional alone. It gives a good picture of the foreigner's concept of the United States. Much of the text, of course, is made up of the kind of materials that have gone into countless emigrant and tourist guides. The material on Louisiana, however, gives definite Southern value to the volume.

311.   Eyma, [Louis] Xavier (1816–1876)

La vie aux États-Unis, notes de voyage par Xavier Eyma. Paris, E. Plon
et Cie., 1876.

307 p.   17½ cm.
Location of copy: University of Kentucky Library.

Eyma, an important author and editor who directed scientific and
educational missions to the United States, traveled up the Mississippi
River at least twice. He describes it as a drainage system, gives some
concept of its lateral streams, and discusses the towns along the great
River. Like most French travelers, he gives a good bit of local history of the places which he describes, but his history has a more
intimate relationship than a bare recitation of encyclopedic facts.

There are good brief discussions of travel experiences aboard
steamboats, the kinds of people who were found on deck, and the
attitudes they had toward the country. Not only were there travelers
who were moving about in the normal course of affairs, but there
were Yankee traders and gamblers who gave some romance and
excitement to river trips.

This is a rather good view of the South through French eyes. Its
tone is quite sympathetic, and in the discussion of newly arrived
immigrants, it gives evidence of the author's comprehension of the
social problems of the American frontier which was absorbing the
influx of Europeans.

Several other works describing Eyma's impressions of American
institutions had appeared between the publication of his first travel
book in 1853 and this last work in 1876. They are as follows: *Les
Peaux Rouges, Scènes de la Vie des Indiens* (Paris, 1854), *Les Peaux
Noires; Scènes de la Vie des Esclaves* (Paris, 1857), *Excentricités
Américaines* (Paris, 1860), *Les Femmes du Nouveau-Monde* (Paris,
1860), *La République Américaine: ses Institutions—ses hommes*
(Paris, 1861), and *La Vie dans le Nouveau-Monde* (Paris, 1862). All
of the above are in the Library of Congress.

312.   Eyma, Louis Xavier (1816–1876)

Les deux Amériques; histoire, moeurs et voyages par Xavier Eyma. Paris,
D. Giraud, 1853.

2 p.l., 374 p.   17½ cm.
Inclusive dates: 1845, 1858–1859.
Location of copy: Harvard University.

Eyma was born in Martinique in 1816 and died in Paris at the age
of sixty. He first visited the United States in 1845 to study the edu-

cational system. Returning in the late fifties, he went to New Orleans, where he "edited the French section of *L'Abeille.*" He traveled extensively in America, and his writings were influential in the formation of French opinion of the United States.

As the title of this book indicates, it treats of the two Americas, and the general approach is a historical one. In the earlier chapters Eyma concerns himself with his first general impressions and the manners of the Americans. Much of this material deals with the surface things to be expected of a visiting foreigner. The vivacity and bustle impressed him. He had the good sense to realize that a traveler had to learn much about the A.B.C.'s of a people before making too many general statements. In his final chapter the author gives a brief résumé of American history of the early federal period. Like so many French visitors, this one kept his route of travel a secret; he did not even mention being in New Orleans.

313. Finch, Marianne

An Englishwoman's experience in America. London, Richard Bentley, 1853.

viii, 386 p. 19½ cm.
Inclusive dates: August, 1850, to June, 1851. In South, May, 1851.
Location of copy: Library of Congress.

Most of this Englishwoman's year in America was spent in New England. She made a three week's trip through the upper South from Washington to Richmond, Lynchburg, across the Alleghenies, and down the Ohio River to Louisville. Natural Bridge and Mammoth Cave impressed her, as did Niagara Falls. She gave some attention to slavery. Her moderate opinions of that institution reflected her reactions to the policies of certain of the militant antislavery leaders, her observations of free Negroes in the North, and her conversations en route with various slaveowners. But in the main, her book centered attention in feminine interests and organizations.

314. Flack, Captain

A hunter's experiences in the Southern states of America being an account of the natural history of the various quadrupeds and birds which are the objects of chase in those countries. London, Longman's, Green, and Co., 1866.

4 p.l., 359 p., 32 p. of ads. and index. 19½ cm.
Inclusive dates: 1850's (?).
Location of copy: Swarthmore College Library.

The comprehensive title and the following prefatory statement by the author give the purpose of this interesting and significant account of wildlife in the South. Flack wrote: "Since my contributions began to appear in the columns of 'The Field' (a British sporting periodical published since 1853) under the nom de plume of 'The Ranger' the frequent questions put to me by sportsmen in search of some region where they might have mild winter quarters, as well as abundance of game, have led me to think that a book on the quadrupeds, game-birds, wild fowl, and other objects of sport in the southern states of (North) America might be both useful and interesting."

This hunter lived for many years in the South during the forties and fifties. Landing at Galveston (p. 233), one of the few cities mentioned in his book, he spent most of his time in the forests, where, in true David Crockett fashion, his gun kept him in "meat, clothes, and money." In 1866, sometime after his return to England, he wrote this account, together with two others, about his American experiences. The latter two were: *The Texan Rifle-Hunter* (London, 1866) and *The Texan Ranger, or, Real Life in the Backwoods* (London, 1866).

Flack, in *A Hunter's Experience in the Southern States of America*, gives no chronology nor itinerary, although he does identify certain general areas where he hunted the various species of game. Each chapter, usually limited to one kind of wildlife, begins with a rather technical but informative treatise on the description and the habits of that animal. Especially well-done and making for exciting reading are his reports on hunting bisons—the monarch of the prairies, "the largest and noblest wild quadruped found on the American continent" (pp. 34–63)—and the black bear (p. 171), playing possum (pp. 209–16), and stalking the wild turkey gobbler—the majestic bird which eluded all of Flack's wiles but finally succumbed to his imitation of the plaintive call of the female of the species (pp. 239–47).

He discusses the fine points of various hunting methods used by the Indians, and he disputes some of the myths and claims presented by earlier writers concerning the habits of American wildlife. He cites from earlier published accounts and relates exploits and legends associated with other noted hunters. The similarity between Revoil's description of being treed by peccaries (first published in 1856) and Flack's experience is very striking and raises the question of the probable originality of some of his other material.

An appendix with detailed information concerning expenses of transportation, recommended equipment and clothing, and favored regions for hunting concludes the work. He estimated £250 as the cost for a six-month hunting trip from Liverpool to the South by way of Galveston or New Orleans.

The outstanding merit of this rare and fascinating book is the author's meticulous attention to detail, based upon his wide range of activity and his particular flare for recording realistically and vividly his pursuit of the fauna of the American South.

315. Fowler, Reginald

Hither and thither; or, sketches of travels on both sides of the Atlantic. London, Frederick R. Daldy, 1854.

> viii, 272 p. 21 cm.
> *Inclusive dates:* Probably 1851 to August, 1853.
> *Location of copy:* Library of Congress.

The author of this book, an English barrister-at-law, returned to Liverpool from New York in August, 1853, after having spent two years traveling in Southern Europe and America (p. 272). Sometime during that period he made a "rather extensive tour" through the Southern and Western states (p. 265), but he made little mention of that part of his trip in this book except for a few very general observations. In a prefatory statement he implied that the public reception of this volume would determine whether he would again venture into print. No evidence could be found of further publications. The book is of little value for Southern travel.

316. Fröbel, Julius (1805–1893)

Aus Amerika. Erfahrungen, Reisen und Studien von Julius Fröbel. 2 vols. Leipzig, J. J. Weber, 1857–'58.

> Vol. I, xvi, 550 p.; Vol. II, xvi, 615 p. illus. 17 cm.
> *Illustrations:* Vol. II: Illustrations of Indian archaeology—picture-writing, etc.
> *Inclusive dates:* November, 1849, to 1857. In South, May, 1850; July, 1850, to ?, 1850; June, 1852; summer, 1853.
> *Other editions:*
> (1) Seven year's travel in Central America, Northern Mexico, and the far West of the United States. By Julius Froebel. London, R. Bentley, 1859. xiv p., 1 l., 587 p. illus., 8 plates (incl. front.). 22 cm.
> (2) A travers l'Amérique, par Julius Froebel. 3 vols. Bruxelles, A. Lacroix, 1861.
> *Location of copy:* Library of Congress.

This former leader of the Democrats in the Frankfurt Assembly of 1848 was condemned because of his political activity. He left Germany for America, where he lived from 1849–57. A onetime professor, interested in mineralogy, he also was well grounded in political theory and history. Later he became an editor and a foreign diplomat. His two-volume work, parts of which were translated for a one-volume English edition in 1859 and a French edition in 1861, must be considered a significant travel account. During his seven years in America, Fröbel traveled extensively through the Southwest, the Far West, and parts of Central America. Much of his travel in the South, except for his two trips into Virginia in May and July, 1850, was en route between New York and the Southwest. He traveled by water from New York to Nicaragua in 1851 because of his interest in a canal across the latter country. In the spring of 1852 he set out for Independence (Mo.) via Cleveland, Cincinnati, and St. Louis to join a wagon train bound for Chihuahua, returning the next year by way of San Antonio, New Orleans, and St. Louis. Later that year he again left for San Antonio, visiting New Orleans and Galveston and then journeying overland to California.

Aside from his broad background of culture, Fröbel had varied opportunities for supplementing his personal observations of American life and institutions. He mingled with many of the leaders, such as William H. Seward, Stephen A. Douglas, and President Fillmore. He spent much time with Peter Force in his library and with William B. Rogers, state geologist of Virginia. His wide reading was apparent from his frequent quotes from newspapers and the books of other travelers. He confirmed the views of Frederick Law Olmstead on slavery and especially recommended the latter's work, *A Journey in the Seaboard Slave States,* as a "positive and objective treatment" of the social and economic aspects of the question in keeping with his own views (p. 127).

The two volumes of *Aus Amerika* are divided into five books. The first volume, including the first three books, was compiled in late 1856 shortly before his return to Germany. It is the most important for Southern travel, for Book I gives Fröbel's rather detailed account of his two visits to Richmond (Va.), his description of the beauty of the "great valley of Virginia," and the five excellent chapters on slavery. These chapters are his real contribution to this study. Fröbel, a liberal, was opposed to slavery, but he did not appear prejudiced. He stressed the basic ideas and theories and the ethics and morals of the question rather than the details (I, pp. 124–88). Yet he did reiterate the figures showing the progress of certain free states (Pennsylvania and New York) as compared with Virginia. He pointed out differences within the latter state between the northern counties where free labor was increasing and those counties where slave labor predominated.

In Book III of the first volume the writer painted with broad and bold strokes the overall picture of American institutions, with their highlights and shadows of regional exceptions. Book IV and V of Volume II are rich in materials describing Texas—the early routes of travel to Galveston, San Antonio, and El Paso, the vegetation and wildlife, German settlers, and geological lore.

317.   Gaddis, Maxwell Pierson (b. 1811)

Foot-prints of an itinerant. Cincinnati, printed at the Methodist book concern, for the author, 1855.

> 546 p. front. (port.). 18½ cm.
> *Illustrations:* Frontispiece: Engraving of author by F. E. Jones, Cincinnati, from a daguerreotype.
> *Inclusive dates:* 1830–1853. In South, July, 1832?, to August, 1842; December, 1842, to May?, 1843.
> *Other editions:*
> (1) Same imprint. 1856.
> (2) Thirteenth thousand. Same imprint. 1857.
> (3) Fourteenth thousand. Same imprint. 1863.
> *Location of copy:* University of Kentucky Library.

During the years that Gaddis served numerous circuits and chapels in the Cincinnati Conference of the Methodist church (1830–53), his failing health made it necessary for him to spend time at some of the mineral springs in Kentucky and Virginia. These were Lower Blue Licks (1832) and Esculapian (1847) in the former state and Kanawha Salines, Blue Sulphur, White Sulphur, and Sweet (July and August, 1842) in the latter state. He describes them in some detail. On December 22, 1842, he left Cincinnati on a six months' trip by steamboat to New Orleans and Mobile. His contributions to travel literature are his descriptions of incidents en route. Henry Clay's visit in New Orleans (p. 334), the inauguration of Governor Mouton of Louisiana at which Clay was also present, and the author's experience aboard a mail packet which caught fire on Lake Pontchartrain. Most of the book is a rambling account of Gaddis' preaching activities.

318.   Girard, Just [*pseud.* for Just Jean Étienne Roy] (1794–1870)

The adventures of a French captain, at present a planter in Texas, formerly a refugee of Camp Asylum. By Just Girard. Translated from the French by Lady Blanche Murphy. New York, Benziger Bros., [1878].

> 180 p. 18 cm.
> *Illustrations:* Frontispiece: Plate by Carbonneau of an Indian ceremony.

Inclusive dates: 1818–1850's (?). In South, 1818–1850's?
Other editions:
   (1) Les aventures d'un Capitaine Français, planteur au Texas, ancien réfugié du Champ d'Asile; par Just Girard [*pseud.*]. Tours, A. Mame et fils, 1860. 185 p. 8vo. (Seven printings were made from this edition, in 1862, 1864, 1866, 1868, 1870, 1872, and 1875).
   (2) Tours, A. Mame et fils, 1877. 191 p. 8vo. (Five printings of this edition were made in 1879, 1880, 1881, 1884, and 1887).
Location of copy: University of Pennsylvania Library.

Just Girard, according to Monaghan, was one of several pseudonyms used by Just Jean Étienne Roy, "one of the most prolific writers of his time." (Eighty-four pages of titles and editions listed in *Catalogue Général . . . De La Bibliothèque Nationale,* Vol. CLVIII, verify this statement.) His accounts of his wide travels were "extremely popular." He may have traveled in Mexico and possibly Texas in the 1850's.

The present book is a translation of Roy's account of what purport to be the experiences of a former Napoleonic officer, recipient of the Legion of Honour, who fled to America after Waterloo. On his last return trip to Paris in 1858, he related the details of his life to Roy who published them in autobiographical and fictional form intended for juvenile readers as *Les Aventures d'un Capitaine Français, Planteur au Texas, Ancien Réfugié du Champ d'Asile* (Tours, 1860).

Landing in Baltimore in 1816, the officer joined a party of French refugees in a futile attempt at a settlement on Galveston Island in 1818. Then followed more than two score years of Texas frontier hardships, settlement failures, and hair-raising adventures, until his ultimate success, following Texas independence, in becoming a prosperous planter on the banks of the Río Brazos in the 1840's and 1850's. Passing in hurried review are this former Napoleonic officer's associations with such Texas frontier figures as Santa Anna, Sam Houston, and Stephen and Moses Austin. An introductory chapter on the geological, topographical, and other features of Texas has limited value. The book, despite its fictional form, has some historical interest.

319.   Gloss, Albert von

Das Leben in den Vereinigten Staaten, zur Beurtheilung von Amerikas Gegenwart und Zukunft. Theilweise für Kapitalisten und Auswanderungslustige in Deutschland. Von Albert Gloss. 2 vols. Leipzig, Georg Wigand, 1864.

   Vol. I, xxviii, 633 p.; Vol. II, xxvi, 688 p.   24 cm.
   Inclusive dates: 1849–1862?
   Location of copy: University of Michigan Library.

The reader will be impressed with the scholarship, variety, and wide range of observations on American life from 1849–62 found in these two thick volumes of some thirteen hundred pages. But the work is a disappointment for Southern travel. Except for slavery, which is described at some length in rather general terms (II, pp. 334–74), and frequent references to Southern slaveholders together with Gloss' comments on a few Southern institutions, such as education in Georgia (I, p. 120) and banking facilities (II, p. 471), there is little in the work that really describes the South. Nor is there evidence that this German traveler journeyed farther South than the "romantic banks of the James" (II, 676). He appeared to have spent most of his time in the East.

Yet Gloss came to New York from Germany in 1849. He lived in America for many years, probably until 1862 or 1863. The only date noted that could be identified with his travels was his visit to Niagara Falls in August, 1850 (I, p. 614). He was thoroughly familiar with the observations of Bromme, Fleischmann, Baumbach, Griesinger, Fröbel, and other German travelers during this period. One of the important chapters in Volume I is an evaluation of their published accounts. He quoted extensively from their writings. He leaned heavily on George Bancroft for much of his information on the slavery question.

Although this work qualifies as a travel account, it is really more of a sociological study of America in the fifties.

320. Goodrich, Charles Augustus (1790–1862)

The family tourist. A visit to the principal cities of the western continent: embracing an account of their situation, origin, plan, extent, their inhabitants, manners, customs, and amusements and public works, institutions, edifices, etc., together with sketches of historical events. Hartford, Case, Tiffany and company, 1848.

> xiv, [15]–640 p., incl. front., illus., plates, ports. 22 cm.
> *Illustrations:* Seventy-eight illustrations, including plates of Mount Vernon, Fort Washington, Count D'Estaing, General Jackson relieving the wounded after the battle, and Mammoth Cave.
> *Other editions:*
> (1) Philadelphia, J. W. Bradley, 1848. xiv, [17]–640 p., incl. front., illus., plates, ports. 22 cm.
> (2) Travels and sketches in North and South America . . . Hartford, Case, Tiffany & co., 1852. xiii, 14–704 p., incl. front., illus., port.
> (3) The land we live in; or, travels, sketches and adventures in North and South America. With descriptions of the towns, cities, states, and territories; their inhabitants, manners, customs . . . etc. Together with sketches of his-

torical events. Rev., cor., enl. . . . . Cincinnati, H. M. Rulison; Philadelphia, D. Rulison, 1857. 1 p.l., vii–xxx, 25–879 p. fold. col. front., illus. (incl. port.), 7 col. plates. 23½ cm.
Location of copy: Library of Congress.

As stated in the preface, the object of this work is to provide "rational entertainment" and to "present an opportunity to the younger classes of society, to become more extensively acquainted with the chief places of the land and the interesting objects which they contain." It is not a book based on the travels of the compiler, C. A. Goodrich, Congregational clergyman and popular author (see the *Dictionary of American Biography*), but rather a description of the important cities of the American continent, including Washington, Alexandria, Richmond, Raleigh, Charleston, Savannah, St. Augustine, New Orleans, and Louisville (see title). Material for the sketches was taken from many of the earlier travel accounts.

321. Goodrich, S[amuel] G[riswold] (1793–1860)

Les États-Unis d'Amérique; aperçu statistique, historique, geographique, industriel et social, a l'usage de ceux qui recherchent des renseignements precis sur cette partie du nouveau monde, par S. G. Goodrich . . . accompagné d'une carte des États-Unis d'après les meilleures autorités. Paris, Guillaumin, 1852.

xvi, 376 p. fold. map. 21 cm.
Maps: Folding map of the United States.
Location of copy: Harvard University Library.

S. G. Goodrich, "author and editor of about one hundred and seventy volumes," best known under his pen name, Peter Parley, was American consul in Paris from 1851–53. There he produced a French edition of his *Standard American Geography*. Characteristic of the Goodrich style, it presents the American scene in a statistical form, giving some attention to surface descriptions, with information that would be useful to immigrants.

322. Grandfort, Marie Fontenay, Mme. Manoël

The new world: translated from the French of Mme. M. de Grandfort by E. C. Wharton . . . New Orleans, Sherman, Wharton & Co., 1855.

[1], 5–144 p., [1] p. 21½ cm.
Inclusive dates: Probably 1852–1855.
Other editions:
    (1) 1st Edition. L'autre monde. Paris, 1855. 4 p.l., 259 p., 1 l.

(2) 2nd Edition. L'autre monde. 2. ed. Paris, Librairie Nouvelle, 1857. 2 p.l., 272 p., 1 l. 18½ cm.
Location of copy: Birmingham (Ala.) Public Library.

Mme. Manoël de Grandfort, pseudonym for Mme. Marie (Barsalou) Laspeyers and later Marie Fontenay de Grandfort, made her appearance in New Orleans in 1852–53 as a public lecturer on French literature. She had recently married M. de Grandfort, publisher of a short-lived French weekly newspaper in New Orleans, the *Coup d'Oeil*. Meeting with only "moderate success" with her lectures, she returned to Paris and published her impressions of America as *L'Autre Monde* (Paris, 1855, and a second edition in 1857). The translator's note, dated June 25, 1855, in this present volume stated that the "situation created among the Creoles of this state (Louisiana) by the recent publication of Madame Grandfort's book . . . caused many persons . . . a desire to have an English version of the work."

This book has been described as a "classic of parody and abuse" (see Monaghan, *French Travelers in the United States,* p. 46). Madame de Grandfort recorded her impressions of America through the experiences of two young Frenchmen, Julian and Richard, who supposedly arrived in New York in 1852. Written in a vivacious and entertaining style, the chapters "New Orleans and Slavery," "Twelve Hundred Miles on the Mississippi," "The Kentuckians," and "Rebecca Smith, the Bloomerite" give colorful though exaggerated pictures of various Southern institutions, including the French quarter in New Orleans, a Negro ball, Creole *soirées,* the palatial hotels, and steamboats. Her extensive report of a Bloomerite meeting in Louisville (pp. 91–112) and her many critical comments concerning American women reflect her own "bitterness and disappointed vanity." At times she could be most generous, as when she described Kentuckians as the "gascons of the United States," the gentlemen who pay their bills the first time they are presented. But the beautiful Creoles "were not women; they were 'Houris'" (p. 84). She charged American women with being "completely ignorant of the art in which French women triumph: the art of dressing in negligie." *Uncle Tom's Cabin,* to her, seemed "romantic nonsense."

323. Griesinger, [Karl] Theodor (1809–1884)

Freiheit und Sclaverei unter dem Sternenbanner; oder, Land und Leute in Amerika, von Theodor Griesinger. Stuttgart, A. Kröner, 1862.

2 pts. in 1 vol. Paged continuously: Part 1, 2 p.l., 480 p.; Pt. 2, 2 p.l., [481]–882 p. fold. map. 19 cm.

Map: Excellent folding map of the United States by C. Bauer.
Inclusive dates: 1851–1856?
Other editions:
(1) Vrijheid en Slavernij; of, Schetsen en tafereelen uit het Amerikaansche volksleven. Naar het Hoogduitsch van Th. Griesinger Rotterdam, H. Nijgh, 1862.
(2) Land und Leute in Amerika. Skizzen aus dem amerikanischen Leben, von Theodor Griesinger. 2 vols. Stuttgart, 1863. fold. map. 17½ cm.
Location of copy: University of Pennsylvania Library.

In the late 1840's, Karl Theodor Griesinger was the editor of a radical German newspaper whose views antagonized the government of Baden and led to his two-year imprisonment. According to an introductory statement in one of his works, after his release from prison he spent five years traveling in the United States, viewing the democracy in an "attempt to give a picture of life in America" in the several books which he would write on his return to his homeland. But he apparently was not pleased with much that he saw of the young nation, for throughout his works there appeared to be a conscious effort to depict more of the sordid shadows of American life and to examine more institutions of the lunatic fringe variety than were in probably any other travel account of the period. His writings, in the words of a present-day scholar, are "all distinguished by a kind of morbid humor and by a sharp sense of frustration."

Griesinger's book, *Sodom and Gomorrha, or New York by Day and by Night* (Stuttgart, 1857), together with chapter titles in other works suggest his particular interests. They cover a wide range of subjects, such as waitresses and barmaids, junk shops, the American Sabbath, the Fifth Avenue man, *Die Mercerstreetdame* (prostitutes), quackery and patent medicine, Shakers, Bloomeries, American sex life, "Ladies Society for the recovery of the drowned," German beggars in New York, prize fights, and icehouses. Many of the chapters portray with stark realism phases of the seamier side of this country, which in the main were not mentioned by most of those who commented about America. In his five years of wanderings, this visitor appears to have had ample time to pry into the nooks and crannies of the American scene, as compared with most travelers who were limited to a few weeks' or a few months' tour.

As a reporter he was meticulous in his detail, and except for an occasional error of fact, he appeared, in spite of his bias, to record accurately those things which he observed. His books are mines of information on aspects of social history of the mid-century, but they appear generally to have been overlooked by historians, especially those of the South.

Unfortunately for a clear record, this German did not give any kind of timetable of his journey. Only in the before-mentioned introduction to what is probably his best known work, *Lebende Bilder aus Amerika* (Stuttgart, 1858), a book in which the author does not make any special reference to the South, does he even mention the routes from Bremen or Hamburg via London, Liverpool, or Le Havre to New York. There is no direct evidence in any of his works that were examined that Griesinger's wanderings took him south of Washington, but it hardly seems possible that his intimate knowledge and familiarity with Southern life and many of its institutions could have been gained solely from secondary sources.

Especially is this true of the two volumes, *Freiheit und Sclaverei unter dem Sternerbanner; oder, Land und Leute in Amerika,* (Stuttgart, 1862), in which almost half of the twenty-eight chapters deal with the South. Here the visitor reveals his extreme dislike for slavery by reporting on its evils with an even sharper pen than that used in his portrayal of New York society and institutions. He spared no details in his picture of the large planter, "the cotton baron of the new world," whom he compared with the feudal lords of medieval Germany (I, p. 86).

Griesinger described the planter's big house, *die Herrenwohnung,* with its balconies, ballroom, and library, in its beautiful and spacious setting, where the owner could "play the role of cavalier" while his sons, educated both at home and abroad, were being prepared to carry on in that tradition (I, pp. 76–77). He had much to say about dueling, the South Carolina code of honor, gambling, concubines, and the political domination exercised by the planter aristocracy, while on the other hand he found little but misery for the three and one-half million slaves—"the niggars," as he identified them, "half animal-half man" (I, p. 195). He emphasized the evils of slavery, calling special attention to the various kinds of punishment, illiteracy, the slave traffic, sex irregularities, and slave markets. All of this reflected his bias toward the system.

Yet this dark and one-sided report on slavery is only a part of this German's picture of the South. Chapters treating the various crops in detail and discussions of American holidays, food, and drink, the excessive use of ice in this country, American music and musicians, and historical and statistical data on Germans in Kentucky, Tennessee, and Texas provide detailed information over a wide range of topics. A long and informative chapter on the origin of American place names, states, cities, and rivers, including a great number in the South (II, pp. 734–818) is another example of the unusual subject matter of the books and makes this work, in spite of the author's bias, an important source concerning American life both north and south of the Mason and Dixon line.

324. Hall, Abraham Oakey

The manhattaner in New Orleans; or, phases of "Crescent city" life. New York, J. S. Redfield; New Orleans, J. C. Morgan, 1851.

> x, 2–190 p. 18 cm.
> *Inclusive dates:* New Orleans, 1846 to 1847?
> *Location of copy:* University of Kentucky Library.

Most of the sketches in this delightful travel account were prepared while the writer, a New Yorker, was in New Orleans in 1846 and 1847 as a newspaper reporter and later as a law student in the office of Thomas and John Slidell. First appearing in various gazettes (*Literary World*), the sketches were later collected and published in book form in 1851, "after much revision and some addition." From the first sketch on "Getting to New Orleans" by packet from New York to the final one on leaving "New Orleans River-ward," the reader is treated to a succession of vivid chapters on subjects such as "Hotel Life in New Orleans" (the St. Charles), "The Calcutta of America," "Yellow Fever," "Street Side Pencilings," "Levees and Crevasses," and "The Picayune and Delta." The latter is especially well done.

The writer's wit and good sense of humor are evident in his sketches on "Rain and Mosquitos," "Watering Places" ("few cities have as much water over, under, in front of, and to its rear" as New Orleans, he says), and "Captain Ric's Epitholamium." Each of these in parts is worthy of a place in an anthology of American humor.

The book was not intended as a profound sociological study of New Orleans' society, nor does it present a rounded picture, for Mr. Hall, who later became a prominent Tammany Hall politician and journalist, has omitted references to the more shady aspects of the "Crescent City's" life. It is a good travel work. The *Dictionary of American Biography* gives a sketch of Hall's career.

325. Hathaway, Gilbert

Travels in the two hemispheres . . . Travels in the Southwest, life in Arkansas and Texas. Detroit, Doughty, Straw & Co., and Raymond & Selleck, 1858.

> vi, 576 p. front. 21½ cm.
> *Illustrations:* Frontispiece: Scenes in Egypt.

[247]

Inclusive dates: Early 1850's.
Location of copy: Grosvenor Library, Buffalo.

This is a "book edition" of the issues of the *Magazine of Travel,* a publication that appeared in 1857, reproduced in this form to "meet the popular demand." Included in the work are the nine letters, each a chapter with the title "Travels in the Southwest, Life in Arkansas and Texas," of Gilbert Hathaway. Hathaway was a doctor from La Porte, Indiana, who in the early 1850's went from the shore of Lake Michigan to St. Louis and down the Mississippi River, then by boat, stage, and wagon through Arkansas and Texas by way of Helena (Ark.), Pine Bluff, Little Rock, Washington (Ark.), and Dallas (pp. 135, 185, 231, 279, 328, 376, 473, 521, 566). His unbiased and unembellished descriptions of that region, its people, and the difficulties and incidents of travel are recorded with a delightful sense of humor and make a significant contribution to the travel literature of the Southwest.

326.　[Hazard, W. P.]

The American guide book; being a hand-book for tourists and travellers through every part of the United States. Embracing full tables of routes and distances from place to place, with clear and accurate descriptions of all the various cities, towns, and natural or artificial curiosities of different routes. The whole preceded with short directions to travellers, remarks on the United States, the manners, etc., of the people, tables of foreign coin in American money, etc., etc. Illustrated with views of the principle cities and maps of the States and the various routes. Part I. Northern and Eastern States and Canada. Philadelphia, George S. Appleton, 1846.

xvi, 256 p. illus., maps. 17 cm.
Maps: Folding map of Northern and Eastern States; several maps of routes and of cities.
Illustrations: Views of points of interest in the Northeast.
Inclusive dates: 1846.
Location of copy: Emory University Library.

The cover title of this work is *Appleton's Hand-Book through the United States,* while an inserted title page gives the title as *A Hand-Book for Travellers through the United States.* A note on the last page (p. 256) states that Part II dealing with "Middle, Southern and Western States, [is] in press and will follow shortly." This implies that a second volume was to be published, but no record could be found of it. Sabin lists Part I.

The first chapter of this work, "A General View of the United States," gives some limited material on the South, but the book is of little value for Southern travel.

327. Herz, Henri (1803–1888)

Mes Voyages en Amérique. Paris, A. Faure, 1866.

> 2 p.l., 328 p. front. (port.). 18 cm.
> *Inclusive dates:* November, 1846, to 1847.
> *Location of copy:* Yale University Library.

Herz was a celebrated pianist, who visited Boston, New York, and Philadelphia before continuing his concert tour through the South to Charleston, Mobile, and New Orleans. In Charleston he found the hotels crowded, and it was necessary for him to go to a boarding-house. He had been invited to stay on the plantation of a Mr. Richard, a French *émigré*, but his time schedule would not permit him to do so.

Here the author saw slaves for the first time. He believed they were better off than many Europeans, for they were happy and seemed to have many material things. Yet the account is a close examination of the subject of slavery in America. Herz compared American slavery with that throughout history and favored that of the South.

He found the Negroes in Charleston fond of music and described their use of the banjo and other instruments. He gave an interesting description of a Negro examining his piano, and he recorded the conversation which took place.

There is a good picture of a slave auction, in which the author quoted what was said. His visits in New Orleans and Mobile did not alter the impressions gained in Charleston. A considerable amount of historical and descriptive material is given, as well as information concerning railroads, Indians, and the press.

This is one of the good French accounts of travel in America. The author had a highly perceptive mind and was able to record his impressions in good style.

328. Hooton, Charles (1813?–1847)

St. Louis' Isle, or Texiana; with additional observations made in the United States and in Canada. By Charles Hooton, author of 'Launcelot Widge,' 'Colin Clink,' 'Bilberry Thurland,' etc. With a portrait and other illustrations. London, Simmonds and Ward, 1847.

> 2 p.l., [vii]–xiii p., 1 l., 204 p. front. (port.), plates. 22 cm.
> *Illustrations:* Frontispiece: Lithograph by A. McCallum of Robert James' por-

trait of Charles Hooton. Five scenes of Texas: Settlers houses on the Prairie, scene on the Bayou, Galveston from the Gulf Shore, General Hospital, and fever burial ground.
Inclusive dates: 1840–1842. In South, March 29, 1841, to 1842.
Location of copy: University of Pennsylvania Library.

The principal object of this prejudiced collection of sketches of Texas was to warn fellow countrymen against attempting the "insane project of dropping themselves down . . . into the heart of [that] burning wild, however luxuriant, amidst lurking savages, reckless and unprincipled outcasts of civilization and fell diseases" (p. 155). The account was written in 1847, six years after the Englishman, Charles Hooton, had spent most of two years in Texas in search of health. He described the "brick-burned earth," "the sweltering bayous," and "the almost inevitable ruin and death" that confronted the emigrant. Yet interspersed among his gloomy sketches were vivid and discerning pictures revealing this traveler's sharp observation. He described Galveston Bay, "the ocean cemetary for ships"; Galveston stores, "a series of modern museums"; and Galveston Island, "the most salubrious portion of the Texas sea-board." His lengthy discussion of the bowie-knife, hunting and fishing adventures, and "sudden death" provide all the color and excitement of a Western thriller.

The last part of the book centers around his five months' residence in New Orleans and discusses its system of street-lighting, the drainage problem, and "people of colour" and the Mississippi River with its wharves, its flat boats, and its "thief boats." He labeled the city "a very gentle sort of pandemonium."

329. Houstoun, Matilda Charlotte (Jesse) Fraser

Hesperos: or, travels in the West. London, John W. Parker, 1850.

2 vols in 1. xiii, 293 p., 279 p.   19 cm.
Inclusive dates: Probably October, 1846, to April, 1847. In South, November to March.
Location of copy: University of Kentucky Library.

Matilda Houstoun, an English writer of some fame and family, landed at Halifax and traveled about the East before leaving Washington for Pittsburgh to journey by river to New Orleans. She spent about four months enjoying planter hospitality in Louisiana and Texas. Her return trip was by way of the Mississippi and Ohio rivers. Much of the last volume of her book presents in readable style her observations on the more obvious features of river travel and planter activity from the point of view of one who, though "aware of the roughness of a less civilized society," was quite in sympathy with the overall picture of plantation life. Although not condoning slavery, the author concludes that it "exists here in its most modified form" and that the accounts of cruelty are "greatly exaggerated." The work, though interesting, is not a penetrating travel account.

Some of Mrs. Houstoun's conclusions were based on experiences of her earlier tour in 1843, which she described in a book entitled *Texas and the Gulf of Mexico; or, Yachting in the New World* (15 cm., Philadelphia, G. B. Zieber & Co., 1845).

330. Howell, Peter (b. 1805)

The life and travels of Peter Howell, written by himself; in which will be seen some marvellous instances of the gracious Providence of God. Newbern, N. C., W. H. Mayhew, [1849].

> 2 p.l., 320 p. front. (port.). 15 cm.
> *Illustrations:* Frontispiece: Steel print of author by J. Telfea.
> *Inclusive dates:* 1805–1848.
> *Location of copy:* Sondley Reference Library, Asheville, N. C.

This is a monotonous account of the life and travels of Peter Howell, itinerant preacher, who was born in Virginia in 1805. Most of the book is a record of the almost daily entries during the years 1840–48, when he was preaching in eastern Virginia and North Carolina. He reported sixty-one services in thirty-seven days on one trip (p. 247) and fifty-eight services in forty-six days on another (p. 270), and he often walked ten to thirty miles between appointments.

Many of Howell's entries consisted of little more than the distances between appointments, the text used for the sermon, and the quality of the hospitality, especially the meals and lodging.

331. Jewell, Henry

Life and writings of Rev. Enoch M. Pingree, who died in Louisville, Kentucky, January 6, 1849. Aged 32 years. By Rev. Henry Jewell, pastor of the First Universalist church, Cincinnati. Cincinnati, Longly & Brother, 1850.

> vi, [9]–385 p. front. (port.). 18 cm.
> *Illustrations:* Frontispiece: Engraving of Pingree from a daguerreotype by C. A. Jewett & W. Anderson.
> *Inclusive dates:* About 1840–1849.
> *Location of copy:* University of Kentucky Library.

This book of the sermons of Enoch Pingree (1817–49) together with an extended biographical sketch was prepared for publication by his friend and fellow Universalist minister, Henry Jewell, from the letters written by Pingree to the editor of *The Star of the West* and the entries in Pingree's "Journal of daily occurrences." His brief comments about his trips to New Orleans, Memphis, Nashville, and Louisville were generally critical of travel conditions. Pingree had a church in Louisville from 1843–49.

332. Jobey, Charles

L'amour d'un Nègre. Paris, M. Levy frères, 1860.

282 p.
Inclusive dates: In South, 1834–1840?
Location of copy: Harvard University.

Jobey says he lived in Louisiana for six years of his life and that his semifictional account of the *Love of a Negro* is a true observation of life in that region. He says he changed names and situations only to avoid embarrassing people. The book is in the form of a travelogue, but it reproduces enough dialogue to give it the earmarks of a novel. The locale is New Orleans, and the tone of the book is a mixture of love and violence.

333. [Jörg, Edward (1808–1864)]

Briefe aus den Vereinigten Staaten von Nord-Amerika von—Leipzig, Verlagsbuchhandlung von J. J. Weber, 1853.

2 vols in one: viii, 274 p.; viii, 358 p. 16 cm.
Inclusive dates: November, 1851, to May, 1852.
Location of copy: Chicago Public Library.

Nothing in this book suggests the identity of the writer or the editor of the twelve long letters which make up this thick little volume in two parts. The Library of Congress Catalog of Printed Cards identifies the writer as one Edward Jörg. The letters written from Highland, Illinois, to friends in Germany were dated from November, 1851, to May, 1852. A prefatory note indicated that the writer made a trip to North and South America to observe the conditions of the German immigrants and felt that he must give his countrymen back home a true picture "of the Germans in America," for he thought that many of the earlier accounts had been exaggerated.

Evidence in the book indicates that this traveler had journeyed from Washington to Norfolk and Charleston. He had visited in Louisville and hunted game in parts of Arkansas and Louisiana. But there is no regular pattern of travel. Many of the letters give a detailed but rather tedious description of the agriculture, wildlife, and living conditions among the Germans in Ohio and Illinois. Some discuss the opposition of Americans to the immigrants, especially in parts of the South, the routes of travel (the writer did not recommend the route via New Orleans, II, p. 273), and politics in certain of the cities, especially St. Louis.

The third letter focused attention on slavery. This traveler, even though opposed to slavery, developed a prejudice against the Negroes. He noted evidences of their debauched condition and thought them incapable of improvement (p. 82). Aside from personal observation, he indicated that the sources of information for his opinions were newspapers and the many books written about slavery as well as conversations with abolitionists and Southern planters. Although he noted many advantages for immigrants in Texas, he advised those with "little capital" to settle in the North.

334. Johnston, James Finlay Weir (1796–1855)

Notes on North America, agricultural, economical, and social; by James F. W. Johnston . . . 2 vols. Edinburgh and London, W. Blackwood and sons, 1851.

> front. (fold. map). 20 cm.
> *Maps:* One: Northeastern America.
> *Inclusive dates:* 1849–1850.
> *Other editions:*
> 2 vols. Boston, Charles C. Little and James Brown, 1851. Vol. I, xvi, 415 p.; Vol. II, xii, 512 p. map. 19 cm.
> *Location of copy:* Columbia University Library.

Professor Johnston, of the University of Durham, was widely known as an expert agricultural chemist. He came to America on the invitation of several societies, including the Agricultural Society, of New York State, and he was a featured lecturer at the New York State Fair in 1849.

His travel book contained a great mass of valuable information pertaining to the Northeastern seaboard states and the St. Lawrence Valley, but unfortunately he did not observe the South with the same degree of acuteness and careful attention to detail. As a matter of fact, Johnston did not go much beyond Alexandria, Virginia. He presented a description of slavery in Virginia and the South without seeing the institution himself. He recorded that the growing number of free Negroes was causing alarm in Virginia. He noted that there were cotton mills in the South and there were apt to be an increasing number of these establishments. He thought that industrial development would fasten slavery more firmly on the region. Johnston did not mention the social and intellectual life of the Southern whites.

This book will prove a disappointment to the student of Southern life. For a more detailed account of Southern life at the same time, see Francis and Theresa Pulszky (*q.v.*), *White Red Black. Sketches of Society in the United States During the Visit of Our Guest* (3 vols., London, 1853). See also *Blackwood's Magazine,* Vol. LXX, pp. 699–718.

335. Jonathan [*pseud.*]

Brieven uit en over de Vereenigde Staten van Noord-Amerika, door Jonathan. Uitgegeven met eene inleiding en bijschritt, door Dr. E. B. Swalue, predikant te Amsterdam. Met platen en eene kaart. Schoonhoven, S. E. Van Nooten, 1853.

> xiv, 304 p. front., plates, fold. map. 22½ cm.
>
> *Maps:* Folding map of the United States.
>
> *Illustrations:* Five plates by C. C. A. Last: Steel engravings of buildings and American scenes, including one of New Orleans (Natural Bridge, Smithsonian Institute, Capital Crystal Palace, New York, New Orleans, Niagara Falls, Bunker Hill, park in New York, Presbyterian Board of Publication), by P. Blommers-te-Hage.
>
> *Inclusive dates:* Probably July, 1848, to January, 1852.
>
> *Location of copy:* Library of Congress.

The fifteen letters in this book appear to have been written by an anonymous Dutch traveler to a friend in Holland and later edited for publication by an Amsterdam clergyman. According to the latter's prefatorial statement, "Jonathan" had been in America a "long time," but except for the dates of the letters over a period of some three years, there was indefiniteness concerning any travel itinerary. Occasionally "Jonathan" cited a personal experience, usually in or about New York, but much of the material was historical and descriptive. He quoted freely from newspapers and secondary works in his efforts to give a rounded picture of the United States.

The author was a European liberal impressed with what he found in America. He noted the greater freedom of American women, the many religious organizations, and the cultural and educational institutions. He described in general terms the chief features of the Southern states as well as many of the important cities. Texas was, to him, the "most beautiful region." Even though opposed to slavery, an institution which he discussed at some length, he did not support the views and methods of the abolitionists. He was much interested in the Republic of Liberia as the possible solution to the problem.

[254]

336. Judson, Edward (1788–1850)

The life of Adoniram Judson by his son, Edward Judson. Philadelphia, American Baptist Publication Society, 1883.

> vii–xii, 601 p. 19½ cm.
> *Location of copy:* University of Kentucky Library.

The Massachusetts-born, thrice married, Baptist scholar-missionary Adoniram Judson returned on furlough to the United States in 1845 after thirty-two years of continuous and significant service in the Burma mission field. He traveled throughout the East and as far south as Richmond (Va.) (p. 474), preaching to large audiences. This account of his life was compiled by his son from family letters and the journal kept by the missionary.

337. Kelland, Professor Philip (1808–1879)

Transatlantic sketches. Edinburgh, Adam and Charles Black, 1858.

> viii, 77 p. 16½ cm.
> *Inclusive dates:* August to October, 1858.
> *Location of copy:* Illinois State Historical Library.

Kelland, distinguished professor and fellow of the Royal Societies of London and Edinburgh, traveled in Canada and the United States in the late summer and fall of 1858 (see the *Dictionary of National Biography,* X, p. 1227). He went by rail from Niagara Falls to Detroit, Chicago, St. Louis, and Louisville. He visited Mammoth Cave before returning to New York by way of Cincinnati and Buffalo. The two lectures which he delivered at the University of Edinburgh were his observations en route.

Kelland noted the things of interest in Mammoth Cave, as well as a Kentucky hotel lobby where the floor was rendered "slippery and unsafe" because of the "monster vice" of "spitting." Even though he predicted the impending doom of slavery, he declined any "indiscriminate censure of slaveholders."

338. "The Clerke of Oxenforde" [Kennedy, John Pendleton (1795–1870)]

The blackwater chronicle, a narrative of an expedition into the land of Canaan, in Randolph County, Virginia, a country flowing with wild animals such as panthers, bears, wolves, elk, deer, otter, badger, etc., etc., with innumerable trout—by five adventurous gentlemen, without any aid of government, and solely by their own resources, in the summer

of 1851. By the "Clerke of Oxenforde" with illustrations from life by
Strother. New York, Redfield, 1853.

> 223 p. front., illus. 18½ cm.
> *Illustrations:* Frontispiece engraving of wildlife by Kennersley and ten sketches
> of humorous situations en route.
> *Inclusive dates:* May 31, 1851, to July ?, 1851.
> *Location of copy:* University of Kentucky (Wilson Collection).

This is an entertaining and, at times, humorous account of the experiences of five Virginians and their two guides, who set out on a
fishing trip from Winchester (Virginia) to the then remote and
almost inaccessible region of the headwaters of the Cheat, the Blackwater, and the Potomac rivers in the early summer of 1851. The
writer centers attention on the natural beauty the wildlife, and the
many adventures of the group in this sportsman's paradise. Interspersed in the narrative are literary, historical, and philosophical allusions somewhat along the pattern of Chaucer's *Tales.* Although the
style differs widely from most travel works, *The Blackwater Chronicle* can be considered as peripheral material for a travel bibliography.

The Library of Congress Catalog lists the work under Philip Pendleton Kennedy (1808?–64) but states that it generally is attributed
to John Pendleton Kennedy.

339. Kirsten, Dr. A.

Skizzen aus den Vereinigten Staaten von Nordamerika. Von Dr. A.
Kirsten. Leipzig, F. A. Brockhaus, 1851.

> xx p., 1 l., 374, [1] p. 17 cm.
> *Inclusive dates:* August, 1846, to July (?), 1847.
> *Location of copy:* Newberry Library.

Perhaps this volume is hardly worth a notation, for the German
author probably never traveled farther South than Baltimore during
his year spent in the United States. But he does discuss in a general
treatment (p. 259–74) the slavery question and its important political
implications.

340. Koch, Dr. Albert C.

Reise durch einen Theil der Vereinigten Staaten von Nordamerika in
den Jahren 1844 bis 1846, von Dr. Albert C. Koch. Nebst 2 Tafeln Ab-
bildungen. Dresden and Leipzig, Arnold'sche Buchhandlung, 1847.

> 2 p.l., 162 p. front., col. plate. 21½ cm.
> *Inclusive dates:* June, 1844, to June, 1846. In South, January, 1845, to June, 1845;
> December, 1845, to January, 1846.
> *Location of copy:* Library of Congress.

Koch was a German geologist who spent most of two years collecting fauna and flora in New England and parts of the South. His most important discovery was a gigantic fossil, "the Hydrareus harlani," which he uncovered in March, 1845, in the Tombigbee Valley near St. Stephens (Ala.). Charles Lyell (*q.v.*), who later visited the site, questioned the "factitious skeleton" and some of Koch's findings (Lyell, *Second Visit,* II, pp. 59, 65). During his visit he met and conferred often with many American scientists, such as Benjamin Silliman of Yale and Dr. Klapp of New Albany, Indiana. Koch was familiar with the work of Charles Lyell.

After some weeks in the East near Holmes Hole and Martha's Vineyard, he went to Cleveland and then south through Ohio via the Ohio Canal to Portsmouth, reaching that river town in early September. The rest of the year was spent investigating several sites along the Ohio and upper Mississippi rivers. He was methodical in reporting day by day progress with dates, distances, and findings together with brief comments on nonprofessional interests, such as religious groups and churches, the campaign of 1844, and travel conditions. The book has limited value except for its interest in natural history. Yet it was considered one of the important travel books in 1848.

Koch returned to New York from Alabama via the river route to Pittsburgh and Philadelphia. He later made another trip South in December, 1845, through Virginia to Enfield, North Carolina, to investigate locations. The rest of the time he spent in the East displaying his collection which he had sent to New York by ship from Mobile and which survived a shipwreck off the Florida coast. He did not follow the common practice of German travelers, who usually gave a concluding summary of impressions of America and advice to future travelers.

341. Lanman, Charles (1819–1895)

Adventures in the wilds of the United States and British American provinces. Illustrated by the author and Oscar Bessau . . . with an appendix by Lieut. Campbell Hardy . . . 2 vols. Philadelphia, J. W. Moore, 1856.

front., plates. 23 cm.
Illustrations: Vol. I: Six sporting scenes from the old Northwest. Vol. II: Six sporting scenes, including River St. John and Florida, by Van-Incen-Snyder. Others by the author and Oscar Bessau.
Inclusive dates: 1846?–1856.

[257]

Other editions:
  (1) London. 1856.
  (2) Second edition. London. 1859.
Location of copy: University of Kentucky Library.

This important collection of Lanman's travels includes four that had already been published in single volumes plus three additional journeys, two of which were in the South. Together the volumes are, according to a prefatory note, "a kind of cyclopedia of American Scenery and Personal Adventure and of Traveling Incidents, calculated to exhibit the manners and customs of our people, and interest the lovers of Natural History and the various Arts of Sporting." The earlier published travels which appear with only minor changes and additions in this work are: *A Summer in the Wilderness* (New York, 1847); *A Tour of the River Saguenay* (Philadelphia, 1848); *Letters from the Alleghany Mountains* (New York, 1849); and *Haw-Ho-Noo; Records of a Tourist* (Philadelphia, 1850).

The only previously unpublished travel account in Volume I, "The Sources of the Potomac," describes Lanman's quick trip in the spring of 1851 through the back country of Maryland and northern Virginia. The other, "A winter in the South," in Volume II is a record of the author's "zig zag journey" from Washington in December, 1853, to Florida and New Orleans and of his return via the rivers to Pittsburg. It is probably Lanman's most significant contribution to Southern travel literature. Accompanied by his wife, he enjoyed the entire trip without a "single accident of movement" to retard him in any way. Traveling most of the distance through the interior he visited many cities en route. Interesting descriptions of Savannah, St. Augustine, Huntsville, Mobile, and New Orleans are given along with those of many lesser places. Lanman was partial to river travel whenever possible. He made several side trips on such streams as the St. Johns, Black Creek, Suwannee, Chattahoochee, Tennessee, Alabama, Tombigbee, and Black Warrior, ever aware of the details of scenic beauty and wildlife. A "desperate journey" of some eighty miles into the interior from Mobile to Augusta, Mississippi, afforded opportunity for further observation of back-country life (pp. 191–97). On this trip, as on all of his previous journeys into the South, he was inclined to record only the "lights" of slavery rather than its "shadows."

Lanman's books are a significant contribution to a clearer understanding of some of the lesser known "areas of Southern life." Usually on horseback or on foot, he moved along routes not often included in the itineraries of travelers. This brought him in closer contact with the natural history and the people. He was a careful observer with many years of experience. His habit of accurate identifications of names and places is also a real value to students of Southern Appl-lachia.

342. Lanman, Charles (1819–1895)

Haw-Ho-Noo; or, records of a tourist, by Charles Lanman . . . Phila-delphia, Lippincott, Grambo and co., 1850.

> 4 p.l., ₁13₁–266 p. 19 cm.
> *Inclusive dates:* No indication of exact dates; probably 1846–1850.
> *Other editions:*
>   In the author's Adventures in the wilds of the United States and British American provinces. Philadelphia, J. W. Moore, 1856.
> *Location of copy:* University of Kentucky Library.

According to Lanman, the word "Haw-Ho-Noo" was originally used by the Cherokee Indians in describing America as meaning "the country upheld on the back of a turtle." Lanman justifies its use in the title of this book, dedicated to William Cullen Bryant, because part of the volume was "devoted to the traditionary (*sic*) lore of the aborigines" but all of it to his native land.

This prolific writer, a native of Michigan, artist, editor, onetime secretary of Daniel Webster, librarian of the War Department and later librarian in the Department of the Interior, nature lover, ama-teur explorer, and devoted Izaak Waltonian made numerous trips through the eastern half of the United States, from the St. Lawrence to the Gulf of Mexico, observing and noting wildlife, piscatorial habits, scenic beauty, and Indians. The three chapters entitled "Ac-comac" (see description of the wild horses of Accomac county, Vir-ginia, pp. 31–33), "A Virginia Barbecue," and "Plantation customs" describe accurately some of the popular and interesting aspects of Southern life. Lanman moderated his early views toward slavery, an institution which he considered evil but not as great an evil as the "fanaticism of the North" (p. 139).

A section on authentic Indian legends collected by the author in-cludes several identified with the Cherokee, the Catawba, and the Choctaw tribes. See the *Dictionary of American Biography* for a complete account of Lanman's life.

The contents of this book were included with a few changes and additions in Volume II of his *Adventures in the Wilds of the United States and British American Provinces* (Philadelphia, 1856).

343. Lanman, Charles (1819–1895)

Letters from the Alleghany Mountains, by Charles Lanman . . . New-York, George P. Putnam, 1848.

> 198 p. 19 cm.
> *Inclusive dates:* April to June, 1848.
> *Other editions:*
> (1) New York. 1849.
> (2) In the author's Adventures in the Wilds of the United States and British American provinces. Philadelphia, 1856.
> *Location of copy:* University of Kentucky Library.

Lanman made a three months' trip through the Allegheny Mountains from Dahlonega in Lumpkin County, Georgia, to Harpers Ferry, Virginia, during the spring and early summer of 1848. He describes his observations on the geology, wildlife, scenery, climate, and people of the western slope of the Alleghenies in a series of twenty-one letters written en route and first published in the *National Intelligencer.* Although most of the book is devoted to the natural beauty and Indian lore associated with such spots as Tallulah Falls, Trail Mountain, Smoky Mountain, the French Broad, Black Mountain, and the Valley of Virginia, Lanman in a short chapter makes a few general but pertinent comments on the lives and economy of the mountain people (p. 151). Concerning the few slaves in that region, he concluded that they were "the happiest and most independent portion of the population." He expressed sincere appreciation and enjoyment of the generous and genuine hospitality of the Southern gentry in Appalachia.

A twenty-five-page addendum, consisting of five letters written by Representative T. L. Clingman, Professor E. Witthell of the University of North Carolina, and Professor C. U. Shepard of Yale University, completes this volume. The letters, previously appearing in the *National Intelligencer,* New York *Albion,* and the *Highland Messenger* (Asheville, N. C.) and reprinted here with the consent of the writers, discuss important data concerning the topography, geology, and resources of the counties in western North Carolina.

344. Lesquereux, Leo (1806–1889)

Lettres écrites d'Amérique. Neuchâtel, De Henri Wolfrath, 1853.

> 2 p.l., 300 p. 20 cm.
> *Inclusive dates:* 1848–1851. In South, at intervals, April, 1850, to April, 1851.
> *Other editions:*
> Lettres écrites d'Amérique, destinées aux émigrants. De M. Léo Lesquereux. Neuchâtel, impr. de H. Wolfrath, 1849–50. 1 l., 116 p. 22½ cm.

Also in:
The Revue suisse, May, November, 1849; January, March, and May, 1850.
Issued in three parts with continuous pagination. Copy 2.
Location of copy: Newberry Library.

Ousted from a Swiss government post as director of peat bogs because of the political upheavals of 1848, this friend and associate of Louis Agassiz and Arnold Guyot landed that year in New York at the age of forty-two. Lesquereux at this time was unable to speak English, and he was "stone deaf." He overcame that handicap by learning to read lips, and he ultimately was "able to carry on conversation with three persons at once speaking English, French, and German in turn, although it was necessary in such cases that he be told in advance the language each was to speak."

His botanical work in the United States in connection with coal flora made him a foremost authority, and he later was honored as the first member to be elected to the National Academy of Sciences after its organization. He continued to reside in Columbus, Ohio, until his death in 1889 (see the *Dictionary of American Biography*).

Lesquereux traveled extensively throughout the United States. He first entered the South at Cincinnati and journeyed to Tennessee in the spring of 1850 (p. 212). The twenty-seven letters of this book, the first edition of which was not seen, appeared to be written from Lesquereux' journal after his return home to Ohio, to friends in Neuchâtel, where they were published in the *Revue Suisse* in 1849 and 1850. They describe his emigration to America and his travels and observations during his first years in this country. There is internal evidence that the botanist was interested in giving prospective immigrants a view of the United States. The book is first-class social and natural history.

The scientist was a careful observer, and he could write clearly. His description of slavery is even tempered and penetrating. He went to a Methodist camp meeting near Nashville, Tennessee, and saw the emotional outburst that took place. He visited Dr. Gerard Troost, the Dutch geologist who had settled in that state, and he went to the Hermitage. He described travel overland and by river. The seven letters pertaining to the South (pp. 215–95) make an excellent chapter on Southern travel.

345. Lewis, Henry (1819–1904)

Das illustrirte Mississippithal, dargestellt in 80 nach der Natur aufgenommenen Ansichten vom Wasserfalle zu St. Anthony an bis zum Golf von Mexico . . . von H. Lewis . . . Nebst einer historischen und geographischen Beschreibung der den Fluss begränzenden Länder, mit besonderer Rücksicht auf die verschiedenen den obern Mississippi bewohnenden Indianerstämme. (Deutsch und Englisch.) Von George B. Douglas. With two portraits of Henry Lewis and an introduction by J. Christian Bay. Leipzig, H. Schmidt und C. Günther; Firenze, Otto Lange, 1923. (Reprints of Rare Americana No. 3).

> 3 p.l., iii, xii, 431 p. illus., 79 plates (78 col., 1 fold.), 2 mounted port. (incl. front.). 26 cm.
>
> *Illustrations:* Frontispiece: Portrait of Henry Lewis in middle age by unknown German artist; portrait of Henry Lewis in old age; 79 plates (78 colored, 1 folded), prints of rare Americana.
>
> *Inclusive dates:* 1847–1849. In South, 1847 and 1848?
>
> *Other editions:*
>
> Das illustrirte Mississippithal, dargestellt in 80 nach der Natur aufgenommenen Ansichten vom Wasserfalle zu St. Anthony an bis zum Gulf von Mexico ... von H. Lewis ... Nebst einer historischen und geographischen Beschreibung der den Fluss begränzenden Länder, mit besonderer Rücksicht auf die verschiedenen den obern Mississippi bewohnenden Indianerstämme. (Deutsch und Englisch.) von George B. Douglas ... Dusseldorf, Arnz & Comp. ₍1857₎. 431 p. front., ₍engr. title₎, illus., 78 col. plates (1 double). 27½ cm.
>
> *Location of copy:* Princeton University Library.

When Henry Lewis, an important though relatively obscure American panoramist, retired in Düsseldorf in 1851 to spend the remainder of his life in Germany, he had successfully displayed, both here and abroad, his sensational and gigantic, "almost a mile long," panorama of the Mississippi Valley from the Falls of St. Anthony to New Orleans. He shortly arranged with a German firm of lithographers to issue *Das Illustrirte Mississippithal.* They made the colored plates from his original sketches, and they used the same text, unaltered, which had been written for the panorama by George B. Douglas, who had accompanied the artist on his two sketching tours and who now translated that text into German for the new publication. (No copy with English text has been located.)

Lewis no doubt wished the many German emigrants to have a "purely descriptive work to facilitate their orientation in the vast country which they [had chosen] for their future home...." But the publishers went bankrupt after turning out only a few copies with board covers (less than twenty of the volumes are known to be in private collections in America). The rest were sold as scrap paper, or the colored plates were given to students who "purchased their books at Lempertz store."

Yet these copies of this rare first edition of 1857 are possibly one of the finest published pictorial portrayals of the mid-century Mississippi Valley in existence. There are seventy-eight full-page colored scenes, alphabetically arranged, some with both English and German titles. In 1923 this work was reprinted in Leipzig without any change except for the addition of a good introduction by the editor, J. Christian Bey of the John Crerrar Library. This edition was used in preparing this bibliography.

Space permits for only the highlights of the artist's career, as taken in part from the editor's account. Born in England, Lewis came to America in 1836, settled in St. Louis as a carpenter, and eventually became a stagehand at a local theater. A self-instructed painter, he was inspired to do a river panorama because of the mounting interest in the new scenic extravaganzas. After attempting to collaborate first with Banvard, then with Pomarede, and also with Stockwell, each of whom produced successful panoramas, Lewis determined to venture alone. He began his first sketching trip from St. Louis to the upper Mississippi in 1847, and later that year he was reported to have gone down to New Orleans. In May, 1848, he set out on a continuous trip along the entire river. The question has been raised whether he visited in person the lower part of the Mississippi Valley. Some investigators claim that he painted the five-hundred-yard southern section of the panorama of the river from St. Louis to New Orleans from sketches made by an artist named Rogers (see *Missouri Historical Review*, Vol. XXVII [April, 1933], 246, and *Minnesota History*, Vol. XVII, [June, 1936], 131–58).

At any rate, the work was finished in September, 1849. The fate of the panorama following its long showing is unknown. But the lithographs of both the first edition and the recent reprint, which give a pronounced German flavor to the urban architecture of those communities portrayed and which graphically depict the steamboats, the Indians, the river plantation scenes, and the many topographical points of interest—all of these have preserved for posterity a good part of Lewis' accurate picture of his contemporary West. Few emigrants probably saw the printed lithographs or read the text of the first edition, but no one can estimate the interest in America generated in the hundreds and thousands of Europeans who were fascinated by the new panorama medium of that period. Of the six known Mississippi Valley panoramists, only Lewis has left substantial tangible evidence for our generation.

Some fourteen of the lithographs and considerable textual material deal with the South. There are excellent river scenes, views of Memphis, Natchez, Baton Rouge, General Taylor's plantation, the spectacular water-front fire in St. Louis in 1849, and a double-page spread of New Orleans. Much of the accompanying information describing the area as a whole, the individual states with their natural products, the social customs, the wildlife and flora, and the plantation economy is rather general in scope. At times excerpts from newspapers, periodicals, and the works of recognized scholars are quoted, but on the whole the narrative seems to be based on personal observation. No effort was made to discuss the political right and moral wrong of slavery, although it was evident that Lewis and Douglas were not in sympathy with that institution. Yet the writer of the descriptive account reported that after "twenty years in slave states" he seldom had seen a character such as St. Clair and never a Simon Legree (p. 373).

Considered solely as a descriptive discourse on the South—its features, its historical development, and its institutions—*Das Illustrirte Mississippithal* probably rates no special consideration over many of the travel accounts, nor do the individual lithographic illustrations have distinctive artistic quality. But from the conceptions of recording the overall grandeur and strength of the expanding American scene with vigorous strokes, this must rank as a unique and significant work of the period.

The original edition of 1857 is listed in the Library of Congress Catalog with a full description.

346.   [Lewis, John Delaware (1828–1884)]

Across the Atlantic. By the author of Sketches of cantabs. London, G. Earle, 1851.

> x p., 1 l., 274 p.   18 cm.
> *Inclusive dates:* June, 1850?
> *Other editions:*
>   [J. D. Lewis]. London, 1851.
> *Location of copy:* Library of Congress.

Arriving in Boston from Liverpool shortly after the death of President Zachary Taylor, John D. Lewis traveled for some months in the East. He went as far south as Virginia, noting American institutions and "laughing at the social manners of the American people." His observations are written up in a series of topical sketches, "light and trivial," supporting and justifying the criticism of such early travelers as Marryat, Dickens, Trollope, and Houstoun. To him America was the "most sublime and the most ridiculous, the most appalling and the most amusing, of all countries."

His firsthand knowledge of the South was probably limited to a few trips across the Potomac from Washington. He regretted the "dilapidated" condition of Mount Vernon. On another occasion he observed some of the lighter aspects of a camp meeting. A chapter on "slaves and slavery" presents without prejudice the pros and cons of the question.

347. Ligeret de Chazey, Madame Eleanor

Les creoles. Response à Madame de Grandfort. New Orleans, imp. de H. Merider, n.d. (1855?).

> 1–42 p. 14½ cm.
> *Location of copy:* The Howard Memorial Library.

Madame Ligeret de Chazey's little booklet is hardly a travel account within itself, but it does comment on the observations of an earlier traveler, Madame de Grandfort. (See de Grandfort, *L'Autre Monde,* Paris, 1855.) The author undertakes to explain the position of the Creole in Louisiana society and to explain the eccentricities which the former author described. This book is too brief to have much value, and it is too defensive in its nature to give more than the point of view of an ante bellum native of New Orleans.

348. Löher, Franz von (1818–1892)

Aussichten für gebildete Deutsche in Nordamerika. Von Franz Löher. Berlin, Julius Springer, 1853.

> iii–vi, 91 p., 1 l. 19 cm.
> *Location of copy:* Detroit Public Library.

As in his earlier work, *Geschichte und Zustände der Deutschen in Amerika* (Leipzig, 1847), there is no mention of the time nor a pattern of travel in this book. Löher records his impressions of his fourteen months' visit in this country in numerous topics of real interest to the social historian. Even though he states that he did not travel in the slave states, he does mention Virginia and Mammoth Cave. He may have gained much of his information on the South from his extended visits to Cincinnati and St. Louis.

349. Löher, Franz von (1818–1892)

Geschichte und Zustände der Deutschen in Amerika. Von Franz Löher. Cincinnati, Leipzig, Eggers und Mulkop (Cinci.), K. F. Köhler (Leipzig), 1847.

> 2 p.l., xii, 544 p. 21 cm.
> *Inclusive dates:* 1845–1847?

Other editions:

Geschichte und Zustände der Deutschen in Amerika. Von Franz Löher. 2 Ausg. Göttingen, G. H. Wigand, 1855. iv p., 1 l., x, 544 p. 21½ cm.
Location of copy: Wisconsin State Historical Society.

Albert Faust, in his *Introduction to The German Element in the United States,* published in 1909, stated that no "historical survey [of German immigration] has . . . existed in the English language nor has one been attempted in German since the publication of Löher." Later in the first volume Faust wrote that Löher was "perhaps the first German traveler and man of letters who felt sincerely interested in the German-American population of the United States." These statements would assure Löher's position as an important figure in spite of the fact that nowhere in the above book does the German scholar and world traveler indicate any itinerary or time of travel nor even suggest that he had been in the United States. Yet in a later work, published in 1853, Löher stated that he had spent fourteen months traveling through all of the states except the Southern slave states. During that time he was in Cincinnati and St. Louis for extended stays, and it is reasonable to surmise that he might have gained much of his information and impressions concerning the South while in those two cities.

This present account traces the historical development of German immigration. In the ten books (chapters) there are a few sections concerning the Germans in the South (pp. 275–80, 316–28, 348–53), but for the most part material on the South must be gleaned from the mass of detail pertaining to the nation as a whole. Because Löher in the first half of this work credits the sources of his information, while in the last part there is virtually no documentation, it is possible that he relied on contemporary travel accounts as well as on personal observation. The book, according to Löher, was published in Leipzig in 1847 and by a friend in Cincinnati in the same year. The Library of Congress does not list the Leipzig edition.

350. Löher, Franz von (1818–1892)

Land und Leute in der Alten und Neuen Welt. Reiseskizzen von Franz Löher. Göttingen, George H. Wigand, 1858. New York, L. W. Schmidt, 1855.

3 vols. in 2; Vol. I and Vol. II in 1. Paged separately: Vol. I, 1–283 p.; Vol. II, 1–281 p.; Vol. III, 1, 292 p. 17 cm. (Göttingen, George H. Wigand, 1853). *Inclusive dates:* 1845–1847?
Location of copy: Library of Congress.

This work furnished a definite clue about the time of Löher's travel in the United States. He must have arrived in New York from Liverpool on the *South Carolina* in the summer or early fall of 1845 or 1846 to begin his more than one-year stay in America. During that time, much of which appears to have been spent in Cincinnati, he completed for publication there (II, p. 56) his *Geschichte und Zustände der Deutschen in Amerika* (Cincinnati, 1847).

Löher ranks as an important German traveler who wrote extensively and intensively about the United States. He differed from most of his compatriots in certain respects: he did not give the usual clear picture of his daily itinerary; he learned to converse with Americans in their own tongue; he reflected his deep interest in Americans, especially German-Americans, by an even greater attention to the details of their everyday living, home life, family relationships, popular customs, and cultural interests; and he made frequent comparisons with old-world conditions, often to the advantage of the United States.

But he did little more than skirt along the northern river border of the South. On arriving in New York, he traveled through parts of Canada and New England before he visited Washington, Pittsburgh, Cincinnati, and St. Louis. He returned to the East by way of the upper Mississippi River and the Great Lakes. His many interesting observations in Baltimore and the nation's capital gave him his first impressions of the South. But his long stays in Cincinnati and St. Louis, his trips on the river steamboats (for an excellent description of the activities on board, see Vol. II, pp. 100–16), his opportunities for contacts with many Southerners, and his wide reading and erudition were his main sources of information concerning the region. He made few references to the South as a particular section of the nation. Most of his observations were intended to be national in scope.

Not until he made his side trip up the Missouri River from St. Louis to Hermann (Mo.) did Löher discuss slavery (II, p. 164) and then only in the limited way in which it affected the Germans in America. Although opposed to the system, he argued that his former countrymen were incapable of being effective slaveowners, for they either worked their Negroes too hard or too easy, and in both cases the results were unsatisfactory (II, p. 167). He observed that those areas in the South with great numbers of German settlers soon became antislavery. Like Moritz Busch, Löher gave attention to the spirituals as a rich source for interpreting the Negro. He thought that the colored folk were the *einzigen naturdichter* in America (II, p. 174).

The last volume of this work, aside from the travelers' occasional references to the South, discusses two topics of regional and local interest: factors contributing to the characteristics of Kentuckians (III, p. 221) and the Cherokee Indians of the Carolinas and Georgia. This substantial three-volume work, together with his two other books on his American travels, make Löher another of the significant German commentators on America in the mid-century.

351. Ludvigh, Samuel Gottlieb (1801–1869)

Licht und Schattenbilder republikanischer Zustände. Skizzirt von Samuel Ludvigh während seiner Reise in den Vereinigten Staaten von Nord-Amerika 1846–1847. Leipzig, W. Jurany, 1848.

viii, 344 p.   18½ cm.
Other editions:
New York, Helmich und Co., 1848.   viii, 344 p.   18½ cm.
Inclusive dates: August, 1846, to March, 1847. In South, November, 1846, to February, 1847.
Location of copy: Library of Congress.

The Austrian-born scholar and writer of this important travel book later returned to the United States to become one of the "great liberal editors among the Germans" in this country. Ludvigh made little mention in this work of his first visit in 1845 (pp. 119, 223). But he returned to New York in the late summer of 1846 and traveled to Philadelphia, Wheeling, Pittsburgh, Cleveland, and Columbus, en route to Cincinnati. Here he spent about two weeks and observed the many points of interest, which he describes at some length. He was irked with the "Puritan Sabbath" and made special note of the various forms of amusement in the city.

After a brief stay in Louisville, Ludvigh went to St. Louis and then proceeded up the Mississippi River to Dubuque (Ia.). From there he traveled across Illinois to Chicago and back to St. Louis—the city which he labeled the "New York of the West." His well-attended lecture in this Missouri city on "The United States and Europe" provoked editorial attacks on him by the native American press.

The last half of the book describes the author's trip through the South. He was much attracted by New Orleans because of its trade potential, its varied population and institutions, and its many contrasting "lights and shadows." He compared it with other great cities and concluded that "there is only one New Orleans." He called it *Die Karrenstadt* because it had many carts instead of carriages. With the thoroughness so characteristic of qualified German travelers, he packed his account of that area with a wide range of descriptive, historical, and statistical information concerning such details as the battleground of 1812, Creoles, flatboaters, quadroons, the market, the charity hospital, shipping, and slavery. Ludvigh did not focus as much attention on the latter institution as most travelers of the period. He liked the South and "chivalrous Southerners" compared to the "gold seeking Yankees," but he made some sharp criticisms of some of the deeper shadows of slavery (p. 311).

Mobile and its "Puritan Sabbath" seemed "dismal" to him after New Orleans. He did not appear impressed with Montgomery, Savannah, or Charleston (S. C.), except for the excellent theater in the latter city. He recorded considerable information about Washington and New York. A final interesting detail is a listing of his itinerary for the entire trip in the United States with the distances between cities and the cost of travel by the various forms of conveyance from town to town. His transportation costs totaled $161.75.

Ludvigh was a candid and objective observer. He had great hopes for America. It is unfortunate that he did not see fit to scrutinize other areas of the South as intensely as he did New Orleans.

352. Lyell, Sir Charles (1797–1875)

A second visit to the United States of North America. In two volumes. New York, Harper and brothers; London, J. Murray, 1849.

Vol. I, vii–xii, 13–273 p.; Vol. II, v–xi, 13–287 p., 12 l. 19 cm.
Illustrations: Several small sketches of geological interest.
Inclusive dates: 1845–1846. In South, December, 1845, to April, 1846.
Other editions:
(1) A second visit to the United States of North America . . . 2 vols. [London, J. Murray, 1849]. illus. 19½ cm.
(2) A second visit to the United States of North America. By Sir Charles Lyell . . . 2 vols. New York, Harper & brothers; London, J. Murray, 1849. illus. 19½ cm.
(3) A second visit to the United States of North America. By Sir Charles Lyell. 2 vols. New York, Harper & brothers; etc., etc., 1850. illus. 19 cm.
(4) A second visit to North America. By Sir Charles Lyell F.R.S. 3rd ed. 2 vols. London, J. Murray, 1855. illus. 21 cm.
Location of copy: University of Kentucky Library.

On the second of his four visits to the United States, the eminent British geologist Charles Lyell, accompanied by his wife, spent five of the nine months traveling through the South and retracing much of the route of his first trip in 1841–42. (See *Travels in North America; with Geological Observations on the United States, Canada, and Nova Scotia (q.v.)* (London, 1845.) Arriving in Halifax in Septem-

A SECOND VISIT

TO

THE UNITED STATES

OF

NORTH AMERICA.

BY

SIR CHARLES LYELL, F.R.S.

PRESIDENT OF THE GEOLOGICAL SOCIETY OF LONDON,
AUTHOR OF "THE PRINCIPLES OF GEOLOGY,"
AND "TRAVELS IN NORTH AMERICA."

IN TWO VOLUMES.
VOL. II.

LONDON:
JOHN MURRAY, ALBEMARLE STREET.
1849.

[270]

ber, 1845, he toured the East and reached Washington in early December. On the sixteenth of that month he started for Richmond. Christmas found him in Charleston, South Carolina, a city that he liked. From there he continued by water to Savannah where he made a side trip to Darien, Butler's Island, and other points along the coast of Georgia. Crossing that state, part of the way by handcar in order to better examine the rocks and fossils in the many grade cuts along the right of way, he moved on to Montgomery and to Mobile along the Alabama, Mobile, Tombigbee, and Black Warrior rivers. Late in February the geologist left for New Orleans. After an extended stay which gave him opportunity for many interesting and significant observations in and about that city, including an investigation of the mouth of the river, he started North, making several side trips en route to examine the varied geological phenomena. The Lyells were in Louisville from April 5–13. Returning to Philadelphia, he made a quick field trip to Richmond, Virginia, on April 29 to re-examine the coal deposits near that city. They sailed from Boston for Liverpool on June 1.

More than half of the two volumes published in 1849 pertain to the South. Lyell's scientific interest took him along the regular routes as well as into the remoter corners seldom seen by other travelers. He visited and conferred with many prominent as well as lesser known persons such as John Bachman, Charles Shepherd, Dr. John Le Conte, Hamilton Couper, David Dale Owen, and J. R. Cotting. From time to time one or more of them accompanied him on some of his expeditions.

Lyell's description of the coastal islands of the southeastern coast (I, pp. 243–73), erosion, topography, and fossils in Georgia and Alabama (II, pp. 26–66) are an important contribution to travel literature, while his detailed observations of the Mississippi Valley from the delta to the mouth of the Ohio River (II, pp. 111–99) equal or excell the accounts of other travelers. He checked and compared his new data with his earlier findings and with those of travelers and scientists such as William Bartram (1739–1823), François Michaux (1770–1855), and Benjamin Silliman (1779–1864), whose works he often cited in the two volumes (II, p. 250).

Lyell's unbiased, careful, and objective observations of the social and economic pattern of Southern institutions are of particular significance. His unhurried travel afforded him opportunities for close contact with virtually all elements of Southern life. He noted the "perfect ease and politeness which a stranger is made to feel" during his fortnight's visit at Hopeton, the home of Hamilton Couper and one of the large, well-managed plantations along the Altamaha River (I, pp. 245–50). Yet he had much to say about the more simple operations of the small farmers in the back country (II, p. 61). He enjoyed the lavish appointments of the St. Charles in New Orleans, but he often shared and endured the frugal fare and rough quarters of the isolated settlers on his many side trips, especially along the Mississippi River. His wife seldom accompanied him on these ventures (II, p. 172).

The reader is kept informed of his schedule of travel, and Lyell was quite meticulous in identifying both places and persons en route. His fame, his wide acquaintance, and his many letters of introduction assured him a welcome everywhere along the way. He ventured few predictions concerning the future of the South, nor did he summarize his conclusions on America as had Alexander Mackay in *Western World* (London, 1849) or Moritz Busch in *Wanderungen zwischen Hudson und Mississippi 1851 und 1852* (Stuttgart, 1854). But throughout the two volumes a wide variety of nonpolitical questions are considered with varying degrees of emphasis. The author seldom missed attending church, and he often commented on the services of the various religious denominations in America. He had a particular interest in Negro sermons, for he made frequent references to them throughout the two volumes. It was evident that the geologist took advantage of his many opportunities to examine objectively the many aspects of slavery. He recognized the complexity of its problems, especially those involving emancipation. He attended slave auctions, inspected living conditions, and observed the various kinds of daily toil. He noted the opportunities for colored artisans in the United States. He called attention to efforts made to improve the conditions of the Negro, especially the attempt of Hamilton Couper to increase the self-independence of slaves. Lyell felt that the intelligence of the colored race increased in proportion to its contacts with the whites. But even though he was opposed to slavery, he vigorously refuted the charges of extreme cruelty to slaves reported by some of the travelers (II, pp. 38, 79, 126). He thought that the colored race, if given opportunity and fair play, "might soon be safely entrusted with equality of civil and political rights." These many realistic yet prophetic observations make Lyell one of the most important among the many travelers reporting on the institution during this period.

The dozen or more small, part-page or marginal sketches, usually of a scientific nature, add some interest to the work, and the ten-page index is a feature not often found in other travel accounts.

The work was published simultaneously in London and New York in 1849 with the same title and collation.

353. Mackay, Alexander (1808–1852)

The western world; or travels in the United States in 1846–47: exhibiting them in their latest development, social, political and industrial. 3 vols. London, 1849.

8 plates.

Inclusive dates: January, 1846, to January, 1847. In South, May, 1846, to early fall, 1846.

Other editions:

(1) . . . including a chapter on California . . . By Alex. Mackay. 2d ed. 3 vols. London, R. Bentley, 1849. fronts.; Vols. I, III, fold. maps.

(2) . . . From the 2d London ed. 2 vols. Philadelphia, Lea & Blanchard, 1849 19½ cm.

(3) Third edition. 3 vols. London, 1850.

(4) . . . With a new map of the United States, showing their recent territorial acquisitions, and a map of California. By Alex. Mackay . . . 4th ed. 3 vols. London, R. Bentley, 1850.

(5) Die Westliche Welt. Reisen in den Vereinigten Staaten. Deutsch bearbeitet und mit Zusätzen aus anderen Reisewerken, sowie nach den neuesten statistischen Quellen bis zum Jahre 1854 vervollständigt von O. L. H[eubner]. 4 vols. Vol. IV, fold. sheet.

(6) . . . Reise durch die Vereinsstaaten von Amerika von Alexander McKay. Aus dem Englischen übersetzt von Marie Heine. Nebst einer Einleitung und vier Illustrationen von Wilhelm Heine . . . Leipzig, C. E. Killmann, 1861. 4 vols. in 2.

Location of copy: University of Kentucky Library.

Mackay, Scottish-born journalist, barrister, and for many years a resident of Canada, from where he traveled extensively throughout the United States, revisited this country in 1846–47 as the correspondent of the London *Morning Chronicle* to report the debates in Congress and to sound out public sentiment on the Oregon question. (See the *Dictionary of National Biography* for a sketch of his life.) Landing at Halifax in January, he visited the important cities along the Atlantic seaboard and reached Washington in early May. Near the end of that month he journeyed to Richmond and proceeded from there by rail through Petersburg, Weldon, Raleigh, and the Dismal Swamp, to Washington, where he boarded a steamer for Charleston. Leaving that city after a two-day stay, he went by train to Columbia, Augusta, and Milledgeville and then endured the discomforts of a stagecoach to Macon, Columbus, and Montgomery. The remainder of his trip through the South was by water to Mobile, New Orleans, Natchez, Vicksburg, Memphis, St. Louis, and Louisville.

THE

WESTERN WORLD;

OR,

TRAVELS IN THE UNITED STATES

IN 1846-47:

EXHIBITING THEM IN THEIR LATEST DEVELOPMENT,
SOCIAL, POLITICAL, AND INDUSTRIAL;

INCLUDING A CHAPTER ON

CALIFORNIA.

———

BY ALEX. MACKAY, ESQ.,

OF THE MIDDLE TEMPLE, BARRISTER AT LAW.

———

IN TWO VOLUMES.
VOL. I.

FROM THE SECOND LONDON EDITION.

PHILADELPHIA:
LEA & BLANCHARD.
1849.

[274]

Early in 1847 he sailed from Boston for England after completing the circuit of the nation from Louisville to Pittsburgh, Niagara Falls, Montreal, and south to New York.

The author diversified his account by inserting chapters on broad national subjects, such as commerce, government, slavery, agriculture, religion, education, and manufacturing, between chapters that are primarily descriptive of his travel route and of local interest. In this way he distilled his many years' experience of wide travel in the United States, careful observations, and understanding into comprehensive analyses of the important forces in American life. Throughout this work he expressed great faith in the progress of America. This is evident in his prophetic final words of the main part of this account, written a century ago, in which he predicted that the "American Republic or Republics, as the case may be" would take over England's position of political and commercial leadership when that power had "fulfilled her glorious mission" and "abdicated her supremacy."

Mackay was objective and unbiased in his data regarding the South. His analysis of the region takes up about one-third of the two volumes. He warned of the dangers of forming impressions from a few days' observation of its "floating population" encountered on steamboats, in railway carriages, and in barrooms. "In the South particularly," he continued, "one must get out of the current if he would appreciate . . . society aright" (II, p. 98 [2d ed.]). His attention centered chiefly on two classes in Southern society—planters and Negroes. Regarding slavery—he devoted two chapters to a moderate but intelligent appraisal of its political, social, and economic aspects—he felt that many "treated it as a cloak which the Republic could lay aside at its pleasure." He stated that he was "neither the apologist of slavery in the abstract, nor the panegyrist of the phase, which as a domestic institution, it has assumed." Mackay noted many instances of race prejudice in this country. He also observed a greater severity in the system as carried on in the cotton-producing areas of the South. Yet he appeared to be vitally interested in enlightening those persons whose candor sought out a "correct estimate of a sad reality."

This visitor was greatly impressed with the hospitality and the commercial opportunities of both Mobile and New Orleans. He noted the steps already underway toward improved sanitary conditions, and he refuted the exaggerated view which was generally held abroad that the unhealthfulness of the latter city was worse than that of other seacoast areas in the South.

[275]

Mackay's droll humor in recording lighter incidents enlivens the narrative. (See his descriptions of the upset stagecoach [II, p. 63], an inquisitive traveler [II, pp. 27–32], a Kentucky rifle match [II, 143], and the posthumous adventures of Picayune Walker [II, 124–26].)

Students interested in the intimate experiences of daily life in the South, specially on the plantations, may be somewhat disappointed in this work, for Mackay did not emphasize them as much as certain of the other travelers. Nor did he devote as much space to the details of society in the states bordering the Mississippi River as in those on the seaboard. In much of the last half of the work he did not indicate the time element in his travel itinerary. Yet as an evaluation of the overall picture of the South this scholarly work ranks as one of the foremost accounts of the period.

354.   Marcy, Randolph B. (1812–1887)

. . . Exploration of the Red River of Louisiana, in the year 1852; by Randolph B. Marcy . . . assisted by George B. McClellan . . . With reports on the natural history of the country . . . Washington, R. Armstrong, public printer, 1853.

> xv, 320 p.   plates, fold. maps.   22 cm.   (32 Cong., 2 sess., Sen. Exec. [Doc.] No. 54).
> *Maps:* Two: Folding maps of the region, in a pocket.
> *Illustrations:* Sixty-six plates of landscapes, geological sections, paleontology, zoology, and botany of the region.
> *Inclusive dates:* April to July, 1852.
> *Other editions:*
> (1) Washington, B. Tucker, Senate printer, 1854.   xv, 310 p.   plates. 22½ cm.   (33 Cong., 1 sess., Sen. Exec. Doc.).
> (2) Washington, A.O.P. Nicholson, public printer, 1854.   xv, 286 p.   plates (1 fold.), fold. maps.   23½ cm.   ([U. S.] 33 Cong., 1 sess., House Exec. Doc.).
> *Location of copy:* University of Kentucky Library.

This work is on the periphery of Southern travel literature, for it is the official report of Captain Marcy's exploring expedition to the headwaters of the Red and Canadian rivers in Louisiana, northern Texas, and New Mexico. Marcy described the natural history of the area, the Indian tribes, and the possibilities of a railroad route.

355.   Marjoribanks, Alexander

Travels in South and North America. By Alexander Marjoribanks. Edinburgh, 1852.

> 486 p.   col. front.
> *Illustrations:* Colored frontispiece: Print of suspension bridge at Niagara Falls.
> *Inclusive dates:* July 11, 1850, to November, 1850.

Other editions:
(1) London, Simpkin, Marshall, and company, 1853. xiv, 480 p. col. front., illus. 20½ cm.
(2) New York, D. Appleton and company, 1853.
(3) Edinburgh, 1854. 460 p.
(4) Fifth edition. London, Simpkin, Marshall and company, 1854.
(5) Fifth edition. New York, D. Appleton and company, 1854.
Location of copy: University of Kentucky Library.

Nothing in this book proves that this British traveler journeyed farther south in the United States than Philadelphia. Yet he devotes four chapters (18–21) to an objective discussion of the slavery question in the South, drawing on the works of earlier travelers such as Houstoun, Martineau, Lady Stuart-Wortley, Buckingham, Johnston, and Charles Lyell. The matter is treated from the historical and topical point of view.

Marjoribanks arrived in Boston from Liverpool and visited in the East and along the St. Lawrence and Great Lakes area. The first part of the work describes a trip from Australia to South America, which appears to have been made earlier, but no date is indicated. Considerable space in this part is devoted to slavery and its history in South and Central America.

The above is apparently the first edition, although Sabin lists an edition published in Edinburgh in 1852. The *British Museum Catalog of Printed Books* gives the date as 1853 for printings in both London and Edinburgh.

356. Marmier, Xavier (1809–1892)

Lettres sur l'Amérique, par X. Marmier. Canada.–États-Unis.–Havana, Río de la Plata. 2 vols. Paris, A. Bertrand, 1851.

Vol. I, 455 p.; Vol. II, 463 p. 18 cm.
Inclusive dates: Summer, 1849–1850. In South, autumn and early winer, 1849.
Other editions:
(1) Lettres sur l'Amérique, par Xavier Marmier. Unis.–Havane, Río de la Plata, Canada.–États. 2 vols. Paris, E. Plon et cie., 1881. 18½ cm.
(2) Cartas sobre la America . . . Traduicidas para El Universal . . . 2 vols. Mexico, impr. del Universal, ₁185-₁. Vol. I, 3–450 p.; Vol. II, 3–434 p. 19 cm.
Location of copy: University of Pennsylvania.

Marmier, traveler, littérateur, and member of the French Academy, entered the South at Washington and traveled across it by way of the Ohio and Mississippi rivers to New Orleans. He was a good observer and gave his two-volume book a ring of trustworthiness. He, like his fellow countrymen, had a great interest in history, and he gives the historical background of the major scenes before him.

Washington and its eternal interest in politics received rather full coverage. The author saw the public buildings and the Patent Office, spent an evening at the White House, and detected an aristocratic movement in the United States.

The letters about America written by this important French traveler first appeared in 1850 in *El Universal,* the *New York Times* of Mexico. They then were published in these two volumes before the French edition came out in 1851. Marmier was a professor of foreign languages on the *Faculté* of Reims and then librarian in the Ministry of Public Instruction, a position which enabled him to travel where he pleased. He covered much of the world and published some thirty or forty books on history, literature, and travel and was honored in 1870 with a membership in the French Academy.

His journey by river to New Orleans excited Marmier's interest in American history, and he explained the sights which appeared before him. Even Louisiana and New Orleans conjured up historical interests. However, slavery received more than a historical treatment. He believed that field hands were unhappy, while household servants were fairly well off. He discussed the divisive influence of slavery in the nation. After leaving the United States, Marmier traveled by boat to the mouth of the Mississippi on his way to Havana.

357. Martin, Horace

Pictorial guide to the Mammoth cave, Kentucky. By the Rev. Horace Martin. Illustrated . . . by S. Wallen, John Andrew, J. W. Orr, and N. Orr. New York, Stringer and Townsend, [1851].

> 4 p.l., [7]–116 p. front., 8 plates, illus.
> *Illustrations:* Ten full-page engravings of scenes inside the cave and many smaller illustrations.
> *Other editions:*
>   (1) New York, 1852.
>   (2) New York, 1853.
>   (3) (Five-page description of Jenny Lind's visit, as described by Julius Benedict, quoted in Jenny Lind in America, by Charles G. Rosenberg. New York, Stringer & Townsend, 1851. p. 193.)
> *Location of copy:* University of Kentucky Library.

The only point of travel interest in this guidebook of Mammoth Cave is the five-page description of Jenny Lind's visit to the cave with six other members of her party in 1851. The trip was described by Julius Benedict, a member of her group. The same material is quoted in a footnote in Rosenberg's *Jenny Lind in America* (New York, 1851) (p. 193).

[278]

358. Massey, S[tephen] L.

James traveler's companion. Being a complete guide through the Western States, to the Gulf of Mexico and the Pacific, via the Great Lakes, rivers, canals, etc. giving full and accurate descriptions of all places on, and in the vicinity of, the western waters; interspersed with historical notes and statistical tables; together with a vast amount of general information not found in other works of a similar character with numerous maps and illustrations. Also, containing all of the principal stage, steamboat, and railroad routes in the West, and the chief routes to Oregon and California, with their respective distances. The whole brought down to the present time. Cincinnati, J. A. and U. P. James, 1851.

vi, 9–224 p. illus., 2 fold. maps (incl. front.). 15 cm.

Maps: Frontispiece: Folding map of Mississippi River; also, folding map of Ohio, Missouri, and Illinois rivers.

Illustrations: Map and view of Cincinnati; view of New Orleans, Louisville, and other important cities.

Other editions:

James travelers companion: being a complete guide through the West and South, to the Gulf of Mexico and the Pacific . . . with historical notes, statistical tables, and a vast amount of general information . . . To which is added a new and complete railroad and route book. Cincinnati, J. A. & U. P. James. 2 vols. in 1. illus. 15 cm.

Inclusive dates: 1851.

Location of copy: Newberry Library.

The title of this compact little guidebook gives a complete description of its contents. Much of the material pertains to the South, including the routes of travel on the Mississippi, the Missouri, and the Ohio rivers and the routes on the Gulf of Mexico.

359. Maury, Sarah Mytton (Hughes), "Mrs. William Maury" (1803–1849)

An Englishwoman in America. By Sarah Mytton. With an appendix containing the history of the Emigrant Surgeons' Bill. London, T. Richardson and son; Liverpool, George Smith, Watts and company, 1848.

3 p.l., [iii]–cxviii p., 1 l., 251, 204, 16 p., 1 l. 19½ cm.

Inclusive dates: May, 1845, to August, 1846.

Other editions:

London, John Murray, 1856. 576 p.

Location of copy: University of Kentucky Library.

An Englishwoman in America was the second work written by Mrs. Maury about her second visit to the United States in 1845–46. (See *Statesmen of America in 1846.*) In contrast to those British travel accounts that were critical of America, this book appears to have been written with the intention of further exalting the United States in general and the South in particular. Also the traveler's experience with smallpox contracted en route to America had prompted her to carry out a campaign in England and the United States for a bill compelling emigrant vessels to "carry a medical officer" and to improve sanitary conditions on board ships. An appendix of 204 pages traces the interesting history of that effort.

The book includes a dedicatory letter to the Secretary of State, James Buchanan, copies of the Declaration of Independence, the Constitution of the United States, and Washington's Farewell Address, which Mrs. Maury states "have never been published in England [and] it is time that these noble documents should be made known to the British public." There are also an extended preface answering the criticism of "her excessive and indiscriminate praise" of the statesmen in her earlier work and an introduction which calls attention to the unfavorable economic opportunities in England as compared with America. The main part of the book is the three chapters entitled: "The Lady's Log," "The Small Pox," and "New York—General Observations." It is this last chapter that contributes to travel literature.

Her comments follow no pattern or route of travel. Much of her information seems to have been garnered in and about New York and Washington. Her observations reveal a wide range of interest and a keen awareness of the problems in the American picture. Yet she was most biased in favor of Southern institutions and life, and she preferred the South and things Southern on the sectional level in much the same way that she favored the United States over England on a national basis. Her close family ties in Virginia and Kentucky account for much of this attitude. Her characteristic of viewing phases of the American scene in the most favorable light possible, as in her *Statesmen of America in 1846,* made this work popular with many readers of a century ago, but definitely limits its merit in an evaluation of travel literature today.

The last sixteen pages of the book give numerous reviews, press notices, and other testimonials concerning the earlier work.

360. Maury, Sarah Mytton (Hughes), "Mrs. William Maury" (1803–1849)

The statesmen of America in 1846. By Sarah Mytton. London, Longman, Brown, Green, and Longman, 1847.

vi p., 1 l., 548 p. 19½ cm.
Inclusive dates: May, 1845, to August, 1846.
Other editions:
  Philadelphia, Carey, 1847. 261 p.
Location of copy: University of Kentucky Library.

Mrs. Sarah Mytton Maury, daughter of a Liverpool merchant and wife of the Virginian who became mercantile agent in the same city, spent more than a year in America (1845–46) for reasons of health and interest in possible emigration opportunities for her eleven children. After a trip of "twelve thousand miles or more" in the land of her husband's family, which she stated included a tour through the South by way of Virginia, the Carolinas, New Orleans, up the Mississippi and the Ohio to Lexington, and on to Washington, Mrs. Maury returned to England "more American than the Americans themselves."

Her opportunities for entree through family connections, letters of introduction, and her radiant yet persistent personality were apparently unlimited. She, of course, reveled in this generous reception. Very much enamored with America, she wrote the twenty-four intimate, rather superficial, but always flattering character sketches of prominent Americans, usually statesmen, which make up this work. It was enthusiastically received in general in this country, but it provoked much irritation across the Atlantic, for all of the figures, including such Southerners as William H. Haywood, John Y. Mason, Edward Hanagan (born in Kentucky), Mathew Fontaine Maury, John C. Calhoun, and Henry Clay, were exalted with no suggestions of weaknesses. This uncritical adulation is the most serious criticism of her work. Then, too, Britain in almost every instance was made to appear in an unfavorable light when compared with the United States.

361.   Miss Mendell

Notes of travel and life. By two ladies—Misses Mendell and Hosmer . . .
New York, for the authors, 1854.

288 p.   20 cm.
Inclusive dates: Uncertain; probably a short visit early in 1853 and another longer trip of several weeks in the summer of 1853 or 1854.
Location of copy: University of Kentucky Library.

Questions were raised in the minds of friends of these two young ladies, one a schoolteacher and both interested in women's rights, when they began their unconventional vacation—journeying about New York state as "book peddlers" in order to see the country. Later they extended their itinerary into the South through Virginia and North Carolina, selling books en route to finance their trip. They reported rather cool receptions both from those who questioned the propriety of two young women traveling unprotected and from others who were either indifferent to the acquiring of books or who generally distrusted "Yankee pedlers."

Their interesting and ofttimes humorous experiences, together with their very penetrating observations concerning the people, institutions, and customs encountered on their travels via Richmond, Petersburg, Norfolk, and Raleigh about 1853, are related in more than twenty-five of the fifty-two letters in this book. Their impressions differed from those of Mrs. Maury, Lady Wortley, and Miss Bremer, who, they said, "saw people on their best behavior and in their best clothes" with no business transactions involved. Misses Mendell and Hosmer saw "men in their homespun and everyday wear and in their true characters as displayed in the ordinary relations of life" (p. 188). They commented on the very sheltered position of woman in the South.

Even though critical of slavery, "they came to see it in part with the South" (p. 249). The book is a real contribution to travel literature.

362.   Menzel, Gottfried (b. 1798)

Die Vereinigten Staaten von Nordamerika mit besonderer Rücksicht auf deutsche Auswanderung dahin; nach eigener Anschauung beschrieben von Gottfried Menzel. Berlin, Georg Reimer, 1853.

viii, 364 p.   21 cm.
Inclusive dates: August, 1849, to June, 1851.
Location of copy: University of Illinois Library.

This German traveler, according to his prefatory statement, thought that many of the published travel books concentrated attention primarily on the personal experiences of the particular traveler and not on the actual conditions and overall situation of the German immigrants in the United States. With this in mind, he spent nearly two years here in various parts of the country in order to be able to correct for prospective emigrants from Germany the "exaggerated condition" pictured in America. His generally objective, detailed, and thorough evaluation is recorded without any identification of routes, time, or events of travel. Occasionally he indicated that he was present at a given place, i.e., a free Negro church service in New Orleans (p. 154), but the book is organized by chapters under the general topics of topography, natural resources, inhabitants, historical development, social and political institutions, occupations, and the pros and cons of German emigration.

There are few aids or short cuts for the reader seeking Menzel's impressions of the South. But there is much information concerning that region. Only in the matter of slavery was the table of contents any assistance. He was critical but candid in exposing the "decline of the South" which he attributed to the institution of slavery. He warned emigrants of the need for rebuilding the soil in Virginia, the effects of erosion in South Carolina, and the cavalier attitude of the Southern planter. Yet he was generally optimistic and regarded Texas as a promising region for German immigrants. In his forthright discussion of the pros and cons of emigration he stressed the many handicaps, in order to counterbalance the excessive optimism of earlier travel accounts. This last chapter sets this work apart from most of the other travel books.

363. Milliroux, J. F[elix]

L'abolition de l'esclavage par l'Angleterre, La France, Les États-Unis. Rapprochements. Paris, E. Dentu, 1866.

> 16 p. 23½ cm.
> *Location of copy:* American Antiquarian Society.

This pamphlet gives a few of the salient historical facts based upon the writer's knowledge and observations of the abolition of slavery in England, France, and the United States. It is of no value in this bibliography of travel.

364. Milliroux, J. F[elix]

Aperçus sur les institutions et les moeurs des Américains. Paris, E. Dentu, 1862.

> vii, 172 p.
> *Inclusive dates:* 1840's–1861?
> *Location of copy:* Princeton University Library.

Milliroux took a look at the United States on the approach of the Civil War, having spent ten years in America (see Monaghan). His book is not so much a travel account, for there is no itinerary, as an attempt to explain historically the sources of conflict in the country. He deals rather heavily with the sectional aspects of the constitutional struggle. According to Sabin, the book was written to "bring into disrepute republican institutions, in the course of which De Tocqueville is assailed and the Monroe Doctrine expounded."

The author does analyze the political and social institutions of the country in nineteen chapters, including such topics as population, agencies of the national government, justice, marriage, slavery, intemperance, Indians, and travel. He gives a good French view of the differences between the North and the South.

365.   Milliroux, J. Felix

Confédération Américaine revue de son passé, conjectures, suggestions. Paris, E. Dentu, 1861.

> 48 p.   23 cm.
> *Inclusive dates:* 1850–1860?
> *Location of copy:* Public Library of City of Boston.

This is a commentary on the divisive sectionalism of the United States in the 1850's. The author devotes much attention to the Southern states, but his material is more in the nature of a historical and descriptive review of conditions than an actual firsthand observation, even though he supposedly spent ten years in America. What he says is interesting though brief. He gives a typical French analysis of American political crosscurrents, indicating some appreciation for the major issues. He disagreed vigorously with some of the earlier conclusions of De Tocqueville.

366.   Montgomery, Cora [*pseud.* for Mrs. William Leslie Cazneau]

The queen of islands, and the king of rivers. Charles Wood, New York; William Adam, Washington, D. C., 1850.

> 3–50 p.   map.   17 cm.
> *Maps:* Map showing free and slave territories.
> *Inclusive dates:* 1849?
> *Location of copy:* University of Kentucky Library.

Mrs. Cazneau, writing under the pseudonym of Cora Montgomery, consented to the separate publishing of the two chapters that make up the title of this brief account, taken from a proposed larger work to be entitled *Our Mother Land.* (No reference was found of its publication.) Both works were projected by the organization "Friends of Cuba and the Union" in the interests of Cuban annexation and the expansion of slavery in the United States.

This book describes the author's travels along the Mississippi River. No regular itinerary was evident. She reiterates the usual economic arguments in support of slavery. The work stresses the unifying force of the Mississippi River, condemns the Indian policy of the free states, describes Louisiana as the land of sugar cane where the "Negro population thrives more gaily" than "in the mildest of the free states," and then predicts the ultimate limitation of slavery. This chapter had appeared earlier as an article in the *Democratic Review* (December, 1849) and had also been published separately as *The King of the Rivers, with a Chart of Our Slave and Free Soil Territory* (New York, 1850).

367. Morineau, [Phillippe] Auguste De

Essai statistique et politique sur les États-Unis d'Amérique, d'après des documents recueillis sur les lieux, comprenant 27 tableaux synoptiques et analytiques de la constitution fédérale et de celles des états particuliers, avec le portrait en pied de Washington. Paris, G. Thorel; Blaye, Chatenet, 1848.

> 2 p.l., v, [1], 5–39 p.   27 double tables.   30½ cm.
> *Illustrations:* Full-page lithograph of Washington in 1793.
> *Location of copy:* Library of Congress.

This is not really a book in the orthodox sense, as the author points out in his preface, but rather a statistical compilation concerning the organization of the states in which there was originally a French influence. Morineau was a traveler who, as he says, spent the best years of his life drifting over the globe and came to the end of his journeyings in the United States. He mentions slavery in a somewhat apologetic vein, and in a statement of general notions he undertakes to set the thinking of his fellowcountrymen aright on the subject of America. His statements about the various states are the usual type, giving information about their political organization, location, and general prospects. The appended tables are much more complete and give a good analysis of the American political organization. This book is useful in portraying the kind of information which one Frenchman conveyed to another about the rather confusing system of democratic government in America.

368. Myers, J. C.

Sketches on a tour through the Northern and Eastern states, the Canadas & Nova Scotia, by J. C. Myers. Harrisonburg, [Va.], J. H. Wartmann and brothers, prs., 1849.

> xvii, [19]–475, [1] p.   16½ cm.
> *Inclusive dates:* May to July, 1848.
> *Location of copy:* University of Kentucky Library.

This Southerner, a native of Winchester, Virginia, comments briefly on conditions he observed in his home state while on a tour of the North and East during the months of May, June, and July, 1848.

369. [Nason, Daniel]

A journal of a tour from Boston to Savannah, thence to Havanna, in the island of Cuba . . . thence to New Orleans and several cities . . . by a citizen of Cambridgeport. Cambridge, printed for the author, 1849.

114 p.   16 cm.
Inclusive dates: November 27, 1847, to July 15, 1848. In South, December, 12, 1847, to January 17, 1848; May 6 to May 22, 1848.
Location of copy: Library of Congress.

The cover title of this little book is *Tour South and West in 1848.* The author, a carpenter and building contractor from Boston, kept a brief and simple diary on his trip from Boston by water to Savannah, Havana, New Orleans, and up the river to St. Louis, Louisville, and Cincinnati. From there he traveled to Lake Erie, Niagara Falls, and home. During a months' stopover in Savannah he noted things of general interest, including a slave auction and the prices paid for slaves. He was employed as a carpenter for two weeks at $10.00 a week. The trip north from New Orleans by steamboat was uneventful, but it provided the opportunity for noncritical comments on prices, slaves, erosion, and Jim Porter, the Kentucky giant.

370. Nichols, Thomas Low (1815–1901)

Forty years of American life, by Dr. Thomas L. Nichols . . . 2 vols. London, J. Maxwell and company, 1864.

22 cm.
Inclusive dates: In South, November, 1845, to March, 1859.
Other editions:
   (1) London, Longman, 1874.   xvi, 509 p., 1 l.   18 cm.
   (2) Forty years of American life 1821–1851 . . . New York, Stackpole sons, [c.1937].   421 p.   23½ cm.
Location of copy: University of Kentucky Library.

This is a rather significant social history of life and institutions in the United States from 1821–61. The New-Hampshire-born author, a "pioneer dietician, hydrotherapist . . . and editor," in picturing American society, identifies at least two trips into the South. One was made with a tubercular companion in the fall of 1845 from New York by easy stages to Pittsburgh via the river to New Orleans. From there they traveled to Galveston and then back to Mobile and Montgomery, reaching the latter city in March, 1846. On another occasion (no date mentioned) Dr. Nichols went from Cleveland, Ohio, by rail to Cairo, and then by steamboat to Memphis (pp. 118–65 [1937 reprint]). He revisited New Orleans in 1859. While most of the book follows a topical organization, the travels are recorded in chronological sequence. The river trip, Creole planters and their plantations, the site of New Orleans, Sunday in New Orleans, the barrooms as commercial exchanges, and yellow fever are described in some detail. He liked Galveston. There he met M. Victor Considerant, French socialist and disciple of Fourier, whose account of Texas had attracted much attention (*op. cit.*). On the trip to Montgomery, Nichols noted the "attractive suburbs of Mobile," Yankee overseers, cotton plantations, and a circus in Memphis.

The author saw little to criticize in the South. In the chapters on Negroes and slavery he accepted the proslavery view that four million slaves were superior in physical comfort and freedom from anxiety to any other similar number of laboring population in the world. Other topics, such as "Political Corruption," "Catholics and Convents," "Recreations and Amusements," and "Peculiarities and Eccentricities," included many significant observations of the Southern scene.

371.   A Northern Man [Anonymous]

The planter: or, thirteen years in the South. By a northern man. Philadelphia, H. Hooker, 1853.

275 p.   19 cm.
Inclusive dates: 1833–1852. In South, 1833–1846.
Location of copy: University of Kentucky Library.

This anonymous Pennsylvanian, possibly a clergyman, had a "loathsome dislike for slavery" before going South in 1833 for his health. Twenty years later, after becoming an ardent proponent of the system, he published this account designed to show that the world abounded in "worse evils far, than Southern slavery even as falsely represented by its calumniators." He intended to prove to the abolitionists that the literature was not all on their side, by marshaling evidence for all aspects of the proslavery argument and pointing out the "blessings of slavery" in the South in contrast to conditions in New England, Ireland, and Africa.

His only itinerary of travel was his arrival by ship at Charleston (S. C.) and his later visit in and about St. Augustine. Here he observed the "spiritual privileges and pastoral care" afforded the slaves.

Except as an interesting example of the extremely defensive view of slavery, the book is of little significance.

372.   Norton, Charles

Der treue Führer des Auswanderers nach den Vereinigten Staaten von Nord-Amerika, Texas und der Mosquitoküste. Ein vollständiges Hand- und Reisebuch über alle diejenigen Theile des amerikanischen Conti- nents, nach welchen in der neuern Zeit die Einwanderungen gelenkt werden. Nebst einer ausführlichen Schilderung aller für den Aus- wanderer wichtigen Verhältnisse in Beziehung auf Ueberfahrt, An- siedelung, Arbeitslohn, Boden, Klima, Gesundheit, Verfassung, Kanäle, Eisenbahnen, Maasz, Gewicht, Münzen u.s.w. und einem ausführlichen Dolmetsch, um sich im gesellschaftlichen und geschäftlichen Verkehr mit Amerikanern und Engländern leicht verständlich zu machen. Re- gensburg, George Joseph Manz, 1848.

> 142, [2], 118, [1] p.   fold. map.   18½ cm.
> *Other editions:*
> (1) Der treue Führer des auswanderers nach den Vereinigten Staaten von Nord-Amerika, Texas und der Mosquitoküste. Ein vollständiges Hand-und Reisebuch . . . Nebst . . . einem ausführlichen Dollmetsch, um sich im gesell- schaftlichen und geschäftlichen Verkehr mit Amerikanern und Engländern leicht verständlich zu machen. Von Charles Norton. 3. ausg. Mit einer neuen Karte der Vereinigten Staaten von Nordamerika. Regensburg, G. J. Manz, 1846. 142, [2], 118, [1] p.   fold. map.   20 cm.
> (2) Der treue Führer des Auswanderers nach den Vereinigten Staaten von Nord-Amerika, Texas und der Mosquitoküste . . . Regensburg, G. J. Manz, 1850. 142, [2], 118 [1] p.   fold. map.   20 cm.
> *Maps:* Folding map of North America.
> *Inclusive dates:* 1846.
> *Location of copy:* The Newberry Library.

The material in the five chapters of this rather unusual guidebook attempts practical answers to the questions of prospective German immigrants to North America. The questions are as follows: who should emigrate—information is given concerning the needs of the various crafts and trades; where should one emigrate—statistics are given for each state, with much additional information on Texas; how should one emigrate—this chapter discusses the procedure, ports of entry, cost of passage, and estimated costs and income from various sized farms in this country; disease; and religious conditions.

Another significant feature of this guide is a large section with words, expressions, and sentences common to various trades or pro- fessions and society in general, given in English with the German pronunciation and interpretation. This is the only guide of this particular kind noted in this period. The above is the 1848 edition.

373. O'Connor, John

Wanderings of a vagabond. An autobiography edited by John Morris [*pseud.*]. New York, published by the author, 1873.

> 492 p. 18½ cm.
> *Inclusive dates:* In South, intermittently, 1830–1858.
> *Location of copy:* University of Kentucky Library.

This informative and, in spots, exciting work might appropriately be entitled, "Anthology of Gambling, 1830–1860." The "gentleman gambler" born in Marietta, Ohio, pictures his career in the larger cities and on the river steamboats, explains the origin and development of "games of hazard," exposes the numerous tricks employed, and describes various gambling emporiums in Richmond, Washington, Baltimore, Lexington, Louisville, New Orleans, and Mobile. O'Connor's book is a rich source for information of a sort on such matters as faro boxes, "Sanded cards," "Strippers," "First class 'Skinning Houses'," "Wolf Traps," "Three-card Monte Throwers," and "River Sharpers."

No chronological pattern of travel is recorded, nor is there much deviation from the central theme, but there are a few sharp pictures of slave traders, Mississippi steamers, and districts in some of the Southern cities. This gambler was hostile toward slavery (pp. 336–37).

374.

Odds and ends of travel; or, adventures, rambles, and recollections, of a trip from Sydney; via South America, Panama, the West Indies, the United States, and Niagara. London, Dean and Son, 1851(?).

> viii, 340 p. 19 cm.
> *Illustrations:* Engraved frontispiece by Henry Wallis of a pastoral sketch by T. Crafton Coker.
> *Inclusive dates:* July 30, 1845, to April 26, 1846. In South, February 19 to March 10, 1846.
> *Location of copy:* University of Kentucky Library.

The anonymous and, at times, intensely critical writer of this book was a globe-trotting Englishman who, after five years in Australia, returned to England by way of Valparaíso, Panama, Havana, New Orleans, Louisville, Lexington, Maysville, and New York. Most of the account, published five years after his return, describes at length his journey through South America. Fewer than fifty pages deal with his trip by river from New Orleans to Wheeling, West Virginia.

This traveler differed from those who wrote authoritatively concerning all phases of American life after a few weeks' visit. He claimed no knowledge of "the domestic life of Americans" but gained his impressions of them at table d'hôtes and in conveyances of various sorts. Much in America did not come up to his expectations. He failed to find the nearly one hundred drinks with "most extraordinary names [such as] ('stone fence' and 'chain lightning')" listed by the earlier traveler, Captain Marryat. He left a quadroon ball after "two or three turns up and down the room," noting that the "beauty of the lower order of Quadroons . . . is utter humbug." His first views of the capitol in Washington, the White House, and Niagara Falls were disappointing.

He was impressed with American hotels, especially the St. Charles which he labeled "the finest in the world," and he liked the river steamboats. He made several interesting and forthright observations of his trip through Kentucky, but in the main, life in this section of the South presented to him a series of killings and duels "splattered with a continual stream of tobacco juice." Yet in his final evaluation of the United States and its people he wrote, ". . . from what I did see of them I would wish were I not an Englishman, to be an American."

375. Olliffe, Charles

Scènes Américaines; dix-huit mois dans le nouveau monde. Paris, Amyot, 1853.

> xvi, 344 p. 18½ cm. 2nd edition.
> *Illustrations:* Frontispiece: Portrait of George Washington; and other illustrations.
> *Inclusive dates:* 1850–1851.
> *Other editions:*
> Scènes Américaines; dix-huit mois dans le nouveau monde (1850–1851), par Charles Olliffe. Paris, Amyot, 1852.
> *Location of copy:* Library of Congress.

Scènes Américaines is an unusually solid travel account by a Frenchman who formerly had edited some of the works of Scott and Washington Irving and had the genuine capacity to comprehend American life. In America he must have had a specific interest in the Ohio and Mississippi valleys, because he jumped from Halifax to Boston and then to Cincinnati before he began recording his impressions. In Cincinnati he viewed "Porkopolis" through more sympathetic eyes than did his famous English predecessor Mrs. Trollope. He saw the slaughterhouses and gave a highly interesting account of the packing industry. Olliffe viewed Cincinnati not as a city of the long squeal and an even louder smell but as a thriving metropolis in a vital part of the country.

From Cincinnati the author went on to New Orleans. His chapters covering this part of the journey give an intimate picture of river travel. As was customary with many nineteenth century French travelers, he brings the history of river transportation up to date. New Orleans appealed to Olliffe, and again like all Frenchmen he gave close attention to both its social life and economic environs. From there the visitor went to Mobile, a city which he liked. He compared its situation with that of New Orleans, and the comparison is to Mobile's advantage.

Olliffe went from Mobile to Havana and then back through Florida to South Carolina. His chapter on South Carolina is a good summary of life there. He quickly sensed what might be called the "South Carolina attitude." Slavery impressed him for the first time in this region, and a good portion of his text is devoted to a discussion of the institution. The author completed his Southern journey when he left Maryland. An especially good chapter describes his visit to Washington. As in the case of Mobile, he describes both the physical and political environment of the place. Of the 344 pages, 143 are devoted to Olliffe's visit to the South.

The first edition appeared in 1852, and the above "second edition contained seven chapters" not included in the original work.

376. Olshausen, Theodor (1802–1869)

Die Vereinigten Staaten von Nordamerika im Jahre 1852. Eine statistische Uebersicht mit besonderer Rücksicht auf deutsche Auswanderer zusammengestellt. Kiel, Akademische Buchhandlung, 1853.

iv, 76 p. 18½ cm.
Inclusive dates: 1852.
Location of copy: Library of Congress.

Olshausen, a German politician and member of the provisional parliament of Schleswig-Holstein in 1848, came to the United States in 1851, settled in St. Louis, and edited a German newspaper until he returned to Germany in 1861.

This work appeared before his two more ambitious publications: *Die Vereinigten Staaten von Amerika geographisch and statistisch beschrieben . . . Theil I: Das Mississippi-Thal* (Kiel, 1853–55) and *Geschichte der Mormonen; oder, Jüngsten-Tages-Heiligen in Nord-Amerika* (Göttingen, 1856).

This is not a travel book, even though Olshausen journeyed through parts of the United States. He wished to present pertinent descriptive, historical, and statistical information for prospective German emigrants.

377. Palliser, John (1807–1887)

Solitary rambles and adventures of a hunter in the prairies. By John Palliser . . . London, J. Murray, 1853.

> 3 p.l., [v]–xiv p., 1 l., 326 p. plates. 18 cm.
> *Illustrations:* Frontispiece, vignette title, and six hunting scenes from the West.
> *Inclusive dates:* February, 1847, to Summer, 1849?
> *Other editions:*
> The solitary hunter; or, sporting adventures in the prairies. By John Palliser, esq. The eighth thousand, with illustrations. London, New York, G. Routledge & co., 1856. xvi, 234 p., incl. front. plates. 16½ cm.
> *Location of copy:* Chicago Historical Society.

Leaving Liverpool early in 1847, Palliser, prominent English geographer-explorer, world traveler, and big game hunter, landed at Halifax to journey southward to Wheeling and down the rivers to New Orleans. He visited there for several weeks before leaving for more than a years' hunting in the Trans-Mississippi West. Most of this book is an exciting narrative of the author's many hunting expeditions. It is flavored with hair-raising incidents and careful observations of the details of wildlife, Indian habits, and suggestions to brother sportsmen.

In October, 1849, Palliser left St. Louis for New Orleans with a varied menagerie "consisting of one very large old bison cow, one black bear, two Virginian deer, an exquisitely beautiful little forcifer antelope," and a tamed wolf. These he shipped to Liverpool while he spent more time hunting in the region south of New Orleans. Then he sailed for Cuba, Panama, and finally back to England.

Many of the first seventy-five pages of this excellent book, written later from a journal kept during the trip, record Palliser's favorable impressions of Mississippi steamboats, the city of New Orleans and its French quarter, an interesting hunting trip up the Arkansas, and a Louisiana sugar plantation. He made a side trip from St. Louis to Mammoth Cave before setting out for the Yellowstone and Big Horn country. He seemed well pleased with conditions of life in America.

378. Patten, Edmund, Esq.

A glimpse at the United States and the northern states of America, with the Canadas, comprising their rivers, lakes and falls during the autumn of 1852; including some account of an emigrant ship. By Edmund Patten, Esq. With illustrations, sketched and zincographed by the author. London, Effingham Wilson, 1853.

> iv, 5–109 p. 21½ cm.
> *Illustrations:* Frontispiece: Niagara Falls; and other illustrations of New York and the Hudson River.
> *Inclusive dates:* August to September 18, 1852.
> *Location of copy:* University of Kentucky Library.

Except for a description of an emigrant ship en route to New York and some condemnations and general conclusions concerning slavery and its ultimate abolition, this English traveler adds nothing to Southern travel literature. Patten felt that much of American greatness and prosperity could be "traced to the Fatherland of the United States—England."

379. Paxton, Philip [*pseud.* for Samuel A. Hammett] (1816–1865)

Piney woods tavern; or, Sam Slick in Texas. By the author of A stray yankee in Texas . . . Philadelphia, T. B. Peterson and brothers, [1858].

> x, 11–309 p. front. 18½ cm.
> *Illustrations:* Frontispiece: Engraving of Texas scene. Added engraved title page.
> *Inclusive dates:* Probably 1836–1850.
> *Location of copy:* Library of Congress.

In this, his second volume Samuel A. Hammett used the pseudonym of Philip Paxton and described phases of Texas life and activity in the thirties and forties. Material evidence indicates that the author-sportsman roamed over much of Texas and parts of Louisiana experiencing and collecting the material for his yarns. Like the preceding volume, *A Stray Yankee in Texas* (*q.v.*), it can hardly be considered a regular travel account but rather an interesting humorous, and at times terrifying descriptive narrative of the Texas frontier.

380. Paxton, Philip [*pseud.* for Samuel A. Hammett] (1816–1865)

A stray yankee in Texas. New York, Redfield, 1853.

> 2 p.l., xvi, 17–416 p. front. 18½ cm.
> *Illustrations:* Frontispiece: Engraving of a Texas mule by A. Kimersby added t.p. mrg.
> *Inclusive dates:* Probably 1836–1850.
> *Location of copy:* University of Chicago.

The author intended to "give a correct idea of scenes and scenery, men and manners, as they exist in . . . [Texas] . . . of which much has been written but little is really known." During the ten to fifteen years spent "South of the Sabine," material in this book first appeared in *The Whig,* the *Democratic Review,* the *Spirit of the Times,* and other publications. *A Stray Yankee in Texas* is not a travel book with a regular pattern or definite period of travel. Rather it is a descriptive narrative of early Texas with an entertaining assortment of homespun tales of hunting experiences, pioneer life and institutions, frontier justice, and incidents of the Texas and Mexican wars. Sam Houston, Lafitte, Santa Anna, Lorenzo de Lavalla, and scores of lesser personalities are identified, as well as events in various towns and particular localities. The last two chapters, "Lynch Law" and "Steam on the Western Waters," are germane to the subject of Texas travel literature.

381. Peyton, John Lewis (1824–1896)

Over the Alleghanies and across the prairies. Personal recollections of the far West, one and twenty years ago. By John Lewis Peyton . . . London, Simpkin, Marshall and co., 1869.

  xvi, 377 p. 18½ cm.
  Inclusive dates: June to December, 1848. In South, June to July (?), 1848.
  Other editions:
   2d ed. 1870.
  Location of copy: University of Kentucky Library.

Peyton, prominent Virginian, author, and Confederate agent, published in 1869 the excellent account of his six months' journey through the Old Northwest in 1848, a trip taken on the advice of his physician. En route from Staunton, Virginia, to the Great Lakes region by way of Pittsburgh and down *la belle rivière* to Kentucky he observed in some detail the historical spots along both sides of the river, thrilled to the mounting excitement of a steamboat race, and survived the terror-striking catastrophe of an exploding boiler. Remaining about a month in Kentucky, Peyton enjoyed the hospitality of Colonel John Taylor, John J. Crittenden, Henry Clay, and other prominent Kentuckians, many of whom he described at some length. His picture of Henry Clay and "Ashland" is especially well done. The work is both contemporary and historical, for he injects much of the history of the region and the many personalities encountered. His family connections afforded him intimate associations with leaders everywhere along the route. Peyton was an unbiased and accurate observer. His work is an important travel account.

See the *Dictionary of American Biography* for a sketch of Peyton's life. A second edition of this work was published in 1870. A note in the second edition states that originally "this work was announced under the title of 'Out West,'" but the author, on learning that a book under that title had been published in 1866, changed to the current title.

382.

Phelps's travellers' guide through the United States; containing upwards of seven hundred rail-road, canal and state and steam-boat routes, accompanied with a new map of the United States. New York, Ensigns & Thayer, 1848.

> 4 p.l., [7]–70 p. fold. map. 14 cm.
> *Inclusive dates:* 1848.
> *Other editions:*
>   New York, 1847.
> *Location of copy:* University of Kentucky Library.

Little is known about the compiler who is credited with this travelers' guide. The work lists the important railroad, stage, canal, and river routes and the distances from place to place, arranged by states from Maine to Wisconsin. The guide, though inferior to many, has the advantage of convenient size.

An earlier work, *Phelps and Ensigns' Travellers' Guide through the United States: Containing Stage, Steamboat, Canal and Railroad Routes, with the Distances from Place to Place* (New York, 1844), apparently was not an earlier edition of the above work.

383. Playfair, Robert

Recollections of a visit to the United States and the British provinces of North America, in the years 1847, 1848, and 1849. Edinburgh, Thomas Constable and Co., 1856.

> viii, 266 p. 19 cm.
> *Inclusive dates:* August, 1847, to August, 1849. In South, July to September, 1848.
> *Location of copy:* Swarthmore College Library.

Playfair, a wealthy Scotsman, and his two young daughters enjoyed the best possible accommodations on his two-year vacation tour in America, and he was favorably impressed by what he experienced. Even though a good part of the trip was spent in two visits to a sister in Nova Scotia, he journeyed through much of the East and parts of the South. From July to September, 1848, he dipped into the latter section from Washington to Richmond, White Sulphur Springs, and down the Ohio River to Louisville, Mammoth Cave, and St. Louis. He seems to have been delighted with the many fashionable resorts and watering places in Virginia and Kentucky, but he attributed both states' "falling behind their free state neighbors" to slavery (p. 195). Yet Playfair's refusal to condemn the institution was based on what he termed an "observation [that] could only be superficial." He commented on the "contented slaves" and the general rule of kind treatment to house slaves in both states.

Playfair, in this simple and unembellished account, noted many of the social habits of Americans, the current books and periodicals that were being read, and the menus, rates, and accommodations at the various hotels and springs that he visited. Seldom did he miss attending church, and he usually commented on the service. The book is interesting reading, but one wishes that this Scotch traveler, with his ample opportunity for unhurried observation, had given a more rounded and penetrating analysis of the American scene.

384. [Potter, Eliza]

A hairdresser's experience in high life. Cincinnati, the author, 1859.

iv, 11–294 p. 19 cm.

Inclusive dates: Probably about 1844–1859. In South, intermittently during these years.

Location of copy: University of Kentucky Library.

About fifteen years of service as a hairdresser, maid, and companion among the "smart set" at Northern resorts in the summer and Southern cities such as Memphis, Natchez, and New Orleans during the winter provide the background for this chatty, intimate, but incoherent account. In "true confessions" fashion, the author exposes the joys and miseries unguardedly revealed in the private boudoir. Many incidents are related in support of the writer's abolitionist sentiments.

385. Prentice, Archibald

A tour in the United States, by Archibald Prentice . . . London, C. Gilpin, 1848.

156 p. 19 cm.

Inclusive dates: May to August, 1848. In Louisville, June, 1848.

Other editions:

(1) A tour in the United States, with two lectures on emigration, delivered in the Mechanics institution, Manchester, by Archibald Prentice . . . 6th ed.

London, J. Johnson; [etc., etc.], 1850. 1 p.l., vi, 217 p. front. (port.), fold. map. 13½ cm.

    (2) Seventh edition. Manchester, 1850. vi, 217 p.

Location of copy: University of Kentucky Library.

Although this former Anti-Corn-Law Leaguer and Manchester editor just touched Virginia and spent only one week in and about Louisville on his three-month circle tour by way of New York, Washington, Louisville, and Niagara Falls, he was observant and collected much statistical material on Kentucky economy. This he augmented by frequent quotations from Charles Lyell and other travelers. He was awed by the prominent, seven-foot, eight-inch Louisville giant, former council member and then tavern keeper, James Porter. Kentucky impressed him as a "Second Garden of Eden," except for the "stain of slavery." His trip to America in 1848 was made to recuperate from the effects of his labors in the Anti-Corn-Law League and the failure of his newspaper.

386. Pulszky, Ferencz Aurelius (1814–1897)

White, red, black. Sketches of society in the United States during the visit of their guest [Louis Kossuth]. By Francis and Theresa Pulszky ... 3 vols. London, Trübner and co., 1853.

    18½ cm.

    Inclusive dates: December 5, 1851, to June, 1852. In South, March 4 to April 15, 1851.

    Other editions:

    (1) Weiss, Roth, Schwarz. Skizzen aus der amerikanischen Gesellschaft in den Vereinigten Staaten ... Kassel, T. Fischer, 1853. 5 vols. in 2. 17 cm.

    (2) 2 vols. Redfield, New York. 1853.

    Location of copy: University of Kentucky Library.

When Ferencz Aurelius Pulszky and his wife Theresa, prominent Hungarian exiles, accompanied their illustrious compatriot Louis Kossuth on his much publicized visit to the United States beginning in 1851, they were afforded a rare opportunity for viewing America. Their impressions, based on first-hand observation, wide reading, and conversations with most of the noted Americans of that day as well as with numbers of persons from the lesser walks of life, were first recorded in a diary kept regularly by Mrs. Pulszky. This diary was then published in 1853 and must be considered a major travel account.

    The South is treated in more than three of the seventeen chapters of the three volumes. The authors record the pleasant five-week journey by canal and river en route from the East by way of Cleveland

and Columbus to Louisville, St. Louis, Vicksburg, Jackson, New Orleans, Mobile, Montgomery, West Point, La Grange, Charleston, Wilmington, Petersburg, Richmond, Washington, and Mount Vernon. The return trip from Mobile was unduly hastened in part because of an urgent invitation from Boston to Kossuth to present the cause of Hungary to the state legislature before it adjourned. At the same time Southern interest in him was noticeably cooler. He had received no official invitation from any of the Southern state legislatures. This was explained on the grounds that only three of them were then in session. Yet they did nothing, nor did the cities of Savannah, Charleston, Wilmington, and Richmond arrange any welcome for him. Consequently the distance from New Orleans to Washington was covered in about two weeks.

The Pulszkys were much impressed by the Kentuckians in Louisville, the hospitality of Governor Foote of Mississippi, the Creoles, the market places, a sugar plantation near New Orleans, their welcome in Mobile, nature's bounteous beauty along the Alabama River, and the neglected condition of Mount Vernon. Injected between entries from the diary are significant discussions of such subjects as religion, the land system, and American slavery. The treatment of this last issue is possibly the outstanding contribution of the book. Concerning slavery, the authors write that they "do not enter into the subject . . . from the moral point of view . . . [they] take the question up entirely on political grounds." Even though they are critical of the system, they attempt an objective presentation. Noting that "the white has no antipathy against the slave but [that] he dislikes the free negro," the Pulszkys sensed in the South some of "the same notions upon which despotism is based in Europe" (II, p. 213). Yet in order that slavery might not be misrepresented abroad and as a "friend of fair play," they quoted from J. D. B. De Bow's *Review* and included in the appendix of Volume II a lengthy abridgement of Chancellor Harper's *Memoir on Slavery,* as "one of the most able defences of the system."

The Fugitive Slave Law was, to them, the "heaviest blow inflicted on the peculiar institution." They reproached the North for the "great prejudice" against colored people. They encountered few in the South who would defend the institution, but they observed the readiness of the many to explain the Southern position for the benefit of "foreigners [who did] not understand . . . slavery."

Other travelers have paid more attention to the interesting details of the Southern scene, but few have equaled the Pulszkys' careful and penetrating observations of major forces operating in that picture.

387. Quentin, Karl

Reisebilder und Studien aus dem Norden der Vereinigten Staaten von Amerika, von Karl Quentin. Zwei Theile in einem Bande. Arnsberg, H. F. Grote, 1851.

> Part I, viii, 152 p.; Part II, vi, 209 p. 20½ cm.
> *Inclusive dates:* June 9, 1850, to November 16, 1850.
> *Location of copy:* Wisconsin Historical Society.

Except for the river trip from St. Louis to Cincinnati with a stop or two in Kentucky towns, this couple, a retired Prussian government official and his wife, did not enter the South on their six months' circle tour in 1850. They arrived in New York and spent most of their time in New England before making a swing westward to Chicago and St. Louis and back via Sandusky and New York by rail. Yet Quentin was one of the few travelers of this period who discussed the current sectional political situation and the events of the compromise settlement of that year and predicted the probable party lineup for the presidential election in 1852. A wide range of subjects of historical, descriptive, and current interest were inserted in the two parts of this book, between sections describing the route of travel. Little of this concerned the South. He gave a good picture of an eight-hour delay on a sandbank near the mouth of the Cumberland River. America to these two travelers was a "glorious country."

388. Raeder, Ole Munch (1815–1895)

America in the forties; the letters of Ole Munch Raeder, translated and edited by Gunnar J. Malmin. Minneapolis, pub. for the Norwegian-American historical association by the University of Minnesota press, [c.1929].

> xxi, p. 1 l., 244 p. front. (port.). 22 cm.
> *Illustrations:* Frontispiece: Photograph of Ole Munch Raeder.
> *Inclusive dates:* 1847–1848. In South, November, 1847.
> *Location of copy:* University of Kentucky Library.

This work has little place among Southern travel accounts, except to record the fact that Raeder, a member of the prominent Norwegian family and one of the important Scandinavian travelers in the United States during this period, journeyed from St. Louis via the Ohio River to Pittsburgh and on to Washington by way of Harpers Ferry. Even though he considered his views on slavery, as expressed in his letters, as "moderate as can possibly be expected," the author was critical of its property relationship.

[299]

389.   Redpath, James (1833–1889)

The roving editor: or, talks with slaves in the Southern states. By James Redpath . . . New York, A. B. Burdick, 1859.

> xvi, 349 p.   front., plate.   18 cm.
> *Illustrations:* Two illustrations of slavery scenes.
> *Inclusive dates:* In South, 1854 and 1859.
> *Location of copy:* Library of Congress.

James Redpath, "fiery abolitionist," newspaper correspondent, editor, and future lyceum promoter, traveled extensively through the Southern states for reasons of health but "chiefly to see slavery . . . and personally to learn what the bondsmen said and thought of their condition." He made one trip in March, 1854, to attend the Southern Commercial Convention in Charleston. Another, a walking trip from Richmond to Montgomery, was taken in the fall of the same year. In 1859 he covered much of Virginia. His diary and letters describing his trips, some of which appeared first in Northern newspapers, make up this book. It was dedicated to John Brown, subject of one of Redpath's most widely read later works, *The Public Life of Captain John Brown by James Redpath, with an Autobiography of His Childhood and Youth* (Boston, 1860). The forty-first edition of the book appeared in 1872.

The Roving Editor presents the reported interviews and the accounts of slaves from all parts of the South. It has significance as an example of the material that was being written by the extreme opponents of slavery in their vitriolic attack on the system.

390.   Reid, Samuel Chester, Jr. (1818–1897)

The scouting expeditions of McCulloch's Texas rangers; or, the summer and fall campaign of the Army of the United States in Mexico–1846; including skirmishes with the Mexicans, and an accurate detail of the storming of Monterey; also the daring scouts at Buena Vista; together with anecdotes, incidents, descriptions of country, and sketches of the lives of the celebrated partisan chiefs, Hays, McCulloch, and Walker. A facsimile reproduction of the original. Austin, Texas, the Steck Company, 1935.

> [10], 251 p.   20 cm.
> *Maps:* Double-page map of Monterey and environs for battle. Drawn by Lieut. Geo. Meade of the U. S. topographical engineers.
> *Illustrations:* Frontispiece: Drawing of General Taylor by the celebrated French artist Auguste Chatillon; daguerreotype of Captain McCulloch by J. McQuire;

daguerreotype of Colonel Jack Hayes by Noeselle; daguerreotype by J. Mc-Quire of Captain Walker; scenes from the war.

Inclusive dates: June 4, 1846, to October, 1846.

Other editions:

(1) The scouting expeditions of McCulloch's Texas rangers; or, the summer and fall campaign of the Army of the United States in Mexico—1846; including skirmishes with the Mexicans, and an accurate detail of the storming of Monterey; also the daring scouts at Buena Vista; together with anecdotes, incidents, descriptions of country, and sketches of the lives of the celebrated partisan chiefs, Hays, McCulloch, and Walker. Philadelphia, G. B. Zieber and Co., 1847. ₁10₁, 251 p. 20 cm.

(2) The scouting expeditions of McCulloch's Texas rangers; . . . Philadelphia, G. B. Zieber and Co., 1848. ₁10₁, 251 p. 20 cm.

Location of copy: Wisconsin State Historical Society.

A member of McCulloch's Texas Rangers, Samuel Chester Reid gives an excellent account of the varied activities of that organization in the Mexican War. Reid left New Orleans on June 4, 1846, and returned from Mexico by way of Houston to the former city in October. Later he assisted his father, a famous sea captain and the designer of the present form of the American flag, in bringing suit against the United States in the court of claims (see the *Dictionary of American Biography*).

The present work is a facsimile reproduction of the original journal published in 1847. It is a good account of the military activity, together with many interesting descriptions of Mexican life, but it has limited value for Southern travel.

391. Revoil, Benedict Henry (1816–1882)

Coups de fusil; souvenirs d'un chercheur d'aventures aux États-Unis. Tours, Alfred Mame et fils, 1882.

7–194 p. front., illus. 17½ cm.

Illustrations: Frontispiece: "Besieged by a herd of peccaries," by Yan 'Dargent. There are some thirty-seven additional illustrations of wildlife and hunting scenes by the same artist.

Inclusive dates: 1841–1849.

Location of copy: Boston Public Library.

This is an abridged edition of the original work published in 1856. It seems evident that the author relied heavily upon David Crockett for information about the opossum, for his drawing of the animal gives a distorted picture of a cunning creature with a long hairy tail.

392. Revoil, Benedict Henry (1816–1882)

The hunter and the trapper in North America; or, romantic adventures in field and forest. From the French of Benedict Revoil. By W. H. Davenport Adams ... London, New York, [etc.], T. Nelson and sons, 1874.

vi p., 1 l., [9]–393 p., incl. front., illus. 17½ cm.
Illustrations: Frontispiece: "Besieged by a herd of peccaries," by Yan 'Dargent. There are a great number of illustrations of wildlife and hunting scenes by the same artist.
Inclusive dates: 1841–1849.
Location of copy: Library of Congress.

This famous French sportsman spent nine years (1841–49) in the United States hunting and fishing in all parts of the country. He kept detailed notes from which he later published several books of his experiences, all written in a simple and animated style yet with unassuming modesty. Revoil had great ability in describing the habits of animals and the beauty of nature. His many accounts are important chapters in the history of American sport.

Monaghan lists some eighteen titles by Revoil. Many of them are new editions or abridgements of the original work. *Chasses et Pêches de l'Autre Monde* (Paris, 1856) appeared in two parts as *Chasses dans l'Amérique du Nord* (Paris, 1861) and *Pêches dans l'Amérique du Nord* (Paris, 1863). The first edition appeared without any illustrations. Later editions were illustrated by Yan 'Dargent, possibly from sketches made by Revoil. The first English edition was published in 1865 as *Shooting and Fishing in the Rivers, Prairies, and Backwoods of North America* (2 vols., London, 1865). A new edition of the latter work appeared in 1874 under a different title, *The Hunter and the Trapper in North America* (London, New York, 1874). The original edition and the 1874 edition were used for this study.

No route of travel nor chronological order were observed in relating Revoil's experiences. Each chapter is a topical discussion of a certain kind of wildlife. He hunted raccoons in Kentucky and South Carolina, eagles along the Mississippi River, peccaries in Texas, turkeys in most of the states, and panthers in Virginia and Florida. Other chapters describe the capturing of wild horses, shooting "cayutes," opossums, prairie dogs, wildcats, stags, elk, and bears. Near the Green River (Kentucky) he witnessed a "pigeon massacre," where fifteen women were kept busy salting and packing the slaughtered birds in barrels. Wagons were filled with pigeons and hauled away, after which the remainder were fed to a "herd of three hundred pigs" driven to the spot by two Glasgow (Kentucky) farmers. Even though this account has the earmarks of a tall tale, the sight of "clouds of pigeons" during this period was verified by other travelers.

Revoil limited his observations to hunting and fishing in this sportsman's paradise. He seldom commented on other aspects of American travel. He identified his activities with the names of places and persons, as well as the dates of his hunting trips.

Other books by Revoil include *Les Peaux Rouges de l'Amérique du Nord* (Limoges, 1881); *Scènes Américaines, au Milieu des Bois* (Limoges, 1881); *À travers le Nouveau Monde* (Limoges, 1882); *Les Drames de l'Amérique* (Limoges, 1882); *Moeurs des États-Unis Amérique* (Limoges, 1882); *Notes d'un Voyageur Moderne* (Limoges, 1882); *Le Sport Américain, Chasses Excentriques dans l'Amérique du Nord* (Tours, 1883); and *À travers les Prairies; les Peaux-Rouges de l'Amérique du Nord; Excursions, Chasses, etc.* (Limoges, 1883).

393. Revoil, Benedict Henry (1816–1882)

Pêches dans l'Amérique du Nord, par Benedict Henry Revoil. Paris, L. Hachette et cie., 1863.

> 2 p.l., 320 p. 18 cm.
> *Inclusive dates:* 1841–1849.
> *Other editions:*
> Pêches dans l'Amérique du Nord, par Benedict Henry Revoil. Nouv. ed. illustré par Yan 'Dargent. Tours, A. Mame et fils, 1886. 2 p.l., [7]–384 p., 1 l. front., illus., plates. 30 cm. (Bibliothèque illustrée).
> *Location of copy:* Library of Congress.

This fascinating book is composed of some new materials and new texts not included by the sportsman Revoil in his original work. In this volume he devotes his attention entirely to fishing in North America. His opening chapters describe the kind of fish and oysters that are to be found along the coast. Chapters XIV to XVII are devoted entirely to the South. His first account of Southern fishing is limited to the Ohio Valley and particularly to Kentucky. Like everyone else who has hunted the famous devilfish off the coast of South Carolina and Georgia, Revoil gives an interesting picture of his experiences in searching for this monster. Finally, he gives a good description of hunting alligators in Texas and Louisiana.

Some of this text gives evidence of being a good fisherman's story, but it is seductive enough to make the reader long for the "good old days" when the fish bit and it was possible to catch a lion's share of the big ones. Revoil's sporting accounts are good, and this book is no exception to his observations on hunting.

394.   Richter, K[arl] E[rnst]

Der treue Freund und Begleiter des Auswanderers nach den Vereinigten Staaten von Nord-Amerika. Neuestes und vollständiges Handbuch, in welchem der Auswanderer alles findet, was ihm für seinem Zweck zu wissen nothwendig und wünschenswerth ist. Dessau, Moritz Katz, 1850.

> vi, 235 p.   17 cm.
> *Inclusive dates:* 1835–1848.
> *Location of copy:* Newberry Library.

This is not a travel guide in the usual meaning of the word. Rather it is a book of advice to prospective emigrants concerning preparations for the trip, problems en route, and opportunities in various trades and professions. Richter, who published his *Reisen nach Nord-Amerika und Zürich in den Jahren 1835 bis 1848* (Leipzig, 1852), warned German emigrants of their disadvantages in the Southern states because of the plantation economy and the power of the planter aristocracy. He had much to say about the systems of free and slave labor. Texas, he thought, was the most favorable location in the South for Germans (pp. 61–63). But the book gives evidence that Richter's information about America was largely limited to his twelve years spent in and about Baltimore with little, if any, travel outside of that area. Valuable features of the book for immigrants were a glossary of common English words and expressions with their German meaning and a copy of the Constitution of the United States.

395.   Richter, Karl Ernst

Reisen nach Nordamerika und zurück in den Jahren 1835 bis 1848. Von Karl Ernst Richter. Zugabe; ein Brief aus Californien von Moritz August Richter. 2 vols. Leipzig, Verlag von Ch. E. Kollmann, 1852.

> Vol. I, [8], 373, [1] p.; Vol. II, [6], 3–272, [1] p.   8vo.
> *Inclusive dates:* 1835–1848.
> *Location of copy:* The New York Public Library.

It is not possible to trace the author's route in America, for he did not record his daily movements. Instead, he wrote a topical description of various phases of American life, including discussions of land and climate, Indians, the churches, and government.

Into these he injected some personal observations. During a part of his stay in America, and perhaps during most of it, Richter was in Baltimore; and he wrote chapters on Baltimore and on the Negro. Except for these, this work contains very little information about the South.

In 1852 and 1853 Richter published three volumes of translations into German of American local-color humor, including Johnson Jones Hooper's *Captain Simon Suggs* and Thomas Bangs Thorp's *The Big Bear of Arkansas.*

396. Ritchie, Mrs. Anna Cora (Ogden) Mowatt (1819–1870)

Autobiography of an actress; or, eight years on the stage. By Anna Cora Mowatt . . . Boston, Ticknor, Read, and Fields, 1854.

448 p. front. (port.). 18 cm.

Illustrations: Engraved portrait of author by H. W. Smith.

Inclusive dates: June, 1845–1853. In South, three tours—1845, 1846, 1852–1853.

Other editions:

(1) 8th thousand. Boston, Ticknor, Reed, and Fields, 1854.

(2) 20th thousand. Boston, Ticknor, Reed, and Fields, 1859.

Location of copy: University of Kentucky Library.

The popular memoirs of this celebrated actress, written while she convalesced from an illness in 1853, contain little of value for an understanding of the major forces in the Southern scene. But they do reveal the enthusiasm with which Southern cities received the famous star of the New York stage on her three tours of the South. Mrs. Mowatt, on her first circle tour, appeared in Washington, Charleston, Savannah, Mobile, and New Orleans. Early in the fall of 1846 she made her second trip, "acting in all of the principal theatres." While in New Orleans and on the return journey by steamboat to Louisville, she enjoyed her frequent associations with Henry Clay. Later, while playing a several weeks' engagement in Louisville, she described that city in mourning at the time of his passing. With much of the city draped in "heavy folds of unrelieved sable," she hung white draperies with festoons of flowers in her windows at the Louisville Hotel as the symbol of the "living freshness, gladness, purity of the new life." An explanation of her unconventional tribute appeared next morning in the Louisville *Journal.* On her last trip south, in the winter of 1852–53, the trip that ended her stage career, she played in Washington, Richmond, Mobile, New Orleans, and Memphis. She was especially pleased with the enthusiasm of her warm welcome in Mobile.

The *Dictionary of American Biography* and *Annals of the New York Stage,* Volume V and VI, by George C. D. Odell (New York, 1927), give detailed information about her career.

397. Robertson, John Blount

Reminiscences of a campaign in Mexico; by a member of the "Bloody-First." Preceded by a short sketch of the history and condition of Mexico from her revolution down to the war with the United States. Nashville, John York and Co., 1849.

[7]–288 p.   18 cm.
Inclusive dates: June, 1846, to May, 1847.
Location of copy: Wisconsin Historical Society.

This is an account of the services of the First Regiment of Tennessee volunteers in the Mexican War. The only value for Southern travel is the description of the trip to New Orleans.

398. Robertson, William Parish

A visit to Mexico, by the West India Islands, Yucatan, and United States, with observations and adventures on the way. 2 vols. London, Simpkin, Marshall and Co., 1853.

fold. fronts. (Vol. II, map).   19 cm.
Maps: Volume II, folding map of Mexico and Texas, engraved by J. Archer Pentonville.
Illustrations: Vol. I, folding lithograph frontispiece by Castro, of the funeral procession of Sr. Iturbide to the Cathedral on October 26, 1838.
Inclusive dates: December, 1848 to December, 1849. In South, October 27, 1849, to November 10, 1849.
Location of copy: Wisconsin Historical Society.

William Robertson, onetime British Consul to Peru and to Ecuador and coauthor of *Letters on Paraguay* (London, 1838) and *Letters on South America* (London, 1843), went to Mexico in 1848 as a special commissioner to negotiate a settlement for Mexican securities held by British investors. On his return in a party of prominent Mexicans in October, 1849, he traveled through the United States via Mobile, New Orleans, Cincinnati, Springfield (O.), Niagara Falls, Washington, and New York.

The author exclaimed over the San Carlos Hotel in New Orleans, the grandeur of the Mississippi River—that "great aqueous highway," and Louisville—the very handsome city "with a regular go ahead population." He was deeply impressed on seeing President Zachary Taylor worshiping in a Washington church without ostentation but with the quiet dignity of any other "plain citizen" (II, p. 453).

Robertson limited his description of the United States to the two last chapters in Volume II. His forthright "conclusions on America" (II, pp. 455–61) give the nation a general treatment. He was pleased

[306]

with what he had observed, except for slavery. The brief comparisons of certain American and English institutions mark Robertson as a discriminating observer.

399. Robinson, Solon (1803–1880)

Solon Robinson, pioneer and agriculturist; selected writings, edited by Herbert Anthony Kellar. 2 vols. Indianapolis, Indiana historical bureau, 1936.

Vol. I, ix–xxv, 582 p.; Vol. II, vii–xvii, 556 p. front., illus., plates, ports., map, plans, facsim. 23 cm.
Illustrations: Vol. I, frontispiece: Photograph of Robinson in 1841; and twelve illustrations. Vol. II, frontispiece: Photograph of Robinson in 1872; and ten illustrations, including New Orleans in 1850, cotton plantations in South Carolina, and the turpentine industry.
Inclusive dates: 1825–1851. In South, August, 1841; January to April, 1845; November 14, 1848, to June, 1849; November, 1849, to June, 1850; December, 1850, to May, 1851.
Location of copy: University of Kentucky Library.

Solon Robinson, a Connecticut Yankee residing in northern Indiana and an important traveler and agricultural writer during the ante bellum period, made at least four extensive tours through the South from 1845–51, preceded by an earlier trip to Kentucky. The latter was made in 1841 from Madison, Indiana, by stage to Frankfort, Lexington, and Maysville and by water to Cincinnati. En route he visited Thomas B. Stevenson, editor of the *Kentucky Farmer,* and Richard Pindel and Judge Adam Beatty, both prominent Kentucky landowners. He described these visits and commented on the farming activities of several other "good farmers" in a series of letters to the Albany *Cultivator* (I, pp. 240–58).

In January, 1845, as "Traveling Correspondent" for the same paper, he set out on his first extensive tour through the South, a two-thousand-mile trip by way of St. Louis down the river to Columbus, Kentucky, overland to Jackson, Tennessee, and the Mississippi towns of Holly Springs, Lexington, Vicksburg, and Natchez. From there he continued south into Louisiana and then back through Arkansas, returning to Indiana in late April (I, pp. 401–95). He made a second trip between November 14, 1848, and June, 1849, this time as a correspondent for the *American Cultivator.* He went along much of the same route and reached New Orleans in the latter part of December. From there he traveled east and north through Alabama and the Carolinas to Washington (II, pp. 124–245). Later the same year he set out again from Washington by water and overland to

Georgia. On this trip he was acting as agent for a "New York Agricultural Warehouse," selling, among other farm items, Peruvian guano, a fertilizer, the sale of which he reported amounted to $20,000 for a ten-day period (II, p. 369). On his last trip South during this period, before going East to take over his new editorial duties, he again traveled from New York to Florida and back between December, 1850, and May, 1851. He visited Richmond, Wilmington, Charleston, Savannah, Macon, Tallahassee, and many other places in Florida before returning over much the same route, observing conditions and promoting the sale of guano.

Robinson's varied interests and his reputation as a traveler and accurate agricultural observer are now too well known to require in this evaluation a listing of all the prominent Southern planters whom he visited and whose activities he described in his letters to the various farm journals in many parts of this country. That list would be a roll call of the well-known landowners and farmers of that day, many of whom read and also contributed to the farm papers. Everywhere he went Robinson was an enthusiastically welcomed guest. Little of interest pertaining to agriculture and the social and economic life of the South escaped his notice. He urged adoption of new methods, improved machinery, and continued experimentation. His letters were packed with statistics on such matters as the cost of producing a pound of cotton, the draining of land, operation of a sugar plantation in Louisiana or a turpentine business in North Carolina, increased yields from use of fertilizers, deep plowing, and the benefits of railroads to agriculture in South Carolina. He considered it his business to note details. He denounced the generalizations in "too many railroad traveller's publications" of the period (II, p. 30). Much of his traveling was "done slowly in [his] own carriage."

Yet Robinson did not give a complete picture of the Southern scene. He avoided any reference to or discussion of the political aspects of the issues of his day. Rarely did he comment on the small farmers and the problem of the free Negroes. He observed the "happy slaves" and emphasized the blessings of slavery. On one trip he reported hearing of only a single plantation where the Negroes were overworked and otherwise abused (II, pp. 295-97). Although he did not condone slavery, he condemned the abolitionists and their press and thought that the matter of change should be left to the people in each state where the system existed. Nevertheless, Robinson ranks as one of the foremost travelers of the period. No serious student of the ante bellum South can afford to ignore this work.

400.   Rosenberg, Charles G.

Jenny Lind in America. By C. G. Rosenberg . . . New York, Stringer & Townsend, 1851.

226 p., incl. front. (port.). 19 cm.

Illustrations: Autographed portrait of Jenny Lind, from a lithograph by Sardny & Major.

Inclusive dates: In South, December, 1850, to April, 1851.

Location of copy: Newberry Library.

The author of this book, an Englishman, was one of the twenty-five or more persons in Jenny Lind's party on her famous Southern tour. In 1850–51 she appeared under Phineas T. Barnum's management in concerts in Richmond, Charleston, New Orleans, Natchez, Memphis, Nashville, and Louisville. Rosenberg's narrative describes the unrestrained and sometimes frenzied enthusiasm of her reception in these cities. He noted the travel accommodations, the scenery en route, and incidents experienced by both the Swedish "nightingale" and members of her group. Statistics given on prices paid for the admission tickets auctioned before each concert, profits of speculators (modern scalpers), guarantees posted to assure her appearance, gross receipts from individual concerts, and the singer's generous distribution of substantial sums of money to various local charities show the South's response to both Jenny Lind and to Barnum's promotion. The $7,000 guarantee pledged by Natchez citizens for a single morning concert demonstrated that city's admiration for Jenny Lind.

In 1850, Rosenberg published a biography of the Swedish artist, in which he commented on excessive use of "pearl powder" and "white paint" cosmetics by women in the Southern cities, "female loveliness in Nashville," comparative magnificence of river steamboats, and local concert halls. He commented little on conditions and events not directly connected with the concert tour.

The book makes an important contribution toward an understanding of Southern cultural history.

401.   Ross, George M. von

Des Auswanderers Handbuch. Getreue Schilderung der Vereinigten Staaten von Nordamerika und Zuverlässiger Rathgeber für dahin Auswandernde jeden Standes. Von George M. v. Ross. Elberfeld, Julius Bädeker, 1851.

xii, 509, [1] p.   18 cm.

Inlcusive dates: 1830?–1850?

Location of copy: Minnesota Historical Society.

According to the prefatory statement, the American-born and widely traveled writer of this guidebook for German emigrants had lived in various parts of the United States. He had farmed "for a long time in the West, the Southwest, and the East," and he had traveled in all of the states. He made several trips to Germany in the interest of German emigrants and was at one time editor of the *Allgemeinen Auswanderungs-Zeitung*.

His first guidebook, *Rathschläge und Warnungen, oder zuverlässiger Führer für Auswanderer nach Nord-Amerika* (Augsburg, 1848), had been published earlier. It was more limited in the scope of its recommendations to prospective immigrants.

The above work is divided into three parts: the general picture of the United States, individual states, and advice to emigrants. The first section gives an overall picture of the United States, with the usual statistical data concerning topography, climate, resources, and historical, political, and institutional development. Included in this section is an objective discussion of slavery (pp. 78–85). The next part discusses each state, with special emphasis on the advantages or disadvantages for German immigrants. Louisiana was unsuited for Germans because of the climate (p. 232); Arkansas was too isolated (p. 229). Parts of Kentucky and Missouri were questionable, while Tennessee and Texas offered the greatest opportunities in the South, especially the latter state near New Braunfels (p. 285). Ross listed the German settlements in the various states.

The third section is packed with practical information and advice concerning the many steps in the emigrants' journey and settlement in America. A detailed list of the items affected by the tariff of 1846 and a complete index concludes this work, which is one of the best of the many German emigrant guidebooks.

402. Ross, George M. von

Der nordamerikanische Freistaat Texas, Nach eigener Anschauung und nach den neuesten und besten Quellen für deutsche Auswanderer, geschildert von George M. von Ross. Rudolstadt, G. Froebel, 1851.

1 p.l., 85 p. fold. map. 19½ cm.
Maps: Folding map of the Southwest.
Inclusive dates: 1830?–1850?
Location of copy: Library of Congress.

The avowed purpose of this little work was to interest prospective German immigrants in the opportunities for settlement in Texas. The American-born traveler apparently had spent considerable time in the Southwest. He presented information concerning economic conditions and resources and some descriptive material about the state. Much of the first half of the book is made up of the constitution of Texas. Even though there is some duplication of the material found in *Des Auswanderers handbuch* (Elberfeld, 1851), on the whole there is more attention to Texiana details.

403. Rostaing, Jules
Voyage dans les deux Amériques; ou les neveux de l'oncle Tom. Paris, Ve L. Janet, [1854].

iii, 240 p. 12 col. plates. 23 cm.
Illustrations: Frontispiece and eleven colored engravings by C. N. Lemercier of scenes of life in the two Americas.
Inclusive dates: 1850's.
Location of copy: Harvard University Library.

This author fell under the influence of Mrs. Harriet Beecher Stowe, and he went forth looking for the characters of the book. He does much tearful hand-wringing while tracing slavery in his terse view through the eyes of Uncle Tom and other Stowe characters. Only one brief section of the book (pp. 15–62) is devoted to the United States. There is neither evidence of travel nor a travel itinerary, yet the author claims to have viewed slavery firsthand. There are three magnificent tinted French engravings of scenes from *Uncle Tom's Cabin*. The popular French concept of the slave was about as pertinent as Longfellow's portrait of the American Indian.

404. A. Rugbaean [*pseud.*]
Transatlantic rambles; or a record of twelve months travel in the United States, Cuba, & the Brazils. London, George Bell, 1851.

vii, [1], 168 p. 17 cm.
Inclusive dates: Probably October, 1849, to October, 1850. In South, December, 1849, to April, 1850.
Location of copy: Library of Congress.

This anonymous English traveler, using the pseudonym "A Rugbaean," spent a year in the two Americas. According to a prefatory remark, much of the material first appeared as letters in "a country newspaper," and later, at the insistence of friends for "their amusement and edification," the letters were revised and printed in six-point type in the present book form. Even though the book is small in size, its page content equals that of much larger books.

The writer arrived in Halifax and journeyed to Washington, D. C., stopping in several of the larger cities en route. Entering the South, he visited Mount Vernon and then traveled by rail and river to Savannah, Augusta, Montgomery, and Mobile. After a trip to Cuba, he returned to New Orleans and proceeded up the river to St. Louis and Cincinnati and then across Ohio by rail to Buffalo and New York. The next six months were spent in Brazil before he returned to Liverpool.

"Rugbaean" was favorably impressed with the United States and American institutions in general. While in the South he appeared much interested in observing the condition of the Negroes and frequently commented on their polite manners, their generally happy dispositions, and the good treatment accorded them (p. 54). New Orleans impressed him more than any other American city, although he thought Creole beauty had been greatly exaggerated (p. 70).

405. Sarmiento, Domingo Faustino (1811–1888)

Viages en Europa, Africa i America. 2 vols. Santiago, J. Belin, 1849–'51.

21½ cm.
Inclusive dates: 1847–1848. In South, winter of 1847–1848?
Location of copy: University of Texas.

Here is a frank yet generally sympathetic and interesting appraisal of parts of the United States by the distinguished Latin-American educator, statesman, and prolific writer who later became the Argentine minister to the United States and then president of the Argentine Republic (1868–74). Domingo Sarmiento came to New York following a tour of Europe probably in late 1847 and spent a few months visiting in the East before taking a trip by river steamer from Pittsburgh to New Orleans. He planned his journey to the latter city in 1848 when the danger of yellow fever had passed for the season. En route he made an extended stay at Cincinnati where he observed in detail the resources of the state of Ohio, the literary, scientific, philanthropic, and educational institutions of the "Queen City," as well as numerous human interest features of the "Porkopolis" of the nation. His companion in America was one Don Santiago Arcos, a compatriot who had followed him through Europe and caught up with him in New York.

Sarmiento described his eleven-day trip from Cincinnati to New Orleans (at a total cost of $15.00) as "one of the most beautiful, most lasting, and placid memories that remained with [him]" (II, p. 197), yet he failed to comment on the cities or points of interest en route.

Two things in particular interested him in the United States:

colonization, or "the way to populate the wilderness," and the American system of government. Then, too, his great admiration for the work of Horace Mann, who became his friend and whose program Sarmiento wished to introduce in Argentina, has significance. American elections in Baltimore did not please him. While he learned much about the United States firsthand, he also gained knowledge from his discriminating reading and his conversations with a wide variety of Americans along the way.

He was opposed to slavery, but he concluded that it "was a question without any solution" because of the problem of the freed Negro. Unlike most travelers Sarmiento thought that New Orleans, after his ten-day stay in that city, "was incurably sick" with yellow fever.

A second edition was published in 1922, entitled *Viages . . . con una Introducción de Julio Noe* (Buenos Aires, 1922. 3 vols. in 1. 22½ cm.). A reprint of the first chapter of Volume II of the second edition appeared in 1942 with the title *Estados Unidos* (Buenos Aires, 1942). The above is the 1922 edition.

406.   Savardan, Le dr. [Augustin]

Un naufrage au Texas; observations et impressions recueillies pendant deux ans et demi au Texas et à travers les États-Unis d'Amérique par Le Dr Savardan. Paris, Garnier frères, 1858.

> 2 p.l., 344 p. 17½ cm.
> *Inclusive dates:* 1857–1858.
> *Location of copy:* Library of Congress.

Savardan has produced an interesting and meaty book concerning the French settlement at Reunion, Texas. He gives definite dates and places in his discussion, and what is more unusual for a French travel book, the author took time to prepare a rather detailed index. In 1854 the phalansterian school, under the leadership of M. Victor Considerant, subscribed 1,800,000 francs for the establishment of a colonization society in Texas. During 1853–56, three hundred immigrants went to Texas from France. In 1857, M. Considerant prepared a report or publication entitled *Du Texas* which appears to have attracted considerable attention in France. The author of this *Un Naufrage au Texas,* who served as the physician in the new colony from 1855–57, examined the materials discussed by M. Considerant firsthand and gave a good analysis of foreigners colonizing in such frontier regions as Texas.

Most of the text deals with life at Reunion, Texas. It treats with such subjects as the economics of the settlement, health, leadership, and even the heat and snakes. No Frenchman should have remained in the dark about Texas after the appearance of this book. It is a good social picture of both Texas and a French immigrant society and community in the Southwest.

According to Monaghan, Savardan traveled overland from Texas to New York by way of Fort Smith, Cairo, and Niagara Falls on his return trip to France in the summer of 1857.

407. Schmölder, Captain B.

Neuer praktischer Wegweiser für Auswanderer nach Nord-Amerika in drei Abtheilungen mit Karten, Plänen und Ansichten. Mainz, Le Roux, 1849, [1851].

> 4 p.l., 120, [84]–153 p., 1 l. front. (port.), 3 plates. fold. map. 23 cm.
> *Other editions:*
> (1) Neuer praktischer Wegweiser für Auswanderer nach Nord-Amerika in drei Abtheilungen . . . Mainz, Le Roux, [1851].
> (2) Neuer praktischer Wegweiser für Auswanderer nach Nord-Amerika . . . mit Karten, Plänen und Ansichten . . . von Capitain B. Schmölder. Zweite Ausgabe, Mainz, 1855.
> *Location of copy:* U. S. Geological Survey Library.

Schmölder was a territorial agent with many years of residence in this country. His guidebook was intended to attract German immigrants to the Middle and Far West, but he did give some practical advice to those who came by way of New Orleans.

The book is divided into three parts. Part I discusses the topography of the Mississippi Valley and the Far West together with the best routes of travel. Schmölder advised immigrants to come to New Orleans in the fall and winter rather than the summer because of the heat. Also, opportunities for earning a stake with which to buy land in Missouri or Iowa were better in the spring. Part II classifies the states and those sections of each state best suited for German settlers. Schmölder publicized Morgan County in Tennessee and Stephen County in Missouri. Part III describes Iowa.

408. Shaw, John

A ramble through the United States, Canada, and the West Indies. By John Shaw . . . London, J. F. Hope, 1856.

> 1 p.l., 370 p. 22 cm.
> *Inclusive dates:* August, 1845, to April(?), 1846. In South, January 1–24, 1846.
> *Location of copy:* University of Kentucky Library.

One chapter in this book describes an English doctor's journey from Washington to New Orleans on his way from Canada to Cuba. Dr.

Shaw stopped briefly at Richmond, Wilmington, Charleston, Montgomery, and Mobile, and his observations en route are recorded with candor, and, at times, a sense of humor. (See pp. 207–10 for his description of a stagecoach journey.) He makes frequent mention of "the extensive pine forests," the many varieties of trees and flora, and the slow speed of travel. He disliked slavery, and at times he assumed a rather condescending attitude toward the South.

409. Smet, Pierre Jean de (1801–1873)

Life, letters, and travels of Father Pierre-Jean de Smet, S.J., 1801–1873; missionary labors and adventures among the wild tribes of the North American Indians, embracing minute descriptions of their manners, customs, games, modes of warfare and torture, legends, traditions, etc., all from personal observations made during many thousand miles of travel, with sketches of the country from St. Louis to Puget Sound and the Altrabasca; edited from the original unpublished manuscript journals and letter books and from his printed works, with historical, geographical, ethnological and other notes; also a life of Father de Smet ... by Hiram Martin Chittenden ... and Alfred Talbot Richardson. 4 vols. New York, F. P. Harper, 1905.

> Paged continuously: Vol. I, xv, 402 p.; Vol. II, vii, 403–794 p.; Vol. III, xi, 795–1211 p.; Vol. IV, vi, 1213–1624 p. fronts., plates, ports., fold. map in pocket, facsims. 23½ cm.
> *Inclusive dates:* 1801–1873.
> *Location of copy:* University of Kentucky Library.

Father de Smet, ubiquitous world traveler and missionary to the North American Indians, visited Louisville and Bardstown, Kentucky, on several occasions and made at least one trip through the South to New Orleans in 1850–51 (II, p. 614). He records no observations on the South other than a general discussion of the sectional conflict in his letters written in 1861–63 (IV, pp. 1431–43). It is unnecessary to include more than this note concerning his work in this connection.

410. Smith, Ashbel (1805–1886)

Notice sur la géographie du Texas, sur la variété de ses productions, de ses animaux, de ses plantes, et de ses richesses naturelles et commerciales, par M. Ashbel Smith, membre de la Société de Géographie.

> In the Bulletin de la société geography, Ser. 3, Vol. I, No. 5, p. 321–44. Paris, Arthur Bertrand, 1844(?), 1851(?).

Inclusive dates: 1839?–1844?
Location of copy: University of Texas Library.

This is one of the descriptive bulletins of the French Society of Geography which devotes full attention to Texas. There is no travel material in this volume, but it is descriptive of general Texas geography with some attention being given to life and general economic conditions. The writer was a onetime surgeon general of the Texian Army who, according to Sabin, earlier had published *An Account of the Yellow Fever Which Appeared in the City of Galveston, Republic of Texas, in the Autumn of 1839.* The present bulletin is characteristic of the multitude of French geographical studies which deal with the obvious and largely overlook the fundamentals. One of the main reasons for this was the fact that much of the material was taken from other highly secondary sources.

411.   Smith, Edward (1818?–1874)

Account of a journey through north-eastern Texas, undertaken in 1849, for the purposes of emigration. Embodied in a report: to which are appended letters and verbal communications, from eminent individuals; lists of temperatures, of prices of land, produce, and articles of merchandize; and of costs of carriage and labour; in several parts of the western and southern states; and the recently adopted constitution of Texas, with maps from the last authentic survey. London, Hamilton, Adams, and Co., 1849.

> vi, [5]–188 p. fold. maps. 18½ cm.
> *Maps:* Folding map of Texas; folding map of "part of North Eastern Texas shewing the route of the inspectors."
> *Inclusive dates:* May 1, 1849, to July 7, 1849. In South, May 10(?) to July 2, 1849.
> *Location of copy:* Wisconsin Historical Society.

The title of this book is a fairly complete statement of its content. The author, who later became a distinguished physician and medical writer, together with a friend, John Barrow, a civil engineer, came to America "at the instance of a body of Gentlemen" who were interested in opportunities for English emigrants (see John Barrow, *Facts Relating to North East Texas, Condensed from Notes Made during a Tour Through That Portion of the United States of America* [London, 1848]). They arrived in New York on May 1, 1849, and traveled to New Orleans via Pennsylvania, Michigan, Illinois, and the Mississippi River. They left Shreveport on May 23, circled through the Texas counties of Cass, Hopkins, Lamar, Collins, Dallas, Kaufman,

Smith, and Harrison, and returned to New Orleans on June 22. Upon reaching Cincinnati on the return trip, they separated. Smith traveled to New York by way of northern Ohio and Lake Erie, while Barrow took the "less expeditious but cheaper and more picturesque route" by way of Pittsburgh, Harrisburg, and Philadelphia.

The report is filled with interesting description and statistical information for prospective emigrants to Texas. Smith discussed the best routes of travel, soils, communications, productivity, natural resources, and the opportunities for settlers. He pictured the area "as a very Goshen" surrounded by "everything which heart could wish," but he pointed out the difficulties that would be encountered especially in matters pertaining to health, which was the field of his professional training and one in which he later achieved marked recognition (see the *Dictionary of National Biography,* XVIII, pp. 439–40).

He noted the information which he had received from other sources. Even though the title of the report states that other Western and Southern states are included, there is little pertaining to anything outside of Texas. The chief exception to this is his very objective discussion of slavery in the United States (pp. 76–86). Although opposed to it, he advised those emigrants adverse to the system "never to speak or think lightly" concerning it nor to agitate against it until public opinion was "sufficiently ripened."

A final chapter of advice to emigrants was intended to anticipate all questions in the minds of those who were making ready to emigrate.

An interesting feature of the report was the appended written and verbal communications from Texas officials and residents.

412. [Smith, John]

Across the Atlantic. By the author of "Sketches of Cantabs." London, George Earle, 1851.

x p., 1 l., 247 p., 1 l.   18 cm.
Inclusive dates: July to October(?), 1850.
Location of copy: University of Kentucky Library.

Although the would-be anonymous English writer of some reputation expected this volume to be a "light and trifling" account for the amusement of his readers, his varied sketches of the American scene add interesting and valuable footnotes to travel literature. He observed the "driving energy" and progress of the young republic, yet he was aware of its "rude vulgarity and want of manners and refinement." He was critical of those English travelers who saw only the crudities of America but were blind to the paradoxes of Britain's social and political system. To him the United States was the "most sublime and the most ridiculous, the most appalling and the most amusing of all countries."

This traveler arrived in New York in July, 1850, and spent several weeks visiting as far south as Richmond. His descriptions of Congressmen Cass, Benton, Butler, and Berrien, the dilapidated condition of Mount Vernon, and the emotional outbursts of a Virginia camp meeting are significant. He had much to say about the pros and cons of slavery. In general he was critical of American abolitionists and those Englishmen who refused to recognize the monetary sacrifice involved in emancipation.

413. Smith, John Calvin

The illustrated handbook, a new guide for travelers through the United States of America . . . By J. Calvin Smith. New York, Sherman & Smith, 1846.

> 233 p. illus., map. 24 cm.
> *Maps:* Folding map of the U. S. in 1849 (1849 edition).
> *Illustrations:* 125? small engravings of scenes from each state.
> *Other editions:*
> (1) New York, Sherman & Smith, 1847. 233 p. illus., fold map. 14½ cm.
> (2) New York, Sherman & Smith, 1849. 234 p., incl. front., illus., fold. map. 14 cm.
> (3) Emigrant's handbook, and new guide for travelers, etc. London, Simpkin, Marshall & co., 1850.
> (4) Smith's hand-book for travellers . . . New York, J. C. Smith & son, 1856.
> *Location of copy:* Library of Congress.

This is one of the better travel guides and handbooks of the mid-century period. Its contents include a general description of each state, followed by a list of points of interest in the important cities. There is other material enumerated in the title, plus descriptions of canals and currency rates. An index of cities and towns facilitates the book's use, and an excellent folding map gives detailed information.

414. Smith, Sidney

The settler's new home: or the emigrants' location, being a guide to emigrants in the selection of a settlement, and the preliminary details of the voyage. By Sidney Smith . . . London, J. Kendrick, 1849.

> 1 p.l., 106 p. 16 cm.

Other editions:

(1) The settler's new home; or whether to go, and whither? Being a guide to emigrants in the selection of a settlement, and the preliminary details. Embracing the whole fields of education, and the most recent information relating thereto. In two parts. By Sidney Smith . . . London, J. Kendrick, 1850. v, 106 p. 16½ cm.

(2) The settlers new home or the emigrants' location, etc. . . . London, n.d.

(3) Whether to go and whither? By Sidney Smith. Being a practical view of the whole Southern field of settlement. New South Wales, Port Philip, South Australia, Western Australia, New Zealand, &c. With authentic information, and the latest particulars from the recently discovered gold regions, and full instructions for intending emigrants. London, John Kendrick, 27, Ludgate Street, St. Paul's, and 4, Charlotte Row, Mansion House. 1852. xxvi, 118 p. *Location of copy:* Newberry Library.

Smith wrote for prospective emigrants to various parts of North America. He tried to answer questions on the advantages of emigration, means of transportation, general quality and price of land, estimated expenditures and possible profits from farming, and many other pertinent hints and aids. Smith quoted extensively from reports of emigration agents, other travelers, and from "intelligent Americans and Englishmen long resident in America." Although fragmentary, the book on the whole is favorable. It contains material concerning farm prospects in Virginia, Kentucky, and Tennessee in a section on the Middle and Southwestern states (pp. 103–24). Prospective settlers to Texas were cautioned against the "recently circulated" exaggerated statements.

415. Smith, Sol[omon Franklin] (1801–1869)

Theatrical management in the West and South for thirty years. Interspersed with anecdotical sketches: autobiographically given by Sol[omon] Smith, retired actor. With fifteen illustrations and a portrait of the author. New York, Harper and Brothers, 1868.

viii, [9]–275 [1] p., incl. illus., port. 22½ cm.

Illustrations: Autographed portrait of author and fifteen illustrations of theatrical scenes.

Inclusive dates: 1823–1853.

Location of copy: University of Kentucky Library.

Except for a few scattered appearances from 1853–63, this actor appears to have performed in many of the cities of the West and South during the years 1823 to 1853. Much of the material in this book is a rehash of the actor's earlier works, *The Theatrical Apprenticeship and Anecdotical Recollections of Sol. Smith* (*q.v.*) (Philadelphia, 1846) and *The Theatrical Journey-Work and Anecdotical Recollections of Sol. Smith* (*q.v.*) (Philadelphia, 1854). Some thirty-five pages describe his experiences from 1845–53, many of which centered in New Orleans.

416. Spalding, Martin John, Archbishop (1810–1872)

Sketches of the life, times, and character of the Rt. Rev. Benedict Joseph Flaget, first Bishop of Louisville. Louisville, Ky., Webb and Levering, 1852.

> xvi, 17–405, [1] p. 19 cm.
> *Illustrations:* Frontispiece: Engraved portrait of Bishop Flaget.
> *Inclusive dates:* 1808–1849.
> *Location of copy:* University of Kentucky Library.

Benedict Flaget (1763–1850), the "first bishop who came to the West" according to his biographer, was appointed Bishop of Bardstown (Kentucky) in 1808. In 1841 the residence was transferred to Louisville. This biography by Bishop Spalding, Flaget's successor, though not a travel book, merits some consideration, for it is in effect a history of forty years of administration, visitations, and establishments of religious and charitable institutions in parts of the West and South, especially Kentucky, from 1808–49. The work is based upon Flaget's reminiscences, his manuscript diaries, and voluminous correspondence. A German abridgment of this book was published in 1844, *Leben des hochwurdigsten Benedict Joseph Flaget, ersten bischofs von Louisville, Ky.* (Louisville, 1884).

417. Stewart, Robert, A.M.

The United States of America: their climate, soil, productions, population, manufactures, religion, arts, government, etc., etc. London, W. Tweedie, 1853.

> 4 p.l., 399 p. front. (fold. map). 17½ cm. (Popular geographical library).
> *Maps:* Frontispiece: Folding map of United States.
> *Location of copy:* Wisconsin Historical Society.

This descriptive account of the United States compiled by an Englishman for *The Popular Geographical Library* is not a travel account. The introductory chapter on the nation as a whole gives a good picture of the Mississippi River in flood stage (pp. 25–34). Most of the book consists of chapters for each state with information concerning geography, natural resources, population, and production. Much of the material was taken from the census reports.

418. Stroyer, Jacob

Sketches of my life in the South. Part I. Salem: Salem press, 1879.

51 p. 16 cm.
Inclusive dates: 1849–1865.
Other editions:
   (1) 1880.
   (2) My life in the South. By Jacob Stroyer. New and enl. ed. Salem, Salem observer book and job print, 1889. 83 p. 18½ cm.
Location of copy: Library of Congress.

Freedman Jacob Stroyer, minister of the Salem, Massachusetts, African Methodist Episcopal Church, was born in slavery on a large plantation in central South Carolina in 1849. In 1879 he wrote this autobiography, hoping to realize sufficient funds with which to continue his education. The book presents both the "lights and shadows" of slavery in a simple yet effective style. He gives some interesting side lights on living conditions, witchcraft, and methods used by slaves in detecting thieves.

419.   Stuart-Wortley, Lady Emmeline Charlotte
        Elizabeth (Manners) (1806–1855)
Travels in the United States, etc. during 1849 and 1850, by the Lady Emmeline Stuart Wortley. New York, Harper & brothers, 1851.
      xii, [13]–463 p. 18½ cm.
      Inclusive dates: May, 1849, to 1850. In South, probably November, 1849, to January, 1850.
      Other editions:
         (1) 3 vols. London, R. Bentley, 1851. 19½ cm.
         (2) Paris: A. and W. Galignani and co., 1851.
      Location of copy: University of Kentucky Library.

Arriving in New York in May, 1849, Lady Stuart-Wortley, "daughter of a duke and wife of a baron," one of the better known and oft-quoted English travelers, toured New England and the East. She visited Washington and then crossed the Alleghenies and entered the South via the Ohio River. Continuing down the Mississippi River to New Orleans, across Lake Pontchartrain to Mobile, she sailed to Central and South America. Only six of the fifty-five chapters pertain to Lady Stuart-Wortley's favorable impressions of her trip through the South.
   The author was both awed and depressed by Mammoth Cave. Louisville was, she thought, the best lighted city in the United States. While there she observed the "preponderating population of pigs" that "push the two legged citizens into the streets." En route to New Orleans she was entertained at Cypress Grove, President Zachary Taylor's plantation, where she noted the "well fed, comfortably

clothed and kindly cared for" Negroes who "seemed thoroughly happy and contented." While critical of overseers, she was quite certain that only a small part of the slaves if liberated would accept their freedom.

Lady Wortley made interesting comments on "Liliputian lancers" (mosquitos), the cemeteries in New Orleans, crevasses, and the magnolia groves of Mobile. She recorded the details with a feminine appreciation for the lighter tones of the Southern life, for she was delighted with most of her experiences in the South. Rarely did she attempt any evaluation of underlying forces.

420. Sullivan, [Sir] Edward [Robert], Baronet (1826–1899)

Rambles and scrambles in North and South America. London, Richard Bentley, 1852.

2 p.l., [iii]–viii, [9]–424 p.   20 cm.
Inclusive dates: June 30, 1850, to February 15, 1851. In South, January? to February, 1851.
Location of copy: University of Kentucky Library.

Some forty pages of Sullivan's account center attention on the South (pp. 190–230). The writer, an English sportsman, came to New York in 1850 "strongly biased" against America. He traveled westward by way of the Hudson River and the Great Lakes to La Point (Wis.) where he cut across to the Mississippi River and journeyed by sleigh down through the prairie country to St. Louis, hunting buffalo en route.

Much of Sullivan's impression of the South was gained from his river trip to New Orleans. He had some harsh words concerning American slavery, and his condemnation of the Negro position in both the North and the South reflected his bias. Yet he pointed out many of the inconsistencies of this basic American problem. He found the trip to New Orleans "very tiresome . . . [and] most irksome," but he enlivened his account with interesting descriptions of river life and humor. He failed to admire the Crescent City and its inhabitants, but he was intrigued with the absence of solid ground for building construction, the cotton market speculation, and quadroon dances. In spite of his sarcastic and oftentimes sharp criticisms, he admitted on leaving that, though most things were well done in England, "they do some things even better in America" (p. 227). He left New Orleans for Cuba and South America in February, 1851.

421.   Surtees, William Edward

Recollections of North America, in 1849–50–51. By W. E. Surtees, D.C.L. ₁London? Chapman and Hall? 1852?₁.

> 2 pts. in 1 vol.   53 p.   21 cm.
> *Inclusive dates:* July, 1849, to September, 1851. In South, the same.
> *Location of copy:* Library of Congress.

This is an account of travels in America by an Englishman who left Liverpool for New York in 1849 and returned via the same route in September, 1851. The material appears to have been first published in the *New Monthly Magazine* in two installments. During two years Surtees made what appeared to be an extensive circle tour from Washington through the South to New Orleans and then northward by way of the Mississippi and Ohio rivers to Louisville. Although the evidence is confusing, he seems to have returned by retracing much of the same route.

Surtees reports being at the St. Charles Hotel in New Orleans when it burned and being in Charleston when that city was mourning the passing of John C. Calhoun. The two greatest American novelties to him were Cuba and Mammoth Cave. In view of the traveler's opportunities for extensive observations the book is a disappointment.

422.   Tallack, William (1831–1908)

Friendly sketches in America. London, A. W. Bennett, 1861.

> xi, 276 p.   19 cm.
> *Inclusive dates:* 1860 (four months).
> *Location of copy:* Library of Congress.

The author, an English member of the Society of Friends, stated that he "crossed the United States from California to Virginia and from Mexico to Canada" during a four-month trip in 1860, visiting the various communities of Friends. But there is little in the book pertaining to the South except a brief discussion of the Maryland, Virginia, and Carolina Friends and a mention of the community of Friendship, Tennessee. He condemned slavery and denounced its Southern supporters (p. 228).

423.   Taylor, Bayard (1825–1878)

Eldorado, or, adventures in the path of empire: comprising a voyage to California, via Panama; life in San Francisco and Monterey; pictures of the gold region, and experiences of Mexican travel. By Bayard Taylor ... 2 vols. London, George Routledge, 1850.

Illustrations: Frontispieces and six other illustrations of Californian and Mexican scenes (colored lithographs) (2d ed.).
Inclusive dates: June 28, 1849, to March 10, 1850. In South, July, 1849; February 27, to March 7, 1850.
Other editions:
    (1) 2 vols. London, H. G. Bohn, 1850.
    (2) 2d ed. New York, G. P. Putnam's, [etc., etc.], 1850. 2 vols. in 1.
    (3) 8th ed. 1856. xiv p., 1 l., 444 p., incl. front., plates. 18½ cm.
    (4) 18th ed. 1859.
    (5) 1868. xiv, 444 p. 18½ cm. (Half title: Prose writings . . . Rev. ed.).
    (6) Household ed., rev. 1882. 4 p.l., [vii]–xiv, 444 p. front. 19½ cm.
(Half title: Prose writings of Bayard Taylor. Rev. ed. v. 5).
Location of copy: University of Kentucky Library.

Bayard Taylor, famous world traveler, writer, and New York *Tribune* correspondent, spent four days in New Orleans en route from New York to California and Panama. His two-page description of the Mississippi River and New Orleans adds little of importance to Southern travel literature. Returning from the "gold diggings" by way of Mexico to Mobile, he mentions Lady Emmeline Stuart-Wortley as a fellow passenger. No details are given of his two-week trip from Mobile to New York through Montgomery, Atlanta, Augusta, Charleston, and Washington. (See the *Dictionary of American Biography,* XVIII, pp. 314–16.)

424. **Thomassy, [Marie Joseph] R[aymond] (1810–1863)**
Géologie practique de la Louisiane par R. Thomassy, ancien élève de L'École Imperiale des Chartes, ancien membre du comité central de la société de géographie de Paris, membre de la société géologique de France, membre de l'académie des sciences de la Nouvelle-Orléans, etc. Nouvelle-Orléans et à Paris, Chez l'auteur, Lacroix et Baudry, 1860.

    lxviii, 263, [1] p. 6 plates (incl. 5 maps). 26 cm.
    Maps: Five: Louisiana in 1684 by Franquelin; the Red River in 1722 by J. F. Broutin; Louisiana in 1719–1720 by De Serigny; entrances to Mississippi River 1722–1731; changing Delta from 1839–1851 from Captain Talcott's map and from the U. S. Coast Survey. Additional sketches of geological and physiological features.
    Inclusive dates: 1682–1858.
    Location of copy: University of Kentucky Library.

This is primarily a report of numerous exploring expeditions into Louisiana during the seventeenth and eighteenth centuries, as well as some of the geological studies to 1858. It is to be considered a piece of travel literature in the sense that any geologist's report is essentially a description of travel. There are many scientific observations accompanied by drawings giving some concept of the physiological conditions of Louisiana. At the same time there are observations on the people of the state and on social conditions.

Obviously one of the subjects which would attract the scientist's attention was the matter of health. There are some good observations on physiological conditions which had a bearing upon human life in the region. Thomassy, who was the author of several historical works, gives a good physiological view of Louisiana, with a generous dash of hydrography thrown in for good measure. An interesting feature of the work is the maps of the rivers and the coastline, the entrances to the Mississippi River, and the changing delta from 1839 to 1851.

425. Thorne, Samuel (1835–1915)

1848—The journal of a boy's trip on horseback kept by Samuel Thorne. New York, privately printed by Riverside Press of Cambridge, Mass., 1936.

> vii, [1] p., 2 l., 47, [1] p., 1 l. front., illus., plates, ports., fold. map. 24 cm.
> *Maps:* Folding map with route of journey in 1848.
> *Illustrations:* Frontispiece: Family circle (Thorne family in 1853); and twelve illustrations of places and persons of the period.
> *Inclusive dates:* April 4, 1848, to June 8, 1848. In South, April 4 to May 23, 1848.
> *Location of copy:* Princeton University Library.

This journal is the day by day entries in his diary, supplemented by the letters written to his parents, by the twelve-year-old Samuel Thorne while he was making his return trip from the South to his home in New York in the early summer of 1848. He had accompanied his father on a business trip by steamer to Charleston and Savannah, and there the young Thorne was allowed to buy a pony and to ride it back home accompanied by an older friend. This simple and straightforward narrative of his experiences and boyish observations was edited and published in 1936 by his grandson, who made no evident attempt to edit the youthful traveler's grammatical irregularities.

Young Thorne noted the first gaslights in Charleston, and he was interested in the turkey buzzards, protected by law, roaming the streets of that city. From time to time he mentioned the slave auctions and the contented Negroes. But most of the entries called attention to the pony, the distances covered (forty miles was the longest day's travel), and the accommodations en route. Charleston and Washington were described in greatest detail.

426.   Tolmer, J.

Scènes de l'Amérique du Nord en 1949. Leipzig, Avenarius and Mendelssohn, 1850.

> vi, 134 p.   18 cm.
> *Inclusive dates:* May to October, 1849.
> *Location of copy:* Library of Congress.

Tolmer traveled in this country from May to October, 1849. He visited Alabama, Louisiana, Texas, Kentucky, and Missouri. His account is in the form of ten letters written to a friend from Petersburg (Va.), New Orleans, St. Louis, Louisville, and Washington. They show a keen sense of humor and a highly observant eye. His visit to Galveston Island came at a time when that famous spot in Texas was gathering in a considerable horde of flotsam and jetsam of the human race. Tolmer was amused to see all of the generals and judges who congregated about the liquor bars. Their antics were enough to amuse even a native. Likewise, some of their violent reactions were enough to excite fear in the timid traveler.

Up the Mississippi and Ohio rivers, Tolmer came upon a western braggart who described the true man of the West as a person who had never been trampled on, who had a keen wit, and whose shoulders were four feet apart. There is also a rather fine, brief dissertation on the term "yankee," which indicated that as early as 1849 this name was well established in the minds of both Southerners and Westerners. This is a brief book, but some of its observations are original and stimulating. It is a good source for a glimpse of rugged frontier social life in the peripheral South.

427.   Tremenheere, Hugh Seymour (1804–1893)

Notes on public subjects, made during a tour in the United States and in Canada. London, John Murray, 1852.

> vi p., 1 l., 320 p., 32 p. of advertisements.
> *Maps:* One folding map of the United States and Canada.
> *Inclusive dates:* August to December, 1851.
> *Location of copy:* University of Kentucky Library.

There is little evidence that Hugh Tremenheere, noted English author and publicist who spent fourteen weeks in America during the fall of 1851, ever traveled south of Cincinnati. He visited several of the larger cities throughout Canada and the northeastern United States, paying particular attention to systems of public education, the development of railroads, and their effects on national trade. He studied the various methods of water supply, voting procedures, and the American press, supplementing his observations with statistics. Wherever he went he was well received, for Tremenheere was a candid, yet discriminating, critic of American social and industrial society. His conclusions displayed an understanding of the problems of a young nation. He refrained from passing judgment on slavery, not because of any feeling of indifference, but because he thought that all comments on the subject by those outside the United States, especially England, did more harm than good. He recognized that it was a "heavy weight on the minds of the most thoughtful inhabitants" in all parts of the country.

428. Wagner, Dr. Moritz (1813–1887), and Scherzer, Dr. Karl (1821–1903)

Reisen in Nordamerika in den Jahren 1852 und 1853, von Dr. Moritz Wagner und Dr. Karl Scherzer. 3 vols. Leipzig, Arnold, 1854.

Vol. I, xx, 471 p.; Vol. II, xiv, 429 p.; Vol. III, xiv, 409 p. 16½ cm.
Inclusive dates: June, 1852–1853. In South, November, 1852, to spring(?), 1853.
Location of copy: Library of Congress.

The three volumes of this comprehensive work, one of the few collaborative studies of the period, is an important travel account. The authors, Dr. Moritz Wagner, German-born zoologist, editor, world traveler, and explorer, and Dr. Karl von Scherzer, Austrian scientist and explorer, were both unusually well prepared to give an accurate report of their travels in North America in 1852–53. Both were to achieve wide recognition for their exploits and their scholarship. Wagner had spent some seventeen years in expeditions to parts of the Near East and Asia seeking scientific data. Scherzer was in the early stages of his professional career. Both were to make several globe-circling expeditions in later years.

The authors arrived in New York from Bremen in June, 1852. For six months each traveled along his own route through different parts of the country. Scherzer covered the East and Northeast and then cut across Ohio and Illinois to St. Louis. From there he traveled south through Kentucky, Tennessee, Georgia, and Alabama. Wagner proceeded along the St. Lawrence and the Great Lakes route and down the length of the Mississippi River to Louisiana. Together they appear to have traveled in most of the states except the Carolinas and Florida. After meeting in New Orleans, they spent the rest of the winter months of 1852–53 collaborating in writing these three volumes.

En route they conferred with prominent leaders such as President Millard Fillmore, General Winfield Scott, and Daniel Webster, who assisted them in access to documents and other material. The travelers acknowledged the aid received from the Jesuit fathers and scientists such as Professor Benjamin Silliman of Yale, Dr. George Engelmann of St. Louis and James D. B. De Bow. Throughout the work there are frequent references to the writings of other scholars and travelers, with whose conclusions they were not always in agreement (III, pp. 339, 460). They followed a division of labor in writing, with Wagner treating the geographical and scientific data, while Scherzer utilized the statistical information concerning the national economy. Ethnological and political materials were discussed jointly. Scherzer initialed his chapters, thus identifying his work for the reader.

The first two books, except for a detailed discussion of Washington and its environs in Volume I, little concern the South. Volume III, however, is a rich source for Southern travel. The two scientists wrote much about St. Louis, the starting point for their respective trips through the South. Scherzer was impressed with Louisville, especially its hotels and its medical school. Mammoth Cave was described in considerable detail (III, pp. 252–74). Nashville was the "friendly city." Life on board a crowded Alabama river steamer, with the smoking, spitting, chewing, and noisy passengers, produced criticism of the rough manners in the South (III, p. 298). Quackery in America, the patent medicine craze, and American doctors inspired caustic comments and warnings to readers to "beware and take care of yourselves."

New Orleans, "the great city," gave both men their opportunity for description and for that meticulous attention to detail that characterized so many of the German travelers. They described at length the city site and port facilities, Canal Street, the St. Charles Hotel, the French quarter, and other features of interest. Social institutions, including the coffeehouses, the bars, the theaters, the opera, the exclusive clubs such as the Pelican and the New Orleans, the elaborate balls, and the brothels, all passed in review. They observed that the appearance of Lola Montez in her "obscene spider dance" previously "banned in Boston" was acclaimed in the Crescent City with much applause.

Both travelers attempted a comprehensive report on the status of German immigrants in and around New Orleans. They emphasized the general prosperity of their countrymen and refuted charges made by those who stressed the low economic level attained by the Germans (III, p. 339). Wagner and Scherzer called attention to the great number of attractive and prosperous looking German-owned houses just north of the city. They surveyed German contributions to various trades and professions, the immigrant press of the city, cultural and literary interests, and state politics and supported their findings with considerable statistical data.

The last hundred pages of Volume III are a comprehensive analysis of slavery, especially on the sugar plantations in Louisiana. There is also a description of the sugar industry in that state. These accounts are based on careful observations and some knowledge of the authoritative writings on the subjects. The authors reviewed the proslavery arguments, the program of the abolitionists, and the economics of slavery and predicted an eventual solution of the problem. While critical of the institution, they were unbiased in their evaluations in this significant work.

429.   Warner, I. W.

The immigrant's guide, and citizen's manual: a work for immigrants of all classes to the United States of North America with directions and valuable information for travelers, by I. W. Warner, A.B. New York, for author by C. M. Caxton, 1848.

> iii-vi p., 1 l., 172 p.   16 cm.
> *Inclusive dates:* 1848.
> *Location of copy:* University of Illinois Library.

Neither Sabin nor the Library of Congress Catalog lists this manual for immigrants compiled by I. W. Warner who, in order to aid them, "sought to gain by condensing into as small a compass as possible the largest amount of useful matter." General chapters on description, government and laws, education, moral and religious conditions, occupations, and communications, together with the specific information on routes, lands, currency and coinage, weights and measures, and much other material make up the guide.

430.   Watkin, Sir Edward William (1819–1901)

A trip to the United States and Canada: in a series of letters. London, W. H. Smith and Son, 1852.

> 2 p.l., vii–xii, 149 p.   18 cm.
> *Location of copy:* University of Illinois.

The prominent "British railroad official and future head of the grand French Railroad of Canada" traveled as far South as the Potomac River on his health trip to Canada and the United States in 1851. Aside from his comments about Washington and slavery in Maryland, his journal in the form of letters has little significance for the

[329]

South, but Watkin predicted a great future for the United States. Later he wrote a more comprehensive book on his experiences in America, entitled *Canada and the States; Recollections, 1851 to 1886. By Sir E. W. Watkin* (London, New York, [1887?]).

431. Weichardt, Karl [ed.]

Die Vereinigten Staaten von Nord-Amerika und deren Territorien, nebst einem Blick auf Kanada, dargestellt nach einer Anzahl der neuesten und besten Reise- und andern Werke, und in einer auszüglichen Bearbeitung von Capitain J. C. Fremont's Reisen nach dem Felsengebirge, Oregon und Nord-Californien in den Jahren 1842–1844 von Karl Weichardt. Pfarrer zu Nermsdorf, bei Weimar. Mit einem Stahlstich und einer Karte. Leipzig, August Weichardt, 1848.

> x, 447, [1] p. fold. map. 20 cm.
> *Maps:* Folding map of U. S. in 1848, from Heinzelmann's Weltkunde.
> *Inclusive dates:* 1830–1846.
> *Other editions:*
> Die Vereinigten Staaten von Nord-Amerika und deren Territorien, nebst einem Blick auf Kanada, dargestellt nach einer Anzahl der neuesten und besten Reise- und anderen Werke . . . Leipzig, A. Weichardt, 1848. x, 477, [1] p. front., fold. map. 21½ cm.
> Also issued without the editor's name under the title Reisen durch die Vereinigten Staaten von Nord-Amerika nebst einem Ausfluge nach Canada. . . . Published in the same year as Vol. IV of Die Weltkunde . . . aufgrund des Reisewerkes von Dr. Wilhelm Harnisch dargestellt und hrsg. von Friedrich Heinzelmann. . . . Leipzig, A. Weichardt, 1847–55.
> *Location of copy:* University of Illinois Library.

The editor of this book, a German clergyman, probably never traveled in America, but according to his last statement in the introduction, he intended to compile "interesting features of a number of the newest and best travel accounts and books about the United States." His list included such travelers as Frederick von Baumer, F. Gerstäcker, Count Bernhard of Saxe-Weismar, M. Beyer, L. Koch, Charles Lyell, Francis Wyse, and De Tocqueville. Yet the book falls somewhat short of fulfilling the expectations created by the introduction. Eight of the chapters (pp. 49–166) describe the more obvious features and institutions of the South on the route from Washington along the coast, the Gulf states to New Orleans, and up the Mississippi and Ohio rivers. Special attention is directed to snakes in Virginia, rice fields in the Carolinas, the Indians of Florida, bear hunts, lynch laws, and itinerant preachers along the Mississippi River. Statistical information for the Ohio Valley, as well as a side trip from Louisville to

Lexington, Kentucky, affords some local interest. Weichardt's views concerning slavery were moderate.

432. Williams, W[ellington]

Appleton's railroad and steamboat companion. Being a traveller's guide through the northern, eastern, and middle states, Canada, New Brunswick, and Nova Scotia. New York, D. Appleton and Company, 1849.

313 p. 30 maps, 26 plates. 15½ cm.

Other editions:

(1) Appleton's railroad and steamboat companion. Being a travellers' guide through New England and the middle states, with routes in the southern and western states, and also in Canada . . . Illustrated with numerous maps and engravings. By W. Williams, New York, D. Appleton and Co., 1847. 1 p.l., 235, [1] p. front., fold. plan, illus., fold maps. 15½ cm.

(2) New York, D. Appleton and Co., 1848.

(3) Appleton's northern and eastern traveller's guide; with new and authentic maps, illustrating those divisions of the country. Forming, likewise, a complete guide to the Middle States, Canada, New Brunswick, and Nova Scotia . . . By W. Williams, New York, D. Appleton and Company, 1850. 313 p. fold. front., illus., fold. maps, fold. plans. 16½ cm.

(4) New York, D. Appleton and Co., 1851. 303 p.

(5) New York, D. Appleton and Co., 1852.

(6) New York, D. Appleton and Co., 1853. 303 p.

(7) New York, D. Appleton and Co., 1854.

Location of copy: University of Kentucky Library.

This is one of the most complete travel guides for the eastern and northern United States and parts of Canada, giving just about all of the information pertinent to rail and water travel in these areas. Also included in the guide are sections pertaining to Washington, the springs of Virginia, and routes to Charleston and New Orleans, but this part of the work is incomplete and rather sketchy (pp. 292–95). The above is the 1849 edition.

433. Williams, Wellington

Appleton's southern and western travellers' guide: with new and authentic maps, illustrating those divisions of the country; and containing sectional maps of the Mississippi and Ohio rivers; with plans of cities, views, etc. Forming a complete guide to the Falls of St. Anthony; Mammoth Cave, Ky., Virginia Springs; the tour of the great rivers of the west: the Great Lakes; the Copper Region of Lake Superior, etc.; and containing full and accurate descriptions of the principal cities, towns, and villages, with distances, fares, etc. By W. Williams. New York, D. Appleton and Company, 1850.

1 p.l., [5]–140 p.   illus., fold. maps, fold. plans.   16½ cm.
Other editions:
New York, D. Appleton and Company, 1854.
Location of copy: University of Kentucky (film copy).

More than one-third of the book gives condensed information on the various items enumerated in the title pertaining to the South (pp. 99–140). Especially significant are the descriptions of the rivers, the cities (including excellent maps of Cincinnati, Louisville, St. Louis, New Orleans, and Charleston), routes and distances between cities, and descriptions of other points of interest such as the Virginia springs, Natural Bridge, and Mammoth Cave. An index is a helpful feature of this guidebook.

434.   Williams, W[ellington]

The traveller's and tourist's guide through the United States, Canada, etc., exhibiting the various routes of travel, with explanatory notes, and other useful information; together with descriptions of, and routes to, the prominent places of fashionable and healthful resort. Accompanied by a valuable and authentic map of the United States. Philadelphia, Lippincott, Grambo and Co., 1855.

iv, [5]–246 p.   fold. map.   14 cm.
Maps: Large folding map of the United States in 1855.
Inclusive dates: 1851.
Other editions:
  (1) The traveller's and tourist's guide through the United States of America, Canada, etc., containing the routes of travel . . . with other useful information . . . By W. Williams. Philadelphia, Lippincott, 1851.
  (2) Philadelphia, Lippincott, 1853.   216 p.
  (3) Philadelphia, Lippincott, 1854.
  (4) Philadelphia, Lippincott, 1855.   iv, [5]–246 p.   14½ cm.
  (5) Philadelphia, Lippincott, 1856.
  (6) Philadelphia, Lippincott, 1858.
  (7) The traveller's and tourist's guide through the United States of America, Canada, etc., containing the routes of travel . . . New and revised edition. Philadelphia, J. B. Lippincott and Co., 1859.   iv, [5]–246 p.   15 cm.
Location of copy: University of Kentucky Library.

One of the features of contemporary time-tables is noted in this travelers' guide, namely, the use of double columns to indicate the distance between each starting point and important cities throughout the United States. In addition to this usual information, Williams also included a tourist guide to "places of fashionable and healthful resort." Those in the South were the Virginia springs, Natural Bridge, Mount Vernon, Warm Springs (N. C.), Mammoth Cave, Drennon Springs (Ky.), Hot Springs (Ark.), and Shannondale Springs (Va.).

435.   Willis, Nathaniel Parker (1806–1867)

Health trip to the tropics, by N. Parker Willis. New York, C. Scribner, 1853.

xiii, [11]–421, xxiii p.   18½ cm.

Inclusive dates: Spring and summer, 1852. In South, May and June, 1852.

Other editions:

London, 1854.

Location of copy: University of Kentucky Library.

When this well-known New York poet, journalist, and traveler left New York in the spring of 1852 seeking a more salubrious climate in the Carribean and the South, he described his journey in a series of forty-three letters written to his business associate, George Pope Morris, who first printed them in the *Home Journal.* They were then published in book form under the title *Health Trip to the Tropics.* Twenty-three of the letters sketch Willis' trip from Cuba to Savannah, Charleston, New Orleans, Mammoth Cave, Harrodsburg Springs, and Lexington. (See the *Dictionary of American Biography.*)

Mammoth Cave, a "mammoth Herculaneum first sepulchered with over-toppling mountains but swept and choked afterwards by the waters of the Deluge," afforded this world traveler an unanticipated opportunity for exercising his descriptive and poetic talents in several letters, for he had arrived in Kentucky thinking that the cave, as an attraction, was probably overrated. His enthusiasm also extended to Harrodsburg Springs and "other points of interest in the state" (Letters 16–26).

Yet in Kentucky, as in other parts of the South, Willis recorded only aspects of life that interested people in the upper strata of society. Although his descriptions of Savannah, Charleston, and New Orleans are delightful, the reader is little aware of the less fortunate classes. In the latter city he noted in some detail "the magnolia-like indolence" of Creole femininity on balconied windows, the physically well-formed quadroons, the alligators, and the boatmen along the levee, "unwashed and half buttoned," too sharp-eyed "to be easy under observation."

The book may be evaluated as an interesting, well written, entertaining, but uncritical travel account.

436.   Wislizenus, Frederick Adolphus [M.D.] (1810–1889)

Memoir of a tour to northern Mexico, connected with Col. Doniphan's expedition, in 1846 and 1847. Washington (Tippin and Stretter, printers), U. S. 30 Cong., 1 sess., Sen. Misc. Doc. 26, 1848.

141 p. fold. plate, 2 fold. maps. 24 cm. (22½ cm.).

Maps: Folding map of tour from Independence to Santa Fé, Chihuahua, Monterey, and Matamoros.

Illustrations: Folding charts giving profile of elevation and geological sketches from Independence (Mo.) to Santa Fé, Chihuahua, and the Río Grande.

Inclusive dates: May 4, 1846, to July, 1847.

Location of copy: University of Kentucky Library.

In the spring of 1846, Dr. F. Adolphus Wislizenus, famous German-born scientist, left Independence with his own expedition to study the geography and natural history of northern Mexico and upper California. En route he spent a week in August in El Paso del Norte, a region which he described in glowing terms as a "most fertile country" with much grain and large quantities of fruits, especially "an excellent grape." The outbreak of the Mexican War forcibly detained him for six months in Chihuahua until the arrival of American troops. He joined Colonel Doniphan's regiment as a physician and returned with it to the "states" by way of Monterey and New Orleans, where he spent a few days in June, 1847.

Wislizenus' report, together with his maps and charts, constituted a valuable contribution to the study of the natural history of southwestern Texas and was ordered in January, 1848, for use of the United States Senate.

437. Witlenborger, J.

Der Rathgeber und Wegweiser für Auswanderer nach den Vereinigten Staaten von Nordamerika und Texas in Beziehung auf Ueberfahrt, Ankunft, Ansiedlung, Arbeitslohn, Boden, Gesundheit, Verfassung, Kanäle, Eisenbahnen Münzen, Maasze, und Gewichte, etc. von J. Witlenborger, Gutsbesitzer im Staat Ohio. 2nd ed., enl. & impr. Heilbronn, C. Dreschler, 1848.

2 l., 141 p., 1 l. fold. map. 14 cm.

Maps: Folding map of United States (German).

Inclusive dates: 1848.

Location of copy: Wisconsin Historical Society.

Valuable information for prospective German immigrants to parts of the South was compressed into this little travel guide, as is indicated by its title. The book is not listed in the *Library of Congress Catalog of Printed Cards,* nor by Sabin. Buck, in his microfilm copy of *Travel and Description, 1765–1865,* states that "no copy of the first edition has been located." Especially significant for Southern travel is the section on the Tennessee Colonization Society of 1848 (pp. 35–52) and the description of each of eleven states recommended for German immigrants. Southern states were Kentucky, Tennessee, Missouri, and especially Texas.

438. Wulfing, Gustavus

The letters of Gustavus Wulfing, collected by his grandson, John Max Wulfing; translated by Carl Hirsch. Printed for private distribution for the Gustavus Wulfing association of St. Louis, Missouri. Fulton, Mo., the Ovid Bell press, inc., 1941.

> 395 p. front., illus. (plans, map), port., facsim. 23 cm.
>
> *Illustrations:* Portraits of Gustavus Wulfing (frontispiece) and one of his wife, Christiane Wulfing; a specimen page of a letter with his signature.
>
> *Inclusive dates:* 1835–1852. In South, 1837–1842.
>
> *Location of copy:* University of Kentucky Library.

Gustavus Wulfing and his family lived in Louisville from 1837–42, following a short stay in Cincinnati after their arrival from Germany. His letters to relatives in Prussia during these five years present a forthright picture of the intimate details of daily family life and the activities of an enterprising merchant who was ever improving his economic status. He moved to St. Louis in 1842 for what proved to be increased business opportunities and in order that his family could "live better in German style," for in Louisville there were only "a few German families" and they were "not well matched." Wulfing's letters are limited in their scope of Southern travel, but they record the activities of a successful German emigrant in Louisville and St. Louis.

439.

A young traveller's journal of a tour in North and South America during the year 1850. With numerous illustrations by the authoress engraved by T. Bolton. Second edition. London, T. Bosworth, 1855.

> xi, 260 p. front., illus. 17 cm.
>
> *Illustrations:* Frontispiece and twelve engravings of American scenes, including a view of the Mississippi River from President Taylor's cotton plantation.
>
> *Inclusive dates:* May 5, 1849, to May 10, 1850. In South, November, 1849, to January, 1850.
>
> *Location of copy:* Mount Holyoke College Library.

Traveling from England accompanied by her mother and a maid, the twelve-year-old daughter of Lady Stuart-Wortley records her day-by-day "childish impressions and observations" in a style that reveals either unusual precocity on the part of the young traveler or editing by a maturer person. The book was intended for children,

[335]

but in many respects it is the equal of many of the travel books of the period.

"V. S. W.," the author's initials used by her in signing her many sketches, visited and sketched points of interest in the East and on the river trip from Pittsburgh to New Orleans en route to Central and South America. She stopped briefly at Louisville, Mammoth Cave, President Taylor's plantation, a Choctaw Indian camp, New Orleans, and Mobile.

No record of the first edition could be found.

PART IV

The South in Sectional Crisis, 1852–1860

INTRODUCTION

TRAVELERS in the South in the decade from 1850–60 were numerous enough, but few of their published accounts possess literary charm or much deep historical value. So wrought up was the nation over slavery that few of the visitors to the region viewed the scene before them with true objectivity. Travelers came with preconceived notions and deep-seated prejudices which blinded them to actual conditions. Their prejudices were not only reflective of personal feelings but of the age itself—an age in which objectivity was difficult to obtain. Reforms, crusades, and isms were characteristic of that prewar America. Passions boiled over into hot disputes, and almost any casual discussion could lead to an impassioned argument.

Abroad and in the North there was underway a crusade for racial readjustment, for justice and toleration, and for a general realignment of society. The crusaders fighting for these ideals were themselves biased, intolerant, and quick of judgment. Obviously many of their conclusions were without validity in fact. It was against this background that much of the travel literature produced in this troubled time was cast. Sectional ideologies, particular social viewpoints, deep-seated antagonisms and prejudices, and the impact of propaganda are all reflected in the travelers' observations.

There were many travelers, of course, who showed a keen awareness of the actualities of life about them. They were able to make wise interpretations of the contemporary scenes and to set their writings in reasonable perspective. Fredrika Bremer was one of these, and her two-volume report, *The Homes of the New World, Impressions of America* (2 vols., New York, 1853), was one of the most important travel books written by a foreigner in this decade. Other foreigners produced commendable travel books, but none was more colorfully descriptive than Charles Mackay's *Life and Liberty in America* (2 vols., London, 1859). Mackay, a journalist and publisher, was well conditioned to view the American scene with insight and understanding.

[339]

Slavery was a focal point of observation. Some travelers visited the South with the avowed purpose of seeing the "unchristian" and "sinful" characteristics of the "peculiar institution," and consequently they closed their eyes and their minds to the more favorable features of Negro servitude. Perhaps the most prejudiced observers were the American abolitionists. Charles Grandison Parsons was typical of this group of travelers. When he was unable to find the anticipated horrors of slavery, he accused masters of teaching their slaves to be deceitful. Although Parson's book, *Inside View of Slavery, or a Tour among the Planters* (Boston, 1855), gave a distorted view of Southern conditions, it characterized abolitionist propaganda.

Fortunately for the historian, there were objective travelers from both the North and Europe who recorded more sensible interpretations of the slave regime. The most important of these was Frederick Law Olmsted, the New York landscape architect, who wrote three long books on the South during 1853 and 1854. Olmsted's works are examined with some detail in the bibliography, but it should be suggested here that his volumes contained the most complete picture of the *rural* South in print at the time of their publication. The Olmsted books have become classics among travel literature related to the ante bellum South.

Slavery, while highly publicized, was, of course, only one feature of Southern life, and the more observant travelers left interesting accounts of the social, political, and economic life of the people. Information pertaining to manners and morals, church services, the theater, sports, music, food, and agricultural and commercial pursuits may be gleaned by the discerning historian from the travel books of the period.

Travel literature for this decade constitutes an important body of contemporary materials. As has been suggested above, the tenor of much of it was of a special-interest nature. Some of it was vicious, some was distorted by lack of information, but most of it reflected the spirit of the age. There are possibly no other sources to which a historian can turn which will reveal so humanly the anxieties and uncertainties of this pre-Civil-War period. Into all this literature there creeps a sense of a great nation in the throes of both economic and social change. If the conflict of sectional war was inevitable as some historians have claimed, then the essence of that inevitability is reflected in contemporary observations. On the other hand, the core of factual and trustworthy materials which are to be gleaned from this mass of published literature removes much of the aura of romance with which a contemporary generation might be tempted to view this past decade.

F. GARVIN DAVENPORT
Monmouth College

440.　Abbott, John Stevens Cabot (1805–1877)

South and North; or, impressions received during a trip to Cuba and the South. By John S. C. Abbott . . . New York, Abbey & Abbott, 1860.

iv, 352 p.　18½ cm.

Inclusive dates: December, 1859.

Location of copy: Joint University Libraries, Nashville, Tennessee.

John Stevens Cabot Abbott was a citizen of Maine, a Congregational clergyman, a historian, and an educator. He was probably best known for his *The History of the Civil War in America* (New York, 1863–65; also a German edition, Norwich, New York, 1863–65).

Abbott entered the South at New Orleans and subsequently visited Mobile, Montgomery, Atlanta, Augusta, and Wilmington (N. C.). The chief characteristic of all of Abbott's publications was extravagant exaggeration, and this book on the South is no exception. He became emotional over the miserable condition of the poor whites and the Negroes, but he never saw the yeoman farmer. Atrocity stories equal to the best the abolitionists could invent were presented with emphasis, but at the same time he admitted that there were many in the North who wished they owned slaves or who wanted to engage in the slave trade. He made a few interesting comments on Southern politicians.

Except as a typical example of distorted observation, this book has no value.

Abbott referred to H. R. Helper, *The Impending Crisis of the South* (New York, 1857). For a contemporary British point of view, see Henry Ashworth, Esq., *A Tour in the United States, Cuba, and Canada* (London, 1861).

441.　Adams, Nehemiah (1806–1878)

A south-side view of slavery; or, three months at the South, in 1854. By Nehemiah Adams, D.D. Boston, T. R. Marvin, [etc.], 1854.

viii, 7–214 p.　18 cm.

Inclusive dates: 1854 (from internal evidence probably April, May, and June).

Other editions:

(1) 3d ed. Boston, T. R. Marvin; N. Y., J. C. Derby, 1855.　viii, 7–222 p. 17½ cm.

(2) 3d ed. Richmond, Va., A. Morris, 1855.

(3) 4th ed. Boston, Ticknor and Fields, 1860. vi, 7–224 p. 18½ cm.

Location of copy: University of Kentucky Library.

Dr. Nehemiah Adams was a well known Boston Congregational minister and author. He was especially interested in evangelical orthodoxy, and many of his publications were concerned with this doctrine. When he left New England to visit the South in 1854 he was a confirmed abolitionist, and one of his last acts before boarding the ship for Savannah was to sign the remonstrance of the New England clergymen against the extension of slavery into the proposed territories of Kansas and Nebraska.

He entered the South at Savannah, expecting to find slavery untenable and the Negroes victims of an inhumane system. He tried to persuade himself that his original theories were correct, but after personal observation in Georgia, South Carolina, and Virginia he concluded that the abolitionists had exaggerated conditions in the South. Although he disapproved of slavery, Dr. Adams found the slaves well treated and contented. He believed that public opinion was a strong factor in protecting the slaves from injurious treatment. He justified the Southern prohibition of abolitionist publications from the mail.

This is an interesting book of minor importance. The picture of slavery is too superficial and there is little data on Southern life in general.

Compare Adams' book with Philo Tower, *Slavery Unmasked* (Rochester, 1856). Tower was as hostile to slavery as Adams was friendly. See also C. G. Parsons, *Inside View of Slavery* (Boston, 1855).

442. Ampère, Jean Jacques Antoine (1800–1864)

Promenade en Amérique; États-Unis–Cuba–Mexique, par J. J. Ampère . . . 2 vols. Paris, Michel Lévy frères, 1855.

Vol. I, 421 p.; Vol. II, 425 p. 22 cm.

Inclusive dates: 1851.

Other editions:

(1) Nouv. éd., entièrement rev. Paris, Michel Lévy frères, 1856.

(2) Nouv. éd., entièrement revue. Paris, Michel Lévy frères, 1860.

(3) 3d edition. Paris, Lévy frères, 1860.

(4) Nouv. éd., entièrement revue. Paris, Michel Lévy frères, 1867.

(5) Nouv. éd., illustrée par les principaux artistes. Paris, Michel Lévy frères, [etc.], 1874. 2 p.l., xliii, 299 p. front. (port.), illus., plates. 27 cm.

Location of copy: University of Kentucky Library.

Jean Jacques Ampère was a teacher, historian, philologist, authority on Scandinavian and German epic poetry, and a member of the French Academy. He made a grand tour of Canada, the United States, Cuba, and Mexico. He traveled south from Washington through Virginia and mentioned such towns as Charleston and New Orleans. He was not in the South long enough to observe Southern life in detail. Only sixty pages in his two-volume work are devoted to what he saw in the Southern states. He showed some interest in cotton, slaves, humane planters, a sugar refinery, and hotels. He was interested also in meeting American and Southern philologists, and he commented on scientific interests around New Orleans.

Aside from its French point of view, this book throws little light on Southern life. For more detailed descriptions, see Fredrika Bremer, *The Homes of the New World;* Charles Mackay, *Life and Liberty in America;* and Frederick Law Olmsted, *A Journey in the Seaboard Slave States,* which are listed in this section.

443. Ashworth, Henry (1794–1880)

A tour in the United States, Cuba, and Canada. By Henry Ashworth, esq. A course of lectures delivered before the members of the Bolton mechanics' institution. London, A. W. Bennett; ʀetc., etc.ʀ, 1861.

> 198 p. 18½ cm.
> *Inclusive dates:* January to June, 1857.
> *Other editions:*
> Recollections of a tour in the United States of America, Canada, and Cuba; delivered before the members of the Bolton mechanics' institute . . . Reprinted from *The Bolton Chronicle.* Bolton, James Hudsmith, 1859. 45 p. 8vo.
> *Location of copy:* University of Kentucky Library.

Henry Ashworth was a founder of the Anti-Corn Law League, friend of Cobden, successful manufacturer, student of agriculture, traveler, and writer.

He entered the South at New Orleans after a visit to Cuba. He gave a detailed description of New Orleans and some interesting data on the school system in Louisville; otherwise most of his descriptive material pertained to agriculture, travel conditions, and slavery. Ashworth presented objectively the case of the proslavery group, and he was impressed by the paternal attitude of planters toward their slaves. He was interested in plantation finance and soil exhaustion. He recognized the yeoman farmers of Tennessee, and he exploded the traditional theory that planters lived a life of ease. On the contrary he discovered that both the planter and his wife frequently worked with extreme diligence and perseverance to overcome obstacles and hardships.

Ashworth was well informed and made some interesting comparisons between Southern cotton culture and that of India. He believed that as long as England enjoyed the benefit of Southern cotton, the English people should not say too much against slavery. It is this logical, common-sense attitude which makes the book valuable.

The material in this book first appeared as a series of lectures in *The Bolton Chronicle.*

The Scotsman, James Stirling, traveled in America at about the same time. See his travel book, *Letters From the Slave States.* See also J. J. Ampère, *Promenade en Amérique.* (Both are listed in this section.) Like Ashworth, Ampère found the planters of the South rather humane when dealing with slaves.

For obituaries, see the *Manchester Guardian,* of May 19, 1880, and the London *Times* of May 20, 1880.

444. Baxter, William Edward (1825–1890)

America and the Americans. By W. E. Baxter . . . London, New York, G. Routledge & co., 1855.

2 p.l., 244 p.   16½ cm.
Inclusive dates: 1846, 1853–1854.
Location of copy: Columbia University Library.

William Edward Baxter was a British merchant and politician. He visited the United States in 1846 and again in 1853–54. After his second and more extensive visit he wrote *America and the Americans.* He traveled over ten thousand miles in the United States, but it is impossible to trace his route since the book does not represent a continuous narrative of the author's wanderings. Instead, Baxter presented a series of essays representing what he considered general observations on American life.

With respect to the South the book contains little reliable information. In fact, the South, except for river boats and slavery, is brought into the text only incidentally. The author described American literary production but did not mention a single Southern writer, not even Poe. Although the author maintained that he was unprejudiced and objective, he did not live up to this claim. There are many ridiculous statements, such as the following: "The stranger may find in the negro-cabins by the wayside in Kentucky . . . little libraries containing the best works of Scott and Byron, Wordsworth and Southey, Chalmers and Hall, Marryatt and Bulwer Lytton" (pp. 84–85).

He quotes several contemporary travelers, including Alexander Mackay, *The Western World* (in Part III, Number 353); Fredrika Bremer, *The Homes of the New World* (listed below); and Charles Lyell, *Second Visit to the United States* (in Part III, Number 352). All of these travel books are superior to Baxter's.

445. Beauvallet, Léon

Rachel and the new world. A trip to the United States and Cuba. Tr. from the French of Léon Beauvallet. New York, Dix, Edwards & co., 1856.

> 2 p.l., ₍iii₎–xiv, 404 p.   18 cm.
> *Inclusive dates:* August, 1855, to January, 1856.
> *Other editions:*
>   Rachel et le nouveau monde, promenade aux États-Unis et aux Antilles. Paris, A. Cadot, 1856. viii, 304 p. 16mo.
> *Location of copy:* Columbia University Library.

This Frenchman was a member of Rachel Felix's opera troop which toured America in 1855–56. The company entered the South via Fredericksburg and stopped at Richmond, Petersburg, Wilmington, and Charleston. Beauvallet was not impressed by the "filthy towns," although Charleston had more appeal than the others. He reported that the slaves were generally happy. Only a dozen pages are devoted to the South. The approach is rather superficial.

446. Benwell, J.

An Englishman's travels in America: his observations of life and manners in the free and slave states. By J. Benwell. London, Binns and Goodwin; ₍etc., etc., 1853₎.

> vii, 231 p. col. front. 17 cm.
> *Inclusive dates:* 1852.
> *Other editions:*
>   London, Ward and Lock, ₍1857₎.
> *Location of copy:* Tennessee State Library.

Benwell entered the South via the Mississippi River. He took a river boat at St. Louis and passed Memphis, Vicksburg, and Natchez on his way to New Orleans. Later he visited Florida, going to such towns as Tallahassee and Fort Andrews, and he finally reached Charleston. He observed little in the towns through which he passed and accepted as truth what irresponsible passengers told him. He was impressed with the wildlife, scenery, and river traffic on the Mississippi but seemed to imagine slave gallows every few rods along the riverbank. He saw only the worst features of slavery and reported that the slaveowners believed that the only way to keep the slaves under control was by means of harsh treatment.

In general, this book represents an intolerant mind and a superficial observer. However, the descriptions of life in Florida, usually overlooked by the travelers of the period, give it a special value. The author described Indian problems, tobacco culture, wildlife, and climatic conditions as they existed in that state.

447. [Bishop, Isabella Lucy Bird] "Mrs. J. F. Bishop" (1831–1904)

The Englishwoman in America. London, John Murray, 1856.

vii, 464 p. 19½ cm.
Inclusive dates: Probably from August, 1854, to December, 1855; the internal evidence is confusing.
Location of copy: University of Kentucky Library.

Mrs. Isabella Lucy Bird Bishop was unknown when she first visited the United States in 1854. Later she became a well known traveler, writer, and reformer.

Her book has no value for students of Southern life because her penetration of the South did not go beyond "a peep into Kentucky." She spent a few hours in Covington and gave an uncomplimentary picture of that town. She was opposed to slavery but did not take time to examine the institution. Mrs. Bishop's ideas on this subject were based on the reading of abolitionist literature and on interviews with Northerners.

448. Bosshard, Heinrich

Auschauungen und Erfahrungen in Nordamerika. Eine Monatsschrift. 3 vols. Zürich, Druck von Zürcher und Furrer, 1853–1855.

Vol. II, plate; Vol. III, col. map. 17 cm.
Maps: Colored map of the U. S. in pocket of Vol. III.
Illustrations: Surveyor's chart of a Wisconsin township in Vol. II.
Inclusive dates: 1853–1855.
Location of copy: Newberry Library.

The contents of this book were prepared as a series of monthly letters published in Zurich from 1853 to 1855. Bosshard was interested primarily in the Midwest, especially Iowa, but he also wrote several letters from Florida during his visit there in 1854. Most of these letters emphasized conditions around Appalachicola. Bosshard made comments about the climate, value of the land, and the sale and transportation of cotton. He also observed the turpentine industry and the native plants such as indigo. The letters from Florida are interesting because very few travelers made detailed observations on this section of the South at this time.

449. Bowen, Eli (b. 1824)

Rambles in the path of the steam-horse. An off-hand olla podrida, embracing a general historical and descriptive view of the scenery, agricultural and mineral resources, and prominent features of the travelled route from Baltimore to Harper's Ferry, Cumberland, Wheeling, Cincinnati, and Louisville. By Ele[!] Bowen . . . Philadelphia, W. Bromwell and W. W. Smith; Baltimore, S. B. Hickcox, agent, 1855.

3 p.l., v–viii, 432 p., incl. illus., plates.   23.3 cm.
Illustrations: 16 full-page sketches and engravings and numerous smaller sketches, wood engravings, and plans. The author did some of the wood engravings; David H. Strother and others did the rest. The engravings were executed by Louduback of Philadelphia. There is no frontispiece, but the title page is done in color (engraved).
Inclusive dates: 1852–1854?
Location of copy: Harvard University Library.

This is a combination travel book and history of the Baltimore and Ohio Railroad in the early days. The author admits his indebtedness to many persons for his details on slavery, coal mining, geologic formations, and commerce. The main value of the book is to be found in the illustrations of trains, stations, bridges, and track construction. There is some interesting material on train crews and their duties, mining equipment, the maple sugar industry, and Ohio River commerce. The towns described include Baltimore, Frederick, Harpers Ferry, Cumberland, Wheeling, Cincinnati, Newport, Covington, and Louisville.

Several other travelers passed over a similar route about the same time, and William Chambers, *Things as They Are in America* (listed below), might be used for comparison. Amelia Murray, in *Letters from the United States* (listed below), made some interesting comments on American railroads in general. Bowen himself quotes George Tinker, *Life of Jefferson,* and apparently received some of his ideas on slavery from this biography. He also knew the works of the English traveler Charles Lyell.

450. Bremer, Fredrika (1801–1865)

The homes of the New World; impressions of America. By Fredrika

Bremer. Tr. by Mary Howitt . . . 2 vols. New York, Harper & brothers, 1853.

Vol. I, xii, 651 p.; Vol. II, 654 p.   19 cm.

Inclusive dates: October, 1849, to September, 1851.

Other editions:

(1) 3 vols. London, A. Hall, Virtue & co., 1853. 1346 p. fronts. 20 cm.

(2) 2 vols. New York, Harper & brothers, 1854. 20 cm.

(3) Hemmen i den Nya Verlden. En dagbok i bref, skrifna under tvenne års resor i Norra Amerika och på Cuba . . . 1.–3. delen. 3 vols. Stockholm, P. A. Norstedt & söner, 1853–54. 17 cm.

(4) Die Heimath in der Neuen Welt. Ein Tagebuch in Briefen, geschrieben während zweijähriger Reisen in Nordamerika und auf Cuba . . . Stuttgart, 1853. 24 pts. in 3 vols. Vol. I, x, 462 p.; Vol. II, xiv, 520 p.; Vol. III, xiv, 534 p. (Das belletristische Ausland, Berlin, 2009–2023, 2114–2122).

(5) De Nieuwe Wereld (Homes of the new world) Naar Fr. Bremer door S. J. van den Bergh. Haarlem, A. C. Krusemen, 1854. 2 pts. 2 plates. 8vo.

Location of copy: University of Kentucky Library.

Fredrika Bremer was one of the best known and one of the most influential Swedish women of the nineteenth century. She was a novelist, social worker, humanitarian, and traveler. Considered the ugly duckling of her own family, she nevertheless inspired admiration for herself and a love for humanity in all those with whom she associated.

The author came to America in 1849 for a two-year sojourn. During these years she traveled extensively throughout the United States and Cuba—always welcomed, always graciously received. She entered the South via the Ohio River route, stopping at, or at least passing by, such cities as Cincinnati, Memphis, Baton Rouge, New Orleans, Mobile, Havana, Charleston, Savannah, Charlottesville, and Richmond. Being a kindhearted (but not sentimental) woman, there were times when she was not as critical of the American way of life as she would have liked to have been, fearing, no doubt, that she might offend the people who had received her with such a show of hospitality. Even so, there were times when she wrote with extreme frankness. Generally speaking, Fredrika Bremer's comments on Southern life were wholesome, intelligent, womanly, and sometimes witty. She was able to examine slavery with considerable objectivity, and while she earnestly prayed for eventual abolition, she was quick to point out what she considered to be the more desirable features of the institution. For example, she was convinced that Anglo-American culture had exercised a deep, beneficial influence on the Negro. But the great mission of the American people with respect to the colored race should not stop here. Having enslaved and improved the Negroes, they should continue the process to the only reasonable

[349]

culmination—emancipation. She was not impressed with the African Colonization Movement, believing that the freed Negroes would be more contented and better able to make their contribution to society by remaining in the South. She had little sympathy for the methods employed by Northern abolitionists and expressed the opinion, especially with reference to Virginia slaves, that this violent movement had interfered with the normal process of manumission. At the same time she pointed out that many Virginians were hypocritical, not only where slavery was concerned, but also with respect to other social evils in the state, including the condition of some of the jails and prisons.

In addition to slavery, this intelligent and observant traveler described various phases of Southern social life, including the opera, theater, domestic life and customs, church services, hotels, public markets, architecture, manners, and the personal appearance and characteristics of the people. Her appreciation of nature was reflected in fine descriptive passages devoted to the scenery that she observed. Her description of New Orleans was critical but more complete than that of any other traveler of this period. Of special interest was her account of a Negro church service. Some of her comments on Southern white women are priceless.

Fredrika Bremer's early travel records were written as letters and were originally not intended for publication. After her return to Sweden, she decided to share her notes and her thoughts with her public. The result was *Hemmen i den Nya Verlden* (Homes of the New World). The letters had a literary charm that was unusual in travel literature.

Selections from the letters were made by Adolph B. Benson and published as Volume XXIII in the Scandinavian Classics series, under the title *America of the Fifties: Letters of Fredrika Bremer* (New York, 1924). Benson's critical introduction to this volume is scholarly and informative.

Charles Mackay (*Life and Liberty in America,* [listed below]) followed approximately the same route. Some of his descriptions, especially of New Orleans, contradicted Fredrika Bremer's. However, he agreed with her that the slaves enjoyed more physical comforts than many European peasants.

451. Chambers, William (1800–1883)

American slavery and colour, by William Chambers . . . London, W. & R. Chambers; New York, Dix and Edwards, 1857.

2 p.l., 216 p. front. (map). 21 cm.
Maps: Map of the free and slave states.
Inclusive dates: September, 1853, to December, 1853.
Other editions:
   London, W. & R. Chambers; New York, Dix and Edwards, 1861. 2 p.l.,
220 p. front. (map), tables. 20.4 cm.
Location of copy: University of Kentucky Library.

William Chambers was well known in Scotland as an author and
publisher of low-priced journals and books for the middle and lower
classes. He possessed no special literary ability, but he could write
in a plain and interesting manner. He published his first travel book,
Tour in Holland and the Rhine Countries, in 1839.

A large portion of *American Slavery and Colour* was devoted to
a review of the historical facts concerning slavery in the United
States, quotations from American newspapers and periodicals, and
speeches of public men. This book was not written according to the
accepted formula for travel accounts but was, in a sense, a sequel to
his earlier book, *Things as They Are in America* (listed below),
which was the actual record of his trip to the United States in 1853.
Except for Covington, Kentucky, and Richmond, Virginia, Chambers saw little of the South. Therefore, this book expresses the author's
views on slavery, but it does not represent firsthand information. He
ridiculed the part of the proslavery argument which declared that
slavery conferred a spiritual benefit on its victims. On the other hand,
he believed that the abolitionists themselves were hypocrites.

Chambers admired the works of Frederick Law Olmsted, especially his *Journey in the Seaboard Slave States* (listed below). One
of his sources was George Fitzhugh, *Sociology for the South* (Richmond, 1854). For statistics he relied on Henry Chase and Charles W.
Sanborn, *The North and The South; A Statistical View of Conditions
of the Free and Slave States* (Boston, 1856).

452.   Chambers, William (1800–1883)

Things as they are in America, by William Chambers. London and
Edinburgh, W. & R. Chambers, 1854.

   vi, 364 p. 19.3 cm.
Inclusive dates: September, 1853, to December, 1853.
Other editions:
   Philadelphia, Lippincott, Grambo, and company, 1854.
Location of copy: University of Kentucky Library.

This was William Chambers' first book on America. A discussion
of slavery was published by the same author in 1857 under the title
American Slavery and Colour (see above).

Since the author barely touched the South, this book is of secondary importance. He described the meat-packing industry at Covington, Kentucky, hastily surveyed Virginia agricultural methods, and witnessed a slave auction in Richmond. After casual examination he pictured Virginia agriculture unfavorably. Chambers thought most travelers exaggerated the tobacco chewing of American men, and he believed Irish immigrants would soon replace Negroes as domestic servants in the South.

Chambers' second book, *American Slavery and Colour,* should be consulted for his opinions on slavery, although they were not made from actual observation. Fredrika Bremer (*The Homes of the New World,* listed above) visited the United States at about the same time. She made a more extensive tour and recorded more detailed observations of life in the South.

Chambers was acquainted with J. C. Nott and G. R. Glidden, *Types of Mankind* (Philadelphia, 1854), and reported that both Northerners and Southerners were inclined to look on the Negro as inferior to other races.

453. [Clinton, Charles A.?]

A winter from home. New-York, J. F. Trow, printer, 1852.

60 p. 18½ cm.
Inclusive dates: Winter of 1851–1852.
Location of copy: Columbia University Library.

Although extremely brief, this little book of sixty pages was well written by an alert observer. The author entered the South via the Potomac, traveled to New Orleans, and returned to the North via the Mississippi River. He passed through Richmond, Petersburg, Wilmington (N. C.), Charleston, Savannah, St. Augustine, Tallahassee, Macon, Montgomery, Mobile, New Orleans, and Memphis. Over half of the book was devoted to a description of conditions in northern Florida, with special emphasis on St. Augustine, the resort springs and watering places, difficulties of travel, forest fires, and food and produce. In general he found the slaves well treated, slave dealers despised, and the life of the planter monotonous.

The chief value of the book is to be found in the detailed description of meats, vegetables, and fruits, native and imported, that were available in Southern markets and in the pantries of the well to do.

Clinton passed Louis Kossuth and his companions, Ferencz and Theresa Pulszky (*q.v.*), on the way.

454. Cobb, Joseph Beckham (1819–1858)

Mississippi scenes; or, sketches of southern and western life and adventure, humorous, satirical, and descriptive, including the legend of Black Creek. By Joseph B. Cobb ... Philadelphia, A. Hart, 1851.

> vii, [13]–250 p. 20½ cm.
> *Inclusive dates:* Before 1851.
> *Other editions:*
> 2 ed. ... Philadelphia, A. Hart, 1851.
> *Location of copy:* Harvard University Library.

This is not a true travel book. It consists mostly of reminiscences and essays supposedly drawn from "real scenes and characters." The author remarks "the models and incidents are alone borrowed and embellished." The locale of the book is Columbus, Mississippi, and its environment. There is an interesting but embellished description of Sol Smith.

For a more thorough interpretation of the region, see Olmsted, *A Journey in the Back Country in the Winter of 1853–4* (listed below); for a lighter point of view, see J. H. Ingraham (ed.), *The Sunny South* (Philadelphia, 1860).

455. Comettant, Jean Pierre Oscar (1819–1898)

Trois ans aux États-Unis; étude des moeurs et coutumes américaines, par M. Oscar Comettant. Paris, Pagnerre, 1857.

> 2 p.l., 364 p. 18½ cm.
> *Inclusive dates:* 1852–1855.
> *Other editions:*
> (1) Deuxième édition, revue et corrigée. Paris, Pagnerre, 1858. 1 p.l., 389, [2] p. 17½ cm.
> (2) Tres ãnos en los Estados-Unidos. Estudio de los habitos y costumbres americanas, por Oscar Comettant. Tr. del francés por los señores d. Santiago Infante de Palacios y d. Federico Utrera, con un estenso prólogo por los traductores. Veracruz, imprenta veracruzana, 1859. 1 p.l., iii, 278 p., 1 l. 21½ cm.
> *Location of copy:* Columbia University Library.

Monsieur Comettant was a prolific writer and published several travel books in addition to the above. He wrote an interesting book on social life in the United States. He was especially interested in amusements, the theater, and music and made some interesting comments on such figures as P. T. Barnum and Jenny Lind. He followed the usual route into the South via Charleston and across the Gulf States to New Orleans. He gave a vivid description of New Orleans' social and religious customs, barroom etiquette, and the Code Duello. A unique feature of the book was a comparison of the typical Yankee type with the typical Virginian.

There were certain features of slavery which Comettant emphasized, such as punishments and rewards and the practice of hiring out certain slaves not needed on the plantation. The author observed that in Louisiana slaves who misbehaved were sent to a place of correction called "the sugar house." At this establishment the slave presented a ticket from his master which stated the nature of the offense and the number of strokes with the lash which he was to receive. Comettant observed that there was little if any pity for the slaves, that they were regarded as property and not as human beings.

This is an interesting book of secondary importance. Comparisons should be made with Frederick Law Olmsted, *A Journey in the Back Country,* and Charles Mackay, *Life and Liberty in America,* both of which are listed below.

456. Cornwallis, Kinahan (1839–1917)

Royalty in the new world; or, the Prince of Wales in America. By Kinahan Cornwallis . . . New York, M. Doolady, 1860.

> xii, 286 p. front. (port.). 17.9 cm.
> *Illustrations:* Frontispiece: H. R. H. the Prince of Wales, from a photograph by Brady.
> *Inclusive dates:* July 10, 1860, to November 15, 1860.
> *Location of copy:* The New York Public Library.

Cornwallis was one of several traveling companions who accompanied the Prince of Wales on his American visit. There is little information on the South. The royal party visited Mount Vernon and later landed at Acquia Creek, Virginia, and went on to Richmond and Petersburg. Cornwallis gave a brief description of the party (including President Buchanan and his cabinet) which accompanied the Prince to Mount Vernon. He commented briefly on fashions and the reception given the Prince by the mayor of Richmond.

For parallel accounts (lacking in detail), see Henry James Morgan, *The Tour of H.R.H. the Prince of Wales through British America and the United States* and Gardner D. Engleheart, *Journal of the Progress of H.R.H. the Prince of Wales through British North America; and His Visit to the United States.* Both are listed below.

457. Crowe, Eyre (1824–1910)

With Thackeray in America. By Eyre Crowe . . . New York, C. Scribner's sons, 1893.

> xvi p., 1 l., 179 p., incl. front., illus. 21 cm.
> *Illustrations:* In addition to the frontispiece showing Thackeray lecturing in

New York, there are 116 sketches of American life and personalities, made by the author.

Inclusive dates: November, 1852, to April, 1853.
Other editions:
    London, ₍etc.₎, Cassell and co., 1893. xii, 179, ₍1₎ p., incl. front., illus. 22½ cm.
Location of copy: Louisville Free Public Library.

This is a delightful book, but its chief value lies in the author's sketches of American life in the early fifties. Unfortunately there is little on the South—only about thirty pages of text. However, the following illustrations are interesting: "Testing Tobacco" and "An American Barber's" (Richmond scenes), "On the Banks of the Appomattox" (Petersburg), "A Negro Ball" (Charleston), "Easter Monday" (Petersburg), "At the Charleston Hotel," "Shopping" (Charleston), and "A Group of Market Women" (Charleston).

The text may be ignored but the pictures are indispensable. The author related that Thackeray was well received in Richmond, lionized in Charleston, and ignored in Petersburg.

Fredrika Bremer traveled in the South at about the same time. For details on social life, see her *The Homes of the New World,* listed above. She described in words what Crowe reproduced in his sketches.

458.   Cunynghame, Sir Arthur Augustus Thurlow (1812–1884)

A glimpse at the great western republic. By Lieut.-Col. Arthur Cunynghame ... London, R. Bentley, 1851.

    2 p.l., 337, ₍1₎ p.   22 cm.
Inclusive dates: September to November, 1850.
Other editions:
    London, R. Bentley, 1863.
Location of copy: Columbia University Library.

Cunynghame was a British Army man. He entered the South via the Mississippi route and passed through St. Louis, Memphis, Napoleon (Ark.), Natchez, New Orleans, Mobile, Stockton (Ala.), Montgomery, Macon, Savannah, Charleston, Wilmington, and Richmond.

He noted that the South had better food and wine than the North and that slavery, while mild, was a curse. He observed the scenery, wildlife, methods of transportation, country inns, and Irish laborers. The highlight of the book as far as the South was concerned was

Cunynghame's description of New Orleans, including details on hotels, churches, cemeteries, markets, gardens, dances, and sports.

The book has definite limitations, but it may be considered one of the better minor travel accounts.

459. De Cordova, Jacob

Lecture on Texas delivered by Mr. J. De Cordova . . . Also, a paper read by him before the New York geographical society, April 15th, 1858 . . . Philadelphia, Printed by E. Crozet, 1858.

> 32 p. 18.2 cm.
> *Inclusive dates:* 1838 (?)–1858.
> *Location of copy:* The New York Public Library.

De Cordova had lived in Texas for twenty years. His lecture, which was delivered in New York, Brooklyn, Newark, Mount Holly, and Philadelphia, was intended to promote emigration to the Southwest. The author gave brief but interesting information on population, education, religion, clubs, banks, labor, agriculture, transportation, and climate. He advised old maids to stay away from Texas.

460. Edwards, Richard, ed.

Statistical gazetteer of the state of Virginia, embracing important topographical and historical information from recent and original sources, together with the results of the last census population, in most cases, to 1854. Edited by Richard Edwards . . . Richmond, for the proprietor, 1855.

> 2 p.l., [53]–456 p. illus. 23½ cm.
> *Maps:* Colored map of Virginia in 1855, with insets of Richmond and Norfolk. Map published by J. H. Colton and co., N. Y.
> *Illustrations:* Illustrated advertisements.
> *Inclusive dates:* 1855.
> *Other editions:*
>   Statistical gazetteer of the states of Virginia and North Carolina . . . Richmond, pub. for the proprietor, 1856. 6 p.l., 601 p. illus. 23½ cm.
> *Location of copy:* Harvard University.

This is not a travel book but a detailed guide to Virginia. Every town and village of any importance is named and located. There are numerous statistics on economic life.

A more extensive interpretation of Virginia can be obtained from Frederick Law Olmsted, *A Journey in the Seaboard Slave States* (listed below).

461. Engleheart, Sir John Gardner Dillman (1823–1923)

Journal of the progress of H.R.H. the Prince of Wales through British North America; and his visit to the United States, 10th July to 15th November, 1860. By Gardner D. Engleheart . . . ⌈London⌉, priv. print., ⌈1860?⌉. (Sabin gives 1861).

> 3 p.l., 110 p., 1 l. illus., 9 plates (incl. front.), 2 fold. maps. 20½ cm.
> *Maps:* Two: Route of the Prince; the North Atlantic.
> *Illustrations:* Numerous sketches in black and white and tinted scenes of the United States and Canada.
> *Inclusive dates:* July 10 to November 15, 1860.
> *Location of copy:* The New York Public Library.

Engleheart was the private secretary to the Duke of Newcastle. He missed a fine opportunity to write an interesting travel book. There is very little on the South. There is a brief description of the Presidential party which escorted the Prince into Virginia, along with a few lines on Richmond.

Henry James Morgan's *The Tour of H. R. H. The Prince of Wales* (listed below) is no better. For a few more details, see Kinahan Cornwallis, *Royalty in the New World* (listed above).

462. Everest, Robert

A journey through the United States and part of Canada. By the Rev. Robert Everest . . . London, J. Chapman, 1855.

> xi, 178 p. 21 cm.
> *Inclusive dates:* Probably winter of 1854–1855.
> *Location of copy:* The New York Public Library.

Everest was a chaplain of the East India Company. He entered the South via the Ohio Valley and passed through Louisville, Frankfort, Vicksburg, Jackson, Baton Rouge, New Orleans, Mobile, Montgomery, Columbia, Wilmington, and Richmond.

The author recorded a variety of facts pertaining to social and economic conditions. He was opposed to slavery but reported that the plantation slaves were as well off as rural laborers in England. He gave a detailed description of New Orleans including statistics on crime. His impressions of dueling, card playing, dancing, river boats, roads, jails, cotton, and wildlife in the South are vivid. This is an interesting book for "atmosphere."

463. Ferguson, William

America by river and rail; or, notes by the way on the New world and its people. By William Ferguson, F.L.S. . . . London, J. Nisbet and co., 1856.

> viii, 511 p. 2 plates (incl. front.). 20.9 cm.
> *Illustrations:* One plate represents Horseshoe Fall, Niagara, by Charles A. Ferrier.
> *Inclusive dates:* February to July, 1855.
> *Location of copy:* Louisville Free Public Library.

Only a small portion of this voluminous work is devoted to the South. The author entered the South via Richmond and passed through Petersburg, Wilmington (N. C.), and Charleston. Most of his observations were made about Charleston.

Ferguson was generally friendly toward the South. He made some interesting comments on the superstitions of the Negroes, their treatment, and their churches and Sunday schools. He reported that treatment of the slaves varied even in a small area. He was opposed to the methods employed by abolitionists but disapproved of slavery. He reported that South Carolina planters believed that slavery was doomed.

The book is interesting but somewhat superficial and is of only minor importance. Compare Ferguson's comments on South Carolina slavery with those of Nehemiah Adams, *A South-Side View of Slavery* (listed above).

464. Foley, Rev. Daniel, D.D.

The people and institutions of the United States of America; a summer vacation tour. Dublin and London, George Herbert (Dublin); James Nisbet and co. (London), 1858.

> 79 p. 18½ cm.
> *Inclusive dates:* August to October, 1857.
> *Other editions:*
> Account of the people and institutions of the United States of America, from personal observations, during a three months' summer tour, in 1857. London, 1858.
> *Location of copy:* Newberry Library.

Foley made a brief tour through Delaware, Maryland, and Virginia, where he visited Mount Vernon. He called slavery "the disgrace of the American people" and expressed the opinion that it would eradicate itself because it did not pay. He admitted that the slaves were well treated. He actually saw very little of the slave system but based his opinions on conversations with free Negroes in the North, a few slaves in Virginia, and whites in the North and South.

465. Foster, Lillian

Way-side glimpses, north and south. By Lillian Foster. New York, Rudd & Carleton, 1860.

> xi, [13]–250 p.   18.6 cm.
> *Inclusive dates:* July, 1853, to July, 1859.
> *Location of copy:* University of Kentucky Library.

This book was written in the letter form made popular by Fredrika Bremer in *The Homes of the New World* (listed above), but it falls far short of the Bremer contribution both as literature and as a travel book. *The Homes of the New World* made literary history, while *Way-Side Glimpses* was intended to be an intelligent travel guide for the businessman. On various trips during a six-year period the author managed to cover the South, and, in addition to descriptions of such towns as Louisville, Vicksburg, Memphis, New Orleans, and Charleston, she included other towns frequently overlooked by travelers, such as Frankfort, Kentucky, Nashville, Tennessee, Columbus and Augusta, Georgia, and Columbia, South Carolina.

This book is of secondary importance. Most of the descriptions and observations are superficial. Lillian Foster exhibited a definite race prejudice, so her favorable impressions of Negro slavery are of little value. She was at her best when describing the social activities on the Mississippi river boats.

Charles Mackay (*Life and Liberty in America*, [listed below]) traveled over similar routes, and his report on American life and customs should be compared with the observations made by Lillian Foster.

466. Grattan, Thomas Colley (1792–1864)

Civilized America. 2 vols. London, Bradbury and Evans, 1859.

> Vol. I, xix, 444 p.; Vol. II, vii, 517 p.   map.   21½ cm.
> *Maps:* One map of the United States.
> *Inclusive dates:* Probably 1839–1854.
> *Location of copy:* Newberry Library.

The author calls his book a "practical essay on a great nation." It is not a typical travel book, but most of the information was secured first-hand. Grattan made several excursions to Virginia, passing through Washington on his way to Richmond and Norfolk. He made superficial observations on slavery and the hospitality of Southerners who, according to Grattan, were constantly either smoking or chewing tobacco.

For a more detailed and interesting account of life in Virginia, compare Grattan with Sarah Mendell and Charlotte Homer, who recorded their impressions in *Notes of Travel and Life* (New York, 1854). Olmsted's *A Journey in the Seaboard Slave States* (listed below) is indispensable for the slavery picture.

467. Gurowski, Adam G. de (1805–1866)

America and Europe. By Adam G. de Gurowski. New York, D. Appleton and company, 1857.

> viii, 411 p. 19½ cm.
> *Location of copy:* University of Virginia Library.

This book consists of topical discussions of American customs before 1860. It is neither illuminating nor convincing. There is a chapter on slavery but no evidence that the author ever saw a slave.

468. Hall, Marshall (1790–1857)

The two-fold slavery of the United States; with a project of self-emancipation; by Marshall Hall . . . London, A. Scott, 1854.

> 2 p.l., [ix]–xiii p., 1 l., 159 p. 2 fold. maps (incl. front.). 17 cm.
> *Maps:* Two: Map of slavery in the United States; map of unfriendliness to the African race.
> *Inclusive dates:* February, 1853, to March, 1854.
> *Location of copy:* Louisville Free Public Library.

Marshall Hall was well known in England for his work in physiology. He entered the South via Richmond, Louisville, St. Louis, and the Mississippi River route. He visited New Orleans and Mobile but had very little to say about any of the Southern towns. Only 23 pages of this publication can be considered a travel record. The remaining 136 pages were devoted to a discussion of the slavery problem. Hall did not believe in colonization or in mass emancipation. He developed an elaborate plan whereby each slave, by being educated and properly disciplined, but more particularly by being paid for "over-work," could eventually buy his freedom. After receiving his freedom, the Negro was to be given the privilege of working for his former master for wages.

This book has no value as a record of travel. However, the sociological theories are interesting. Olmsted had similar ideas pertaining to self-emancipation. See below, Frederick Law Olmsted, *A Journey in the Seaboard Slave States.*

[360]

469.   Hundley, Daniel Robinson (1832–1899)

Social relations in our Southern states. By D. R. Hundley ... New York, Henry B. Price, 1860.

> vi, [7]–367 p.   18.6 cm.
> *Inclusive dates:* About 1850–1860.
> *Location of copy:* University of Kentucky Library.

Daniel Robinson Hundley was born in the South and educated at several institutions in the North and South. He studied law at Bacon College in Kentucky. When he wrote this book he was a seasoned traveler and observer, having been at one time or another in every state in the Union.

This is not a typical travel book, and yet it is based on the author's many years of observations in various states under varying conditions. He described the Southern gentleman, the "cotton snobs," the yeoman, the middle classes, and what he called the Southern Yankee, those Southerners who were always after the almighty dollar. In addition, he included descriptions of the Southern bully, poor white trash, and slaves.

Although this book does not follow the traditional travel formula and is frequently overlooked by students of the period, it is one of the few books published before 1860 which attempted to describe all levels of Southern society. The book is not a scholarly product, but it is thought-provoking, enlivened unexpectedly with flashes of humor and biting sarcasm. Although unique and unorthodox, it is an important book on the late ante bellum South.

It is interesting to compare Hundley's book with the following contemporary publications: C. G. Parsons, *Inside View of Slavery;* Nehemiah Adams, *A South-Side View of Slavery;* Frederick Law Olmsted, *A Journey in the Seaboard Slave States* and *A Journey in the Back Country* all of which are listed in this section; and Hinton Rowan Helper, *The Impending Crisis of the South* (New York, 1857). Hundley and Parsons often reached similar conclusions although by different means and for different reasons. Olmsted had contacts with Hundley's "cotton snobs."

470.   Hussey, H.

The Australian colonies; together with notes of a voyage from Australia to Panama, in the "Golden age." Descriptions of Tahiti and other islands in the Pacific and a tour through some of the states of America, in 1854. By H. Hussey. London, Blackburn & Burt; Adelaide, E. S. Wigg, [1855].

vi, 174 p. 17 cm.
Inclusive dates: 1854.
Location of copy: The New York Public Library.

This book contains very little on the United States and still less on the South. However, the author did pass through Wheeling and Bethany, West Virginia, which gave him an excuse to devote several pages to Alexander Campbell and the Disciples of Christ. He mentioned the *Millennial Harbinger*. This book is relatively unimportant.

Amelia M. Murray passed through the same section of Western Virginia at about the same time. See her book, *Letters from The United States, Cuba, and Canada* (listed below). See also Marianne Finch, *An Englishwoman's Experience in America* (in Part III, Number 313).

471. Jobson, Frederick James (1812–1881)

America, and American Methodism. By the Rev. Frederick J. Jobson. With a prefatory letter by the Rev. John Hannah, D.D. Illustrated from original sketches by the author. London, J. S. Virtue, 1857.

xvi, 399 p. front., illus., plates. 19.8 cm.
Illustrations: Four by the author: The capitol at Washington; the Mississippi; Falls of Niagara; bird's-eye view of Niagara.
Inclusive dates: April to June, 1856.
Location of copy: University of Virginia Library.

Frederick James Jobson was a Wesleyan minister who attended the General Conference of the Methodist Episcopal church of America held at Indianapolis during May and June, 1856.

He did not see much of the South. He stopped at Wheeling, then in Virginia, but proceeded immediately to Cincinnati on his way to Indianapolis. However, he commented on the underground railway and slavery and called Kentuckians "genteel Irish."

The book has little value for the student of the South since the author secured his information about the region secondhand. For more details on Southern life at about the same time, see Amelia Murray, *Letters from the United States, Cuba, and Canada*. The standard travel references for the period are Frederick Law Olmsted, *A Journey in the Seaboard Slaves States* and *A Journey in the Back Country* (New York, 1860).

472. Kingsford, William [?] (1819–1898)

Impressions of the West and South during a six weeks' holiday. Toronto, A. H. Armour and co., 1858.

THE SOUTH IN SECTIONAL CRISIS, 1852-1860

83 p.   21 cm.
Inclusive dates: November to December, 1858.
Location of copy: Columbia University Library.

William Kingsford was probably the author of this book which was published anonymously. The author entered the South via the Mississippi River, going southward from St. Louis and passing Memphis, Natchez, and New Orleans. He went to Mobile, Montgomery, Macon, Charleston, Wilmington (N. C.), Petersburg, and Richmond. New Orleans and Charleston were the only towns that made an impression on him. He was not impressed with Memphis and Vicksburg and was unable to see much of Natchez. He reported that "Natchez under the hill" had lost its earlier shady reputation.

An entire chapter was devoted to New Orleans, and his description of the town is the most interesting in the book. Kingsford reported that while certain architectural features gave a foreign air to the city New Orleans was still very much an American port. The people enjoyed their leisure but there was considerable business efficiency. There were no commercial "swells" of the New York type. The author decided, however, that New Orleans, when compared with Boston, was not as productive intellectually. The theaters, opera, and churches were well supported, and the opera in particular, he thought, deserved special notice. He was impressed with the theater and the actors in Charleston, too, and also with the police in that South Carolina city. He described the police organization as a perfect *gens d'armerie.*

Interesting items pertaining to commerce, travel conditions, natural scenery, and morals and manners were included. The river boats made a deep impression on the author and he described them in detail. He reported that Spanish moss was used to stuff sofas and mattresses. Slavery is mentioned only incidentally.

This book is brief and often superficial, but for a study of New Orleans, Charleston, and Mississippi River travel conditions, it should not be overlooked.

Amelia M. Murray visited New Orleans at about the same time. See her *Letters from the United States, Cuba, and Canada* (listed below). Charles Casey, *Two Years on the Farm of Uncle Sam* (London, 1852), was interested, too, in the Mississippi river boats.

473. Mackay, Charles (1814-1889)

Life and liberty in America; or, sketches of a tour in the United States and Canada, in 1857-8. By Charles Mackay . . . 2 vols. London, Smith, Elder and co., 1859.

Vol. I, [2], 343 p.; Vol. II, [2], 336 p. front., plate. 20 cm.

Illustrations: Ten: Levee at New Orleans, torch-light procession of firemen in New York; American Indians waiting for the president; banks of the Ohio; Mississippi steamboat *Philadelphia,* cemetery of Bonaventura, capitol at Washington; break-up of ice on the St. Lawrence; Victoria Tubular Bridge, Montreal; and Toronto.

Inclusive dates: October, 1857, to May, 1858.

Other editions:

(1) 2d ed. London, Smith, Elder & co., 1859.

(2) With ten illustrations. New-York, Harper & brothers, 1859. 1 p.l., [v]–viii, [9]–413 p., incl. plates. 20 cm.

Location of copy: University of Kentucky Library.

Charles Mackay was a well known British poet, song writer, journalist, and publisher and should not be confused with Alexander Mackay, who wrote *The Western World* (in Part III, Number 353). He was educated in Scotland and on the continent and in addition to his literary interests developed a fondness for foreign languages, becoming proficient in French, German, Spanish, and Italian. From time to time he was connected with various British newspapers and magazines. In 1850 he was editor of the *Illustrated London News,* and during the American Civil War he served as special correspondent for the *New York Times.*

Mackay arrived in the United States in 1857 on a lecture tour, crossed the country from Boston to New Orleans by way of the Ohio and Mississippi rivers, and returned overland through the slave states to Washington and New York. In addition to the towns mentioned, he passed through Wheeling, Cincinnati, Louisville, St. Louis, Memphis, Natchez, Mobile, Montgomery, Savannah, Charleston, Petersburg, Richmond, and Mount Vernon. This author wrote in a light, fast moving style, and his material often approached superficiality. He sometimes resorted to journalistic tricks that, while pleasing to the casual reader, left a void where details could be expected. For example, the trip from St. Louis to New Orleans was described in verse. Again, while crossing North Carolina and Virginia he recorded very little except his impressions of the train and the railroad stations. However, he recorded some interesting descriptions of river boats, Southern swamps, a rice plantation, food, and tobacco chewing. His description of New Orleans is noteworthy.

Mackay's views on Southern life and slavery were favorable. He believed that the abolitionists were unfair to the South and that many of them were hypocrites. He observed that while Northern men talked about the political rights of the Negro they degraded and oppressed him socially. Northern men turned up their noses at the slightest physical contact with the Negro, while the Southerner did not object to the close proximity of the colored people. They used them as nurses for children, house servants, and personal maids. This traveler asserted that some slaveowners "cohabited" with the more attractive young female slaves.

Although he observed the strained sectional relationship, Mackay failed to fully appreciate the danger it involved. Like so many travelers, he overlooked the yeoman farmer in the South.

The original London edition of this book was published in two volumes in 1859. There was a New York edition in the same year.

In spite of its "blind spots" this is an important travel book, although it is below the standard set by the author's namesake, Alexander Mackay. For more detailed descriptions by an American traveler who covered the same general area, see any edition of Frederick Law Olmsted's *A Journey in the Seaboard Slave States* and *A Journey in the Back Country* (listed in this section). Mackay's descriptions of the Sea Island area of Georgia may be compared with Frances Anne Kemble, *Journal of a Residence on a Georgia Plantation, 1838–1839* (in Part II, Number 187). For a critical essay on Mackay's travel book, see *Debow's Review,* Vol. XVIII (1860), pp. 48–66.

474. Mitchell, David W.

Ten years in the United States; being an Englishman's view of men and things in the North and South. By D. W. Mitchell . . . London, Smith, Elder and co., 1862.

xii, 332 p. 19.7 cm.
Inclusive dates: 1848–1858.
Location of copy: University of Kentucky Library.

David W. Mitchell claimed that he lived in the United States (mostly in Richmond, Virginia) for a period of ten years (1848–58). This book, which is based on his observations while a resident of the United States, is generally favorable to the South and to slavery. He thought the abolitionists did the Negroes an injustice when they made a moral issue out of slavery, and he asserted that the Negro (who was regarded as a nuisance by Northerners and an economic necessity by Southerners) was and would be better cared for by Southern masters than by Northern politicians. He emphasized certain fallacies in abolition statistics concerning the superiority of the North over the South.

This is an opinionated book of minor value. For a more valuable parallel study, see Frederick Law Olmsted, *A Journey in The Seaboard Slave States* (listed below).

[365]

475. Moelling, Peter August

Reise-Skizzen in Poesie und Prosa. Gesammelt auf einer sieben-monat-lichen Tour durch die Vereinigten Staaten von Nord-Amerika. Galves-ton, Texas, Gedruckt in der Office des "Apologeten" und daselbst zu haben beim Verfasser, [1857?].

> 384 p. 21½ cm.
> *Illustrations:* Nine line-sketches, mostly of ministers whom the author met on his travels. The frontispiece shows the author himself.
> *Inclusive dates:* Probably June to December, 1857.
> *Location of copy:* Newberry Library.

As a minister from Bavaria, Moelling had a special interest in churches and religious activities. He toured the entire Mississippi Valley from Galveston to Toledo and included New Orleans, Memphis, and Natchez on the Northern trip and Newport, Kentucky, Louisville, and St. Louis on his trip back to the deep South. The book has a definite religious flavor, but the author's comments on the habits of the people and their economic life are generally objective. There is a good description of the churches in New Orleans.

476. Moor, Allen Page

Letters from North America, written during the summer of 1853. Can-terbury, St. Augustine's College press, 1855.

> 72 p. 20 cm.
> *Inclusive dates:* 1853.
> *Location of copy:* Newberry Library.

Moor did not travel below St. Louis. He said there was nothing to be seen in St. Louis, so he returned to Chicago. His work is of no value to the student of the South.

477. Morgan, Henry James (1842–1913)

The tour of H. R. H. the Prince of Wales through British America and the United States. By a British Canadian. Montreal, printed by J. Lovell, 1860.

> 2 p.l., ix, [11]–271, [1] p. front. (port.). 21½ cm.
> *Illustrations:* Frontispiece: Albert Edward, the Prince of Wales.
> *Inclusive dates:* July 10 to November 15, 1860.
> *Location of copy:* Joint University Libraries, Nashville, Tennessee.

This book gives only a brief itinerary of the Prince of Wales during his visit to Mt. Vernon and Richmond. For another account of the journey of the Prince, see Gardner D. Engleheart, *Journal of the*

Progress of H.R.H. the Prince of Wales through British North America, which, unfortunately, is little better than Morgan's book. Somewhat more detailed is Kinahan Cornwallis, *Royalty in the New World.* Both are listed above.

478. Murray, Hon. Amelia Matilda (1795–1884)

Letters from the United States, Cuba and Canada. By the Hon. Amelia M. Murray. New York, G. P. Putnam & company, 1856.

2 vols. in 1.   402 p.   18.4 cm.

Inclusive dates: July, 1854, to October, 1855.

Other editions:

(1) 2 vols. London, J. W. Parker and son, 1856.   Vol. I, ₍2₎, viii, ₍2₎, 320 p.; Vol. II, viii, ₍2₎, 317 p.   fold. map.   20 cm.

(2) New York, G. P. Putnam & company, 1856.   410 p.   19½ cm.

Location of copy: University of Kentucky Library.

Amelia Murray was well known in British social and political circles. She was a writer, botanist, artist, social worker, and traveler.

This is one of the better English travel books. The author entered the South via Richmond and passed through Charlottesville, Staunton, Lexington (Va.), Natural Bridge, Petersburg, Wilmington (N. C.), Charleston, Savannah, Jacksonville, New Orleans, Galveston, Mobile, Montgomery, Atlanta, Nashville, Mammoth Cave, and Louisville. She made interesting and intelligent observations on social life, architecture, church services, railroads, hotels, slavery, flora, fauna, and fossils. She was slightly bewildered by the heavy thunderstorms of the South and referred to New Orleans as "amphibious." She asserted that the slaves were better cared for in the Southern states than they were in Cuba and that the house servants in particular enjoyed food and clothing superior to that which was supplied to the average British apprentices. She thought that Negroes in the North exhibited more signs of discontent than did slaves in the South. Her favorable impressions of slavery are noteworthy when it is remembered that she had a preconceived prejudice against the institution when she left England to visit the United States.

For a contrasting, unfavorable report on American and Southern life and institutions, see James Stirling, *Letters from the Slave States.* Since Amelia Murray was interested in natural science, Robert Russell's *North America Its Agriculture and Climate* should be listed here. For a Continental interpretation of Southern life, consult Fredrika Bremer, *The Homes of the New World.* All are listed in this section.

479. Murray, Henry Anthony (1810–1865)

Lands of the slave and the free; or, Cuba, the United States, and Canada. By the Hon. Henry A. Murray . . . 2 vols. London, J. W. Parker and son, 1855.

> 980 p. plates, maps (1 fold.). 19½ cm.
>
> *Maps:* Two: One of the United States showing slave and free states; the other of Croton Aqueduct. (In 2d ed.).
>
> *Illustrations:* Eleven, including frontispiece of a Mississippi steamer. Other illustrations: A coffee planter's residence; a railway carriage; a locomotive; a yacht; a Negro; St. Charles Hotel, New Orleans; a Cuban hawker; Gerard College; Toronto Normal School; Hudson River steamer. (In 2d ed.).
>
> *Inclusive dates:* 1852–1853(?).
>
> *Other editions:*
>
> London, New York, G. Routledge & co., 1857. xxiii, 480 p. front., plates, maps (1 fold.). 18 cm. ("Second and cheap edition").
>
> *Location of copy:* University of Virginia Library.

Henry Anthony Murray was a Captain in the Royal Navy, and he was not very well disposed towards democracies. However, on his tour of the South he noted many features of social and economic life. The dates in this book are most confusing since the author quotes from newspapers and magazines published after he made his trip. There is also some doubt about the exact line of his journey, but he apparently passed through Louisville, St. Louis, New Orleans, Havanna, Key West, and Charleston and then perhaps went up the coast through Maryland. He was interested in duck hunting, rural outhouses, circus life, methods of transportation, hotels, and servants. He found his room at the St. Louis Hotel in New Orleans to be like a dog kennel, and he noted that most of the servants were Irishmen. New Orleans people impressed him with their hospitality, but as a city he preferred Charleston, where the fire department in particular attracted his attention. He showed little interest in Southern slavery, although he made observations on the institution in Cuba.

The text of this book is of uneven quality. Some of the observations are interesting and the author occasionally displays a good sense of humor, but in general it is superficial and poorly organized. The origin of the commercial statistics is in doubt.

Compare Captain Murray's book with Amelia Murray, *Letters from The United States, Cuba, and Canada,* listed above.

480. Oldmixon, John W.

Transatlantic wanderings: or, a last look at the United States. By Capt. Oldmixon . . . London, New York, G. Routledge & co., 1855.

iv, 189, [1] p. 17 cm. (Routledge's new series).
Inclusive dates: Probably from the autumn of 1852 to the spring of 1853.
Location of copy: Tennessee State Library.

Oldmixon was a captain in the Royal Navy. From Baltimore he traveled west to Louisville and then to Natchez, Baton Rouge, New Orleans, Mobile, and Pensacola. He recorded some facts on shipping, steamboating, and social life in the towns, but only a few pages were devoted to the South. The book is superficial and of minor importance.

Oldmixon mentioned William Chambers' book, *Things As They Are in America,* but Chambers recorded little about the South. For detailed descriptions, see Frederick Law Olmsted, *A Journey in the Seaboard Slave States* or Fredrika Bremer, *The Homes of the New World.* All are listed in this section.

481.   Olmsted, Frederick Law (1822–1903)

A journey in the back country in the winter of 1853–4. New York, Mason brothers, 1860.

xvi, [11]–492 p. 19 cm. (Our slave states. III).
Inclusive dates: Spring, 1854 (based on internal evidence; the title is misleading).
Other editions:
    (1) London, S. Low, son & co., 1860.
    (2) New York, Mason brothers, 1861.
    (3) The 2d ed. 1863.
    (4) (Originally issued in 1860). 2 vols. New York, [etc.], G. P. Putnam's sons, 1907. 22½ cm.
Location of copy: 1907 reprint in the Transylvania College Library.

Frederick Law Olmsted was one of the most important observers of Southern life in the ante bellum period. He was born in Hartford, Connecticut, in 1822. His father, John Olmsted, was a successful merchant who was very much interested in geography, wildlife, and people. Frederick inherited these interests, and when he was only sixteen he had over four thousand miles of travel to his credit. Before he made his first journey to the South, he visited China and toured Europe and England. His experiences in England brought forth his desire to write, and in 1852 he published his first travel book, *Walks and Talks of an American Farmer in England.* In addition to his travels Olmsted had various experiences as an engineer, a landscape architect, a student at Yale, and a farmer in New York State. Among his architectural accomplishments may be listed Central Park in New York City, the preservation of the natural beauty of Niagara Falls, and numerous park systems throughout the United States.

In the decade before the Civil War, Olmsted was disturbed by the propaganda of the more violent abolitionists, and gradually the desire grew within him to study the South at firsthand and to present a more objective picture of slavery and plantation life. He entered the South fully aware of the fact that slavery was an integral part of the nation's historical development and not the result of the evil wishes of certain Southern men. He was equally convinced, however, that eventual emancipation was necessary. He asserted that not to plan for the eventual and gradual freeing of the Negroes was as impractical as the demands of the Garrisonians who demanded immediate emancipation. Nothing which he observed in the South changed this initial desire, although he was to be disappointed in what he found and he was to become increasingly critical and hostile where slavery was concerned. He was especially disappointed to discover that what he termed the Christianizing and cultural influence of the whites did not, as he had hoped, offset the more undesirable aspects of slavery. It seems evident, furthermore, that his disillusionment in this respect tended to sour slightly his attitude toward the South in general and caused him to minimize the actual benefits which the Negroes had derived from close association with the whites. These benefits varied, of course, both in kind and degree from town to town and from plantation to plantation but were important enough to change the total picture.

In all, Olmsted wrote three travel books on the South: *A Journey in the Back Country in the Winter of 1853-4, A Journey in the Seaboard Slave States with Remarks on Their Economy,* and *A Journey Through Texas; Or, a Saddle-Trip on the Southwestern Frontier.* In each book, but especially in the first two named, he used many arguments and thousands of words developing his thesis that slavery was uneconomical. Many of these arguments are difficult to follow and are not too convincing, although there is little doubt today that slavery was not as efficient as the best white free labor. Among other things, Olmsted explored the old alibi that the white men could not work in the heat of the Southern sun. He saw white men and even women working in the fields all the way across the South without any evil effects. In some cases these white laborers were not the best physical specimens, but this was the result of poor diet and insufficient housing conditions and had nothing to do with their outdoor labor. Having disposed of the climatic argument, Olmsted next proved to his own satisfaction, at least, that a slave could do only one-eighth as much work as a hired white man. He admitted that in certain cases Southern planters had matched free labor with slave and that the results had been unfavorable to the free labor, but he explained this on the basis that only free laborers who had been debilitated by slavery were used in the experiments. Had the slaves been matched with the best white labor, he claimed, the results would have been quite different. The poor whites in the South were themselves the victims of the institution of slavery and should not be considered typical of free labor.

With respect to the poor whites in the South, Olmsted had the opinion that they were lower, socially and morally, than the lowest class in the North. Only the slum classes in New York City approached the depravity of the Southern poor whites, and he expressed the mistaken idea that these slum classes would disappear in a few years. He made similar comparisons with respect to education and general culture. He compared the number of schools in the North, for example, with the number in the South, without making allowances for differences in the density of population and for certain frontier conditions still very much in evidence especially in Mississippi and Alabama. Strangely enough, he recognized the frontier influence in certain sections of Mississippi but was blind to the fact that similar conditions were just as much in evidence in Iowa at the same time.

Although Olmsted painted a drab picture of life among the lower classes, he did not look upon these people with disdain. To the contrary, his sympathies were definitely with the underdog. For this reason he was more interested in the field hands than in the house servants and gave more attention to rural life than to city life. He usually described conditions among the poor whites and the lower type of slaves with pity and sympathy. On the other hand, he was very critical of those in power. But whether he was describing the wealthy planter, the field hand, or the poor white, he believed that he was being realistic. He did describe what he saw without resorting to the verbosities and extravagances so prevalent in the writings of the controversialists on both sides of the Mason and Dixon line.

In some respects, there is a reasonable doubt that Olmsted was not as honest and impartial an observer and recorder as he claimed to be. Perhaps he himself was unaware of any distortion of fact. Certainly his reputation was above reproach. He possessed an enviable reputation for integrity, honesty, and tolerance among his friends and acquaintances. So perhaps wherever he lost his objectivity it was not deliberate but motivated by some subconscious force or personal characteristic which was so much a part of the man that he never suspected its influence. This idea is developed in an interesting manner by Broadus Mitchell in his study of Olmsted, entitled *Frederick Law Olmsted, A Critic of the Old South* (Baltimore, 1924).

But regardless of the cause, Olmsted's descriptions were at times misleading. He was especially critical of little things. He was intolerant of many Southern habits and characteristics probably because he loved order and precision; he was, as a matter of fact, an old maid in many respects. He was especially critical of the many little inefficient habits of the Southern farmer, of the uncomfortable hotel, and of private accommodations. He made a great noise over what he called the poor management of Southern farms, apparently forgetting that his own farm on Staten Island was about to pass out of his hands because of the same type of bad management.

It may have been that his method of travel—mostly on horseback—while affording unusual opportunities for observation, sapped his strength and his patience until he was quite capable of seeing the worst in every situation. He was at his best when he forsook his horse or the stagecoach and traveled on the river boats. For example, his description of a trip on the Red River is one of the most delightful in travel literature. He was rested when he boarded the boat, having been in New Orleans for several days, and he saw the humorous side of a situation that would have been almost intolerable had he been as travel-worn as he so frequently was when he crossed the countryside on horseback—perhaps losing his way, going miles through a roadless wilderness, often drenched with rain.

Olmsted's greatest weakness was his ability to make mountains out of unpleasant molehills while he over colored the contrasting better features of Southern agricultural life. An example of this was his complimentary description of German towns and German farms in Texas. These were superior in Olmsted's eyes because they offered a rather sharp contrast to many of the nondescript settlements of the Americans which he had passed through.

In spite of certain faults and slight exaggerations (deliberate or subconscious), Olmsted's three travel books were unique. They constituted the most detailed picture of the South, especially the rural South, which had been attempted up to that time. He was one of the few who recognized the existence of a yeoman class, especially in the back country. He was one of the first to explode the idea that the South presented a solid front and that the only distinction was one of color. He pointed out the fact that there was no such thing as solidarity among the whites. There were regional differences and prejudices that caused the Southern white element to be disunited.

A Journey in the Back Country is a record of Olmsted's observations made during a trip through Mississippi, Alabama, Tennessee, and the back country of the Carolinas and Virginia. He passed through such towns as Woodville (Miss.), Natchez, Jackson, Vicksburg, Memphis, Tuscaloosa, Asheville, and Richmond. However, the value of the book lies in his description of rural life.

The author found more wealthy planters in Mississippi than he had seen in the seaboard states, but most of them were the "vulgar-rich." He hastened to point out that there were men of refinement in Mississippi, but without just cause he asserted there were more newly rich, ignorant people in Mississippi than in any other part of the United States. He found the people of the uplands more sociable, cheerful, and liberal than the planters of the lowlands. He believed that they were more ambitious and more intelligent than the poor nonslaveholders of the Black Belt. Even where he found the people ignorant, as in northern Alabama, they exihibited many worthwhile characteristics, especially self-reliance. But here Olmsted's sympathies with the lower classes caused him to draw some doubtful conclusions. For example, he placed too much emphasis on the few new houses he saw, taking these structures as indicative of the increasing prosperity of the people.

In this book Olmsted revealed that he considered slavery a very undesirable institution, although he cautioned against immediate abolition. Since this was the last of his travel books, he seemed to desire to point out that he no longer had any illusions about the South and slavery. At times he was too didactic.

One of the outstanding features of the book is the author's attempt to compare and contrast the various social classes of the North and South. Although it is known that Olmsted privately acknowledged that there was a great deal of rowdyism and commonness among the Northern farmers and laborers and no true aristocrats in the Southern sense, still he avoided this in his writing and played up what he considered the higher general level of culture in the North as compared with the general backwardness of the South. For this reason many contemporary Southerners believed that he deliberately misrepresented the facts.

Olmsted quoted liberally from the contemporary press and from *DeBow's Review*. An additional parallel source is DeBow, *The In-\dustrial Resources, Statistics, Etc., of the United States and More Particularly of the Southern and Western States* (3 vols., New York, 1854). See also D. R. Hundley, *Social Relations in Our Southern States* (listed above) and his *Seventh Census of the United States, 1850* (Washington, 1853). Olmsted had read in addition Robert Russell, *North America* (listed below) and Henry Caswall's books, especially *The Western World Revisited* (in Part III, Number 285).

482. Olmsted, Frederick Law

A journey in the seaboard slave states, with remarks on their economy. By Frederick Law Olmsted . . . New York, Dix & Edwards; London, S. Low, son & co., 1856.

3 p.l., ₍ix₎–xv, ₍1₎, 723, ₍1₎ p. illus. 17.8 cm.

Illustrations: Ten drawings representing various phases of country life by Peter Paul Duggan (1810–1861). Duggan worked in oils occasionally, but he was noted for his crayon drawings.

Inclusive dates: 1853–1854.

Other editions:

(1) New York, Mason brothers, 1859.

(2) New York, Mason brothers; ₍etc., etc.₎, 1861.

(3) (Originally issued in 1856). With a biographical sketch by Frederick Law Olmsted, jr., and with an introduction by William P. Trent . . . 2 vols. New York, London, G. P. Putnam's sons, 1904. front. (port.). 22½ cm.

Location of copy: Lexington Public Library.

Olmsted started his trip through the South in Virginia. Among the towns and cities which he passed through were Norfolk, Richmond, Alexandria, Fayetteville (N. C.), Gaston, Raleigh, Wilmington, Beaufort (S. C.), Charleston, Savannah, Columbus, Macon, Mobile, Montgomery, New Orleans, and Natchitoches. Although he was more interested in rural life, his comments on these towns are interesting.

Olmsted was a sharp observer, and the book contains a great variety of detail pertaining to agricultural methods, the inefficiency of slave labor, the uncomfortable homes of the planters, soil exhaustion, the use of guano, rice culture, Dismal Swamp and other physical features, Creoles, and wildlife. In addition to this detail on the numerous subjects observed, the book contains considerable speculation based on the author's wide reading of government reports, newspapers, and local histories. These arguments are rather tiresome and are not as valuable as the records of actual observation.

The author discovered that the slaves in the seaboard states were generally well treated. They received enough food to keep them in good physical condition. However, Olmsted believed that the slaves were not as well fed as American free laborers, and he devoted considerable space to one of his favorite theories, namely, that slavery was a destroyer of self-respect and initiative. But he added a qualifying statement to the effect that neither slavery nor democratic free labor offered any insurance against occasional suffering, mistreatment, and even starvation. In this book Olmsted proved that he was a social thinker as well as a journalist, and he worked out and described an interesting plan whereby the slaves, through a system of debits and credits, might be given the opportunity to buy their freedom from their masters.

This was the first of the Olmsted travel books on the South. It is more objective than *A Journey in the Back Country* and better written than *A Journey through Texas*. For an overall picture of the South as seen through Olmsted's eyes and in order to secure a better evaluation of Olmsted's social theories and his interpretation of Southern social institutions, the three books should be treated as one unit.

A contemporary traveler who gave a British interpretation of slavery and Southern life was James Stirling, *Letters from the Slave States*. A more favorable American point of view will be found in Nehemiah Adams, *A South-Side View of Slavery*. An interesting Southern point of view is expressed in D. R. Hundley, *Social Relations in Our Southern States*. (All three are listed in this section.) For other contemporary observations, see *DeBow's Review*. See the *New York Times* for February 16, 1853, and subsequent issues for the original Olmsted letters which formed the basis for *A Journey in the Seaboard Slave States*. The best book on Olmsted is by Broadus Mitchell, entitled *Frederick Law Olmsted, a Critic of the Old South* (Baltimore, 1924).

483.   Pairpoint, Alfred J.

Uncle Sam and his country; or sketches of America in 1854–55–56. By Alfred Pairpoint . . . London, Simpkin, Marshall, & co., 1857.

2 p.l., vii, 9–346 p.   19½ cm.
Inclusive dates: 1854–1856.
Location of copy: University of Kentucky Library.

Although this book has one section of nineteen chapters, entitled "My Trip to the South," there are actually only three sketchy chapters on Mount Vernon, a tobacco plantation, and a Richmond tobacco factory. The text consists of unenlightening conversations and superficial descriptions. What the author related about New Orleans, which he never saw, was hearsay.

For a detailed description of Virginia agricultural life at this time, see Frederick Law Olmsted, *A Journey in the Seaboard Slave States* (listed above).

484. Parsons, Charles Grandison (1807–1864)

Inside view of slavery: or, a tour among the planters. By C. G. Parsons, M.D., with an introductory note by Mrs. H. B. Stowe. Boston, J. P. Jewett and company; Cleveland, O., Jewett, Proctor and Worthington, 1855.

> xii, [13]–318 p. 19½ cm.
> *Inclusive dates:* 1852–1853.
> *Other editions:*
>   4th thousand. Boston, J. P. Jewett and company; Cleveland, O., Jewett, Proctor and Worthington, 1855.
> *Location of copy:* University of Kentucky Library.

Charles Grandison Parsons was a Maine physician, abolitionist, and temperance leader. For many years he believed that a man could form his opinion of slavery without ever thoroughly investigating the institution as it actually operated in the South. He had condemned it on principle as a sin and an evil blight on the nation. But in 1852 he tired of abstract principles and decided to view slavery with his own eyes.

He traveled through Virginia, Tennessee, Alabama, the Carolinas, Georgia, and Florida. However, this book was based on observations made by the author in Georgia alone. He made Savannah his headquarters and, having engaged in various types of business, he was able to see slavery "from within." He was convinced that slaveowners deliberately trained their slaves to deceive all travelers into believing that they (the slaves) were happy and contented with their lot.

Parson's book may be classed as abolition propaganda. The author never forgot what he called "the superior intellectual character" of the people of New England, and he judged all other people accordingly. The best passages in the book described the South's natural resources and commercial activities. The list and description of plantation torture instruments was intended to shock Northern readers. Parsons seemed to have been shocked by the amount of liquor consumed by Southern gentlemen, although he admitted that they did not drink as much at one time as some of his Northern acquaintances.

Harriet Beecher Stowe wrote a brief introduction to Parsons' book. She asserted that the volume was "the simple, straightforward narrative of an impartial witness."

For the opinion of another New Englander on slavery, see Nehemiah Adams, *A South-Side View of Slavery* (listed above).

485. Pelz, Eduard

Handbuch für Reisende durch die Vereinigten Staaten Nordamerikas.
Hamburg, Verlag der Buchner'schen Buchhandlung, 1854.

viii, 95 p. 17 cm.
Maps: One, showing railroads and canals of the United States.
Inclusive dates: 1854.
Location of copy: Newberry Library.

This tourist guide contains certain statistics on the Southern states
of interest to travelers and settlers, including climate, minerals, chief
products, and a brief comment on major towns.

486. Phillippo, James Mursell (1798–1879)

The United States and Cuba. By James M. Phillippo . . . London, Pew-
tress & co.; New York, Sheldon, Blakeman, & co., 1857.

xi, 476 p. 19 cm.
Location of copy: Columbia University Library.

Phillippo was a Baptist missionary. Apparently he entered the South
via Richmond and then passed through Raleigh, Wilmington,
Charleston, Savannah, St. Augustine, Pensacola, Mobile, New Orleans, and Louisville. With the exception of New Orleans, there was
very little in these towns that impressed him.

Although this book was a popular guide in its day, it seems obvious
that the author drew heavily on published materials, and for this reason his book was more of a compendium than a conventional travel
book. Compared with several other travel books published at about
the same time, Phillippo's book is relatively unimportant.

487. Pierce, George Foster (1811–1884)

Incidents of western travel: in a series of letters. By George F. Pierce . . .
Ed. by Thomas O. Summers, D.D. Nashville, Tenn., E. Stevenson and
F. A. Owen, 1857.

x p., 1 l., 13–249 p. front. (port.). 18½ cm.
Illustrations: Frontispiece of the author, engraved by T. B. Welch of Philadel-
phia from a daguerreotype.
Inclusive dates: September, 1855, to December, 1856.
Location of copy: Nashville Public Library.

George Foster Pierce was a bishop of the Methodist Episcopal church,
South. He left Georgia and traveled west through Nashville, Louisville, and Memphis, and after a swing through the plains, he returned
via Texas and Louisiana through Marshall, Shreveport, New Orleans,
Mobile, and Montgomery.

In addition to some interesting observations on the Choctaw Indians west of the Mississippi River, Pierce noted with some detail life on the rivers, commercial activities, manners, and morals. Towns usually overlooked by travelers in this period (Shreveport and Greenwood, La., and Marshall and Galveston, Texas) were included in the author's observations. The book was marred by too much moralizing.

Pierce's book should be compared with Frederick Law Olmsted, *A Journey Through Texas* (mentioned above). See also, the *Atlanta Constitution* of September 4, 1884.

488.   Pollard, Edward Alfred (1828–1872)

Black diamonds gathered in the darkey homes of the South. By Edward A. Pollard ... New-York, Pudney & Russell, 1859.

> xiv, [17]–122 p.   19 cm.
> *Inclusive dates:* 1858.
> *Other editions:*
> New-York, Pudney & Russell, 1860.   4 p.l., [xiii]–xv, [17]–155 p.   18.7 cm.
> *First published under this title:*
> The southern spy; or, curiosities of negro slavery in the South. Letters from a Southerner to a northern friend. Washington, H. Polkinhorn, printer, 1859. 72 p.   18½ cm.
> *Location of copy:* Joint University Libraries, Nashville, Tennessee.

Edward Alfred Pollard was a well known Virginia historian and biographer. His works, however, were usually journalistic and prejudiced. He toured the South to correct "the false views of northern spies" who had traveled in the region in disguise. Among the towns he visited were Macon, Charleston, Briarcliff, and Addebary, Maryland. Except for Macon, Georgia, Pollard said very little about the towns. He wrote an interesting description and evaluation of the Negro character and mind. He was also interested in Negro religion and superstition. He believed that the social and spiritual improvement of the Negro justified slavery.

As a travel book, this publication is of minor importance. William Kingsford toured the South at about the same time and left a detailed description of town life in his *Impressions of the West and South during a Six Weeks' Holiday* (listed above).

489.   Reid, Hugo (1809–1872)

Sketches in North America; with some account of Congress and of the slavery question. By H. Reid. London, Longman, Green, Longman, & Roberts, 1861.

vi p., 1 l., [9]–320 p.   16 cm.
Inclusive dates: 1859–1860.
Other editions:
  Published under this title:
  American crisis; or, sketches in North America. With some account of Congress and of the slavery question. By H. Reid. London, Ward & Lock, 1862.
Location of copy: Columbia University Library.

Hugo Reid does not mention his route of travel. He wrote a chapter on slavery, but apparently he gathered his material from newspapers and Congressional records. There is no evidence that he observed the institution firsthand. He asserted that American rowdyism was worse than slavery.

490.   Reid, John Coleman (b. 1824)

Reid's tramp, or a journal of the incidents of ten months travel through Texas, New Mexico, Arizona, Sonora, and California. Including topography, climate, soil, minerals, metals and inhabitants; with a notice of the great inter-oceanic rail road. By John C. Reid. Selma, Ala., printed at the book and job office of J. Hardy & co., 1858.

237 p.   21 cm.
Inclusive dates: September 1, 1857, to July, 1858.
Other editions:
  Reprint: Austin, Texas, the Steck company, 1935.   4 p.l., 7–245 p.   illus.
  22 cm.   (Original narratives of Texas history and adventure).
Location of copy: Harvard University Library.

This is the record of the journey of the Messilla Valley Company and of Reid's tramps in the Southwest. The group left Marion, Alabama, and proceeded to Mobile and New Orleans. From this port they went by ship to Galveston. From Galveston the trail led through San Antonio, Castroville, El Paso, Tucson, San Diego, and San Francisco. Reid returned by way of Panama, Havana, and New Orleans.

The book contains brief notes on towns and villages along the route, the Mexican character, German immigrants, Indian life, flora and fauna, and the agricultural possibilities of the area. Of special interest is the inclusion of the articles drawn up by the Messilla Valley Company to govern its members.

With respect to Texas, this book has little value when compared with Olmsted's *A Journey Through Texas* (New York, 1857, 1860). However, Reid's comments on the Mexican session are interesting if scanty.

491. Rey, William

L'Amérique Protestante; notes et observations d'un voyageur. 2 vols. Paris, De Soye et Bouchet, printers, 1857.

>Vol. I, vii, 326 p.; Vol. II, 370 p. 17½ cm.
>*Inclusive dates:* 1853.
>*Location of copy:* Newberry Library.

With the exception of St. Louis, Rey saw little of the South. There are eighteen pages of interesting and objective observations on St. Louis. He reached there by way of Chicago. He was favorably impressed with St. Louis but was opposed to slavery. His observations pertain to the people of the city, the hotels, the river traffic, and the agricultural life of Missouri.

492. Robertson, James

A few months in America; containing remarks on some of its industrial and commercial interests. By James Robertson . . . London, Longman & co.; ［etc., etc., 1855］.

>vii, 230, ［8］ p. 18.9 cm.
>*Inclusive dates:* November, 1853, to April, 1854.
>*Location of copy:* Louisville Free Public Library.

Robertson was a British businessman. He entered the South via Virginia and passed through Richmond, Wilmington (N. C.), Charleston, Savannah, Montgomery, Mobile, and New Orleans. After a visit to Cuba, he returned to the United States and went up the Mississippi River.

Because of his own business interests, he noted in detail various features of Southern commerce, agriculture, and industry. He observed, also, social life and customs, including amusements, lectures, theaters, and dances. He had no personal interest in slavery, but he believed the lethargy in the South was due to this servile institution. With the possible exception of Charleston, he was unimpressed by Southern cities.

The value of this book is to be found in the intelligent discussion of economic life. The author's interpretation of social life is biased.

For more interesting and intelligent observations on social life (including slavery), see Amelia M. Murray, *Letters from the United States, Cuba, and Canada* (listed above). See also *The Seventh Census of the United States, 1850* (Washington, 1853).

493. [Rogers, Carlton H.]

Incidents of travel in the southern states and Cuba. With a description of the Mammoth cave . . . New York, R. Craighead, printer, 1862.

> 2 p.l., ₍iii₎–viii, ₍9₎–320 p. 18.6 cm.
> *Inclusive dates:* February to May, 1856.
> *Location of copy:* Tennessee State Library.

> Rogers was a resident of Palmyra, New York. He entered the South via Virginia and visited Richmond, Wilmington, Charleston, Havana, Key West, Savannah, Macon, Columbus, Montgomery, Atlanta, Chattanooga, Nashville, and Mammoth Cave.

> Rogers made observations on city and country life, travel conditions, hotels, architecture, public institutions, markets, moral conditions, and slavery. His comments on the backwoodsmen and poor whites were unusually tolerant. He seemed to be anxious to give a well-balanced picture of the South, and he gave the best with the worst characteristics. One of the features of the book is a detailed description of his trip through Mammoth Cave. The notes on slavery are incidental.

> This is one of the better travel books of the period. For the slavery side of the picture, see Frederick Law Olmsted, *A Journey In the Seaboard Slave States* and *A Journey in the Back Country*. For observations on industrial life at about the same time, see James Robertson, *A Few Months in America*. All are listed above.

494. Routledge, George

Routledge's American handbook and tourist's guide through the United States. London, George Routledge and Co., 1854.

> vi, 216 p. 16½ cm.
> *Inclusive dates:* 1854.
> *Location of copy:* Newberry Library.

> As the title indicates, this is not a travel book but a tourist guide. It is characteristic of its kind, having mileage charts and general information about all the states and towns, including those of the South. There are notes on Southern hotels, food, amusements, agriculture, and hunting and fishing.

495. Ruffin, Edmund (1794–1865)

Agricultural geological, and descriptive sketches of Lower North Carolina, and the similar adjacent lands. By Edmund Ruffin, of Virginia. Raleigh, printed at the Institution for the deaf and dumb, and the blind, 1861.

xi, [13]–296 p. 22 cm.
Illustrations: One diagram illustrating method of plowing a tidewater field.
Inclusive dates: 1856.
Location of copy: Harvard University Library.

This is a semiscientific study of the soils of the tidewater South and especially of North Carolina. Edmund Ruffin, well known farmer, journalist, and politician of the Old South, was considered one of the nation's most progressive agriculturists. In addition to describing the soils of the area he visited, the author presented a good argument for diversified crops and truck gardening in the North Carolina lowlands. In addition, he described methods of plowing and draining lowland fields.

This is not a typical travel book, but it is valuable as an item of Ruffiniana and has a special interest for students of Southern agricultural history. Ruffin's book is based in part on articles published at an earlier date in *The Farmers Register,* especially in Vols. IV, VII, VIII, and IX.

496. Russell, Robert (d. 1871)

North America, its agriculture and climate; containing observations on the agriculture and climate of Canada, the United States, and the island of Cuba. By Robert Russell, Kilwhiss. Edinburgh, A. and C. Black, 1857.
4 p.l., 390 p. front. (fold. col. map), 8 plates (charts, part fold.), diagrams. 23 cm.
Maps: Ten. Only one, showing the Missouri Compromise line, is political. Nine are scientific maps. There are also charts and meteorological registers.
Inclusive dates: August, 1854, to April, 1855.
Location of copy: University of Kentucky Library.

Robert Russell was a British naturalist, but this book was not devoted entirely to scientific matters. Russell entered the South through Virginia via Richmond, Wilmington (N. C.), Charleston, Savannah, Key West, New Orleans, Natchez, Mobile, and Montgomery. Apparently he did not enter Kentucky, but he talked with Kentucky farmers attending a fair at Springfield, Ohio, and he gained some knowledge of the Bluegrass State from these interviews and from secondary sources. The book indicates that the author had done wide reading of government publications and agricultural journals. He was especially interested in rice culture, and he has a detailed description of this agricultural pursuit both in South Carolina and in Louisiana. Sea Island cotton attracted his attention. He gave an objective picture of slavery but asserted that slave labor was less efficient than free labor. He took a special interest in erosion and worn out land, and he believed that the only way a worn out plantation could be made to pay would be to divide it into small farms for free labor.

Except for the scientific facts pertaining to climatic and soil conditions, there is very little in this book that is not better described by Olmsted in his *A Journey in the Seaboard Slave States* and *A Journey in the Back Country* (both listed above). Russell was acquainted with *Debow's Review* and Debow's *Industrial Resources, Statistics, Etc., of the United States and More Particularly of the Southern and Western States* (3 vols., New York, 1854).

497. Sears, Robert (1810–1892)

A pictorial description of the United States. New York, Robert Sears, 1855.

vii, 648 p. illus. 24 cm.

Illustrations: Numerous imaginary sketches.

Inclusive dates: About 1855.

Other editions:

(1) A pictorial description of the United States; embracing the history, geographical position, agricultural and mineral resources . . . etc., etc., of each state and territory in the Union. Interspersed with revolutionary and other interesting incidents, connected with the early settlement of the country. New York, Robert Sears, 1860.

(2) A pictorial description of the United States; embracing the history, geographical position, agricultural and mineral resources . . . etc., etc. Interspersed with revolutionary and other interesting incidents connected with the early settlement of the country. Boston, J. A. Lee & Co., 1876.

Location of copy: Newberry Library.

This is not a travel book but a compilation of facts pertaining to each state in the Union. All the Southern states are included, and the data is arranged according to a pattern of area, agricultural production, antiquities (history), government, latitude and longitude, population, and a brief description of cities. Except for the historical oddities, most of the information can be secured from more reliable census reports and other publications, including DeBow, *The Industrial Resources, Statistics, etc., of the United States and More Particularly of the Southern and Western States* (3 vols., New York, 1854).

498. Stirling, James (1805–1883)

Letters from the slave states. By James Stirling. London, J. W. Parker and son, 1857.

viii, 374 p. front. (map). 19.8 cm.

Maps: One, showing the author's travel route.

Inclusive dates: August, 1856, to May, 1857.

Location of copy: University of Kentucky Library.

LETTERS

FROM THE

SLAVE STATES.

BY

JAMES STIRLING.

LONDON:
JOHN W. PARKER AND SON, WEST STRAND.
1857.
[*The Author reserves to himself the right of Translation.*]

[384]

This Scotsman gave a critical and sometimes biased picture of the American way of life. He never forgot his own origin and native heath and believed that all the slaves in the South looked up to England as the goddess of liberty.

He entered the South via the Ohio River and passed through Louisville, New Orleans, Montgomery, Mobile, Columbus, Macon, Savannah, St. Augustine, Charleston, Columbia, Aiken (S. C.), Knoxville, and Richmond.

Stirling was often inconsistent. While he made the traditional statement that the South was made up of rich planters and poor white trash, he acknowledged the presence of the yeoman farmers and asserted that these middle-class people operated slavery in its mildest form. Apparently he believed all the slave atrocity stories. Slavery itself he blamed on the aristocratic tendencies of the Southern people.

At best, this book is only of secondary importance, but if read with caution and compared with more reliable travelers, such as Olmsted, it is usable.

499. Thornbury, George Walter (1828–1876)

Criss-cross journeys. By Walter Thornbury . . . 2 vols. London, Hurst and Blackett, 1873.

Vol. I, 329 p.; Vol. II, 342 p.   18.6 cm.
Inclusive dates: Autumn of 1860.
Location of copy: Columbia University Library.

George Walter Thornbury was a "miscellaneous writer," traveler, and journalist. The title of this book aptly describes his route in the South, for he had no definite travel plans. It is likely that he entered the South through Kentucky and visited Mammoth Cave. After this he went to Nashville, Memphis, Vicksburg, New Orleans, Charleston, and Richmond. He made observations on travel conditions, hotels, agriculture, slavery, fairs, and elections. He was favorably impressed with the Mississippi boats but found the towns dirty and unfinished.

The book is often superficial, but the description of the Richmond Fair and loading operations at the Mississippi river-boat landing saves it from being useless.

Compare Thornbury with William Kingsford, *Impressions of the West and South During a Six Weeks' Holiday* (listed above). See also the *Illustrated London News* of June 24, 1876.

500. Tower, Philo

Slavery unmasked: being a truthful narrative of three years' residence and journeying in eleven Southern states: to which is added the invasion of Kansas, including the last chapter of her wrongs. By Rev. Philo Tower ... Rochester, E. Darrow & brother, 1856.

> xv, [17]-432 p. front. 18½ cm.
> *Illustrations:* Sketch of an imaginary plantation.
> *Inclusive dates:* 1853-1854.
> *Location of copy:* Fisk University Library.

The Reverend Tower toured the South with two of his colleagues. He was a New Englander who found the South very dull, although he was shocked constantly by Sabbath desecrations, horse races, lewd women, and the sins of slavery.

He entered the South via the Potomac route and passed through Richmond, Wilmington, Charleston, Columbia, Savannah, New Orleans, Vicksburg, Natchez, and Louisville. He predicted the Civil War and called upon all Americans to either choose the flag of freedom or the dark flag of slavery drenched in the blood of murdered bondsmen. Atrocity stories, especially those involving female slaves, were given special emphasis.

Although prejudiced, the book is amusing. It is a good example of abolition propaganda. Compare Tower's book with Nehemiah Adams, *A South-Side View of Slavery* (listed above). See also De-Bow's *Industrial Resources, Statistics, Etc., of the United States and More Particularly of the Southern and Western States* (3 vols., New York, 1854).

501. Trotter, Isabella (Strange) (1816-1878)

First impressions of the New world on two travellers from the Old, in the autumn of 1858. London, Longman, Brown, Green, Longmans, & Roberts, 1859.

> xi, 308 p. front. (fold. map). 19.6 cm.
> *Maps:* One: United States and Canada, 1858.
> *Location of copy:* The New York Public Library.

Mrs. Trotter did not go south of the Potomac, but she did tour Kentucky and visit Louisville, Frankfort, and Lexington. She was impressed with Louisville's artesian well, hotels, and book store. She made a favorable comparison between the Bluegrass area and the English countryside. She described the state capitol at Frankfort and visited Henry Clay's home and the fairgrounds in Lexington. She was opposed to slavery but found the slaves in Kentucky generally well treated.

The book has little value as a regional description, but the few pages on Kentucky are worth reading. Lady Emmeline Stuart-Wortley toured Kentucky at an earlier date (*Travels in the United States*), but for a better feminine interpretation of the South see Hon. Amelia M. Murray, *Letters from the United States, Cuba, and Canada* (both listed above). See also *Frasers Magazine*, Vol. LXI, pp. 276–88.

502. Turnbull, Jane M. E.

American photographs. By Jane M. E. Turnbull and Marion Turnbull. London, T. C. Newby, 1859.

> 2 vols. in 1. Vol. I, vi, 329 p.; Vol. II, iv, 298 p.   17.6 cm.
> *Inclusive dates:* 1852–1857.
> *Location of copy:* Joint University Libraries, Nashville, Tennessee.

Jane and Marion Turnbull were the daughters of an English physician. They toured the United States, Canada, and Cuba, entering the South at New Orleans after their trip to Havana. They passed through such towns as Mobile, Montgomery, La Grange, Augusta, and Charleston.

The book is not too interesting and reads like a travel guide. It is noteworthy, however, for its descriptions of a trip on the Alabama River, a Negro dance, and social life in Charleston.

Lillian Foster visited many of the places described by the Turnbulls at about the same time. See her *Way-Side Glimpses, North and South*. However, Fredrika Bremer observed and recorded more than any other woman traveler in the decade. See her *The Homes of the New World*. Both are listed above.

503. Van Buren, A. De Puy

Jottings of a year's sojourn in the South; or, first impressions of the country and its people; with a glimpse at school-teaching in that Southern land, and reminiscences of distinguished men . . . Battle Creek, Mich., Review and Herald, 1859.

> x, 11–320 p.   19.8 cm.
> *Inclusive dates:* November, 1857, to November, 1858.
> *Location of copy:* University of Kentucky Library.

Van Buren was a Michigan schoolteacher who spent a year in the Delta region of Mississippi, living with wealthy planters and teaching school for a short time.

As far as slavery is concerned, the book has no value because the author ignored the institution. With respect to social life, the book has little value because Van Buren looked at everything through rose-colored glasses and made the mistake of picturing the entire Southern region as he found it on a few ideal plantations in the Yazoo basin. He believed that the South had no plain "country girls"; to him they were all gracious ladies. There are descriptions of sailing parties, balls, reading habits, the Negroes at Christmas, etc. There is one chapter each on the Southern lady and the Southern gentleman, Yazoo style.

504. Vandenhoff, George (1813–1885)

Leaves from an actor's note-book; with reminiscences and chit-chat of the Green-Room and the stage, in England and America. By George Vandenhoff ... New York, [etc.], D. Appleton and company, 1860.

> vi, 347 p.   19½ cm.
> *Inclusive dates:* 1842–1855.
> *Other editions:*
>> *Published also under this title:*
>> Dramatic reminiscences; or, actors and actresses in England and America. By George Vandenhoff. Ed., with preface, by Henry Seymour Carleton. London, T. W. Cooper & Co., [etc.], 1860.   xvi, 318 p.   20½ cm.
> *Location of copy:* University of Virginia Library.

To borrow an appraisal from the *Dictionary of American Biography,* Vandenhoff's book "shows him a man of breeding, taste, and good sense." It recounts a theatrical career begun in the year 1839 when the author, a young lawyer in Liverpool with a promising career in sight, suddenly turned to the stage. Three years later he came to America where he remained for much of the rest of his life, first as a popular actor, then as a teacher of elocution and a reader of plays from the lecture platform.

He entered the South with a case of sherry via the ship route from Boston to New Orleans. When he entered New Orleans he found the St. Charles hotel in ashes and the American theatre closed for want of support. He made interesting and pertinent comments on social and political life and customs in New Orleans and Mobile in particular. He met Sol Smith, investigated society balls, quadroons, and hotels.

This is a fascinating book, but only a few pages are devoted to the actor's experiences in the South.

505. Weld, Charles Richard (1813–1869)

A vacation tour in the United States and Canada. By Charles Richard
Weld . . . London, Longman, Brown, Green, and Longmans, 1855.

xi, 394 p. 19.6 cm.
Inclusive dates: Either 1854 or 1855; internal evidence and biographical material conflict on this point.
Location of copy: University of Kentucky Library.

Charles Richard Weld was secretary to England's Royal Society. He
was a lawyer, scientist, and authority on Polar expeditions. He was
especially noted for his *A History of the Royal Society* (London,
1848).

Weld was a half-brother of Isaac Weld (1774–1856), whose book
Travels through the States of North America (London, 1799) had
made a deep impression on the British public. He seemed to regard
his own publication as a sequel to the earlier book. It is well written
but contains very little on the South. He described a slave market and
a tobacco factory in Richmond, Virginia. He relied on Richmond
newspapers for some of his material.

For more detail on Virginia and the South Atlantic States, see
Frederick Law Olmsted, *A Journey in the Seaboard Slave States*
(listed above). The files of the *Richmond Examiner* from 1853–55
should prove useful for background. See also the London *Times*
of January 19, 1869.

506. William, Father [*pseud.*]

Recollections of rambles at the South. By Father William [*pseud.*].
New-York, Carlton & Phillips, 1854.

196 p., incl. front., 4 plates. 14½ cm.
Illustrations: Five black and white line sketches.
Inclusive dates: Probably 1849.
Location of copy: Harvard University.

The author was a New England farmer and schoolteacher who
traveled through parts of the Carolinas and Virginia. He visited
Charleston, Columbia, Fayetteville, Norfolk, and Yorktown. Although Father William had numerous experiences, the book is dull.
His comments on cotton culture, Negro laborers, naval stores industry, bad roads, the scarcity of taverns, and the general hospitality of
the people (especially the Virginians) are more or less orthodox.

A more detailed picture of this region can be better obtained from
Olmsted, *Seaboard Slave States* and Charles MacKay, *Life and Liberty in America,* especially Volume II. Both are listed in this section.

[389]

INDEX

TRAVELS IN THE OLD SOUTH

has been set in several sizes of Linotype Granjon.
On the title page, set by hand, appear
Bruce Rogers' nobly proportioned Centaur capitals,
cut by the Monotype Corporation, Ltd., of England.
The fleurons on the same page, composed into
a triangular shape,
are probably of Renaissance origin, and are
also from Monotype.